A Son's Return

A Son's Return

~SELECTED ESSAYS OF STERLING A. BROWN ~

Edited with a foreword by MARK A. SANDERS

NORTHEASTERN UNIVERSITY PRESS ~   BOSTON

Library of Congress Cataloging-in-Publication Data
Brown, Sterling Allen, 1901–
    A son's return : selected essays of Sterling A. Brown / edited by
Mark A. Sanders.
        p.   cm.—(The Northeastern library of Black literature)
    Includes bibliographical references (p.   ).
    ISBN 1-55553-274-8 (cl. : acid-free stock). — ISBN 1-55553-275-6
(pbk. : acid-free stock)
    1. Afro-Americans.   2. American literature—Afro-American authors—
History and criticism.   3. Afro-Americans—Folklore.   4. Folk
literature—United States—History and criticism.   5. Afro-
Americans—Politics and government.   I. Sanders, Mark A., 1963–.
II. Title.   III. Series.
E185.615.B736   1996
973'.0497—dc20   96-1192

Designed by Ann Twombly

Composed in Bodoni Book by Coghill Composition, Richmond, Virginia.
Printed and bound by Thomson-Shore, Inc., Dexter, Michigan. The paper is
Glatfelter Supple Opaque Recycled, an acid-free stock.

MANUFACTURED IN THE UNITED STATES OF AMERICA
00 99 98 97 96   5 4 3 2 1

Contents

REVIEWS ❧

Acknowledgments

⫘ ALL BOOKS come about through the concerted efforts of loving communities—relatives, friends, intellectual sparring partners all committed to psychic and emotional growth. As this volume and editor strive to pay homage to Sterling A. Brown's example and legacy, I would like to thank some of these communities for making these attempts possible. Earl A. Sanders and Dr. Arthrell D. Sanders are due the highest honor for their instruction, challenges, and guidance. My gratitude goes as well to Dr. Claire A. Sanders, for the example of excellence toward which I continue to aspire.

I would also like to thank my colleagues Rudolph Byrd, Trudier Harris, and Frances Smith Foster, for their help in the conception and development of this project. A thanks is due, too, to Michael Antonucci for his crucial help in the physical preparation of this manuscript. I would also like to extend my sincere gratitude to Michael S. Harper for his timely encouragement.

Finally, I would like to reserve a special thanks for my wife, Dr. Kimberly Wallace Sanders, colleague and loving confidante, for her support, those daily affirmations vital to psychic sustenance.

This book is dedicated to the loving memory of Purvis Anthony Haggai Dixon.

"Negro Character As Seen by White Authors" is reprinted from the *Journal of Negro Education* 2 (April 1933). Used by permission of the *Journal of Negro Education.*

"The American Race Problem As Reflected in American Literature" is reprinted from the *Journal of Negro Education* 8 (July 1939). Used by permission of the *Journal of Negro Education.*

"Count Us In" is reprinted from Sterling A. Brown, *What the Negro Wants,* edited by Rayford Logan. Copyright 1944 by the University of North Carolina Press. Used by permission of the publisher.

"Athletics and the Arts" is reprinted from *The Integration of the Negro into American Society,* edited by E. Franklin Frazier (1951). Used by permission of the Moorland-Spingarn Research Center of Howard University.

"The New Negro in Literature (1925–1955)" is reprinted from *The New Negro Thirty Years Afterwards,* edited by Rayford W. Logan, Eugene C. Holmes, and G. Franklin Edwards (1955). Used by permission of the Moorland-Spingarn Research Center of Howard University.

"Folk Literature" is reprinted from *The Negro Caravan,* edited by Sterling A. Brown, Arthur P. Davis, and Ulysses Lee (1941). Used by permission of Ayer Company Publishers, Inc.

"Luck Is a Fortune" by Sterling A. Brown is reprinted from the October 16, 1937, issue of the *Nation.* Reprinted with permission from the *Nation* magazine. Copyright The Nation Company, L. P.

"An Annotated Bibliography of the Works of Sterling A. Brown" by Robert G. O'Meally is reprinted from *The Collected Poems of Sterling A. Brown,* edited by Michael S. Harper. Copyright © 1980 by Sterling A. Brown. Reprinted by permission of HarperCollins Publishers, Inc.

Foreword

 VERY LATE in his career, well after all the exhausting work for the Federal Writers' Project and the Gunnar Myrdal study, well after the accolades won through *Southern Road* and *Negro Caravan*, Sterling A. Brown reflected on a long, sometimes controversial career and quipped: "I am unique in that I'm the only person at Howard who was hired, fired—and I was, I'm not ashamed of it, I'm proud of it, I'm not going to tell you why but the cause was good—but I was hired, I was fired, I was rehired, I was retired, I was again rehired. If I tell many lies tonight and you get them taped, I may be refired."[1] In an address at his alma mater, Williams College, Brown effectively deflected, in a passing joke, the frustration and anger marking too much of his final years. Indeed, Brown, to a large extent, had been ignored or taken for granted, his poetry allowed to go out of print, and his criticism, while generally acknowledged as extremely influential, relegated to the margins of critical debate. By 1973, when he went back to Williams and made these remarks, Brown was, in his own words, "in the rocking chair," quietly lamenting the long years of critical neglect. Fortunately, in 1980, Michael S. Harper brought out *The Collected Poems of Sterling A. Brown*, initiating a recovery project that has yet to be completed, a project that not only pays tribute to an enormously important figure, but offers substantive responses to compelling questions concerning race and cultural plurality, aesthetics and political ideology, and the relentless demands of participatory democracy. For Brown's work, both artistic and critical, addresses that defining tension in American society that Ralph

1. Sterling A. Brown, "A Son's Return: 'Oh, Didn't He Ramble,' " in *Chant of Saints: A Gathering of Afro-American Literature, Art, and Scholarship*, ed. Michael S. Harper and Robert B. Stepto (Urbana: University of Illinois Press, 1979), 3.

Ellison describes as "the conflicts within the human heart which ar[ise] when the sacred principles of the Constitution and the Bill of Rights clash with the practical exigencies of human greed and fear, hate and love."[2]

While his comments refer overtly to Brown's poetry, Kimberly Benston's apt appraisal effectively extends to encompass the scope and profundity of a full career of artistic and critical contributions: "For well over half a century, Brown has pushed our estimation of Afro-American expression past cliché, ideology, and narrow preconception toward an ever-wider and more complex awareness of black tradition's vitality. A long distance runner and long breath singer, he has remained the guide to yet another generation of performers and their kin."[3] Indeed, the full range of human complexities, expressed through American and African American art and culture, constitutes the central concern of Brown's critical career and specifically this collection. Brown's commitment to political redress, democratic access, and economic opportunity; his investment in the concept of history, and his attention to the pragmatics of historical accuracy; his emphasis on African American culture as an ever-adaptive dynamic, capable of transforming both conceptual and physical surroundings; and his ear and eye for aesthetics, insisting upon form and style as a medium of substance, culminate in his overriding project of African American visibility, both political and cultural.

Much of Brown's commitment to liberating politics finds its origins in the New Negro Movement, as Brown often identified himself with contemporaries such as W. E. B. Du Bois, Paul Robeson, Mordecai Johnson, and James Weldon Johnson. Born in 1901 in Washington, D.C., to a struggling middle-class family, Brown had a background nearly prototypical for the New Negro intellectual. His father, a former slave, worked his way to and through Fisk University, then attended Oberlin College Seminary, where he received his formal religious training. Sterling Nelson Brown presided over Lincoln Temple Congregational Church (a church well known for hosting debates and conferences of national importance) and headed the School of Theology at Howard University. Adelaide Allen, Brown's mother, was also a graduate of Fisk, and an avid patron of the literary arts; she introduced Brown to poetry and to the pleasures of reading.[4] Growing up practi-

2. Ralph Ellison, "Brave Words for a Startling Occasion," in *Shadow and Act* (New York: Random House, 1964), 104.

3. Kimberly W. Benston, "Sterling Brown's After-Song: 'When de Saints Go Ma'ching Home,' and the Performance of Afro-American Voice," *Callaloo* 14 and 15 (1982): 33.

4. See Joanne V. Gabbin, *Sterling Brown: Building the Black Aesthetic Tradition* (Westport: Greenwood Press, 1985), 15–19.

cally on Howard University's campus and in a family active in the intellectual life of Washington's African American communities helped to cultivate in Brown an appreciation for aesthetics and art, particularly literature.

But beyond that cultivation, Brown's family and community inculcated in him a defining New Negro ideology that would inform his entire critical career. In reaction to radical change in African American outlook and philosophy at the turn of the century, the New Negro took on the responsibility of reconstructing the conceptual, cultural, and political apparatus for rationalizing African American life. In short, the New Negro Movement constituted the politically self-conscious attempt on the part of African Americans to define themselves as a post-slavery, post-agrarian people. As a result of massive migration from the south to the urban north and midwest, a significant percentage of the African American population was, for the first time in African American history, no longer rural but urban, no longer farmers but wage earners. And thus both African American individual and collective identities were forced to adjust to the new demands of city life and industrialization.

Simultaneously, the sobering reality of dismantled Reconstruction compelled African Americans to develop a new political self-awareness. This generation, born toward the end of the nineteenth century, constitutes the first full generation born free. Not only Brown, but Zora Neale Hurston, W. C. Handy, James Reese Europe, and a host of others were born to former slaves, and so stood as direct heirs of Reconstruction and its promises of full citizenship. Yet this generation experienced from birth the systematic exclusion from the political access guaranteed them by the Thirteenth, Fourteenth, and Fifteenth Amendments. The reaction to America's theoretical promise of equality and the palpable reality of peonage was black America's first collective assertion of citizenship. The "newness" of the New Negro, then, stemmed largely from an aggressive claim to political inclusion, economic and cultural participation, and fundamental equality. Or, in Alain Locke's words: "With each successive wave . . . the movement of the Negro becomes more and more a mass movement toward the larger and more democratic chance—in the Negro's case a deliberate flight not from countryside to city but from medieval America to modern."[5]

Thus, political figures, many born during Reconstruction, helped to form organizations such as the Urban League and the NAACP, pursued

5. Alain Locke, "The New Negro," in *The New Negro*, ed. Alain Locke (New York: Albert and Charles Boni, 1925), 6.

litigation challenging the notion of "separate but equal," and aggressively campaigned for a federal anti-lynching law. In the respective realms of the arts, education, housing, public accommodations, and job opportunities, this generation agitated for desegregation and equal opportunity. But for Brown the New Negro Movement was more than simply an intellectual or political movement: it encompassed the broad cultural transformation emerging from a fundamental shift in African American self-conception, a shift that traversed class, regional, and educational boundaries. Brown found in both African American music and idiomatic expression a dynamism and cultural modality that again suggested a new and vital self-awareness.

I stress here the importance of New Negro self-conception as a pervasive political and cultural phenomenon largely because so much of Brown's artistic and critical work sought to correct the middle-class exclusivity that dominated New Negro publications. Both Brown's poetry and critiques of folk culture attempted to include extra-literary modes of self-articulation, thereby acknowledging and celebrating the multiple ways in which New Negroes formulated and expressed their modernity and claim to full participation. In this sense, an eclectic array of contemporaries including Nate Shaw, Ida B. Wells, Ma Rainey, W. E. B. Du Bois, Anne Spencer, and Duke Ellington reflect plurality in terms of class, education, region, and modes of expression, and at the same time a unanimity in conception of citizenship and participation.

Brown published his first essay, "Roland Hayes," in *Opportunity* in 1925. Shortly thereafter, publishing a series of extremely well received poems in *Opportunity, Crisis,* and Countee Cullen's *Caroling Dusk,* Brown quickly became an innovative force in the artistic wing of the New Negro Movement. In "The New Negro in Literature (1925–1955)" Brown makes a critical distinction between the Harlem Renaissance and the New Negro Renaissance. Objecting to limiting the era to the 1920s and to focusing exclusively on Harlem, Brown rejects the term "Harlem Renaissance" as a misnomer, insisting upon terminology that encompasses the geographical breadth and artistic eclecticism of his generation of artists. Brown took the distinction quite personally, once stating, "when you say that I belong to the 'Harlem Renaissance' you are insulting me, but if you say I belong to the 'New Negro Renaissance' then I will feel . . . proud."[6]

6. Sterling A. Brown, "Ragtime and the Blues," in *Sterling A. Brown: A UMUM Tribute,* ed. Black History Museum Committee (Philadelphia: Black History Museum UMUM Publishers, 1982), 81.

When his first book of poetry, *Southern Road,* was published in 1932, it was unanimously hailed as a radical reconfiguration of African American poetics. Luminaries such as Louis Untermeyer and Alain Locke sang Brown's praises, particularly for his ability to reinvent dialect poetry, freeing it from the oppressive politics of plantation tradition caricature. Brown revisited folk forms such as blues, ballads, and work songs, and found there the foundation of a poetics stressing agency and modality inherent in folk culture. In his review of *The Collected Poems of Sterling A. Brown,* Henry Louis Gates, Jr., summarizes the extraordinary achievement of this first collection:

> Not only were most of Brown's poems composed in dialect, but they also had as their subjects distinctively black archetypal mythic characters, as well as the black common man whose roots were rural and Southern. Brown called his poetry "portraitures," close and vivid detailings of an action of a carefully delineated subject to suggest a sense of place, in much the same way as Toulouse-Lautrec's works continue to do. These portraitures, drawn "in a manner constant with them," Brown renders in a style that emerged from several forms of folk discourse, a black vernacular matrix that includes the blues and ballads, the spirituals and worksongs. Indeed, Brown's ultimate referents are black music and mythology. His language, densely symbolic, ironical, and naturally indirect, draws upon the idioms, figures, and tones of both the sacred and the profane vernacular traditions, mediating between these in a manner unmatched before or since.[7]

Throughout the 1930s Brown continued to pursue his poetic innovations, writing two collections of poetry. He attempted to publish his second volume, *No Hiding Place,* in 1937, but because of complications never fully illuminated, Brown's publisher declined to bring it out.[8] As a result, Brown stopped soliciting contracts for his collection until 1975, when *The Last Ride of Wild Bill and Eleven Narrative Poems* was published by Broadside Press. Not until 1980, in *The Collected Poems of Sterling A. Brown,* did *No Hiding Place* finally appear in print.

Despite the problems Brown encountered trying to publish his poetry

7. Henry Louis Gates, Jr., "Songs of a Racial Self: On Sterling Brown," in *Figures in Black* (New York: Oxford University Press, 1987), 227–228.

8. For a more thorough discussion of the controversy surrounding the rejecton of *No Hiding Place* see Sterling Stuckey, Introduction, *The Collected Poems of Sterling A. Brown,* ed. Michael S. Harper (New York: Harper & Row, 1980), 3–13.

toward the end of the 1930s, he continued to produce major critical projects concerned with the particular ways in which literary representation packages and transmits ideological presuppositions. Brown wrote two books critiquing African American characters in literature, *The Negro in American Fiction* and *Negro Poetry and Drama*, both published in 1937. The former, for which the essay "Negro Character As Seen by White Authors" serves as a precursor, examines the pervasive use of racial stereotypes in American literature. The latter constructs a previously ignored history of African American writers and literature. Though written under severe page limitations and thus containing more cursory than in-depth analysis, both studies constitute the first book-length considerations of African American representation (and its attending politics) in American literature. This mode of critical inquiry has given rise to a rapidly expanding body of criticism, of which Toni Morrison's *Playing in the Dark: Whiteness and the Literary Imagination* is a recent example.

Brown addresses the same set of concerns in *Negro Caravan* (1941), coedited with Ulysses Lee and Arthur P. Davis. An anthology amassing the widest array of African American writing to date (and perhaps since), and including blues, spirituals, and folk ballads, the collection attempts to present a "true mosaic" of African American cultural life. Specifically answering *American Caravan* (the annual anthology of the era supposedly representing American literature, but excluding black authors), *Negro Caravan* sought to broaden dramatically the conceptual framework applied to African American expression. Though its limited representation of African American women qualifies the volume's breadth, *Negro Caravan* was the first such anthology to present a multiplicity of voices and forms in order to stress cultural plurality and complexity. The volume still looms as a monumental achievement, to which John Edgar Tidwell aptly attests:

> In 1,082 pages, the literary history of Blacks had been turned on its axis. Who could ever again assert that Blacks had no literary past? What "scholar" could confidently claim Blacks contributed nothing of significance to American letters? Didn't the *Caravan* put to rest an already tiresome argument that Black literature started with the publication of Wright's *Native Son?* Wasn't the canon of American writing considerably enlarged by historicizing unfamiliar Black names and previously unconsidered genres?[9]

9. John Edgar Tidwell, "Oh, Didn't He Ramble! Sterling A. Brown (1901–1989)," *Black American Literature Forum* 23, no. 1 (Spring 1989): 111.

Subsequent anthologies (particularly Michael S. Harper and Robert Stepto's *Chant of Saints*) championing eclecticism in form and voice owe a great deal to *Negro Caravan*'s example.

Brown's most productive period, 1929–1945, during which most of the essays in this volume were written, self-consciously responds to its immediate political and cultural context, one that viewed African Americans and their literature as anomalies, aberrations by definition at odds with American norms. To a large extent mainstream American culture either negated the existence of African Americans or relegated them to severely circumscribed symbolic spaces. Exacerbating the problem, many of Brown's white academic contemporaries constructed literary histories that aggressively denied the ongoing contributions of African Americans. Equally important, numerous writers, particularly those portraying southern life, traded upon ossified stereotypes of African American. Reductive poses of the Mammy, the Sambo, the contented slave, the exotic primitive, and so on (all of which Brown examines in "Negro Character As Seen by White Authors") serve to negate African American presence and agency, thus affirming the assumptions of black aberration and deviation.

Too often, Brown found the various responses of African American critics and writers just as restricted as the statements of their white counterparts. Many New Negro writers asserted a contrasting set of poses, presenting African American gentility and middle-class respectability as the antidote to the myriad dehumanizing caricatures. Thus, those whom Brown terms the "NAACP programmatic writers" used the novel of manners as the vehicle to show the African American middle class as strikingly similar to the American mainstream. W. E. B. Du Bois in 1926 initiated in the *Crisis* a debate over the representation of African Americans in which he aggressively urged the propagandistic use of literature: "all Art is propaganda and ever must be, despite the wailing of the purists. I stand in utter shamelessness and say that whatever art I have for writing has been used always for propaganda for gaining the right of black folk to love and enjoy."[10] The logical outcome of this formula, for Du Bois and others, was literature that represented the black middle class and intelligentsia, in effect literature that put the best face on African American life. In addition to Du Bois's *Dark Princess* and *Quest of the Silver Fleece*, Jessie Fauset's *There Is Confusion* and Nella Larsen's *Passing* (at least as it was originally received) serve as apt examples of the propaganda school.

10. W. E. B. Du Bois, "Criteria of Negro Art," Chicago Conference of the National Association for the Advancement of Colored People, Chicago, June 1926, quoted from *A W. E. B. Du Bois Reader*, ed. Andrew G. Paschal (New York: Collier Books, 1971), 94.

Simultaneously, authors such as Benjamin Brawley, Georgia Douglas Johnson, William Stanley Braithwaite, and Leslie Pinckney Hill pursued a romantic tradition in poetics, one that avoided the hardships of African American peonage in favor of romantic love and the celebration of nature. Brown referred to this tradition as both "escapist" and "derivative," arguing that it suppressed, through erasure, the compelling complexities of African American life.

Still a third group of young New Negro writers claimed an unprecedented level of artistic independence, declaring the right (indeed the responsibility) of the writer to interpret and represent the surrounding life and culture just as he or she saw fit. Thus attempting to free themselves from the limitations of caricature (regardless of political motive) while attending to a dynamic range in African American representation, writers such as Zora Neale Hurston, Langston Hughes, Jean Toomer, and Sterling Brown celebrated African American complexity and artistic vision as the real criteria for innovative cultural work. In what has come to be known as the manifesto of young New Negro artists, "The Negro Artist and the Racial Mountain," Hughes writes:

> We younger Negro artists who create now intend to express our individual dark-skinned selves without fear or shame. If white people are pleased we are glad. If they are not, it doesn't matter. We know we are beautiful. And ugly too. . . . If colored people are pleased we are glad. If they are not, their displeasure doesn't matter either. We build our temples for tomorrow, strong as we know how, and we stand on top of the mountain, free within ourselves.[11]

Both Brown's poetry and criticism pursue the freedom called for by Hughes. As a result of Brown's extensive work in African American folk culture, he was well prepared to present his vision to a wider audience when the opportunity arose. The Gunnar Myrdal study was one such opportunity.

When Gunnar Myrdal first came to the United States from Sweden in 1938 to begin his study, which would become *An American Dilemma: The Negro Problem in Modern Democracy*, "he knew practically nothing about

11. Langston Hughes, "The Negro Artist and the Racial Mountain," in *Speech & Power: The African-American Essay and Its Cultural Content, from Polemics to Pulpit*, vol. 2, ed. Gerald Early (Hopewell, N.J.: Ecco Press, 1993), 91; originally published in the *Nation*, June 23, 1926.

black Americans."[12] Indeed, Myrdal had been selected by the Carnegie Corporation because, according to the panel's thinking, his lack of familiarity with America's long and conflicted history of racial inequities afforded him an "impartiality" that would lend greater credibility to his findings. Because of his ignorance of African American culture and politics, Myrdal relied heavily upon a staff of researchers, many of whom were charged with writing manuscripts to be included with the larger work. The most prolific and perhaps most influential aide, Ralph Bunche, prepared a 3,000-page manuscript that proved to be "the most complete and articulate statement of a black intellectual of the current goals and status of the race."[13] Because of the fact that "of all of Myrdal's collaborators, Brown had the most subtle understanding of Afro-American folklore and the traditions of resistance developed by blacks in the rural South,"[14] he was hired as well, and he took it upon himself to expose Myrdal to the intricacies of African American culture. "Reading his poetry, reciting ballads, and playing blues records,"[15] for Myrdal and taking him to Harlem jazz clubs, Brown attempted to affect one of the most influential studies of African American life by presenting the cultural agency and complexities so often ignored or erased.

During his tenure on the Myrdal study, from 1938 to 1940, Brown further amplified his career-long study of African American culture. The unpublished essay "The Negro in American Culture"[16] came directly out of this study. But more importantly, "Count Us In," perhaps his most ambitious essay to emerge from this period, provocatively exposes the politics creating African American subjugation, and the essay displays the critical acumen Brown brought to bear on all of his projects, both academic and creative. As Brown plays on the highly ironic tension between African American cultural presence and political invisibility—that is, the peculiar ways in which African Americans do and do not "count"—he critiques the larger American paradox: the reality of economic and political servitude at radical variance with the highest ideals of the republic. Thus, Brown's examination of African American participation in World War II, southern politics, and Jim Crow points toward the larger issues of citizenship, toward African Americans being "counted in" as full participants.

12. Walter A. Jackson, *Gunnar Myrdal and America's Conscience: Social Engineering and Racial Liberalism, 1938–1987* (Chapel Hill: University of North Carolina Press, 1990), xiii.
13. Ibid., 132.
14. Ibid., 131.
15. Ibid.
16. Ibid., 151.

During this period Brown also served as national editor of Negro Affairs for the Federal Writers' Project. From 1936 until 1940, Brown supervised the research and writing on African American culture in the guide books for individual states and oversaw the creation of two monumental FWP publications: *Washington: City and Capital* (1937), and *The Negro in Virginia* (1940). Brown's second major essay of this period, "The Negro in Washington," opens the former work, focusing on the sobering paradox of black peonage at the very site of American democracy. In an era that effectively sought to render invisible the plight of African Americans, Brown's essay, in Jere Mangione's words,

> constituted the most forthright analysis of the plight of blacks in Washington ever to be published under government auspices. . . . His prose, though well-tempered, enunciated a forceful indictment of the forces in White America that kept Negroes subjugated in the ghettos of the nation's capital, some in the very backyard of the Capitol itself.[17]

Brown's aggressive critiques in both "The Negro in Washington" and "Count Us In" function as the broadest and most extensive statements in the opening section of this collection, "African Americans and American Politics," exploring the highly conflicted relationship between culture and politics. The more narrowly focused articles in the section, "The American Race Problem As Reflected in American Literature" and "Athletics and the Arts," emphasize historical accuracy, insisting upon the ongoing impact of African Americans upon American culture.

The second section, "American Literature," examines the complex relationship between African American and American literature. Stressing the premise that "without great audiences we cannot have great literature," Brown, in "Our Literary Audience," criticizes the often simplistic and inconsistent ways African American audiences judge black representation in literature by both black and white writers. The second essay, "Negro Character As Seen by White Authors," takes up the larger argument for inclusion and focuses more sharply on literature, exposing the ideological biases transmitted through fiction. Indeed, through Brown's "pioneering critical surveys which began the necessary work of tearing down the icons of misconception, stereotypes, and ignorance that stood fast in American society,

17. Jere Mangione, *The Dream and the Deal: The Federal Writers' Project, 1934–1943* (Boston: Little, Brown, 1972), 210.

he l[ays] the foundation for the study of Black images in American fiction, poetry, and drama."[18] Furthermore, contemporary cultural criticism (by Herman Grey, Patricia Turner, Marlon Riggs, and others) examining black images in the media finds its roots in Brown's groundbreaking work. And, finally, "The New Negro in Literature (1925–1955)" redefines the first moment of African American artistic modernity, again stressing an eclecticism in artistic and cultural expression as an essential strength in New Negro artistry.

The third section of this collection features Brown's influential work on African American folk culture. "Brown's essays on folklore, music, and history," writes Gabbin, "identified the cultural values that pervaded the society." She goes on to assert that "Brown put into place an aesthetic philosophy which has the folk tradition as the basis of art."[19] These essays assert folk expressive culture as a viable vehicle for rationalizing and reshaping one's political and cultural environment. Ultimately, Brown illuminates folk culture as a historically dynamic presence informing the development of American art and culture in the main:

> Whatever may be the future of the folk Negro, American literature as well as American music is the richer because of his expression. . . . Folk Negroes have themselves bequeathed a wealth of moving song, both religious and secular, of pithy folk-say and entertaining and wise folk-tales. They have settled characters in the gallery of American heroes; resourceful Brer Rabbit and Old Jack, and indomitable John Henry. They have told their own story so well that all men should be able to hear it and understand.[20]

Again, the essential inextricability of American and African American culture for Brown points toward egalitarian ideals.

Brown's concise history of early jazz, "Stray Notes on Jazz," ends this section. As he displays his nearly encyclopedic familiarity with jazz history and personnel, Brown offers a subtle comment on the distortions of historical record, particularly by those either unfamiliar with major trends and their influences or bent on a narrow premise. As he draws a sharp demarcation between African American and Euro-American forms of jazz, between origin and derivation, Brown examines a complex cultural process of inno-

18. Gabbin, *Sterling Brown*, 185.
19. Ibid.
20. Sterling A. Brown, "Negro Folk Expression: Spirituals, Seculars, Ballads and Work Songs," *Phylon* 14 (Winter 1953): 61.

vations, adaptations, and marketplace appropriations. Accepting the exigencies of production and consumption, he concludes that jazz continues to thrive as a telling sign of African American cultural modality.

The last section of this volume consists of reviews. Throughout the 1930s Brown wrote a monthly column for *Opportunity:* "The Literary Scene: Chronicle and Comment." Gabbin recounts, "Brown commented on the modern developments in American literature: the trend toward regionalism, the newer traditions of realism and naturalism, the dominance of the lowly subject matter, the use of dialect to achieve local color, and the rising tide of social protest in literature."[21] Brown also published reviews in the *Journal of Negro Education,* the *Nation,* the *New Republic,* and others, covering major writers and publications, both black and white. The selections here feature a fairly diverse set of critical responses to contemporary literature. In "A Romantic Defense" Brown responds, with cutting sarcasm, to Robert Penn Warren, John Crowe Ransom, Allen Tate, and others, specifically their reactionary and nostalgic portrait of black and white life in *I'll Take My Stand* (1930): "The white man's burden. Oh the pity of it, Iago." Though quite brief, Brown's unequivocal dismissal serves as an essential political gesture, a vehicle through which a major New Negro publication denounces the Fugitives, as they were called, and the reigning manifesto of southern intellectual racism. The political clout the Fugitives wielded in academic and publishing circles was not insignificant, particularly as publishers became more hesitant about African American writers as the Depression persisted. For Brown and *Opportunity* to condemn the Fugitives bespeaks the journal's investment in inclusive and ultimately democratic politics. By the same token, Brown challenges both Fannie Hurst and Hollywood, finding *Imitation of Life* (1935) trading on "the old stereotype of the contented Mammy, and the tragic mulatto; and the ancient ideas about the mixture of races."[22] Though Zora Neale Hurston "does not dwell upon the 'people ugly from ignorance and broken from being poor,' "[23] Brown finds *Their Eyes Were Watching God* (1937) an apt corrective, which avoids the pose of "naive primitive" while providing a fuller account of black life. So, too, Brown lauds Langston Hughes's first novel, *Not Without Laughter* (1930), as fiction not only committed to accurate and intricate black portraiture, but also capable of exploring "problems that

21. Gabbin, *Sterling Brown,* 187.
22. Sterling A. Brown, "Imitation of Life: Once a Pancake," *Opportunity* 13 (March 1935): 88.
23. Sterling A. Brown, "Luck Is a Fortune," *Nation* 145 (October 16, 1937): 410.

are universally human."[24] Rounding out this section is Brown's poignant review of an overlooked postbellum account of slavery, Louis C. Hughes's *Thirty Years a Slave* (1897). While Brown finds the lack of emotion or psychological depth in the narrative disturbing, he interprets the omission not as erasure but as survival strategy. Again, Brown makes explicit his assumptions of African American complexity while consistently critiquing denials of that complexity.

I have chosen to open this collection not with an essay in the strict sense, but with Brown's address, late in his career, to his alma mater, Williams College. A rambling reminiscence of his college years, during which he learned the forms and functions of critical reading and thinking, "A Son's Return" levels balanced praise and criticism at both Williams College and Brown himself; in doing so, the address presents both the institution and the man as deeply flawed, yet aggressive in pursuit of their own perfection. But just as much as the address provides crucial information about Brown's intellectual maturation, it reveals a persona poignantly representative of the intellectual and personal rigor sustained across a lifetime of writing. In the mode of the liar, the tall-tale teller more than willing to sacrifice the accuracy of fact for the truth of metaphor, Brown represents the very best of that relentlessly dynamic, undeniably hybrid American tradition of grand storytelling. In this sense, too, "A Son's Return" gestures toward the ensuing collection, revealing Brown's critical acumen and commitment to inclusive politics, while presenting him as consummate stylist, the raconteur taken with the near-limitless possibilities language offers.

MARK A. SANDERS
Emory University

24. Sterling A. Brown, "Not Without Laughter," *Opportunity* 8 (September 1930): 280.

WORKS CITED

Benston, Kimberly W. "Sterling Brown's After-Song: 'When de Saints Go Ma'ch-ing Home,' and the Performance of Afro-American Voice." *Callaloo* 14 and 15 (1982): 33–42.

Brown, Sterling A. "Imitation of Life: Once a Pancake." *Opportunity* 13 (March 1935): 87–88.

———. "Luck Is a Fortune." *Nation* 145 (October 16, 1937): 409–410.

———. "Negro Folk Expression: Spirituals, Seculars, Ballads and Work Songs." *Phylon* 14 (Winter 1953): 45–61.

———. "Not Without Laughter." *Opportunity* 8 (September 1930): 279–280.

———. "Ragtime and the Blues." In *Sterling A. Brown: A UMUM Tribute*, 76–88. Ed. Black History Museum Committee. Philadelphia: Black History Museum UMUM Publishers, 1982.

———. "A Son's Return: 'Oh, Didn't He Ramble.' " In *Chant of Saints: A Gathering of Afro-American Literature, Art, and Scholarship*, 3–22. Ed. Michael S. Harper and Robert Stepto. Urbana: University of Illinois Press, 1979.

Du Bois, W. E. B. "Criteria of Negro Art." In *A W. E. B. Du Bois Reader*, 86–96. Ed. Andrew G. Paschal. New York: Collier Books, 1971.

Ellison, Ralph. "Brave Words for a Startling Occasion." In *Shadow and Act*, 102–106. New York: Random House, 1964.

Gabbin, Joanne V. *Sterling Brown: Building the Black Aesthetic Tradition*. Westport: Greenwood Press, 1985.

Gates, Henry Louis, Jr. "Songs of a Racial Self: On Sterling Brown." In *Figures in Black*, 225–234. New York: Oxford University Press, 1987.

Hughes, Langston. "The Negro Artist and the Racial Mountain." In *Speech & Power: The African-American Essay and Its Cultural Content, From Polemics to Pulpit*. Volume 2, 88–91. Ed. Gerald Early. Hopewell, N.J.: Ecco Press, 1993.

Jackson, Walter A. *Gunnar Myrdal and America's Conscience: Social Engineering and Racial Liberalism, 1938–1987*. Chapel Hill: University of North Carolina Press, 1990.

Levine, Lawrence W. *Black Culture and Black Consciousness: Afro-American Folk Thought from Slavery to Freedom*. New York: Oxford University Press, 1977.

Locke, Alain. "The New Negro." In *The New Negro*, 3–16. Ed. Alain Locke. New York: Albert and Charles Boni, 1925.

Mangione, Jere. *The Dream and the Deal: The Federal Writers' Project, 1934–1943*. Boston: Little, Brown, 1972.

Murray, Albert. *Stomping the Blues*. New York: McGraw-Hill, 1976.

Southern, Eileen. *The Music of Black Americans: A History*. 2d ed. New York: W. W. Norton, 1983.

Stuckey, Sterling. Introduction. In *The Collected Poems of Sterling A. Brown*, 3–13. Ed. Michael S. Harper. New York: Harper & Row, 1980.

Tidwell, John Edgar. "Oh, Didn't He Ramble! Sterling A. Brown (1901–1989)." *Black American Literature Forum* 23, no. 1 (Spring 1989).

A Son's Return:
"Oh, Didn't He Ramble"

~ THANK YOU A GREAT DEAL. Fifty-one years is a long time. I was happy to be invited. I'm somewhat melancholy now, which is not my usual state. I've seen briefly the campus. I've seen the changes. I've seen the Observatory that was way back, and it's right here now on the street. I've forgotten many of the street names. I've never been in Griffin Hall before. This was for government and history. I've been looking at a *Guliel-mensian* and memories have come back, some bitter, some happy. I've thought about the return ever since I was invited back. When I heard the introduction, which was overgenerous, I thought this must be old folks' week, and you're good to gray hairs and bent-over people. I am grateful to you young people that you respect your elders, but I thought of the Playboy of the Western World who, in his coffin, hearing the eulogies about him, rose up and said, "Is it me?" and I always wonder is it me? At my age, these compliments, whether they are true or not, are awful damn good to hear. I talked to Robert Burns Stepto. It's no accident that Robert Burns is one of my favorite poets, and if Robert Burns Stepto keeps introducing me like this, he's one of my favorite people. These notes are not for the "Images and Reality" lecture. I gave that talk at Brown, and I will give it again elsewhere, and I will write an article about it, but I'm talking tonight on a son's return, not a prodigal son, though I'm certainly getting the fatted calf.

The subtitle comes from an old famous folksong that is well known on college campuses, and that is "Oh, Didn't He Ramble"—because I'm a ramblin' wreck, not from Georgia Tech, but I am going to ramble. I am 72 years old, and if I give three minutes to each year that is a long ramble. At Howard University I have been returned. I am the oldest person on the

~ Professor Brown delivered this speech at Williams College on September 22, 1973.

Howard University campus now in active duty. I am older than any maintenance man, any gardener. I am the oldest so and so at Howard, and I am unique in that I'm the only person at Howard who was hired, fired—and I was, I'm not ashamed of it, I'm proud of it, I'm not going to tell you why but the cause was good—but I was hired, I was fired, I was rehired, I was retired, I was again rehired. If I tell many lies tonight and you get them taped, I may be refired.

Oddly enough there are a host of my students down at Amherst and at the University of Massachusetts. And you know Williams' attitude to Amherst. But there's a colony of Howard people at Amherst, and some of them are here, and I'm glad to see them. I don't think they heard my lecture which was a few years back—no, that was at Brown. I get all these Ivy Leagues mixed up, you see, in my rambling way.

I am doing my autobiography at Howard, and they're taping me. I think they have hours and hours, let us say sixty-some hours they have taped me, and I'm now at the fourth grade at Garnet-Patterson School. Frank Marshall Davis, a very good poet who has gone to Hawaii, came back, and we had him read some poems, and I told him about my autobiography. His is finished, and I told him that I was at the fourth grade, and he said, "You must be a slow learner." I did not appreciate that. I am not a slow learner. I *am* a long talker. And I remember vividly, and I'm in two traditions. One is the tradition of Mark Twain. I remember vividly what happened and also a large number of things that did not happen, but sound good. I am the best yarnspinner at Howard University. I am the best liar at Howard University, in the Mark Twain tradition. I can outlie Ralph Bunche, who was a great liar. I'm not talking about the Nobel Peace Prize winner—oh no, oh no. Ralph could tell a wonderful story, but Ralph's political science experience stood in his way: he didn't have Mark Twain behind him. He had a Harvard Ph.D., but he told a good lie. E. Franklin Frazier was a great liar, and our President Mordecai Johnson was a tremendous liar. And these are meant as words of praise. The Mark Twain yarn, this is the anecdote with a point, with pith, sometimes with a little profanity. But of course I would not do that, not always. J. Saunders Redding stated that one quality of Negro folklore was that they had no dirty stories except in the dirty dozens. And I want to know what fraternity houses J. Saunders Redding did not go into. Now I am going to say something that may hurt your feelings, but the dirty story is important in American literature, and I point to Mark Twain. But certainly in our tradition some of the finest dirty stories that I have heard from people—I'd better not say it, but they are close to the theological department at Howard. I am not going to tell you a dirty story. I'm trying to point to a tradition. Of course, I learned this at Williams. I did not read Mark Twain's "1601—A Social Conversation in the Time of the Tudors" under Sam Allen—"Straw Allen"—or under George Dutton, but I learned a great respect for Mark Twain, and I learned a great respect for the tradition of the anecdote.

But I'm going to be serious tonight for about five minutes of these seventy-two and talk about Williams. Why did I come to Williams? I came to Williams because I grew up on the Howard University campus, and my father knew that I was not going to do any studying there. I knew the Howard University campus like the back of my hand. I was mascot at Howard when I was seven. I would get up at five o'clock in the morning. They had a great team in those days. They had a guy whose name, whose nickname, was Bulldog. Bulldog was really a wonderful fullback. At seven years old I would go out in the early morning and struggle under all those sweaters and helmets and whatnot and carry the water bucket, and I used to have to carry the water bucket to them, and in the football games I carried the water bucket to them and also carried signals in. And I'll never forget how red the water bucket was. The sponge of course you know, but I saw all this gore and so forth. But I would tell 'em go over left end, or the right end was laggin' or something. In those days it was shock freelance football. A wedge, you know, like push forward and then just pile over. It was rough and tough football. I was the mascot. I grew up on the campus. I knew it inside out. My father said, "Go to Williams." At Dunbar, they had the tradition of giving annual scholarships to Williams and Amherst and Bowdoin and Bates and Dartmouth, but chiefly Williams. Williams would give a scholarship to Dunbar, and the top man got it. Generally he was the "greasy grind," and the athlete got into Amherst. I was the "greasy grind." I may have been greasy, but I was not exactly a grind. But I had read a lot of books. My house was full of teachers. Everybody in my house was a teacher. Most of them had gone to Howard. I grew up with books. My mother came from Fisk. She was valedictorian of her class. My father met her at Fisk. They were there when Du Bois was there.

I met Du Bois, and Du Bois said, "Who are you?" I said, "I'm Sterling Brown," and he said, "Who was your father?" and I said, "Sterling Nelson Brown." And then Du Bois grabbed me and hugged me. And that is the only time I have known him to hug me. And I think it is the only time I've known him to hug a man. But Du Bois certainly would hug the ladies, for which I am very proud. I am very proud of Du Bois for his great affection for people, including the ladies. I knew Du Bois quite well. I love him. I admire him, and one of the things I admire is what I mentioned.

I won the scholarship to Williams, and I came here to Williams. Now I came here in the SATC. I am a veteran. I am an army veteran. I was wounded on Cole Field. I was also wounded. I don't know which direction, but which is Vermont? There is a plateau on a mountain up there. There is a mountain dome and a plateau, and they had a rifle range up there. And you went straight, and this guy in front of me had his rifle over his shoulder, and he poked me in the eye. And I should have a hash mark. I was in the SATC, which is not to be confused with the ROTC. I was in the Student Army Training Corps, and I got thirty dollars per month. I put my age up to get in because my friend, named Axe Ellis, was eighteen and he wanted to go; and the men that I respected—like Rayford Logan, people of that sort—they were drafted, and they had gone into the Army Training Corps, so I wanted to fight for my country and beat the Kaiser and whip the Huns. But the main thing, I wanted to be with the guys who were going. I always went with older men, so I put my age up and got thirty dollars per month. And when my father found it out he wanted to shoot me or something, and he said that I did it for the thirty dollars. The thirty dollars went nowhere because the junior, Carter Marshall, would beat me and make me buy him soda pop and chocolates, and my thirty dollars went for nothing. I had a uniform. I was fed, and I started as a corporal, and was busted. I ended up as number four in the rear rank of the first squad of D Company, which I resented because I had been a major in the cadets at Dunbar. And I showed off, and we had a little man who didn't finish Williams but he had learned in some summer camp, and he came here and he threw his weight around. And he made wrong orders and I would say, "As you were." And he resented that and he busted me. And he said, "Mr. Brown, when Major General Pew was talking to the troops you were standing like this (*slumps*)," which I was, because Major General Pew was long-winded. Major General Pew used to sing us a song, "Only the Gamefish Swim Upstream," and he was a game fish if there ever was one. Pew was talking and I was loafing, but I was a corporal and the shavetail said, "Do you know, Corporal Brown, how you were standing when Major General Pew was talking? You were standing like this (*slumps*)." And I said, "Do you know how you were standing? You were standing like this (*slumps*)." So he busted me, and I was four in the rear rank . . . and Carter Marshall got to be corporal.

Now Carter Marshall was another one of the token Negroes. Carter was a junior. He had come here earlier, and he was accommodated. Henry Adam Brown was not old enough; he was the sophomore. And so you had a junior and a private, and of course he was number four in the front rank, and I was number four in the rear rank. As we marched to this hill to go to the Commons Club to eat, I would trip Carter Marshall. He would turn around and throw me down in the snow. We were in D company, that was the last company. All the others had gone in to eat, and Carter and I were back here cavorting, which shows the kind of military life I had. But I had bad eyes. I had to memorize the letters in order to get in. So I signed up for the artillery, because I couldn't make the rifle range and I was good in mathematics. I was shooting right-handed, and my right eye wasn't any good, and I didn't have glasses. And so the sergeant said to me, as I would shoot away, "Pull the trigger," and they would wave down there that I had missed the target completely. So he said, "Are you afraid to shoot?" I said, "No, my father's a great hunter; I shoot, but I just can't see it." So he said, "Try left-handed," and the bolt came over this way, you see, you couldn't shoot left-handed. So he put me down in the pit. And in the pit the boys were shooting craps to decide what numbers to put up there. And they would say, "Give him an eight, give him a ten." They were shooting dice. They had no money. It was a beautiful experience. It was freezing cold. That is where I got what nearly caused my early death. It was the coldest place. With raincoats—we had slickers, no overcoats. You climbed up this plateau, and then I went and got down in the pit. And of course I don't like to gamble, but I had to go along with my peers!

What was Williams? Was it just the joy? The SATC was good. It was democratic. A lot of the boys were brought in from North Adams and Williamstown. Carter Marshall and I lived in Williams Hall, and I can't remember whether we lived on the top floor or the first, because we had a roommate, a Jewish fellow named Victor Leo Jacobson. And Victor Leo Jacobson was not tall enough to be in our squad. He was short, but he was long on knowledge. He was from Cleveland. He was long on knowledge that I didn't know much about. And I don't know whether he was first floor or not, but he left the room, and we had to puff his pillow and things to make it seem that he was in the bed, because he was out with women from North Adams. I think he was on the first floor because I think we put the window up to let him in. I do not remember for sure. But he was not letting the army interfere with what he would call his "basic training." Victor Leo Jacobson did not return to Williams. But he was our roommate, he selected me and Carter as we had something of his kind of situation. He was in our squad; he could not drill. He didn't do anything except to go out with the women and never get caught. The SATC ended with Armistice Day. I was to go to artillery camp, and Carter Marshall was to go to infantry camp. Well, now I've already taken a whole lot of time on SATC.

The second year that I was here . . . I was looking at the *Gulielmensian*, and I noticed that everybody had "East Hall" or "West Hall" or "—Fraternity" except me and Ralph Winfield Scott, who was then a freshman. I was a sophomore, and beside our names was the expression—"Mrs. Hogan's." Beside Carter Marshall's was "East College" and beside Henry Brown's was "East College." But they lived at Mrs. Hogan's too. President Harry Garfield was not here, and I don't know who it was, but somebody said that Negroes at Williams would be happier together. So they put all four of us at Mrs. Hogan's. And Mrs. Hogan's was between the tailor shop on Spring Street and Jessup Hall. It was not an alley, but it also was not a street. Mrs. Hogan, I can't remember; I know she was delightful. But we paid our rent, and we were told that the reason we were there was that we had not paid our advance on the dormitory room. I know that was true of Carter because he was poorer than I, and Henry A. Brown was even poorer than he, but my father had put down some money on my room. Nevertheless we were all four there.

I had the largest room because, I think, my father had paid something for Berkshire Hall. Ralph Scott, the freshman, had a fairly small room, and Henry Brown and Carter had the double. We lived there for a year, and the statement was made that the college was looking out for our happiness. They thought we would be happier together. And I know, this is very arrogant for me to say it, but I was the spokesman even though I was the sophomore. And I said that we came to Williams for an education, and let Williams give us the education and we would look out for our own happiness. And I would still say that, except I might be a little more profane and state what kind of g.d. happiness I am going to look out for! But I looked at the pictures that I had taken then, and there was a great deal of bounce and resiliency. One picture that I'm going to show Robert Burns Stepto— but I couldn't bring it up—is a picture of me sitting in shirtsleeves in six feet of snow, fanning, and I sent it down to Washington, and all my schoolmates had it, and I'm fanning and I'm grinning. I was doing a lot of grinning then, and I had a lot of bounce. Now in my melodramatic moments, and having heard a lot of propaganda, much of which I agreed with, I've been told that Williams was a traumatic experience. And you know I had fallen for that and sometimes later spoke of how unhappy I was. I was not unhappy. My letters home were not unhappy. And I've been thinking about it. Why should I expect graduates of Andover, Exeter, and Groton to take me in and know me? They had never seen a Negro, and I had never seen a white man their age. Until I came to Williams, I had never spoken to a white boy except the little son of the drugstore man where we used to go to get sundaes for my family; and he and I were friends until Negroes came around with me or whites came around with him. Then we didn't know each other. But until that point we would speak. You know. So this was the separation that was strong.

So, when I came to Williams, I have mentioned, I met with (I think it's President Nixon who said it) "benign neglect." I did not meet with anything blatant. I did not meet with anything flagrant. Carter Marshall was called a "nigger" on Main Street, and he knocked the guy down. And I was right behind him to help on that. I was not a fighter, but I had my race to defend. And that's the only time I heard the word "nigger." I've talked to other people and Rayford Logan says that a professor from Louisiana teaching Kipling threw in the word "nigger" unnecessarily, and he told me that he thought that no Negroes should study under this man. I did, and I'll tell you about that a little later.

One of the big shots in my class from Louisiana would come to us (we were knickerbockers in those days), and he would say "Look at the little 'knickers'?" but you didn't know whether it was *ck* or *gg*. And the last lie I want to tell is that they used to call me Brownie. But how the hell could I object to them calling me Brownie? My name was Brown, but they never missed on Brownie. I was Brownie.

During the Depression, a man as seedy looking as I, as indigent as I and as much in need of relief as I, met me at Times Square and he said to me, "Brownie, are they doin' you all right?" This cat was one of the best artists at Williams; and for the *Purple Cow* he drew beautiful cartoons. He was in French class with me and a very nice guy, and I know that he knew during the Depression, if I needed any help, he would help. I think I could have helped him. I was not professor at Howard, I was assistant professor, making the glamorous amount of $1500 a year. This is not Depression time, this was before Depression. So I might have helped him, but the business of Brownie and the rest was there. Now, I have not been a good son of Williams in respect to contributions to the alumni fund. I have not done as well as I should. Nor has the Class of '22, according to the *Record*. I know that is wrong, every now and then I have sent my . . . my modicum. And I'm going to send a lot more now that I'm back here, because the place is very dear to me. Now why is the place dear to me? I owe this place more than this guy at Times Square could tell me. I learned how to read at Williams. I learned how to teach at Williams. I want to read what your new president has said. Your new president, in greeting the freshmen, has said:

These next four years will come to represent many things to you. Friendships that you will cherish for the rest of your life. The development and enjoyment of a variety of skills. Growth in social skills and self-confidence. Other skills—theatrical, athletic, and musical. But I hope you will perceive your stay at Williams, *principally*, as a unique opportunity for the development of a range of intellectual skills and habits that will stay with you for a lifetime and add to your enjoyment, stature and usefulness as a human being.

I did not store up this friendship, except for the nucleus of Negro students. I got to know Allison Davis very well. I got to know Carter Marshall and Henry Brown well. Allison Davis and Ralph Scott and I used to go for long walks, and we decided the race problem, we decided the problem of women, which was a serious thing here.

This was a monastic institution, and the opportunities for, let us say, for conversation with the fair sex were limited. The dirtiest thing I did at Williams was when I went over to be initiated into the Omega Phi Psi fraternity. I went to Boston, Massachusetts, and I had never seen so many beautiful women in my life. Of course, male Bostonians stated that they were not beautiful; I had just not seen women, period. But anything I saw was beautiful. I went over there and the fraternity guys said to be at the fraternity house at midnight, dressed up for this rough initiation. I came to the fraternity house at one o'clock in a blue coat and white flannel britches and was not bothered about the initiation. I had just fallen in love with six different women. I'm going to call up five of them on this trip—and their grandchildren, I'd like to send some of their grandchildren to Williams. Not out of any paternal relationship, but out of love of both Williams and these lovely things. So I went to this fraternity house late, and they nearly killed me. These were people from Lincoln University and Howard, and they resented my going to Williams anyway, you know, and me, Ivy League conceited egotist and wearing white flannel britches. They wore those britches out. They beat me up and down the Charles River. They beat me in South Boston, Somerville, North Cambridge, Arlington, Boston Common. I died on Boston Common, a death that Crispus Attucks never suffered. I still cannot sit down on my memories of the Boston Massacre. I had on my breast, or chest, or whatever a man has—I had Omega Phi Psi all over me. I went down later to Tuskegee, where the guys from B.U. were, and they had become great lawyers and doctors, but they nearly killed me.

I came back to Williams, and I had both consecutively cut and I had also overcut, and that was bad. We had to make chapel at seven forty-five every day God sent, including holidays. Not on Sunday, that was later and longer. But we had seven forty-five chapel, because of eight o'clock classes.

Seven forty-five you went in there, you had to go in. Most guys went in pajamas and heavy coats. They bet. (I was not alienated: I participated.) They bet on what would be the length of the prayer—six minutes, seven minutes, eight minutes. They'd bet on anything. They were not very religious. Nor was I. So, you could not cut consecutively, you could not overcut . . . and I had overcut and consecutively, and Dean Howes said, "Mr. Brown, you have got to go. You have got to be suspended." I knew that as much beating as my fraternity brothers had given me that was nothing to what my father was going to give me. I committed one of the worst deeds of racism in my career. I said to Dean Howes, "You would not do this if I were not a Negro." It was the college law, he would have put out Nixon's son or daughter. He would have put out anybody—I had broken the law. I threw race at him and said he's picking on a poor little Negro. And it worked. He was the descendant of abolitionists. This man's grandfather had probably fought at Chickamauga or something, and he nearly cried. He said, "Mr. Brown, do you really feel that?" I said, "Yes, and the other fellows feel it too." From then on I not only consecutively cut, you know, I ain't thought about chapel. That's not true really, but it's a good lie.

So at Williams I made friends with people who have been good friends, good mentors, brothers. Allison Davis is now John Dewey Professor at the University of Chicago. He's been there thirty years, almost, on the faculty. He's a great guy. A great teacher. Rayford Logan was before me. Rayford Logan is a professor emeritus at Howard. He's teaching courses at Howard. He's one of the oldest people. He's older than I, but not in length of service. Rayford has received from Williams an honorary degree. He's Ph.D. from Harvard. He got an A.B., an M.A., and a Litt.D. from Williams, and he is one of my best friends. We were close. He was not here with me, he was three or four years ahead of me. Allison was here, Carter Marshall became a noted doctor, taught at Yale, taught at Howard. Ralph Scott, first rate in government and history, was a principal at a school in Washington, and died untimely. Mortimer Weaver made Phi Beta Kappa here, taught at Howard. Made Delta Sigma Rho. I didn't make Delta Sigma Rho. I won one oratorical contest, was second once, and made alternate on the debating team. When they had the debate, I wore a full dress suit. I got a picture in the *Gulielmensian* of me in a full dress suit. I have on a white tie, and I'm sitting there conceited, posing unnaturally, and the full dress suit was green with age. It had been worn by Montgomery Gregory, who was on the Harvard debating team, about ninety years before. He was my Sunday

School teacher, and he let me have it. It did not fit well, but you can't tell that in the picture.

And we had a great tennis team. There was this man named Chapin. I was number one on the Commons Club tennis team. I learned playground tennis in Washington, which was scrambling like Bobby Riggs tried to against that woman champion, you know, way back, that proved women's superiority. And I had the scrambling game, and then I learned to drive. I had a good forehand. And when I went back to Washington they said, "You play like a fay boy"; I had learned to drive at Williams. I always had a weak backhand, and I ran around it; therefore I was vulnerable. But I was the best man on the Commons Club team. And Chapin was a great player, and there was a guy named Bullock who was the captain. He was a pretty good player. Allison Davis and I were the Commons Club's doubles team, and we were pretty good. I had to play for the Commons Club against the fraternity, and they brought in a guy whose service I have not seen until yet. And this guy was a great baseball player and was seldom on the courts, and so I thought I had something good. I have never seen the ball. He had all the stuff that is today known, you know that Ashe would have, that Smith would have, and whatnot, and I've never seen the ball. It was a shame. The ball would fly off my racket. We were playing in front of Williams Hall, and I was hitting the ball in the Grace Auditorium. But I was a good tennis player.

I was good in track in SATC. They thought I had to be a good runner because all Negroes can run. We got longer heels in the back. You know, that kind of nonsense. So I was fast and they put me in a race, but they put spikes on me and I'd never had spikes on. And get on your mark, get set, go . . . and I'm stuck in the heel with those spikes on me, and I've never had spikes on. And I came in last. I'll tell you one last lie about athletics and Du Bois's double consciousness. I rooted strongly for Williams all the time. Ben Boynton was one of the greatest athletes Williams ever had. He played professional football, and I saw him at the Griffith Stadium in Washington. He remembered me. So I was all for Williams until Amherst would come over with the track team and there were boys I had grown up with. So I wanted to cheer for purple Williams, but Amherst was also wearing purple and white, and they were my buddies at Dunbar High School. So I would be cheering for Percy Barnes, who became professor of chemistry at Howard—a great guy at Amherst, Phi Beta Kappa—Montague Cobb, and Bill Hastie, and Charlie Drew. I would cheer for them all when they ran against Williams. What happened was there was a man over there named Parker who ran a two-mile race and we're cheering for all the Negroes on the team, 'cause we wanted the race to be well represented. But in the two-mile race Parker came in about a mile and a half behind everybody, and we wanted to lynch him. He was the slowest man. I was not too fast. I was fast in the SATC. So athletically I did not achieve a great deal.

I learned how to read, however. And I want here to give my testimony to great teachers here at Williams, because the whole business of teaching is very important to me. I want to read what was said by ex-President Pusey of Harvard speaking of Colonel Williams's legacy. He says here:

> Teaching is a very demanding profession. If your college has spoken to you truly and deeply you have seen in your relationship with one or more of your teachers, what teaching can be, and what it can mean in life. It is no secret that the profession does not hold out promise of financial reward. [Amen.] There are very few places in American society where the results of selfish material greed have shown itself more hideous than in the relative depressed condition of the profession of teaching. Did we think clearly, this career would certainly be held to be one of the most deserving of all. These unfortunately are facts one cannot ignore.

He mentions then that

> All professions in the full range of calling make a legitimate claim on me and on you, but if you have the skill, personal gift, and love of the enterprise which might enable you to become a truly great teacher, may I urge you not to close your eyes to this road without giving it careful consideration. For if you can be a teacher, you are needed more, more than ever before.

At this stage in my life, it is a good thing to hear that kind of statement, when you find out your life has not been completely empty. My students have meant a great deal to me. Now, in my seventh decade, I hear from Kenya that "I am your son." An article says I have no sons—I have no children. I have an adopted son and this guy writes me from Kenya and tells me he is my son and I've got thousands of them. I don't know whether I got thousands, but I have plenty of them. Some of them are in here now. That's a very important reward and I'm glad to hear that from President Pusey. And we have here something about Ephraim Williams's remarks on Mark Hopkins and the little log:

There was a rare simplicity in Hopkins's approach to his pupils. He sought to train them to think their way into the hearts of things and to think in such a fashion that life would have meaning, and they could use their powers to the best advantage.

Pusey continues:

Our need today is to convert his age old persistence into a steady stream of able young people who with the spirited zeal of a pioneer like Colonel Williams will homestead our contemporary educational frontier and keep alive and extend the faith.

I want to pay tribute here to some of the English teachers. I cannot give you a list of the great teachers I had at Williams. I look at the *Gulielmensian* and I remember a man like Professor MacElfresh in physics. I remembered Professor Carl Whetmore. I met only recently a novelist, married to a poet in Washington. He heard that I was coming to Williams, and said he was Karl Weston's nephew. But I want to speak of four men in the English department. One of them is Carroll Maxcy, who had been dean of Williams, who taught me Chaucer, who taught me Rhetoric 7-8, he taught me the Lincoln-Douglas debates, he taught us argumentation and debating. He has a statement I was going to read later. There was one who was called "Straw" Allen. His name was Samuel S. Allen. They say he was a poor student who paid his way to Williams with a load of straw. He was a very democratic, excellent, rather dry teacher of American literature. He was an excellent friend who wrote me a beautiful letter when *Southern Road* came out. I didn't know he even knew about it. And the third was a man named Albert Licklider and Licklider was the man I was told never to study under. Licklider was a Princeton man. One of the lesser ambitions of Williams in those days was to be a second Princeton. Which I could never understand, because I didn't think much of the first Princeton, which of course never let a Negro in there unless he was waiting tables at a fraternity, and they didn't have many of them. That has changed. I have lectured at Princeton. Will Thorpe is one of my good friends. He went to Hamilton; but he went to Hamilton, he didn't go to Princeton. Princeton was one of the worst. Harvard, as far as my people are concerned, was one of the best. Yale was one of the worst and Williams, with its Haystack Monument, was one of the leaders.

But Williams fell down at a certain time, I think under President Dennett, when it was said Negroes would be happier elsewhere, but more than that, Williams should be democratic, and being democratic it should get students from the South. And these students from the South should be white and they may reject Negroes being here; therefore in the spirit of democracy let us leave Negroes out of here. Fortunately, that did not prevail, that failed, according to one of the trustees—he has told me much about this. But when we were staying in Mrs. Hogan's, Harvard was keeping people out of its dormitory. Princeton was not letting anybody in, nor was Vassar, and I taught at Vassar when they didn't even have the token they had in my day here. So there was this whole picture in American life. Rayford Logan said he had no problems about living here because the law was you could not live in a dormitory.

Now Williams has had the Haystack Monument tradition and it has had these excellent men. This is a lead-up to Licklider. Licklider was from the Deep South and would let you know it. I was told not to take Licklider. I took him and I got "A" almost all the way with Licklider. I heard nothing—there was nothing at all of disparagement or whatnot. He treated me well and made no racial statement. I took a course in creative writing and he said, "Mr. Brown, you have no sense of rhythm." I was the only Negro in the class and everybody else was rhythmical except me. Which was ridiculous. I have a marvelous sense of rhythm, not because I am a Negro but because I am rhythmical. Or, as Louis Armstrong says, "rhythmatical." I am a good dancer and I know a whole lot of Negroes are not good dancers. And when you start talking about all Negroes having a sense of rhythm, ask a lot of girls they've been dancing with recently. Take a lot of Mississippi fieldhands who just came from plowing that mule and put them in the country dance and ask the girls, "Have they got rhythm?" This whole nonsense about racial rhythm is ridiculous. But this man had said I had no sense of rhythm for this reason. He was giving us French poems to translate, and I was a first-rate student of Jean and Albert Cru and Karl Weston, and I knew a lot about French and was giving a literal translation, getting the meaning of the French. The boys—the other guys in the class did not know French, and all they knew was beat, so they had the iambs going but the French was bad. So he said you have no sense of rhythm. So I gave him three poems I had just written to three girls—one in Boston, one in Baltimore, and one in Washington. Because I was a *true* Williams Man. I believe in spreading the blessings around. I wrote a beautiful poem with a beautiful beat and he said, "Mr. Brown this is much more like it."

My last problem with Licklider was that I could not meet a deadline. So I got an "incomplete" in my senior year in rhetoric, whatever was the number, creative writing. There I saw the loyalty of my classmates, because they wanted to raise the devil because they said Licklider, from the Deep South, is pressing this poor Negro, you know. So they sided with me. Because they felt a kind of neglect from him, they were still from the North. So they fought my battle. But I said "nay, nay, my work is late." At 11:59 on the deadline date *I stuck it under the door* of the faculty club over there off Spring Street and I got my B with him. I didn't get an A. I took Shakespeare with him, Elizabethan drama and creative writing. It was not my lack of rhythm that got me the B; it was that the work came in late.

Now the important man is George Dutton. George Dutton was sarcastic, sharp witted; he didn't suffer fools gladly, he was a tough guy. He taught me English 5-6, he taught me the Romantic movement, he taught me the modern novel. He was in bad at Williams because he had written an article in the *Redbook* on modern ficton. And that was too advanced. You must remember that this was in the twenties and American literature was unpopular. He taught the English novel but he made us read *Madame Bovary*, he made us read *Brothers Karamazov*, he told us of Dostoevsky, Tolstoy, he told us about the new Sinclair Lewis. He taught me critical realism. He was a tremendous influence. I learned to read at Williams College. I could not stand the cold up there. I was from the Deep South, Washington, D.C., and I could not stand this weather. So I caught either the pleurisy, pneumonia, or something, and was out of school but I could go to the library. So in the library, right across from here, in about two days I read Thomas Hardy's *Return of the Native*, George Meredith's *Diana of the Crossways*, and Balzac's *Père Goriot*. I could not do it now. I could not read *Diana of the Crossways* now in six months. Back there I was very bright and I read. I learned then. I was a junior then. I learned then what reading meant. Last anecdote about Dutton. Dutton was teaching Joseph Conrad. He said Joseph Conrad was being lionized in England—H. G. Wells and Galsworthy and all the ladies and lords and the rest were making over Joseph Conrad and whatnot, and Conrad was sitting over in the corner, quiet, not participating. Dutton said he was brooding and probably thinking about his native Poland and the plight of his people. He looked straight at me. I don't know what he meant, but I think he meant, and this is symbolic to me, I think he meant don't get fooled by any lionizing, don't get fooled by being here at Williams with a selective clientele. There is business out there that you have to take care of. Your people, too, are in a plight. I've never forgotten it. He was a great man. He was a man who was forbidding until he knew you. He was one of the warmest human beings I have ever met. I said this once and his son heard it. His son, who graduated from Williams, has written me a letter. I'm going to write him about my return. Dutton *taught* me, he *taught* Allison Davis, he *taught* Mortimer Weaver. He was a great teacher. He was not alone. Williams was full of great teachers. One last thing. (I've taken up 72 years almost.) I want to read what Carroll Maxcy wrote about another great teacher whom I had at Harvard. And this man's name is important in the history of Williams. This is Bliss Perry. Bliss Perry was at Harvard and he also taught at Williams. (I studied at Harvard in '23 and then I went back in '31; I took courses with Bliss Perry both times.) Carroll Maxcy said:

> Whatever fame Professor Perry may have attained in the field of literature, to Williams men he is the teacher. In the amateur spirit he has written, "Your born teacher is as rare as a poet. Once in a while your college gets hold of one. It does not always know that it has him, and proceeds to ruin him by overdriving the moment he showed power; or let another college lure him away for a few hundred dollars more a year. But while he lasts—and sometimes, fortunately, he lasts until the end of a long life—he transforms a lecture hall by enchantment. Lucky is the alumnus who can call the roll of his old instructors, and among the martinets, and the pedants, and the piously insane can here and there come suddenly upon a man."

And that was Dutton and that was Bliss Perry. Upon a man, a man who taught him to think or help him to feel and thrill to a new horizon. And Maxcy said of Bliss Perry, "scholarly in his taste, clear in his thinking, simple and direct in the expression of his thought and always human in his personality. He taught us to *think* he helped us to *feel* and he *thrilled* us to a new horizon. To us he seemed the ideal teacher. And this teacher, and this man withal, he has won the loyalty of Harvard, Princeton and Williams men alike." This was written by Carroll Lewis Maxcy, class of '76 and appeared in a Williams anthology in 1921.

These men taught me to think. At Harvard, I went into careful study of American poetry. I learned from Edwin Arlington Robinson's *Tilbury Town*, where he took up the undistinguished, the failures, and showed the extraordinary in ordinary lives. I learned Robert Frost. I learned from my own; the man I was brought up on was Dunbar. I learned from Claude McKay. I participated in what I called the New Negro Renaissance. I wrote poetry. I went South. I taught at Virginia Seminary, where I learned a great deal that I could not learn at Williams, I learned the strength of my people, I learned the fortitude. I learned the humor. I learned the tragedy. I learned from a wandering guitar player about John Henry, about Stagolee, about "The

Ballad of the Bollweevil." I learned folktales. I learned folkstuff. I was like a sponge. I had a good eye. I had a good ear. I had a good mind trained by people like Dutton. I learned how to read American literature and found out how much stupid stereotyping of my people there was. I read all the Jim Crow *additions* to the history of American literature. I read nonsense from people who talked about *the Negro,* who probably knew their cook and would generalize from that. I read the nonsense of people like Thomas Nelson Page. I saw the limitations of Joel Chandler Harris, of whom the first historian of the Negro in literature said that in sixteen lines of Brer Turtle you have the whole range of Negro character. That kind of nonsense I read. I wrote *The Negro in American Fiction.* I wrote many essays. I am still writing them. Howard University is bringing out a book of mine. It is called *To a Different Drummer* and I pay credit, of course, to Thoreau, whom I learned of in "Straw" Allen's class and under George Dutton. *Southern Road* is going to be reprinted. I'm bringing out a book of poems, *Thirty-six Poems Thirty-six Years Later,* because friends of mine, like Stokely Carmichael and the rest, think that I wrote the poems after discussing these things with them.

I am an *old Negro* and I am proud of it. My students get angry because I do not use the word "black." I do use the word "black." If a person wants to call himself black, fine. I am very glad the word "black" has different connotations now than what it had. I am an old Negro, as W. E. B. Du Bois is an old Negro, Paul Robeson is a Negro, James Weldon Johnson is a Negro, Mordecai Johnson is a Negro, Jack Johnson is a Negro, and a whole lot of other Johnsons are Negroes. I am not a worshipper of the bourgeoisie. I am not one who has piled up money at the cost of my deprived brethren. There are a whole lot of people who called me a "bourgeois Babbitt" whom I am going to meet on the shores when they come to Africa, but I am not going back to Africa tomorrow . . . I am going to Tipton, Mississippi. They need me over here and a whole lot of Africans don't. I was taught Sunday School by an African. Many of my best friends, this is an awful thing to say, I'll change that, my best students, friends, teachers and the rest are Africans. I have had a love for Africa since I was a child. But I know a whole lot of people who are talking about going to Africa are going to stop in Paris on the way over. A lot of them are not going to stay over there because it is tough and rough there, and many are copping out on what is tough and rough here.

I am an integrationist, though that is an ugly word, because I know what segregation really was. And by integration, I do not mean assimilation. I believe what the word means—an integer is a whole number. I want to be in the best American traditions. I want to be accepted as a whole man. My standards are not white. My standards are not black. My standards are human. I love the blues. I love jazz and I'm not going to give them up. I love Negro folk speech and I think it is rich and wonderful. It is not *dis* and *dat* and a split verb. But it is "Been down so long that down don't worry me," or it is what spirituals had in one of the finest couplets in American literature: "I don't know what my mother wants to stay here for. This old world ain't been no friend to her." I'm teaching spirituals at Howard. You get a lot of nonsense about the spirituals talking about the good ole days, or when the Negro sings of wanting to be free he means freedom from sin. So when he says, "I've been rebuked and I've been scorned" that means, you know, that he hasn't been baptized yet or something. That kind of nonsense. Newman White, who was a great scholar on Shelley, says the Negro seldom contemplated his low condition. And I want him to ask . . . his mama where he heard that the Negro did not contemplate his low condition. Which Negro, which cook, said that to him and how much winking did the Negro do after he said what he did? The whole picture of the Negro I saw was flagrantly ridiculous. Sometimes the motive was not ignorance, but evil, and that I have fought and am continuing to fight.

Now I want to close this with a statement from another of the people about Williams. But I think the business of the teaching and the importance of Williams to me is there. I learned here to think, I try to make my students think. I learned, I say, critical realism. I want my students to be critically realistic. I want them to look at what is on the page, and think about it.

One last anecdote. I like to send out the audience laughing. I had a room in Berkshire Hall about as big as a telephone booth, but that was all my father could afford. My father had two jobs. He was professor of theology at Howard, and he was a minister; and he got no money for either job. My sisters taught school and put me through. I waited tables at Zeta Psi fraternity for one year. Then I ate on Spring St. and I lived on Western sandwiches, which I still love, and Lorna Doones and water. This is not *Black Boy* . . . I ate, as you can see I have an *embonpoint* (French for belly). I was skinny then, but I was eating enough. I was eating a kind of monotonous diet. But I still love Lorna Doones. They are better than ordinary crackers; they got a little butter or shortening or something in them. But I ate Westerns. I had Westerns, I had Easterns, and I had milkshakes. I spent most of my money across the street at Bemis's store, buying second-hand books that the Williams students had sold there. I have a beautiful library, and that was the nucleus of it—a lot of books—from Williams

1913, Williams 1919. Fine books, 'cause Williams made you buy good books. So I ate on Spring St. and starved. When I went to Boston to join the fraternity, I didn't eat for a while, but I made it. I made it down to the present until I have, you know, a "bay window."

Carter was even poorer. We went to a dance in Pittsfield one cold night. We did not have many clothes, and Carter did not have a full suit with long breeches. We were wearing knickerbockers which we got at Rudnick's; these were second-hand knickerbockers. Lots of people wore rough clothes then. This was after World War I. Carter Marshall comes to a dance—a full-dress dance at Pittsfield. Everybody else is there in full dress. I had on a suit. Henry had on a part suit. Carter came in with a long coat and nothing but golf stockings showing beneath. Looked very bad. And he says to me, in front of these people who were running the dance . . . they did not like us much, we were intruders. Carter has to explain why he comes there in a long coat and his skinny legs in golf stockings and his great big shoes. He says, "Sterling, the news of the dance came to me when I was on the links. And I could not go home and change." There was six feet of snow on the ground. Carter Marshall did not know which end of the golf stick to use. And this guy comes telling me that "I was out on the links." Good God Almighty!

The last lie is that I had a kind of literary group in this telephone booth in Berkshire. And a lot of the intellectuals and the mavericks—you know, the ones who didn't mind being known to associate with a Negro—the rebels—they would come in there. You can always find five or six of them. We were sitting there one night and in comes Gyp Symonds with a hat on, a kind of Alpine hat, knickerbockers, and a cane. He comes in and he starts with the Latin: *Non sum qualis eram bonae sub regno Cynarae.*

All of us looked at him like he was crazy, which he was. He was a great guy. He was a fine poet and I looked for great things from him, but I think he went the other way. He intoned:

> Last night, ah, yesternight, betwixt her lips and mine
> There fell thy shadow, Cynara! thy breath was shed
> Upon my soul between the kisses and the wine;
> And I was desolate and sick of an old passion,
>   Yea, I was desolate and bowed my head:
> I have been faithful to thee, Cynara! in my fashion.

And then he went through the next two stanzas and closed with

> I cried for madder music and for stronger wine,
> But when the feast is finished and the lamps expire,

Then falls thy shadow, Cynara! the night is thine;
And I am desolate and sick of an old passion,
    Yea, hungry for the lips of my desire:
I have been faithful to thee, Cynara! in my fashion.

Oh, he was great. I learned the poem by heart. I quoted it all up and down the Atlantic seacoast. I won my wife by reciting it, "I have been faithful to thee, Cynara!—in my fashion."

It introduced me to Ernest Dowson. We had studied Swinburne. But here was a better Swinburne and he was something! So, Symonds broke up the meeting; we had never heard such things. That was the temper of the times. But when I went to Harvard, I learned about Edwin Arlington Robinson, Edgar Lee Masters, and that monstrosity written by Vachel Lindsay called "The Congo." When I read this poem to my classes they love it and I say, "think about it": and then they hate it. "Then I saw the Congo creeping through the black, cutting through the jungle with a golden track!" I tried to write a parody, with Severn cutting through the Anglo-Saxon, but I couldn't get a rhyme for "Anglo-Saxon" except "claxon" and "claxon" is a bad horn. So I had to give it up. But I do have a poem called *The New Congo.* And it is a killer.

Now I'm going to close this with a poem from a man who taught at Dartmouth. He comes from this neighborhood and he wrote about New Hampshire and north of Boston, a man who has meant a great deal to me. Langston Hughes has meant much to me, Richard Wright, Claude McKay, Ralph Ellison, and I have learned also from people like Robert Frost. And this is the end of my 72nd year to you. I swear I'm not going to say one word after I explain this poem. I must explain it. Because you will say, "Why does a man who studied T. S. Eliot and Ezra Pound give us this doggerel?" It is not doggerel. This, to me, says more than a whole lot of the *Cantos,* which I have read, and have not dug completely, as many critics haven't. I read T. S. Eliot's *Waste Land* when I was at Harvard. I bought a copy at the Harvard Co-op and I worked out at that time a good exegesis of it. And I knew a lot about those allusions. "And April is the cruelest month." I knew it almost by heart. So I had my Eliot period, and I've also had my falling out with the Anglican so forth and so forth and so on.

This poem is called "In Dives' Dive." I met Robert Frost once and quoted this to him and he said that I was the only person he knew that knew this poem and respected it. I loved it. He asked me did I play poker and I told him no and he said that he didn't play good poker either. We talked about poker and there were a whole slough of new poets there. He and I were the old poets talking about "Dives' Dive." Ladies and gentlemen, from an Old Book known as the Bible, there was a character named Dives. And in the spiritual it is:

> Rich man Dives he lived so well, don't you see
> Rich man Dives lived so well, don't you see
> Rich man Dives lived so well,
> When he died he found a home in hell
> He had a home in that Rock, don't you see.
>
> Po' boy Lazarus, po' as I, don't you see
> Po' boy Lazarus, po' as I, don't you see
> Po' boy Lazarus, po' as I,
> When he died he found a home on high
> I got a home in that Rock, don't you see.

So Frost takes Brother Dives. Ladies and gentlemen, the word "dive" means a low place. It means a haunt of iniquity. It means what you privileged children know nothing about. This is not worth going into. That is what a dive is. There is gambling there and many other things unmentionable in a mixed society. I am trying to give you now an exegesis in the manner of the New Critics. I want you to understand the language and then you get the meaning. And of course the structure of the poem is the important thing. The biography of the author has nothing to do with it. So you get your meaning, but I want you to know *what in the hell I'm talking about*. They're talking about a game named "poker." I've got to explain it afterwards, because if you don't like this poem my evening is ruined. And don't throw "Ash Wednesday" at me either. This is a poem for me. This is an autobiographic "sounding off."

> It is late at night and still I am losing,
> But still I am steady and unaccusing.
>
> As long as the Declaration guards
> My right to be equal in number of cards.
>
> It is nothing to me who runs the Dive
> Let's have a look at another five.

Now this means that Frost is gambling, and he has been a loser all of his life. As far as I am concerned, I have been a loser most of my life. But in the seventies, I've been a winner; you know like coming back to Williams, etc. "It is late at night": Frost was in his seventies or later, that's what "late at night" means. It is late at night and still I'm losing. But *still I* am steady and unaccusing. He is not laying blame on anybody. If I lose I am not singing blues about anybody else causing it. I am steady and unaccusing. As long as the Declaration—*the Declaration of Independence* as long as the Declaration guards—g-u-a-r-d-s. "As long as the Declaration *guards* my right to be *equal* in number of cards." You don't have any more cards than I have. I don't have any more than you have. We got the same number of cards. As long as the Declaration guards my right to be equal in number of cards, it does not matter to me who runs the dive. Now that's where a lot of my liberal friends disagree, and I too would agree with them somewhat. It matters who runs it. But he is saying it does not matter who runs the dive. I, Frost, an American individual, will take my chance. I'm not a good poker player, but I'm not complaining. It does not matter to me who runs the dive. Let's have a look at another five. That means he wants five more cards, his right in the game. I'm going to play my hand out with the cards that come. And that to me is a strong statement of a man's belief in America and in himself.

And that is the last of my 72 years speech to you.

∼African Americans
and American Politics

The Negro in Washington

~& THE HISTORY OF WASHINGTON so far sketched has been a
chronicle of events from the city's distant beginnings to its indelible present, concerning itself mainly with the white population. But the story would
remain incomplete without a discussion of the Negro in Washington who,
from the start, exerted a profound influence upon the city's destiny. Aside
from the fact that at the present day the Negro population constitutes more
than one-fourth of the city's total, the Negro's subtler influences are by far
greater than might be apparent on the surface.

Chronologically this subject lends itself to treatment in three distinct
periods.

I. FROM THE BEGINNINGS TO THE CIVIL WAR

Benjamin Banneker, a Negro mathematician, was appointed by
George Washington to serve on Major L'Enfant's commission for the surveying and laying out of the city. Though this might be considered symbolic
of the Negro's later participation in Washington life, the lot of Banneker's
fellows, even in our times, has hardly been so auspicious. Viewing Washington in its early years Thomas Moore found

Even here beside the proud Potowmac's streams . . .
The medley mass of pride and misery
Of whips and charters, manacles and rights
Of slaving blacks and democratic whites . . .

Though spoken by a pro-British son of Erin, his indictment is substantiated
by other sources.

It was not alone the shabby contrast between the profession of democracy and the practice of slavery that struck the observer, nor was it chiefly the brutality of the working and living conditions of slaves in the District of Columbia. Although conditions hardly deserved to be called ideal, still the cook, coachman, and artisan, in Alexandria, Georgetown, or Washington, or the truck-farmer in the rural areas surrounding these towns was generally better off than the field hand in the deep South and Southwest. What brought ill-fame to the District was the extensive slave trading conducted here. Because of its location, the District served as a natural outlet for both the coastwise slave ships and the overland coffles and was rightly called the very seat and center of the domestic slave traffic.

The District of Columbia, too small for slave rearing itself, served as depot for the purchases of interstate traders, who combed Maryland and northern Virginia for slaves. Since the slave jails, colloquially known as "Georgia pens," and described by an ex-slave as worse than hog holes, were inadequate for the great demand, the public jails were made use of, accommodations for criminals having to wait upon the more pressing and lucrative traffic in slaves. There were pens in what is now Potomac Park; and one in the Decatur House, fronting on what is now Lafayette Square. More notorious were McCandless' Tavern in Georgetown; in Washington, Robey's Tavern at Seventh and Maryland Avenue, and Williams' "Yellow House" at Eighth and B Streets SW. In Alexandria, the pretentious establishment of Armfield and Franklin, who by 1834 were sending more than a thousand slaves a year to the Southwest, was succeeded and surpassed by the shambles of the much-feared Kephart.

In 1819, when Miller's Tavern at Thirteenth and F Streets NW. was on fire, a bystander, William Gardiner, refused to join the customary bucket brigade and loudly denounced the place as a slave prison. The resulting controversy conducted in newspaper columns revealed the tragic past of the tavern. A Negro woman, about to be sold South apart from her husband, had leapt in frenzy from an attic window, breaking both arms and injuring her back, but surviving. This focused attention upon the local slave trade. Humanitarian Jesse Torrey came to Washington shortly after the attempted suicide, visited the injured woman, and discovered two kidnaped Negroes in the attic. He began suit in the circuit court for their freedom, the expenses being defrayed by a group of persons headed by Francis Scott Key, who gave his legal services gratis. It is highly probable that the stir attendant upon this celebrated case urged the slave owner John Randolph to that bitter invective in which he said:

You call this the land of liberty, and every day that passes things are done in it at which the despotisms of Europe would be horror-struck and disgusted. . . . In no part of the earth—not even excepting the rivers on the Coast of Africa, was there so great, so infamous a slave market, as in the metropolis, in the seat of government of this nation which prides itself on freedom.

A chorus of voices rose in harmony with Randolph's. The sight recorded by Torrey, and engraved as the frontispiece of his *Portraiture of Domestic Slavery*, of a coffle of manacled slaves, like a butcher's drove of hobbled cattle, passing along the east front of the ruined Capitol, became a familiar figure in the many orations attacking the traffic. The struggle for abolition in the District recruited such men as Benjamin Lundy, Salmon P. Chase, Charles Miner, Charles Sumner, William Lloyd Garrison, Henry Wilson, William H. Seward, and Abraham Lincoln when serving as Congressman. John Quincy Adams' famous fight for free speech and against the "gag rule" in Congress was prompted by the refusal of the two Houses to hear petitions for the abolition of slavery in the District of Columbia. But the forces commanded by men like Calhoun were too great, and while solicitude was expressed by Northerners and Southerners, Congress, which had the power to abolish, refused to act. The District, wedged in between two slave States, was kept slave territory, and the slave trade prospered until the Compromise of 1850. The black code of the District was even more severe than the codes of Maryland and Virginia of which it was the reeanctment, and the "stealing" of free Negroes was shamefully widespread. William Wells Brown, in *Clotel*, the first novel by a Negro, has one of his heroines jump into the Potomac to escape slave catchers.

The Negroes of Washington, both free and slave, at times took matters into their own hands against these flagrant abuses. The Underground Railroad had important stopping places in Washington; ex-slaves today remember churches whose basements served as layovers, and out-of-the-way Georgetown homes that were specially marked for the fugitives. One of the famous trails started at a cemetery skirting the stage road leading north from the city. It is probable that Harriet Tubman, "the Moses of her people," the greatest underground agent, worked around Washington as well as on the Eastern Shore. Legend has it that she was discovered by her friends asleep in a local park beneath a sign advertising a reward for her capture, which meant nothing to her, as she could not read.

In 1848, 77 Negroes under slave and free Negro leadership, took advantage of the relaxed patrolling of Washington while it was celebrating the liberty of the new French Republic, and escaped on board Captain Drayton's *Pearl*. But at Cornfield Harbor, 140 miles from Washington, contrary winds forced the schooner into shelter and an armed steamer captured the runaways and the crew. The manner of flight had been betrayed by a Negro hackman. Captain Drayton was mobbed (an Irishman cutting off a piece of his ear), sentenced to a fine of $10,000, and imprisoned until Sumner prevailed upon President Fillmore to intercede. For captured Negroes there was only occasional intercession. Emily and Mary Edmondson, long coveted by the trader Bruin, were sold South, but later were redeemed through Henry Ward Beecher and other sympathizers. Another Emily, who had hoped to reach her mother in New York, met with a different fate. Said to be the "finest looking woman in this country," and destined as a "fancy article" for New Orleans, she died from exposure on the overland trek. Her mother, who had bought herself free by labors over the washtub, thanked God.

In 1830 there were 6,152 free Negroes in the District of Columbia compared with 6,119 slaves; in 1840, 8,361 compared with 4,694 slaves; and in 1860, 11,131 compared with only 3,185 slaves. Thus, in 30 years, the free colored population was nearly doubled, while the slave population was halved. It would be inaccurate to infer from this that there was any wholesale manumission or that the District was a haven for free Negroes. The free Negroes were of several classes: Those whose antecedents had never been slaves, such as descendants of indentured servants; those born of free parents, or of free mothers; those manumitted; those who had bought their own freedom, or whose kinsmen had bought it for them; and those who were successful runaways. These free Negroes were an ever present "bad example" to the slaves of the District and of the surrounding slave States, and the more they prospered, the "worse example" they became.

Especially stringent regulations affecting free Negroes were added by the District Common Council to the slave codes. Every free Negro was required: (1) to give the mayor "satisfactory evidence of freedom," plus $50 for himself, and $50 for each member of his family; (2) to post a bond for $1,000 and to secure five white guarantors of good behavior. It was necessary to show manumission papers in order to remain free; even so, gangs bent on kidnaping could and frequently did seize and destroy them. No Negro, slave or free, could testify against whites. The jails were crowded with captured free Negroes and suspected runaways; there were 290 of these in the city jail at one time. Many were sold for prison fees, ostensibly for a fixed period, but really for life. Meetings for any other than fraternal and religious purposes were forbidden. After Nat Turner's insurrection in Virginia in 1831, colored preachers were banned. Curfew rang at 10 o'clock for all Negroes, free or slave.

In spite of all this the class of free Negroes increased and, in the main, advanced. Though forbidden by law to do so many succeeded, through the connivance of friendly whites, in opening and running such businesses as hotels, taverns, saloons, and restaurants. In the District, as in so many southern cities, they had a monopoly of barbering and free colored boys were porters and bootblacks. Waiters were numerous and, in the gay hospitality of a southern city, were comparatively well paid. There were many skilled carpenters, bricklayers, shoemakers, stonemasons, wheelwrights, blacksmiths, plasterers, printers, cabinetmakers, cab drivers, and draymen. For free colored women the opportunities were limited to dressmaking, laundry work, nursing, and general housework.

With chances for a livelihood scanty, many Negroes were driven to petty larceny. The newspapers, as is their custom, interpreted this frequently as grand larceny. The Old Center Market was the resort of plundering marauders. Many Negroes ignored or violated the laws, particularly the curfew. Race riots developed in spite of the fact that the penalty for striking a white man was the cropping of the ears (exacted in the District until 1862). Mulattoes sometimes set up invidious self-defeating distinctions against their darker brothers. Frequently the blacks retaliated. There were unfortunate examples of Negroes serving as informers, as catchers of runaways, as hat-in-hand seekers of personal favors, and ex-slaves still speak with hatred of one Stonestreet, a Negro slave-kidnaper. But more often there was co-operation, the Resolute Beneficial Society being founded for concerted action toward the betterment of conditions. Occasionally free Negroes owned slaves. However, they were usually wealthier Negroes buying kinsfolk for liberation.

The free Negro was avid for education. In 1807, shortly after the first two white schoolhouses had been built, three recently freed Negroes who could not read or write hired a white teacher and set up the first school for Negroes. More successful were the ventures of such pioneers as Louisa Parke Costin, Mary Wormley, Arabella Jones, Father Vanlomen, and Maria Becraft. John F. Cook, a shoemaker, set up a school in 1834, 8 years after his aunt, Alethia Tanner, had purchased his freedom. The Snow Riot gave a set of hoodlums the excuse for attacking his school. Cook fled to Pennsylvania, but returned a year later, doggedly intent upon his mission. Myrtilla Miner, a white woman from New York, driven from place to place in the city in her attempt to establish a Negro school, finally purchased the entire square between what are now Nineteenth and Twentieth and M and O Streets. Harriet Beecher Stowe's donation of $1,000 helped her greatly in this purchase, and Johns Hopkins was one of the trustees. Her students were insulted and attacked by white men along the streets. The buildings were stoned and set afire. But Miss Miner stood her ground. Using some of their leisure time, she and Emily Edmondson (of the famous case of the *Pearl*) warned hoodlums of their mettle by firing pistols at a target in the yard.

The education of Negroes was frowned upon by the majority of whites in the District, especially after Nat Turner's famous uprising. Negroes paid taxes for the support of white schools, but received no consideration themselves. Private Negro schools continued to spring up and no school closed its doors for lack of "scholars." In 1860 there were more than 1,200 free colored children in school.

Church was the solace of the free Negroes. Negro Methodism in the District started in 1820 when a group of free Negroes withdrew from Ebenezer Church and formed a separate congregation. After 1831 when obvious discrimination started in most of the white churches, other Negro groups withdrew from congregations. At St. Johns Church an outside stairway leading to the gallery was called the "niggers' backstairs to heaven." But the Negro members decided that there must be other ways to get there and left the church. In 1833 the First Baptist Church, moving from Nineteenth and I Streets NW. to a new edifice which later became Ford's Theater, instituted segregation. Negro members stayed in the old home. One feature of the churches was the popularity of Sabbath schools among adults as well as among children because they furnished instruction in the three R's. Taking advantage of every chance, the free Negro frequently left Jonah waiting and the Walls of Jericho standing while he fathomed the mysteries of the alphabet.

The houses in which free Negroes lived ran the gamut from hovels to commodious homes. The first were remote from slave quarters, and crouched behind the imposing dwellings of employers, or were grouped in hidden alleyways. The homes of the well-to-do, scattered here and there, were purchased before the law forbidding free Negroes to own property was passed, or later in defiance of it. There were some separate communities, especially in Southwest Washington, "on the island" (so-called because the Tiber and the old canal cut it off from the city). Many free Negroes were poverty stricken, and gave point to the proslavery argument of the wretched freedman, but with the odds against them, it is surprising that this impoverished class was not larger. Many, comparatively wealthy, owned property in such a valuable section as Fifteenth and New York Avenue; many had homes on Sixteenth Street; and a feed dealer, Alfred Lee, purchased the mansion on H Street which had been the British Embassy. In 1865, when scoffers charged that Negroes did not own $40,000 worth of property in the whole city, it was proved that in one square their holdings aggregated $45,592. At the time of the Emancipation Act, Negroes in the District of Columbia were paying taxes on $650,000 worth of real estate.

II. FROM THE CIVIL WAR TO THE TURN OF THE CENTURY

In 1862, the year in which slavery was abolished in the District, President Lincoln authorized the enlisting of Negroes as part of the Army. Two regiments were soon mustered in from the District and vicinity, the First organized at Washington in May 1863, and the Second at Arlington a month later. These regiments served with honor at Fair Oaks, Petersburg, Fort Taylor, and in other battles. It is estimated that the District supplied over 3,000 colored troops of the 200,000 in the Union Army. Negro contrabands, male and female, had earlier crowded to the camps, eager to serve as teamsters and road builders, laundresses, and cooks for "Marse Lincum's boys."

As early as 1862 more than 13,000 refugees had collected in Washington, Alexandria, Hampton, and Norfolk. The Emancipation Proclamation in 1863 was an added stimulus to Negroes to flee to the Union lines. Washington, strategically located for slave trading, now became the favorite place toward which contrabands headed. The mustering out of Negro regiments in Washington at the close of the war further increased their number in the District. Washington became a Mecca for Negroes in the next two decades, and in 1880 there were 59,696 in the city and its immediate environs. The proportion to the city's population (about one-third) remained fairly constant.

The picture therefore is greatly changed from what it had been in 1867, when one-fifth of all owners of real estate had been Negroes. In the main the refugees were illiterate and penniless. At their best, these people were intelligent and eager to help themselves; at their worst they showed, in the words of a Federal chaplain, "cringing deceit, theft, licentiousness, all the vices which slavery inevitably fosters." They constituted a grave problem for the District. One proposed way out was colonization. President Lincoln favored this, and Congress appropriated funds for transportation to Liberia or Haiti. Several hundred former slaves were shipped to the Island of Vache, Haiti. But when their plight became desperate, a warship was sent after them. They were settled in Arlington in a place known as "Freedmen's Village," very near a tract left by George Washington Parke Custis to his colored daughter, Maria Syphax. Appeals were made to encourage Negroes to migrate en masse to sections farther north, or to return to the plantations in the South. But the majority chose to remain in Washington.

The first contrabands during the war were housed in the old "Brick Capitol," on the site of the present Supreme Court Building. They were then moved to what was Duff Green's Row, east of the Capitol. As the flood swept in, McClellan's Barracks housed them, and then numerous barracks were built in Washington and Alexandria. Two hundred tenements were fitted up at Campbell Hospital. Many Negroes settled in the neighborhoods of the old forts. The Fort Reno settlement in Tenleytown is one of the last of these to succumb to fine suburban developments. In the main, however, philanthropic efforts did not prove equal to the housing shortage. Real-estate agents floated a project that resulted in Washington's notorious alley system." The deep back yards, and even the front yards provided by L'Enfant's plan, were found to promise more alluring rewards than lovely gardens. Lots were divided and the rear portions sold separately. The first of the ill-fated alleys, as the present day Washington knows them, were laid out in 1867. In 1897 there were 333 alleys, inhabited by approximately 19,000 people, more than three-fourths of them Negroes. Shacks costing as little as $10 proved highly profitable investments. Here, in these disease-infested sties, ex-slaves got their first taste of freedom. And it is here that, in too large numbers, their children's children still drag out their lives.

Negro communities had such suggestive names as Goose Level, Vinegar Hill, Froggy or Foggy Bottom, Hell's Bottom, Swampoodle, and Bloodfield. Cowtown, so-called because, outside of the city proper, cows and hogs and chickens ranged at will on sidewalks and streets, was the present Barry Place. Of a somewhat higher level were the communities across the Anacostia: The Flats, Hillsdale, Barry Farms (an earlier settlement of race-conscious slaves), Stantonstown, Garfield; those in the northeast at Benning, and Burrville; and Brightwood, in the vicinity of Fort Stevens and Fort Slocum. Georgetown had its goodly share of oldest inhabitants, who sat aloof, gazing with well-bred disdain at the ignorant trespassers. Other prosperous Negroes were scattered in almost all of the quiet residential sections.

For new arrivals, accustomed chiefly to manual labor in the fields, there was little employment to be found in a city predominantly governmental and residential. Pauperism forced many to eke out a living by pickings on the dumps. Many took to pilfering. It is hardly a matter of wonder that the rate of crime was high. The paths of many Negroes led straight from the alley to the workhouse. Crimes of violence were numerous. In 1891 the superintendent of police attributed much of the crime to the neglected state of the Negro child. Illegitimacy was frequent. Health conditions were wretched. The death rate in 1891 for Negroes was nearly double that for whites, and both were far too high. The death rate was largely increased by infant mortality. In spite of all this, Negroes were unwilling to go to the poorhouse. Perhaps they saw no reason merely to change addresses.

And yet the grimness of the picture is not without some relief. The Freedmen's Bureau, missionary organizations, and Negroes themselves with their lodges, churches, and schools, waged a determined though hard-pressed battle against prejudice, poverty, and ignorance. The Freedmen's Bureau was created by act of Congress in 1865, for "relief work, education, regulation of labor, and administration of justice," among the freedmen. Major General Oliver Otis Howard, who had lost an arm at Fair Oaks but had returned to serve under Sherman and as commander of the Army of Tennessee, was named commissioner. Unable to cope successfully, for all its gallant efforts, with the problems of destitution and housing, the Freedmen's Bureau exerted its greatest influence in the establishing of Freedmen's Hospital, Howard University, and a number of schools for Negroes that eventually became a part of the city school system. Some of the officials of the Bureau were connected with the Freedmen's Savings and Trust Company which, contrary to the opinions of some, was never controlled by Negroes. This company did not withstand the contagion of the Gilded Age. With its central bank in Washington and 34 branches in the South, it "received in the aggregate deposits amounting to $57,000,000 from more than 70,000 depositors, chiefly Negroes." It taught valuable lessons in thrift, but when, following the panic of 1873, the imprudence of its investments and the dishonesty of certain directors forced it to close its doors, it taught the freedmen an embittering lesson.

Although an act of Congress ruled that Washington and Georgetown should allocate to the trustees of colored schools a proportionate part of all moneys received, the corporation of Washington refused to do this as late as November 1867. After this Negro schools fared well. The northern missionary associations which had conducted schools in temporary barracks and basements of churches joined forces. A high school was organized in 1870. One of its frequent removals found it in Myrtilla Miner's famous building. Then in 1891, M Street High School was erected. Night schools, privately maintained for day-time workers, became part of the public-school system in 1886. George F. T. Cook, son of the militant educator John F. Cook, was appointed superintendent of schools in 1868. A heated contest was waged in 1871 under the leadership of William H. A. Wormley and William Syphax to remove all restrictions of color from the public schools, but those opposing segregation were defeated by whites and some Negroes who feared that mixed schools would return the issue to local politics, and mean the death of the progressing schools.

The old Negro preacher in Georgetown who said of the freed Negro: "Fifteen years after he came out of slavery, what did he do? Sat down by the River of Babylon and sang, 'Peace at home and pleasure abroad', and went to sleep down by the weeping willows for 25 years," was overstating the case. There was definite, if gradual economic advance. Many made their living as domestics, barbers, cobblers, grocers, dry-goods merchants, artisans, contractors, real-estate operators, hucksters, market vendors, saloonkeepers, and hotel-keepers. Others inherited property, made prudent investments, and became prosperous. Colored firemen were appointed on a full-time basis in 1870; colored policemen have been on the force since the Metropolitan Police was organized in the sixties. A colored policeman arrested General Grant for speeding; whether the culprit had set his people free or not, the law was the law.

At Fifteenth and H Streets stood one of Washington's most exclusive hotels, catering to family patronage and the congressional and diplomatic sets. This was owned and managed by a Negro, Wm. Wormley, close friend of Charles Sumner. Many Negroes found employment in the Government service, most of them as laborers, messengers, a few as clerks. Certain political plums fell to Negroes such as the positions of the fourth Auditor, the Register of the Treasury, and the Recorder of Deeds. There was an increasing professional class of doctors, lawyers, preachers, and teachers. Professors were ubiquitous, professors of music, of the dance, of the cake-walk, of algebra, and of penmanship. The title is not so comic when one recalls how rarely a Negro is granted the title "Mister."

Though politically well informed and articulate, the Negro of Washington in this period exerted little force. His newly acquired suffrage was swept away by the disfranchisement of the District in 1874, an act which was definitely influenced by the fact that Negroes comprised one-fourth of the population. Political figures among them, however, were numerous. There were over a score of Congressmen, many intelligent and able. Those whose imprint was most lasting upon Negro history were Robert Brown Elliott, John M. Langston, and John R. Lynch, who later corrected many of Rhodes' inaccuracies in reconstruction history. Representative Ransier caused a commotion during one session while John T. Harris of Virginia was declaiming: "And I say that there is not one gentleman upon this floor who can honestly say that he really believes that the colored man is created his equal." Ransier interrupted with a casual "I can." Later, Ransier, listening to a Negro-baiter who insisted that the Civil Rights Bill meant that Negroes would absorb the whites, stated with suavity that "If we are powerful, we know how to be merciful." Negro Senators were Hiram R. Revels and Blanche Kelso Bruce, both of Mississippi. P. B. S. Pinchback, after a picaresque career culminating in the lieutenant governorship of Louisiana, and Francis Cardoza, State treasurer of South Carolina, were prominent newcomers. Finally there was Frederick Douglass, justly famed fugitive and antislavery orator, later Marshal and Recorder of Deeds for the District, and Minister to Haiti, who spent his last years in the old Van Hook Mansion on Cedar Hill.

The Republican Party was favored in these years. Frederick Douglass' statement: "The Republican Party is the ship, all else the sea," was held axiomatic to such a degree, that when at the Second Baptist Lyceum (a free forum) a paper endorsing the Democrats followed one endorsing the Republicans, the audience hissed; newspapers called it "double play," and the chairman was accused of traitorous intentions against the entire Negro race. The most exciting political campaigns were contests for delegates to the Republican National Convention. The Blaine Invincible Republican Club and the W. Calvin Chase Republican Club were elaborately organized. The Cleveland administration, however, left not a few Negro Democrats in its wake.

For many years after the Civil War, Washington was said, with some justice, to have "the most distinguished and brilliant assemblage of Negroes in the world." The reputation was sustained by cultural societies such as the Second Baptist Lyceum, the Congressional Lyceum, and the Bethel Literary Society. The National Negro Academy had upon its rosters such scholars as W. E. B. Du Bois, of Atlanta, the Grimke brothers, W. S. Scarborough, J. W. Cromwell, and Kelly Miller. At the close of the century Paul Laurence Dunbar, best-known Negro writer, lived here. From 1897 to 1898 he was assistant to another Negro, Daniel Murray, who held a high place in the Congressional Library. Dunbar wrote and gave readings of his poetry, reciting with gusto of the Negro peasant. Will Marion Cook, similarly distinguished in music, collaborator with Dunbar in such musical shows as *Clorindy* and *In Dahomey*, was for a number of years a resident of Washington. The two leading Negro newspapers of the period, W. Calvin

Chase's Washington *Bee* ("Watch the Sting") and E. E. Cooper's *Colored American*, are not only valuable as indices to social life, but also refreshing because of the occasional highly personal combats between the editors.

Despite the destitution and the earnest fight to keep the grudged gains, there was still a gay social life for some Washington Negroes. Negro lodges were convivial as well as "mutually benevolent." Conventions of elders and bishops made Washington their Mecca. G. A. R. encampments in Washington gave excuses for lavish hospitality. The Emancipation Day ceremonies were for a long time popular turnouts, until rivalries terminated them. Two rival factions, urged by President Cleveland to reconcile their grievances, persisted in holding parades with brass bands and "queens of love and beauty" for each. The celebration did not survive this contretemps. Inaugural balls for Negroes, held on March 5 after the official ball, were likewise causes for dissension between groups claiming to represent Negro Washington. Other balls and banquets were numerous and prodigal in the dozens of hotels, buffet-cafes, and saloons. Churches and clubs had frequent excursions down the river to Marshall Hall, Notley Hall, and Chapel Point. There was a flamboyant sporting life; political dignitaries at times had to yield to a visitor like Peter Jackson, heavyweight champion of Australia, against whom John L. Sullivan drew the color line, or Isaac Murphy, noted Negro jockey of the eighties. Major Taylor, "the champion colored bicycle racer of the world," defended his title and, in spite of foul play, defeated all comers at the old Washington Coliseum.

Before the Civil War the elder Joseph Jefferson, lessee of the Washington Theater, had petitioned the city fathers to change the curfew law, as it affected "a great proportion of our audience of this [Negro] caste" and lessened his box-office receipts. This interest in drama persisted into the period under consideration. Musicals were very popular. A Negro opera company founded in 1872 gave several performances at Ford's Theater. Williams and Walker and Cole and Johnson, "in the brightest ebony offering, *A Trip to Coontown*," were viewed by Washington Negroes with only occasional disputes with the theater management over the sale of orchestra tickets. Sissieretta Jones, "Black Patti," sang in 1892 for President Harrison's White House reception; she returned in 1900 with her troubadours in *The Essence of Ole Virginny*. The biggest musical event in years was the first all-colored oratorio, *Emmanuel*, directed by Prof. J. Henry Lewis. He was versatile enough to train a chorus of 70 for "A Mammoth Cake Walk and Jubilee Entertainment in Convention Hall." The Fisk Jubilee Singers and other school choruses sang in Washington to raise funds for their institutions. Some musical organizations were the Dvořák Musical Association, the Amphion Glee Club, the Washington Permanent Chorus, and the Georgetown Musical Association.

III. THE TWENTIETH CENTURY

The first decade of the twentieth century was marked by a consolidation of some of the gains and a loss of others. Negro leaders, attracted by the period's visions of reform, turned more hopefully to the "race problem." In 1903 at Lincoln Temple Congregational Church there was a conference on "How to Solve the Race Problem." Suggested solutions were the setting up of a forty-ninth state, the conciliatory gradualism of Booker T. Washington, and the demanding of full citizenship rights. It was urged that a "Commission to Consider Every Phase of the American Race Problem" be appointed by Congress, and a "Permanent Commission on the American Race Problem" was set up. Many of the militant members of the conference, hardly to be satisfied with commissions and committees, later joined forces with liberal movements which in 1910 culminated in the National Association for the Advancement of Colored People.

With America's entry into the World War, advice came from Negro leadership to forget grievances and close ranks for the sake of democracy. In Washington this was enthusiastically heeded. The First Separate Battalion, the Negro National Guard unit, which had previously served on the Mexican border, was called upon to guard Washington. This battalion was the first in the District to be mustered to war strength. Its commanding officer, Maj. James Walker, was the first District officer to die in the line of duty. When the Three Hundred and Seventy-second Regiment was formed, the First Separate Battalion was included. Overseas this regiment was brigaded with the "Red Hand" Division of the French Army. Of nearly 600 Washington Negroes in the outfit, more than 200 were wounded and 33 killed. One of the first to fall fatally wounded was Private Kenneth Lewis, a mere youngster, just out of the high-school cadet corps. He was awarded the *Medaille Militaire*. A score of Washingtonians received the *Croix de Guerre*, and the Three Hundred and Seventy-second Regiment had its colors decorated with the *Croix de Guerre* and palm for distinguished service.

In October 1917 Emmett J. Scott was appointed by Newton Baker as Special Assistant to the Secretary of War, in order to promote "a healthy morale among Negro soldiers and civilians." Attempts were made in his office to iron out cases of discrimination and injustice. A campaign was zealously initiated to obtain a separate training camp for Negro officers, since no Negro, regardless of qualifications, was permitted to enter the other camps. The spearhead of this movement was found in the newly established office and at Howard University. After much hesitation, authorization of a camp at Des Moines, Iowa, came on May 9, 1917. It is perhaps more than a coincidence that four days earlier, Henry Johnson and Needham Roberts, enlisted Negroes of the Fifteenth New York, had performed feats of valor for which they were later cited by General Pershing. From Des Moines 700 commissioned officers were sent out, the majority to serve in the Ninety-second Combat Division. Many were Washingtonians and of these several were cited for bravery, especially in the Argonne offensive. Over 5,000 Negroes from the District came into service through the operation of the selective draft law. World War veterans were organized in the James Reese Europe Post No. 5, and the James E. Walker Post No. 26 of the American Legion.

The hopes expressed "that the American people will be disposed more and more to remove such handicaps and to right such injustices as we now struggle against after the settlement of this great emergency which now faces our common country" turned barren in the post-war years. A bloody riot had taken place in East St. Louis during the war; on July 19, 1919, the Washington riot started. Inflammatory headlines announced a wave of assaults on white women by Negroes; several of these earlier publicized attacks were shown to be false, and later ones were definitely invented as whips for the mob. A number of white soldiers, sailors, and marines proceeded to southwest Washington and beat up several innocent Negroes. Negroes retaliated and beat up several innocent whites. Street fighting was fierce, if sporadic. On July 21 a newspaper announced a "mobilization of every available service man stationed in or near Washington or on leave . . . the purpose is a clean-up." Negroes mobilized likewise, alley dwellers and most respectable burghers, side by side, and there was no clean-up. The bitter resistance of Negroes, the calling out of regular troops (officially this time), and a rainstorm helped the authorities to disperse the mobs. A year later, a Negro charged with murder confessed to the attacks for which two Negroes (positively identified by the women in the cases) were serving undeserved long-term sentences in penitentiaries.

The great forces opposed to the Negro, however, were not mobs that could be stopped at a brick barricade at Seventh and M Streets. These were, as they have always been, poverty, ignorance, disease, and crime. The extensive migration from the South, accelerated in the years of the war because of the cutting off of European immigration, the demand for industrial labor in the North and Midwest, and a growing resentment at conditions in the South, stranded many Negroes in Washington. Other cities were prepared for the mass invasion of industry, but Washington, even though it was growing by leaps and bounds, had little work for the newcomers to do. There was an aggravation of the post–Civil War problems of housing, health, and employment. At the collapse of the boom period, Negroes preferred the word "panic," depression being what they had experienced in the days of "prosperity."

Negroes of Washington total 27 percent of the population. At one time as many as 4 out of 10 were unemployed. Over 70 percent of the relief cases in 1935 were Negro, almost in inverse ratio to the racial distribution of the population. Many of these unemployed live in the 200 alleys which remain in the slum sections of Washington. An Alley Dwelling Elimination Act was enacted June 12, 1934, contemplating the riddance of inhabited alleys before July 1, 1944. Until then it is likely that these alley dwellings, for which exorbitant rents are charged, will continue to breed vice, crime, and disease.

Negroes who are able to make a living do so generally in domestic and personal service, and in manufacturing and mechanical pursuits (generally unskilled labor). A large number are in various departments under Civil Service; only a few of them, in spite of their capabilities, ranking as clerks or foremen. About 4,000 are listed in trade, and about 3,500 in the professions. The New Negro Alliance was founded in 1933 to demand equal working opportunity for Negroes in Negro areas. One of its slogans is "Don't Buy Where You Can't Work." But in spite of its picketing and boycotting, there has been no large gain in jobs. The struggling Negro business concerns cannot furnish much employment. Regardless of qualification, the Negro worker meets with definite discrimination. Many American Federation of Labor unions exclude him; even more than the white worker, he remains poorly led and unorganized. The Joint Committee on National Recovery, with headquarters in Washington, was active in focussing attention upon and fighting Nation-wide discrimination against, and exploitation of, Negroes.

Many of the slum streets are close seconds to the alleys in squalor, and a mushroom shanty-town at Marshall Heights on the outskirts of the city is much like the camp of the bonus-marchers, with "shelters" made out of pieces of tin, cast-off lumber and beaverboard. Prosperous Negroes live in all sections of the city and Negro expansion into areas of better homes has been bitterly, and at times unscrupulously, contested. "Covenants" to bar Negroes from certain sections were upheld by the Supreme Court in the Curtis case. But the "covenant," while a powerful weapon, frequently cuts both ways. During this century the fastnesses of Le Droit Park were penetrated and transformed to a Negro section. Newer additions to Deanwood and Burrville in the northeast are Kingman Park, Capitol View, and De Priest Village, pleasing, well designed communities for the Negro middle class. Langston Terrace was sponsored by the Public Works Administration to afford better housing for Negro families of low income. The bulk of the Negro population, however, is still in the northwest, where the Negro business area is located.

The health situation resulting from the crowded slums is a grave menace. Only one city in the United States has a higher death rate from tuberculosis than Washington; over half of the tubercular cases in 1935 were Negroes. Other forces playing havoc are infant mortality, social diseases, accidents in the home, and disintegrated home life. Negro patients are received in segregated wards at most of the hospitals, while some of the hospitals afford clinic service only. Freedmen's Hospital, founded by the Freedmen's Bureau and supported by the Department of the Interior, is the Negro general hospital. Its facilities are utilized by the Howard University Medical School. There are also private hospitals conducted by leading surgeons of the race. Although in comparison with the rest of the country Washington has a heavy concentration of medical practitioners, the number is still not large enough to cope with the health problem. Recognition of the socio-economic causes of the high mortality rate is becoming more apparent in recent surveys and their resultant recommendations.

Crime is correspondingly high; areas found to be dense in disease are classed in police reports as dense in crime. Some alleys are "no man's land" for any stranger, Negro or white. Knives flash and pistols bark to terminate crap games and domestic brawls. Rasped nerves and short ugly tempers are not soothed by the heavy drinking of liquor which is as likely to be "canned heat" as corn whisky. Efforts of the police to ferret out crime are not helped by the furtiveness of the alley dwellers, who consider "John Law" to be their natural enemy—with good reason, at times, in light of police brutality. The "numbers" game, an American form of gambling, is popular in the alleys as it is on the avenues. The money that dribbles away to the number "baron" and "runner" could well be used for bread, milk, and shoes, but these poor people look upon the number slip as a magic sesame to momentary affluence.

Agencies struggling to improve these conditions are few in number and lack money. The Twelfth Street Branch Y.M.C.A., erected in 1912 in Hell's Bottom, has its boys' clubs and summer camp, Camp Lichtman; fosters dramatics, athletics, and forums; and attempts to aid employment. The Phyllis Wheatley Y.W.C.A., founded in 1905, aims at similar community service for women and girls, with Camp Clarissa Scott operating in the summer months. The Department of Playgrounds is coming to recognize the needs of this fourth of the city's population. Important playgrounds are the one at the historic Barry Farms, the Howard Playground, the Cardoza Playground, the Willow Tree Playground, Lincoln Playground, and the new Banneker Center. The 30 others are as crowded and active, and all are important. Community centers and settlement houses have programs of wide variety. In all of these, the paid Negro personnel is too small, and still underpaid.

Some other agencies in social welfare are the Washington Corps No. 2 of the Salvation Army and the fraternal organizations which launch occasional programs for civic betterment. Although the Police Boys' Clubs date back to 1933, plans for the inclusion of Negro boys in the surmised benefits are still in the making. The first lesson in civics for these boys seems to be their segregated status.

Athletics are, of course, popular. In the earlier years there was a strong governmental baseball league as well as many sand-lot teams. The present Washington Elite Giants, not indigenous like the old popular Le Droit Tigers, are successful in the National Negro League and therefore in good favor. Against such teams as the Pittsburgh Crawfords, the New York Black Yankees, the Homestead Grays, they put on colorful shows in the Griffith Stadium. Local basketball teams have become nationally known. Howard University and Miner Teachers College have heavy schedules in football and basketball against many of the best Negro collegiate teams, and the high schools are bitter athletic rivals. There are frequent track meets. Jesse Owens gave exhibitions at one of these. This was his only possible performance in Washington, as white colleges in the District do not allow Negroes to participate in their open meets. Tennis enthusiasts in Washington had a great deal to do with the founding of the American Tennis Association. Washington has had many Negro tennis champions, but with the paucity of the courts, public and private, tennis for a time declined. Negroes box in the District on "all-Negro" cards. Negro golfers have only one inadequate golf course in the city. In spite of this, golf is increasing in popularity.

Baptists are the most numerous of the churchgoers in Washington; second to them are the Methodists, divided into several branches. There are churches of other denominations together with many independent storefront churches. The churches frequently have duplicated names, because of "splitting," or because of the shifting of population. Famous preachers of the early century were the Reverend George Lee, whose pulpit power was commensurate with his vast bulk, and the scholarly Reverend Walter

Brooks and Reverend Francis Grimke. "Black Billy Sunday," the Reverend Alexander Willbanks, combined the resources of southern camp meetings with the tricks of his model. But even more spectacular have been the careers of Elder Solomon Lightfoot Michaux and Bishop "Daddy" Grace. The first of these, whose "Happy Am I" chorus and sermons are broadcast over Station WJSV, preaches to crowds in his Georgia Avenue tabernacle, with seats reserved for delegations of whites. Elder Michaux has experimented with communal ventures in lodging, and at present runs a One-Cent Cafe founded for him by Bernarr Macfadden. "Daddy" Grace, whose churches have swept from New Bedford to Augusta, Ga., has set up a House of Prayer at Sixth and M Streets NW. Store-front churches attract attention with crudely lettered signs, their unconscious humor checked by their patent sincerity. In one backward section a little church given over to noisy rousements and sing-song "gravy-giving" sermons is neighbor to a chapel of quiet, dignified services, pastored by a devoted and scholarly man who, without reaching a wide audience, has left a deep impress upon the community. That is a familiar contrast in the church life of Washington, and the less spectacular preachers who speak with quiet authority are not to be underestimated. Andrew Rankin Memorial Chapel at Howard University attracts some of the best known liberal preachers of both races, and the Howard University School of Religion aims to train a graduate ministry and to advance the admittedly backward condition of Negro preachers.

Out of more than $11,000,000 appropriated in 1936 to the public schools of the District of Columbia, approximately one-third was devoted to the colored schools. Education for Negroes in the District has come a long way from the first school founded by illiterate ex-slaves to the teachers' college, 3 senior high schools, 2 vocational schools, 6 junior high schools, and 40 elementary schools, with 1,004 teachers and 35,739 students. These schools are under the direction of Garnet C. Wilkinson, First Assistant Superintendent, divisions 10 to 13. Two other Negroes serve as second assistant superintendents, there is a Negro examining board and there is proportional membership on the Board of Education. The teaching force is unusually well prepared and the salaries are on the same scale as the salaries of the white teachers. The fact of segregation, however, must still be reckoned with. The theory of equal, though separate, accommodations breaks down into the fact of unequal facilities and equipment. Negro high schools are badly overcrowded and too often, instead of new structures, school buildings abandoned by whites are used for Negroes.

Howard University, called by some the "capstone of Negro education," is for the first time headed by a Negro, Dr. Mordecai W. Johnson. Under

President Eugene Clark, Miner Teachers College, in spite of its youth, has received high rank from accrediting agencies. Frelinghuysen University, with Mrs. Anna J. Cooper as president, gives college instruction to students who must attend night classes. Miss Nannie Burroughs is the founder of the National Training School for Women and Girls, the school of the three B's: the Bible, the Bath, and the Broom, called the "nickel and dime school" because it depended for support almost wholly on contributions from Negroes who could not afford to give more.

Because of these universities there are many Negroes of ability in the humanities, and the social and natural sciences. Frequently their influence is greater than academic. At Howard University the *Journal of Negro Education* is ably edited. Carter G. Woodson edits the pioneering *Journal of Negro History* and directs the Association for the Study of Negro Life and History in this city. The weekly *Afro-American*, with a Washington edition, and the semiweekly Washington *Tribune* are the city's Negro newspapers, both tending to develop race consciousness.

These give some point to the boast of Washington's "cultural supremacy" among Negroes, but the boast is not too well founded. There is little literature even attempting to do justice to the facets of Negro life in Washington. There have been literary circles with a few poets, dramatists, and writers of fiction. The Little Theatre movement, initiated among Negroes by Alain Locke, editor of the *New Negro*, and Montgomery Gregory at Howard University, has only partially succeeded.

In 1903 the British Negro composer, Samuel Coleridge-Taylor, sponsored by a society named in his honor, conducted in Washington the first American performance of his *Hiawatha* trilogy. Other musical organizations of the century were the Clef Club and the Amphion Glee Club. The Washington Folk-Song Singers, directed by Will Marion Cook, presented as soloists Abbie Mitchell, Lottie Wallace, and Harry T. Burleigh, all later to become widely famed. The Washington Conservatory, under Mrs. Harriet Gibbs Marshall, was an important factor in musical education. Roland Hayes sang in Washington churches on his long, uphill road. Lillian Evans Tibbs, better known in opera as Madame Evanti, was one of Washington's well-known soloists. Of national popularity is the Howard University Glee Club under the direction of Roy W. Tibbs and Todd Duncan. The latter carried the role of "Porgy" in Gershwin's *Porgy and Bess*. Among jazz composers and orchestra leaders there are many Washingtonians; chief among these are Claude Hopkins and Duke Ellington, who has as one of his "hot" numbers, *The Washington Wabble*.

Although politically voluble, Negroes in Washington are still politically ineffectual. The hey-day of important political figures has passed. Oscar De Priest, Republican Congressman from Illinois, was followed by Arthur Mitchell, Democratic Congressman from the same State. There are still staunch Republicans and a Young Republican Club, and some of the old school have espoused the Liberty League; but there are many Democrats as well. The number of Negro appointees to administrative posts in the New Deal, while by no means adequate, is greater than in previous administrations. Many of these appointees are Washingtonians. Although political disquisitions may still stir the somnolence of barber shops, or break up friendships quadrennially, and although job-seekers abound, disfranchisement makes most of the Negroes politically apathetic. There is likewise a civic apathy. Civic organizations bringing grievances are often treated with scant courtesy by municipal authorities; without the vote they have little redress. There is a growing liberalism among Negroes who understand their plight, but the urging of such groups as the National Negro Congress and the N.A.A.C.P. too often meets with inertia and confusion. Segregation in Washington seems an accepted fact. Public buildings and public conveyances are not segregated, although on every southbound train Negro passengers are "jim-crowed." Negroes are not served in restaurants, saloons, hotels, movie-houses, and theaters, except those definitely set aside for them. Some stores will not accept their trade. Some governmental departments have separate accommodations, and some discriminate in the type of work offered to Negroes.

One boast, perhaps better founded than those of culture or civic status, is that Washington Negroes have a good time. Dances range in full plenty from the "house shouts" to the "bals masqués" of Washington's mythical Negro "400." Social scribes flatteringly speak of Negro "Mayfair" with no sense of incongruity. Social clubs are legion; the What-Good-Are-We Club (composed of ex-Howard students), is widely known for intensive hilarity. Though college sororities and fraternities seem to be awakening to social realities, their lavish "formals" are still the most important events on their schedules. Washington Negroes are great "joiners"; the largest orders are the Elks, Odd Fellows, Knights of Pythias, and the Masons, but some with an ancient history like "Love and Charity" linger on. The Musolit Club and the Capital City Pleasure Club have large memberships.

The movie-houses attract great crowds of Negroes. Of the chain theaters owned by the Lichtman's, three are located on U Street, the thoroughfare of Negro businesses and pleasure-seekers. The Howard Theater, something of a theatrical institution, affording both movies and fast-stepping, high-hearted shows, attracts an audience of both races. Poolrooms, short-lived

cabarets, beer gardens, and eating places, from fried-fish "joints," barbe-
cue, and hamburger stands to better-class restaurants, do an apparently
thriving business. And yet, when the outsider stands upon U Street in the
early hours of the evening and watches the crowds go by, togged out in
finery, with jests upon their lips—this one rushing to the poolroom, this
one seeking escape with Hoot Gibson, another to lose herself in Hollywood
glamor, another in one of the many dance halls—he is likely to be unaware,
as these people momentarily are, of aspects of life in Washington of graver
import to the darker one-fourth. This vivacity, this gayety, may mask for a
while, but the more drastic realities are omnipresent. Around the corner
there may be a squalid slum with people jobless and desperate; the alert
youngster, capable and well trained, may find on the morrow all employment closed to him. The Negro of Washington has no voice in government,
is economically proscribed, and segregated nearly as rigidly as in the
southern cities he contemns. He may blind himself with pleasure seeking,
with a specious self-sufficiency, he may point with pride to the record of
achievement over grave odds. But just as the past was not without its honor,
so the present is not without bitterness.

In spite of the widespread segregation of the Negro in the District of
Columbia, his story as told here has not concerned him solely. From the
outset, white humanitarians have protested his enslavement and abuse, and
farsighted statesmen have worked toward his integration in the total pattern. His schooling resulted from cooporation between Negroes and whites.
Interracial organizations have worked toward an abolition of the injustices
he faces. Governmental and municipal agencies have attempted to deal out
to him a measure of what is his due. Today he is no longer asking, if he
ever asked, to be considered as a ward. He asks to be considered as a
citizen. But fulfillment of this hope seems still desperately remote.

The Negro has been donor as well as recipient. His contributions cannot be limited to those of menial or entertainer, as those who stereotype his
character would insist. Many of the oldest inhabitants of the city who happen to be Negroes, and many newcomers, can boast of a record of citizenship as honorable as any. Culturally, the Negro has much to give, and, in
spite of its being grudgingly received, has given much. No city can afford
to disdain the creative potentialities of the Negro in music, drama, literature, and the arts. The scholars concentrated in Washington have a function
greater than that of Negro scholars. They are American scholars who happen to be Negroes, and Washington and America have need of them. The
Negro professional class of Washington, limited to service among Negroes,
could contribute greatly to the advance of the entire city. The Negro has

contributed. What could be a greater contribution is held in check by segregation.

From the preservation of the color-line in the District grave consequences arise. Educationally, segregation means the maintenance of a dual system—expensive not only in dollars and cents but also in its indoctrination of white children with a belief in their superiority and of Negro children with a belief in their inferiority, both equally false. Politically, it is believed by many that the determination to keep the Negro "in his place" has lessened the agitation for suffrage in the District. Economically, the presence of a large number of unemployed constitutes a critical relief problem; the low rate of pay received by Negro workers lowers the standard of living and threatens the trade-union movement. Socially, the effects of Negro ghettos are far-reaching. One cannot segregate disease and crime. In this border city, southern in so many respects, there is a denial of democracy, at times hypocritical and at times flagrant. Social compulsion forces many who would naturally be on the side of civic fairness into hopelessness and indifference. Washington has made steps in the direction of justice, but many steps remain to be taken for the sake of the underprivileged and for the sake of a greater Washington.

The American Race Problem
As Reflected in American Literature

INTRODUCTION

⚘ IN "CALLING AMERICA," the special number of the *Survey Graphic* which sprang from American concern with the plight of minorities in Europe, William Allan Neilson writes:

> The greatest of the minority problems in the United States concerns *the Negro*, involving as it does some 10 per cent of our population. . . . It would be flagrant hypocrisy to pretend that the position of the Negro in the United States is in harmony with the principles of democracy and equality of opportunity to which we habitually pay lip service.[1]

W. E. B. Du Bois considered that the problem of the twentieth century is the problem of the color line. In a blither spirit a historian of Reconstruction assures the readers of *The Road to Reunion* that "The Negro Problem Always Ye Have With You." An alarmist "scientist" titled his book on the Negro *America's Greatest Problem.* American literature seems to second the warnings and the assurance: the problems attendant upon the presence of the Negro in America have engaged the attention of writers from the earliest years of our national literature.

It is the purpose of this essay to trace what American writers have said about "the Negro problem." Difficult of precise definition, and therefore not defined here, "the Negro problem" is recognizable enough for such a purpose.

1. William Allan Neilson, " 'Minorities' in Our Midst," *Survey Graphic* (Calling America), 28:102, 103 F 1939.

This essay will be confined chiefly to creative literature in which poets, dramatists and fiction writers attempt to reflect the "Negro Problem." The voluminous literature on "the problem" under which library shelves sag has been made use of only to show how influential the ethnologists, psychologists, sociologists, theologians, and historians have been upon the creative artists, who admitted that they were writing fiction.

The essay is divided chronologically into three periods: (1) the antebellum, (2) reconstruction to the turn of the century, and (3) the twentieth century.

Kelly Miller in one of his aphorisms states that "The Negro must get along, get white, or get out." Creative artists have agreed with these as solutions. They see "the problem" or "problems" differently, however. For instance, proslavery authors see the Negro as failing to get along when he was discontented as a slave, or free in the North; antislavery authors when he was treated as a chattel; most Negro authors when he is denied citizenship. The problems then are of two sorts: the problem that the Negro's presence caused those who believed in a white America, *i.e.*, the problem of the Negro to whites; and the problems that the Negro has met with in America, *i.e.*, the problem of America to Negroes.

It is not a purpose of this paper to discuss the question of propaganda in literature, or to evaluate the points of view expressed, although evaluations have not been avoided. This is one of the most controversial subjects in American literature. If one is a good American, it is very difficult to enter this ring where such a rousing battle royal is going on without once raising his arm and letting fly.

THE ANTE-BELLUM PERIOD

American readers had abundant opportunity to learn of the gravity of the problem of slavery from the reports of English travelers such as Charles Dickens, Harriet Martineau, and J. S. Buckingham, and of Northerners such as Frederick Law Olmsted. But such testimony could be dismissed as British or Yankee prejudice. Often too realistic for comfort, the analysis of slavery as an injury to Negroes and a cause of general Southern backwardness was shunted aside.

Creative artists stated the same conclusions in more emotionally stirring forms. Richard Hildreth, an American historian, was the first to use the novel for antislavery opinions. Published in 1836 as the memoirs of an educated slave, his work was enlarged after the great success of *Uncle Tom's Cabin* and renamed *The White Slave* (1852). Considering the pastoral picture of slavery to be largely mythical, Hildreth, like so many of his followers, stressed the slave's basic humanity, introduced Negro runaways, "maroons," insurrectionists; and described with realistic detail the callousness of the domestic slave-trade, the inevitable miscegenation and the brutalities. In the latter section of the book, Hildreth permits his characters to debate slavery at length. One enlightened slave-owner is a mild colonizationist:

> The late president Jefferson . . . [remarked] that we hold the slaves like a wolf by the ear, whom it is neither safe to hold nor to let go. . . . It seems to me that we whites are the wolf, and the unfortunate negroes the lamb . . . whom, if we only had the will, we might let go without any sort of danger. Why can't we allow freedom to the negroes as well as to the Irish or the Germans? But with the inveterate prejudices of our people . . . [they] would be all up in arms at the very idea of it. The more low, brutal, and degraded a white man is, the more strenuously does he insist on the natural superiority of the white man, and the more he is shocked at the idea of allowing freedom to the "niggers." Our colonization system yields to this invincible feeling.[2]

Hildreth does not disguise his belief that colonization is a visionary solution, that Negroes if set free would prosper, and that the whites more than the Negroes need to be readied for the emancipation of the latter. He tells approvingly of a planter's scheme for freeing his Negroes and setting them up on a plantation in a free state.

The antislavery literary crusade took its start from people whose sense of human dignity was shocked by the idea of men and women being held as property. Transcendentalists like Theodore Parker and Thoreau, Quakers like Whittier and Thomas Garrett, agitators like Garrison and Theodore Weld saw slavery as a curse, in Longfellow's words as "a blind Samson in the temple of our liberties." They wanted the curse removed, the Samson throttled. Attack upon the evil was the pressing task for many of the poets and novelists, and they were not perturbed about what would follow its abolition. Happy endings were fashioned for their heroes and heroines: the octoroon Camilla marries her Northern white rescuer; the white slave Archie Moore at last finds his lost wife and sails for England; broken families are happily united in Canada.

2. Richard Hildreth, *The White Slave*. Boston: Tappan and Whittemore, 1852, p. 273.

Fugitive slaves, like Frederick Douglass, William Wells Brown, Lewis and Milton Clarke in their autobiographies, and Harriet Tubman, Josiah Henson, and William and Ellen Craft in their dictated narratives told chiefly of the practical, immediate problems of food, clothing and lodging, of avoiding the slave-buyer, of staying out of the ill graces of the driver, the overseer or the slave-breaker, of finding trustworthy mates to dare an escape, of guarding against treacherous slaves, of dodging the patrol, of checkmating the slave-hunters and kidnappers. With such problems solved, it is no wonder that the spirit of much of their writing was that of the fellow who, spirited away by Harriet Tubman to Canada, threw himself upon free soil and shouted his thanks to God that he was free at last. Some of the noted fugitives, especially Douglass, turned their thoughts to the new set of problems, but most of the autobiographies of ex-slaves close with jubilees.

Some of the novelists, however, although deploring slavery, viewed with distrust the presence in America of free Negroes. Some were like Hildreth in fearing race prejudice; others, believing the Negro to have his peculiarities, could not visualize two races living side by side in harmony. This second attitude goes far back: in one of the earliest antislavery pamphlets, *The Selling of Joseph*, Judge Sewall writes:

> Few can endure to hear of a Negro's being made free; and indeed they can seldom use their freedom well; yet their continual aspiring after their forbidden Liberty, renders them Unwilling Servants. And there is such a disparity in their Conditions, Color & Hair, that they can never embody with us, and grow up into orderly Families, to the Peopling of the Land: but still remain in our Body Politick as a kind of extravasat blood.[3]

In *The Spy* Cooper expresses both hope for gradual emancipation and anxiety over the increasing class of free Negroes, vagrants "without principles and attachments."[4] Melville includes antislavery passages in *Mardi* (1849), but convinced that tampering with the peculiar institution will cause secession and revolt, he concludes gloomily that "Time must befriend these thralls!"

At the time of *Uncle Tom's Cabin* (1851) Harriet Beecher Stowe was

3. Samuel Sewall, *The Selling of Joseph* in Warfel, Gabriel, and Williams, *The American Mind*, p. 64.
4. James Fenimore Cooper, *The Spy*. New York: Charles Scribner's Sons, 1931, p. 44.

perplexed about the future of the free Negro. George Harris' reunion with Eliza in Canada is not unadulterated bliss. His future course is a quandary. He decides that "passing for white" would be disloyal to his mother's race and that his individual fight in America for abolition would be ineffectual. In Africa, however, he dreams that a republic, a nation of his people, is rising that will

> roll the tide of civilization and Christianity along its shores, and plant there mighty republics, that growing with the rapidity of tropical vegetation, shall be for all coming ages.

He knows that colonization has been used to retard emancipation, but there is a "God above all man's schemes" who will use it to found a Negro nation. The Negro has rights to be allowed in America, "equal rights . . . as the Irishman, the German, the Swede," and the added claim of "an injured race for reparation." But George does not want those rights.

> I want a country, a nation of my own. I think that the African race has peculiarities yet to be unfolded in the light of civilization and Christianity, which, if not the same with those of the Anglo-Saxon, may prove to be morally, of even a higher type.[5]

In *Dred*, her second antislavery novel, Mrs. Stowe does not dispatch her Negro heroes and heroines to Africa, but leaves them in Canada. Like Harriet Tubman, Mrs. Stowe seems to believe that after the Fugitive Slave Bill fugitives can be safe only near the defending paws of the British lion.

Mrs. Stowe believes that the African race (her militant and intelligent heroes and heroines are almost always nearly white) has its peculiarities (generally of a higher moral caliber than the Anglo-Saxon's). She pleads for humane treatment of Negroes in the North in order to enable them to attain the "moral and intellectual maturity" requisite for missionary service in Africa. Influenced by Mrs. Stowe, H. L. Hosmer's *Adela, The Octoroon* after describing the misery of Mississippi slaves and of Northern free Negroes, shows Liberia to be a happy land of opportunity.

When Frederick Douglass opposed colonization as "an old enemy of the colored people in this country,"[6] he expressed the animus of the out-

5. Harriet Beecher Stowe, *Uncle Tom's Cabin.* New York: The Macmillan Company, 1928, p. 417.

6. Frederick Douglass, "Speech in Faneuil Hall," June 8, 1849, in Woodson, Carter G., *Negro Orators and Their Orations.* Washington: The Associated Publishers, 1925, p. 178.

right abolitionists, who, like Garrison, assaulted caste as well as slavery. But Douglass' scornful addition that "almost every respectable man belongs to it by direct membership or by affinity," was true of some antislavery writers. During the Civil War, the *Saturday Review* in England commented upon the strange illusion

> that any respectable party or body of Northerners honestly propose to put the negro on a perfect level with white men . . . neither sober American citizens . . . nor sober Englishmen who have visited . . . The West Indies, will give the slightest adhesion to a principle which makes the negro the social equal of the white man, and encourages the dusky pets of the platform to aspire to a matrimonial alliance with white women.[7]

Besides men like Benjamin Lundy and Joshua Coffin who opposed slavery because of its wrong to Negroes, there were other Southern writers who opposed it as working injury to non-slaveholding whites. J. J. Flournoy, convinced that Negroes were "constitutionally ignorant and uncouth, malicious when in power [written in 1836], and proud without beauty—blasphemous and full of obloquy" and therefore "not fit to associate with the whites," founded a sect called "The Efficient and Instantaneous Expulsion Association of Philosophic and Fearless Patriots."[8] Nearly twenty years later, Hinton Rowan Helper developed Flournoy's ideas. Protesting his dislike for Negroes, he still believed that slavery was a great wrong, and that the system of logic that justified it, merely because "Nature had been pleased to do a trifle more for the Caucasian race than for the African," was "antagonistic to the spirit of democracy." Helper produced "expulsion" as the only stay of the impending ruin.[9]

Many non-slaveholders agreed with Helper, but his book was judged to be as incendiary as *The Liberator,* and the poets and novelists strung along with the master class. They countered Helper's strictures on the waste of slavery with paeans about its blessings to planters and slaves, with the latter chief beneficiaries. They agreed with Helper, however, that Negroes—if free—should be ejected from the paradise.

Proslavery authors found biological warrant for their beliefs in the work

7. Cedric Dover, *Know This of Race.* London: Secker and Warburg, 1939, p. 97.

8. William Sumner Jenkins, *Pro-Slavery Thought in the Old South.* Chapel Hill: University of North Carolina Press, 1935, pp. 92–93.

9. Hinton Rowan Helper, *The Impending Crisis of the South.* New York: A. B. Burdick, 1860, p. 184.

of savants whom Helper characterized as "ethnographical oligarchs." The Negro's "different bodily formation" was one of the ways by which Providence assured his political condition. *The Bible Defense of Slavery* established that the Negro was the natural born slave in such ways as citing the great length and width of his foot, "the extraordinary protrusion of the heel backward, placing the leg nearly in the middle of the foot in many instances"; the skin where the "Divine hand" has placed "myriads of little cups of pellucid water minged with the capillary vessels" to throw off the sun's rays and avert sunstroke.[10]

A later book embodying many of the scientific justifications of slavery was *White Supremacy and Negro Subordination* or *The Negro, A Subordinate Race and (So-Called) Slavery Its Normal Condition.* To its author, C. J. H. Van Evrie, M.D.:

> The beard symbolizes our highest conceptions of manhood—it is the outward evidence . . . of complete growth, mental as well as physical—of strength, wisdom and manly grace.[11]

But the Negro cannot raise a beard, being capable at his best of only "a little tuft on the chin and sometimes on the upper lip, . . . nothing that can be confounded with a beard." He goes on:

> The negro, lowest in the scale, presents an almost absolute resemblance to each other [sic]. . . . Except where wide differences of age exist they are all alike, and even in size rarely depart from that standard uniformity that nature has stamped upon the race. The entire external surface, as well as his interior organism, differs radically from the Caucasian. His muscles, the form of the limbs, his feet, hands, pelvis, skeleton, all the organs of locomotion are . . . radically different from the Caucasian.[12]

The Negro's beardlessness, uniformity, and the other biological differences do more than doom him to subordination. They likewise are reasons why "Music is to the Negro an impossible art, and therefore such a thing as a Negro singer is unknown" and why a correctly proportioned brain "could no more be born of a Negress than an elephant could be!"[13]

10. Josiah Priest, *Bible Defense of Slavery.* Glasgow, Ky.: W. S. Brown, 1851, p. 51.
11. C. J. Van Evrie, *White Supremacy and Negro Subordination.* New York: Van Evrie, Horton & Co., 1870, p. 102.
12. *Ibid.,* p. 106.
13. *Ibid.,* p. 130.

Theological warrant for slavery could be quite as fantastic. When Ham laughed at his father's drunkenness and disarray, he and all of his descendants were doomed to perpetual servitude. "Cursed be Canaan; a servant of servants shall he be unto his brethren." For the Fugitive Slave Bill divine sanction could be derived from God's commanding the runaway Hagar to return to her mistress Sarah (Genesis XVI:9). So ran some of the biblical arguments.

It was to the biological, psychological, and theological sanctions that the creative authors turned rather than to the more hard-headed political economy which held that slavery has its *raison d'être* in the need for "sordid, servile, laborious beings" to perform "sordid, servile, laborious offices." J. P. Kennedy's *Swallow Barn* (1832) praised slavery as a beneficent guardianship for an "essentially parasitical race" noted for "intellectual feebleness." William Grayson in a long poem, *The Hireling and the Slave* (1856), described the life of the slaves as "unassailed by care," full of "blessings claimed in fabled states alone." Slavery was the design of Providence to transfer the Negro from bestiality to "celestial light." The hero in Caroline Lee Hentz's *The Planter's Northern Bride* cribs arguments from *The Bible Defense of Slavery* to prove the Negro to be divinely ordained to pick his cotton:

> In the first place, his skull has a hardness and thickness greater than our own, which defy the arrowy sunbeams of the South. Then his skin ... secretes a far greater quantity of moisture, which like dew, throws back the heat absorbed by us. I could mention many more peculiarities which prove his adaptedness to the situation he occupies. . . .
> The mountains and the valleys proclaim it.[14]

The fantasies of the scientists and the theologues were dressed up in sentimentality and melodrama by the romancers. They made slavery, according to a Southern critic, into an "unbroken Mardi Gras." But they admitted that a few problems existed. There were serpents in this Eden: abolitionists sneaking about stirring discontent, short-sighted Southerners who would teach Negroes to read and write, and fractious Negroes who resented what was for their best good.

Thus Kennedy regarded the interference of abolitionists as "an unwarrantable and mischievous design to do us injury," sometimes resented "to

14. Caroline Lee Hentz, *The Planter's Northern Bride*. Philadelphia: Perry & McMillan, 1854, II, p. 4.

the point of involving the innocent Negro in the rigor which it provokes."[15]
W. L. G. Smith in *Life at the South* or *Uncle Tom's Cabin As It Is* shows an abolitionist worming his way into the confidence of honest, unspoiled Negroes and changing their happy lives. *A Yankee Slave Dealer* has an abolitionist foolishly trying to decoy satisfied Negroes; Mrs. Hentz's *The Planter's Northern Bride* has a Dickensian villain preaching liberty and causing an abortive revolt.

Vigilance could of course lessen the impact of the abolitionists. Much graver to proslavery authors was the increasing class of free Negroes, some runaways; some manumitted as natural children of white fathers, or as reward for services; some who by hiring themselves out, scraping and hoarding had saved enough money to buy their own bodies. These, not the safely stowed slaves, constituted the Negro problem to slaveowners and their literary men.

W. J. Grayson gave classic form to the Southerners' concept of the free Negro in the North:

> There in suburban dens and human sties,
> In foul excesses sunk, the Negro lies;
> A moral pestilence to taint and stain,
> His life a curse, his death a social gain,
> . . . with each successive year,
> In drunken want his numbers disappear.[16]

William Thompson in a book of burlesque travels in the North, loses his tone of burlesque in writing of the Northern free Negroes. He can only pity the "pore, miserable, sickly looking creaters . . . diseased and bloated up like frogs—[in a condition] to which the philanthropists . . . wants to bring the happy black people of the South." Uncle Tom, in *Life at the South* finds labor for hire in Canada to be harder than slavery in Virginia, and discovers Negroes frozen to death in snowstorms in Buffalo. Crissy in *The Planter's Northern Bride* runs away from unfeeling Northerners to get back to the freedom of the plantation—a sort of Underground Railroad in reverse. The consensus is expressed by Uncle Robin in John W. Page's *Uncle Robin in His Cabin:* "Dis, sir, is no country for free black men: Africa de only place for he, sir."

15. J. P. Kennedy, *Swallow Barn.* New York: G. P. Putnam's Sons, 1895 (reprint), p. 453.
16. W. J. Grayson, *The Hireling and the Slave.* Charleston, S.C.: McCarter & Co., 1856, p. 69.

Proslavery authors sometimes caught up with the spirit of their age and suspected that slavery could not be permanent. W. L. G. Smith writes in the Preface to *Life at the South:*

> The day will yet come when the descendants of Ham will be gathered in the land of their ancestors, and Liberia, in God's own good time, will take its position among the independent states of the world.

W. J. Grayson waxes poetic at the prospect of the Negro (no longer necessary for the development of the South) returning to Africa on missionary duty now instead of agricultural:

> To Africa, their fatherland, they go,
> Law, industry, instruction to bestow:
> To pour, from Western skies, religious light,
> Drive from each hill or vale its pagan rite,
> Teach brutal hordes a nobler life to plan,
> And change, at last, the savage to the man.[17]

This was to take place, however, "In God's own good time."

RECONSTRUCTION AND AFTER

The Emancipation Proclamation ended one phase of the Negro problem, but only aggravated others. Abraham Lincoln illustrates the indecision that plagued so many humanitarians. In his campaigning for office Lincoln had disclaimed any purpose to introduce political and social equality between the races. "There is a physical difference between the two, which in my judgment, will forever forbid their living together in perfect equality." Lincoln's earlier sponsorship of colonization had resulted in an attempt to settle a cargo of freedmen on the Island of Vache in the West Indies. That ill-fated experiment taught him the futility of colonization, but he was not to live long enough to see the results of his other plans for the freedmen.

Walt Whitman, as contradictory as usual, turned upon the freedmen with surprising invective:

> As if we had not strained the voting . . . caliber of American democracy to the utmost for the last fifty years with the millions of ignorant

17. W. J. Grayson, *op. cit.*, p. 73.

foreigners, we have now infused a powerful percentage of blacks, with about as much intellectual caliber (in the mass) as so many baboons.[18]

Whitman described a parade of freedmen in Washington as "very disgusting and alarming in some respects," the jubilant Negroes looking "like so many wild brutes let loose."[19]

Lincoln's perplexity and Whitman's disgust were prevalent among Northern writers who had been humanitarians toward the slave. Few retained the staunchness of such equalitarians as Garrison, Stevens, and Sumner. One honorable exception was David Ross Locke, who, under the pen-name Petroleum V. Nasby, attacked copperheads and "dough-faces," laid the bogey of Negro domination, caricatured Southern chivalry, and ridiculed the superstition that the Negro out of slavery would perish like a fish out of water. But another humorist, Marietta Holly, after describing the horrors of the Klan in *Aunt Samantha on the Race Problem*, could counsel colonization as the only solution, even as late as 1892. Another Northerner in the South, Constance Fenimore Woolson, was shocked by the hopelessness of doing anything for the freedmen, and reserved her pity for the suffering master class.

With reconciliation the watchword of many Northerners, the South seized the opportunity to glorify its lost cause, and to persuade the North to leave the Negro problem in Southern hands. This campaign started almost with Appomattox. J. H. Van Evrie republished his book at the close of the Civil War with such prefatory remarks:

> We will return to the Constitution and the "Union as it was"; and every man, and woman too in this broad land must accept the simple but stupendous truth of white supremacy and negro subordination, or consent to have it forced on them by years of social anarchy, horror, and misery![20]

His book was intended to prove that what was called slavery was not slavery at all, "but a natural relation of the races." Whenever the two races "are in juxta-position, the normal condition of the Negro . . . is to be guided and controlled socially and politically by the white race."[21]

18. V. F. Calverton, *The Liberation of American Literature*. New York: Charles Scribner's Sons, 1932, p. 296.
19. Newton Arvin, *Whitman*. New York: The Macmillan Co., 1938, p. 32.
20. J. H. Van Evrie, *op. cit.*, VI.
21. *Ibid.*, VIII.

Literary artists, with superior skill, sold Van Evrie's ideas in a more sophisticated, convincing version to the North which, wearied after the long war, was ready to forget, forgive and concede. Their contrivance was simple. Slavery was to be shown as not slavery at all, but a happy state best suited for an inferior, childish but lovable race. In this normal condition, the Negro was to be shown thriving. Then came his emancipation, which the better class of Negroes did not want, and which few could understand or profit by. Freedom meant anarchy. Only by restoring control (euphemism for tenant farming, sharecropping, black codes, enforced labor, segregation and all the other ills of the new slavery) could equilibrium in the South, so important to the nation, be achieved.

Thomas Nelson Page is the chief of these glorifiers of the Old South and alarmists about the New. His old relics of slavery, Charley McCarthys in black-face, breathe forth sighs for the vanished days when Negroes were happy: "Dem wuz good old times, marster—de bes' Sam ever see!" Reconstruction showed servants corrupted by scalawags, carpetbaggers, Yankee soldiers and schoolmarms: faithful housedogs injected with hydrophobia. *In Ole Virginia* is a plaintive cry for the lost heaven; *Red Rock* is a turgid description of the new hell. When the "new issue" Negroes, struggling for schooling and for property, do not enrage Page, they succeed in making him laugh as *Pastime Stories* (1899) indicates. An old Negro, approved by Page (he softens his attacks when dealing with decrepit graybeards whose days of menace are over) says:

> You knows de way to de spring and de wood pile, and de mill, an' when you gits a little bigger I's gwine to show you de way to de hoe-handle, an' de cawn furrer, an' dats all de geog-aphy a nigger's got to know.

Joel Chandler Harris has his pet, Uncle Remus, likewise scornful of "nigger 'book-larnin' ":

> Hits de ruinashun er dis country. . . . Put a spellin' book in a nigger's hans', en right den an' dar' you loozes a plow-hand. I kin take a bar'l stave an' fling mo'sense inter a nigger in one minnit dan all do schoolhouses betwixt dis en de state er Midgigin.

Harris was fundamentally of greater decency than Page, but he still has his mouthpiece Uncle Remus speaking too often the social policy of white Georgians rather than of his own people.

The author who most strongly urged that the Negro be kept "in his place" was Thomas Dixon, whose fiction embodied the creed of the Ku Klux Klan. Dixon makes use of one old trick of the racialist: he equates political equality with sexual license. The argument runs crudely: keep the Negro from the ballot-box, keep him underpaid and uneducated, or else the purity of white womanhood is threatened.

As far back as the Lincoln-Douglas debates, Lincoln was taunted with sponsoring intermarriage when he urged merely that the Negro has "the right to eat the bread which his own hands have earned. . . . Judge Douglas infers that because I do not want a Negro woman for a slave, that I must want her for my wife." In the Reconstruction, intermarriage was dragged out in a more sinister guise. The pat response to assertion of Negro rights became "Would you want your daughter [sister, kinfolks, as the case might warrant] to marry a Negro?" For this, Thomas Dixon and his school are largely responsible. The only Negroes for whom Dixon has any respect are those who dislike Yankees, worship their old masters and mistresses, and prefer slavery. The Negroes engaged in politics are uniformly vicious. The height of their ambition seems to be to make love to a white woman. Negro soldiers abduct white brides; Negro half-wits assault white children. Dixon revels in describing rape. The Ku Klux Klan, the Red Shirts, and other vigilante groups indulge in terroristic activity not for economic or political advantage but to preserve white chastity. A whole school of authors, dreading amalgamation (a bit belatedly) followed Dixon's lead.

Lafcadio Hearn, as fascinated by Negroes as Dixon was repelled, nevertheless expressed one article of the Reconstruction creed. Where Dixon, in company with many others, believed social and political equality would enable a minority to engulf a majority, Hearn foresaw Negro extinction. Freedom would be destruction for "the poor, child-like people":

> Dependent like the ivy, he [the Negro] needs some strong oak-like friend to cling to. His support has been cut from him, and his life must wither in its prostrate helplessness.[22]

Certain Southern writers like George Washington Cable and Mark Twain were sympathetic to the struggles of the freedmen. But Cable's best creative work, where it deals with the tragic injustice of the Negro's lot, is set in the antebellum past and chiefly concerns the abuses of the *Code Noir*

22. Lafcadio Hearn, *Letters from the Raven.* New York: A. and C. Boni, 1930, p. 168.

and the women of mixed blood. Cable does connect the problems of the old South and the new by pointed asides, and he protests current abuses. At the price of ostracism he condemned the convict lease system and the silence of the South on the general indecency of race relations. But this protest was conveyed in polemical essays, not in fiction. Mark Twain, perfectly aware of America's sorry defaulting of its debt to the Negro, still did not reveal this awareness in creative work.

Albion Tourgee, a Northerner who became part of North Carolina's Reconstruction government, used fiction for propaganda purposes. He showed what his contemporaries refused to touch: the slow but steady progress of the freedmen in education, manliness, social awareness, self-sufficiency; the terrorism of the secret orders; the fraud and violence resorted to in order to reduce freedmen to serfs. He felt that he was waging a futile fight, not because of the unreadiness of the freedman but because of the solidifying South. The titles of his best-known books indicate his doubt; they are *A Fool's Errand* and *Bricks Without Straw.*

Negro writers, however, took up the challenge that Tourgee had spoken. Charles Waddell Chesnutt in his fiction included many of the problems of the color line: the problem of the "half-caste" heroine (overemployed even by this time); of the professional man, hampered by prejudice from performing his best service; of the double standard of morality; of convict labor; of mob violence. Chesnutt handled as well problems within the race which later Negroes have shunted aside: the problem of intraracial color prejudice, of the cleavage between the classes and the masses; of treacherous "hat-in-hand" tactics. Chesnutt wrote melodramatically, but his social understanding should not be underestimated.

Dunbar, Chesnutt's contemporary, was more conciliatory. His dialect poetry was often of the plantation tradition idealizing slavery, or was gently pastoral. His protest was confined to his standard English poems, and those, since they inclined to the romantic school, were inexplicit on the causes for protest. In his fiction, especially *The Sport of the Gods,* Dunbar occasionally confronted problems, but in general he elected to portray the less disturbing aspects of Negro life.

THE TWENTIETH CENTURY

Many of the Negro writers of the early twentieth century preserved their trust in conciliatory tactics, in appeals to the Christianity of white America. Some counselled that no wrong this side of heaven was too great to be forgiven since "Christ washed the feet of Judas," or that "Vengeance is Jehovah's own. . . . Let us live like loving men," or that

> The heart of the world is beating
> With the love that was born of God.

Leslie Pinckney Hill in "Self Determination (The Philosophy of the American Negro)" enumerates "four benedictions which the meek unto the proud are privileged to speak": refusal to hate, philosophic mirth, idealism, and unwavering loyalty. There were others who spoke of the wrongs guardedly, abstractly: "We wear the mask"; "We ask for peace"; "At the Closed Gate of Justice": "To be a Negro in a day like this, demands forgiveness . . . rare patience . . . strange loyalty."

> Alas! Lord God, what evil have we done?

This poetry is melancholy with the self-pity of the "talented tenth," but it goes no farther in protest. The dialect poets aimed at farce or sweet bucolics.

But there were some who, disillusioned at the results gained by forbearance, realized that if the struggle for equal rights was to be a long pull, there was even less need to postpone the starting. Novelists, angered at the scorn and hatred of Page and Dixon, retaliated in kind. In their counter-propaganda Negroes were generally faultless victims of white villains, who were generally "poor whites." The heroines were beautiful maidens, the heroes intelligent, militant race-leaders: "As to color he was black, but even those prejudiced as to color forgot that prejudice when they gazed upon this ebony-like Apollo."[23] One novelist had no patience with the school of Booker Washington: "What are houses, land and money to men who are women?"[24]

W. E. B. Du Bois recognized the importance of creative writing as a vehicle for propaganda. He made effective use of many types: chants and short stories denouncing prejudice and mob violence, satires of the shams of democracy, essays combining scholarly research with the emotions of an embittered participant. His first novel, *The Quest of the Silver Fleece*, melodramatic and idealized, was crowded with informed discussions of the "problem"; his second novel *The Dark Princess* shares the preoccupation,

23. Sutton Griggs, *Unfettered.* Nashville, Tenn.: Orion Publishing Co., 1902, p. 71.
24. J. W. Grant, *Out of the Darkness.* Nashville, Tenn.: National Baptist Publishing Board, 1909, p. 19.

presenting mordant and convincing realism in the sections dealing with America.

Early poems of James Weldon Johnson presented his deliberation on the "problem"; asserting the Negro's right to be in America because of his service and achievement; expressing faith in God's will; posing the question "To America": "How would you have us. . . . Men or things":

> Strong, willing sinews in your wings?
> Or tightening chains about your feet?[25]

Johnson's novel *The Autobiography of an Ex-Colored Man* (1912) was the first by a Negro to deal with the dilemmas of the mulatto who, finally beaten by prejudice and lack of opportunity, decides to "pass" for white. Like Chesnutt and Du Bois, Johnson reveals many aspects of the problem, subordinating character and action to its exposition.

Most white writers of the early years of the century followed Page and Dixon, urging that the extension of civil rights to Negroes was equivalent to producing a "mongrel race" in America, or else, satisfied that the Negro problem had been safely handled, viewed Negro life jocularly. John McNeill, for instance, in a poem called "Mr. Nigger" comforted his addressee that he should no longer fear expatriation, since minstrel shows, politicians, planters and lynching mobs depended upon him. The poem is intended to be amusing. More honest writers, realists aware of the tragic uneasiness of American life, occasionally wrote of Negroes in a different vein: Upton Sinclair shows Negro strike-breakers in *The Jungle* (1905) and Stephen Crane and Dreiser recorded brutalities. Mary White Ovington continued the abolitionist tradition in *The Shadow* (1920).

After the War to Make the World Safe for Democracy, Negroes began to write more defiant challenges and more ironic appraisals of America. Fenton Johnson might have produced a parallel to *The Spoon River Anthology*, had he continued delineation of what he started in "Tired" and "The Scarlet Woman." Johnson found brooding defeatism instead of gayety and optimism on the other side of the tracks. Claude McKay's poetry protested "the bread of bitterness" America fed him, and described the Harlem streetwalkers, the workers lost in a city of stone and steel, the menials trying to forget their unhappiness in gin and carousing, the lynching mobs. His best known poem "If We Must Die" was a rallying cry in the epidemic of riots during the post-war years.

25. James Weldon Johnson, *Fifty Years and Other Poems*. Boston: The Cornhill Publishing Co., 1917, p. 5.

Although some of McKay's characters talk lengthily of race, McKay's fiction was like so much of the Harlem school. Written during a "boom period" of culture, the Harlem novels generally showed a life free of perplexities graver than boy getting girl. Wallace Thurman's *Blacker the Berry* (1929) approached an intraracial problem generally shied away from: the predicament of the darker woman in upper-class "society." But Thurman showed little depth in characterizing his heroine. He probably shared the flippancy of many of the literati whom he described, not without caricature, in *Infants of the Spring* (1932). These were riding a crest, and Harlem to them—a small, select circle—seemed to be a Mecca of gay abandon. These younger "intellectuals" of the Harlem province, if we are to believe Thurman and their own confessions, sent in repeated orders for the gin of existence and let the bitters go. Others—Rudolph Fisher, George Schuyler, and Countee Cullen—intelligently aware and quite concerned about the Negro's predicament, still wrote good-natured "spoofs" of what they called professional race-men and their organizations.

But the carelessness of the hedonist and the lighter touch of the satirist were not the chief fashions in fiction. Some Negro novelists felt that wonders would be accomplished by revealing to white America that Negroes had a cultivated middle class—that "we aren't all alike." Many saw lynching as the most flagrant wrong to be attacked. Walter White's *Fire in the Flint* is the classic example of the lynching novel: two upstanding ambitious Negroes become victims of mob violence, the first for avenging an insult to his sister, and the second for attending a white patient, which is interpreted as assault. As long as lynching remains the sole American crime protected by filibustering congressmen it is likely that it will be written of by American artists. But many writers isolate lynching as the chief problem of Negroes and, without much knowledge and understanding of the South, handle it in a stereotyped, unconvincing manner.

Another problem unduly emphasized was that of the "passing" heroine, the octoroon of long standing in American literature. Contemporary white writers still celebrate her misery: "It must be unbearable to have to live on that side of the barrier," they say from their side. "I won't be black," says their octoroon, marked with what Artemus Ward jokingly calls the "brand of Kane." Negro novelists insist upon the octoroon's unhappiness when she "passed" from her people, whose gifts are warm humanity and philosophic mirth. Both sets of interpreters made more of her problems than they seem to deserve. Graver problems, even concerning the mulatto, awaited and await interpretation.

For the statements of these, especially in the South (a section not written of by young Negro writers as much as one might expect) one must resort frequently to southern white novelists. The better known, like Julia Peterkin and DuBose Heyward, while writing with sympathy of their characters, deal little with social and economic hardships, showing tragedies caused by fate, or if made by man, springing from the violence of a primitive folk. As Irvin Cobb has said: "Ef you wants to perduse a piece showing a lot of niggers gittin' skinned, let it be another nigger w'ich skins em . . . an' whatever else you does don't mess wid no race problem."[26]

But all Southern writers have not heeded Cobb's injunction. E. C. L. Adam's *Nigger to Nigger* (1928) is one of the sharpest indictments of Southern race relations. A chorus of unfooled folk Negroes speak their minds on the travesty of Southern justice, the fraud and violence with which white "supremacy" is maintained, the daily insults, the high hurdles in the Negro's way to minimum decency of living. The dialogue discussing the Ben Bess Case, where a Negro was jailed for thirteen years on the trumped up charges of a trollop is worth far more than pretentious propaganda. *Nigger to Nigger* is a remarkable book to have been written by a white Southerner. Paul Green's *In Abraham's Bosom* courageously recorded the struggle of a Negro for schools for his people against the fear and hostility of whites and the fear and inertia of Negroes. T. S. Stribling, tracing both the white and Negro branches of a Southern family, is likewise convincing in his portrayal of callous brutality, sanctioned by Southern custom. Erskine Caldwell in his short stories—"Kneel to the Rising Sun" is probably the most effective in this regard—shows the Negro to be an exploited serf, only nominally free, a catspaw for sadistic landlords and their minions. "Niggers will git killt," says his Tobacco Road philosopher. Grace Lumpkin in *A Sign for Cain* (1935), Theodore Strauss in *Night at Hogwallow* (1937) and other left wing writers see the Negro problem now as a challenge to democracy. Like the best of the old abolitionists, they stress the basic humanity of the Negro. They are more interested in his problems as a member of the working class than as a member of a race. Sympathetic in recording his struggles, his aspirations and his tragedies, they have told valuable truths about him, and incidentally have gained stature as artists.

The picture would be false, however, if certain white authors who differ from the liberals and radicals were omitted. There are strange survivals today of the attitudes and proposals of the antebellum and Reconstruction

26. Irvin Cobb, *Jeff Poindexter, Colored.* New York: George H. Doran Co., 1922, p. 138.

periods. Vachel Lindsay's vision of the "Congo creeping through the black," is coupled with his vision of a Congo paradise with "sacred capitals, temples clean":

> 'Twas a land transfigured, 'twas a new creation
> Oh, a singing wind swept the Negro nation.[27]

Donald Davidson, distrusting so many things—industrialism, democracy, etc.—warns the Negro, now "perhaps unfortunately . . . no longer a child":

> There is the wall
> Between us, anciently erected. Once
> It might have been crossed, men say. But now I cannot
> Forget that I was master, and you can hardly
> Forget that you were slave. . . .
> Let us not bruise our foreheads on the wall.[28]

Others continue the plaint of the feebleness of the Negro, without the guidance of the Southern white, in the perplexed modern world. These characterize the North as proslavery authors did, as the graveyard for the Negro, deploring factors as diverse as Harlem, schooling, factory work, voting, etc., as murderous of the finest qualities of the race. They mourn as Page did for the departed old Negro, pitying what one author has called "the helplessness of a simple jungle-folk . . . set down in the life of cities and expected to be men."[29]

Younger Negro artists consider their people not "helpless simple jungle-folk," but an exploited American minority. Unlike earlier race-apologists who expressed the injuries to heroes of the "talented tenth," these social realists are interested in the submerged nine-tenths. Langston Hughes catches the spirit of the elevator boy "climbing up a mountain of yessirs," hears the tragic undercurrent in the minstrel man's laughter. The little boy in *Not Without Laughter* is turned away from the carnival on Children's Day with: "I told you little darkies this wasn't your party." Hughes believes that some day the Negro will no longer "eat in the kitchen" and he trusts to working-class unity to bring this about. His *Ways*

27. Vachel Lindsay, "The Congo (A Study of the Negro Race)" in Untermeyer, Louis, *Modern American Poetry*. New York: Harcourt Brace & Co., 1930, p. 317.
28. Donald Davidson, *The Tall Men*. New York: Houghton Mifflin Co., 1927, p. 39.
29. Eleanor Mercein Kelly, "Monkey Notions," in Williams, Blanch Colton, *O. Henry Prize Stories of 1927*. Garden City: Doubleday Doran & Co., 1927, p. 207.

of White Folks is an ironic series of short stories showing race prejudice in many of its guises.

George Lee's *River George* is the first novel by a Negro to deal specifically with the evils of sharecropping. Frank Marshall Davis writes vigorous poems of American hypocrisy, and lashes out as well against the sham, the striving and the cowardice to be found in Negro life. Richard Wright in *Uncle Tom's Children* has conveyed with brilliant effectiveness several of the problems of the Southern Negro. His stories are all violent, but they show convincingly how precarious the Negro's hold is upon life and happiness. Self defense in an accidental quarrel, the protection of one's home, the organization of a hunger march, all are due cause for the mob to punish or kill. And the paralyzed fear that Wright shows creeping over the Negro community is eloquent illustration of what life in America means to far too many Negroes.

Not many Negro writers have followed Art for Art's sake. Even so since there are few Negro writers, many problems remain untouched. Especially is this true of intraracial problems. Since the race is so frequently on the defensive, counter-propaganda seems to be called for. Too often the problem is simplified: victimized Negro versus villainous white. Writers analyzing complexities within the race, stating disagreeable truths, and satirists of what could well be satirized are accused of treason. Social realism is a new literary force, and like other important contemporary trends has made incomplete impression on Negro writers. Of the numerous books on Harlem, for instance, there is not one even attempting to do what Michael Gold did in *Jews Without Money* or Farrell did in the Studs Lonigan trilogy. Problems of the Negro middle-class, Northern and Southern, and of the working-class are abundant. The field, except in well-ploughed patches, has barely been scratched. Certainly it has received only the first turning over.

CONCLUSION

From the earliest, American creative writers have recorded the Negro problem. Many wrote protesting his enslavement, some believing that with emancipation the problem would be solved. Others were humanitarian towards the slave, but believed that the free Negro had no place in America and should be colonized. Southern antislavery writers agreed that free Negroes belonged in Africa. Proslavery authors saw no problem if Negroes were left under "beneficent guardianship" suited to their peculiar endowment. The only problematical Negroes were free Negroes; these they intended to keep at a minimum. When slavery should end, and some authors foresaw this eventuality "in God's good time," Negroes were to be sent back to carry to benighted Africans the torch lighted in American bondage.

In Reconstruction, some writers—the minority—described the wrongs heaped upon the freedmen and, following equalitarians like Stevens and Sumner, wished to see the Negro integrated in America as a citizen. The majority of white authors who dealt with the Negro were Southerners who dictated national conciliation upon Southern terms. The Negro problem to these was keeping the Negro in his place, which was away from the ballot box, the schoolroom, and the real estate office. The Negro's problem to these was keeping alive, since the Southern white man's beneficent guardianship had been removed.

In the twentieth century, creative artists have become more and more the defenders of democracy. Realism, recording life as it is in America, has revealed much that is tragically out-of-joint. Realistic observation has developed into social protest. The treatment of the Negro problem, or problems, reflects this major interest of American literature. American treatment of the Negro is now seen to be one of the greatest challenges to democracy. Negro writers, becoming more and more articulate and socially aware, are joining in the depiction of the problems faced by Negroes. Writing from the inside, they are often powerfully persuasive. But they are still very few to harvest the wide field. Nevertheless, even though few, if they believe that literature has social pertinence, that it should interpret what the artist knows most fully, and should help to effect changes that he desires most deeply, they should be challenged by the opportunities that wait.

Count Us In

COUNTED OUT

    🙠 A YOUNG EUROPEAN scholar, back from a swift trip through the South, picked up from my desk a copy of Hal Steed's *Georgia: Unfinished State*. A passage on the last page confused him. It read: "I would not say that the Anglo-Saxon is superior to other races, but that this race makes up nearly one hundred per cent of the populations of the South augurs well for unity—unity in political beliefs, in religion, in social problems."[1] The European was amazed at the figure—nearly one hundred per cent Anglo-Saxon. "But I saw so many Negroes there," he said.

I could have mentioned other oddities in the enumerating of the Negro, from the adoption of the Constitution when a Negro slave counted as three fifths of a man, to the present when a Negro is counted as a unit, a fraction, or a zero, according to the purpose of the counter. Instead I assured him that the evidence of his eyes could be trusted: the gatherings at one side of the depot to see the train go through, the hordes in the ramshackly slums of the cities, the crammed Jim Crow waiting rooms and coaches. Negroes were there all right. Even the publicists who excluded Negroes as part of the population would admit that they were there. Too much so, some might say ruefully, pointing out the large numbers of Negroes as the cause of the poverty and backwardness of the South, apologizing for the belt of swarming cabins engirdling the cities, hoping that the stranger might soften his verdict on the town until the business section around the depot slowly came into view. Too numerous, therefore Negroes had to be kept in their places, the argument might run. Such spokesmen would have a glib reply to recon-

1. Hal Steed, *Georgia: Unfinished State* (New York, 1942), p. 336.

cile the statistics of "nearly one hundred per cent Anglo-Saxon" with the patent reality: "Oh, that's easy to understand. By population we mean the people that count."

I knew that longer study of the South would convince the visitor that in certain respects Negroes definitely counted. He might learn how it was that one scholar called them "the central theme of southern history" running constantly through the record of the section. It would be easy for him to see how the presence of Negroes was chiefly responsible for the political "solidifying" of a region, so far from solid in many other respects. Fear of Negroes' voting had been the primary cause for a poll-tax peculiar to the region, resulting in the disfranchisement of ten millions of American citizens, half again as many whites as Negroes. This disfranchisement, he might learn, exerts more than a sectional influence, since it has been estimated that one poll-tax vote is worth more than five votes in states with no poll-tax. Many poll-tax Congressmen seem to have a permanent tenure on their seats in Congress, and their resulting seniority gives them a power disproportionate to the number of people who voted them into office, to say the least. The European might learn that the Federal ballot for soldiers was most forcefully opposed by those who feared that Negro soldiers might vote; that Federal aid to education was defeated because the race issue was raised; that the "G.I. Bill of Rights" providing unemployment insurance for returning soldiers was jeopardized because of what the Senator in charge of the bill calls the "hatred of certain Congressmen for the colored portion of our armed forces." He might learn how a program of social reform—the Farm Security Administration—though it aided Southern whites as much as Negroes, was in danger of being scuttled by those who feared it meant that the Negro would "get out of his place."

Just how the Negro counted might be clarified should the visitor read Lillian Smith's "Two Men and a Bargain: A Parable of the Solid South," in which the rich white man says to the poor white man:

> There's two big jobs down here that need doing: Somebody's got to tend to the living and somebody's got to tend to the nigger. Now, I've learned a few things about making a living you're too no-count to learn (else you'd be making money same way I make it): things about jobs and credit, prices, hours, wages, votes and so on. But one thing you can learn easy, any white man can, is how to handle the black man. Suppose now you take over the thing you can do and let me take over the thing I can do. What I mean is, you boss the nigger, and I'll boss the money.[2]

2. Lillian Smith, "Two Men and a Bargain," *South Today*, VII (Spring, 1943), 6.

The visitor would thus learn that the Negro counted, and still counts in this "Anglo-Saxon" section. But he would learn also what the Southern spokesmen mean by "people that count."

Negroes have lived too long with this paradox, as with so many others, to be confused by it; they understand the reality behind it. They have been counted out for so long a time.

"Sure, the Negro is all out for the war," my friend the sociologist told me. "He's 72 per cent all out for it." Some might consider this estimate to be cynicism, others optimism. The general conclusion is hardly to be disputed: that for all of its high promise, this war has not summoned 100 per cent of the Negro's enthusiasm and energies.

Before attacking this apathy as short-sighted, it might be wise to look for its causes. They are unfortunately too ready at hand to require much searching. On a six months' stay in the deep South of wartime I saw my fill of them; even casual observations in a border city and on trips to the North have heaped the measure to overflowing.

Documentation of the refusal to count the Negro in the war effort is hardly needed. Discrimination in industry was so flagrant, North and South, East and West, that Executive Order 8802 was issued to ban discrimination in wartime industrial jobs, and the President's Committee on Fair Employment Practices was set up to investigate cases of alleged discrimination. While Negro employment was definitely aided, progress has not been in a straight line. All sorts of obstacles have been in the way: Congressmen and pressure groups continue to snipe and blast at the Committee; the governor of a Southern state openly violated the Executive Order; the railroads have defiantly challenged a showdown. The integration of Negroes into industry has been opposed even with violence; strikes have been called because Negro workers were upgraded; and one of the causes of the Detroit riot is said to be the influx of Negro workers. In spite of welcome gains, Negroes are far from convinced that fullest use is being made of Negro manpower, North or South.

A powerful symbol to the Negro of his "not belonging" was the refusal of the Red Cross to accept Negro donors to the blood bank. Against the medical authorities who stated that there was no such thing as Negro blood, that blood from the veins of whites and Negroes could not be told apart, the Red Cross sided officially with Congressman Rankin, who saw, in the proposal that Negroes too might contribute much needed blood, a communist plot to "mongrelize America": "They want to pump Negro or Japanese blood into the veins of our wounded white boys regardless of the dire effect it might have on their children." The establishment of a segregated blood bank—needless, complicated and irrational—did not help matters much. Nor did the fact, publicized by the recent Spingarn Award, that one of the most important men in the successful establishment of the blood bank was Dr. Charles Drew, a Negro.

In the armed forces, advances have certainly been made over World War I. Drafted to their full quota, Negroes are supposed to be serving in all branches of the Army. Only recently it was reported that Negro para-troopers in Atlanta proved to white paratroopers that they really belonged to the dare-devil's branch. Except in training for pursuit piloting, Negro officers are trained along with white. There are more Negro officers than in the last war, several officers of the rank of colonel and one brigadier gen-eral. Negro airmen are now being trained as bombardiers and navigators. Negro squadrons have seen action in the hot fighting in the Mediterranean theatre, and have been highly commended by military authorities. The long-closed ranks of the Marine Corps are now open, and Marine officers praised Negro Marines as "good Marines," to be used everywhere and exactly as other Marines. In the Navy, Negroes have finally been admitted to other capacities than messboys. Some are to serve as seamen on patrol boats and destroyer escorts. The first ensigns have been commissioned. The record of the Coast Guard toward Negroes has been a good one, and the Merchant Marine, with its Negro officers and mixed crews, is looked upon as an achievement in democracy.

Advances have been made, but the Negro was so far behind in opportu-nity that he does not let his glance linger on the gains; he looks ahead along the road to full participation. This is good Americanism rather than ingratitude. The gains are not unmixed: there still seem to be, for instance, a ceiling on Negro officers and an opposition to having white officers serve under Negro officers. Negroes are dubious about the large number of Negro troops in the service and non-combat units; when the famous Tenth Cav-alry, a source of historic pride, was assigned to service duties, Negroes were disturbed in spite of the assurance that military necessity required the transfer. And the Negro still looks askance at the Navy.

In the South I met on every hand the sense of not belonging. On a bus near Baton Rouge, conversation had hardly started with my seat-mate, a little fellow who looked like a black Frenchman, when he offered me a sure way of staying out of the army: I was to roll a piece of "actican" (Octagon) soap in a pellet of bread and eat it just before the physical examination. He himself knew it would work, he said in his patois. He didn't have nothing against the Germans or Japs, neither one, but he did know some enemies over here. I found the same embittered spirit in a young Negro lieutenant who wanted to get overseas, anywhere, where he could find an enemy *to shoot at*. At the Negro section of an air base, segregated from the rest by a marker reading Beale Street, I found the men not proud of belonging to the Air Corps, but disgruntled at the type of menial labor they were called on to perform. I talked with a well-educated young Negro corporal, who had felt that some meaning might be given to his work in the Army when he learned that he was to be sent to an "area and language" school, but who on the eve of going was told that the school had suddenly been closed to Negroes. I talked with Negro pilots, who in the long hours of the day were learning the intricacies of high-powered P-40's, reading the involved instrument boards, soaring into the "wild blue yonder," with their lives and planes dependent on split-second judgments, developing the aggressiveness and self-reliance necessary for combat pilots. At night, these men were forbidden by curfew to be seen in the downtown section of Tuskegee. This kind of thing, and so much else, rankled.

With a few honorable exceptions, newspapers, radio programs, and motion pictures (omitting of course, Negro newspapers and newsreels for Negro theatres only) have done little to convince Negro soldiers of belonging. Some Northern periodicals, *PM* outstandingly, may publicize Negro military service. But in practically all Southern newspapers, the daily row on row of native sons with the armed forces never showed a dark face. I should have known better, perhaps, than to look for one: pictures of Negroes in these papers were traditionally confined to those of prizefighters or recently deceased ex-slaves. In the North the practice is little better. In a Northern railroad station, a picture, "blown up" by marvelous photographic technique, showed departing soldiers what they were fighting for: a sea of American faces looking out, anxiously, proudly. All were white. An observer saw a contingent of Negro troops entraining; they gave the eye-catching picture a swift glance, and then snapped their heads away, almost as if by command. He wondered, he told me, what thoughts coursed through their minds.

"The Negro Soldier" is a first-class picture, wisely aimed at offsetting some of this indifference and ignorance concerning one-tenth of our armed forces. But only when the picture reaches American white people will Negroes believe its real service to be achieved.

The situation that I found in the South was not solely that of whites refusing to count Negroes in, and of Negroes sensing that they did not and could not belong. It would be inaccurate to omit the friendliness that undoubtedly exists in the South between many whites and many Negroes. Though exaggerated by sentimentalists into a mystical cult of mutual affection instead of a human attachment, certain Southern whites have for a long time protected "their Negroes" and have cherished them with a fondness that has been gratefully received. But, as is frequently pointed out, this has generally been on a basis of master and underling. It has been affection rather than friendship, patronage returned by gratefulness, not the meeting of friends on a plane of mutual respect. It has been Santa Claus and the child. In certain phases—in the courts for instance—when a white man protects *his* Negro regardless of innocence or guilt, the relationship is dangerous. Kindness can kill as well as cruelty, and it can never take the place of genuine respect. Those who boast of the affection between the races below the Mason-Dixon line must be brought up sharp when they realize that one of the worst insults to a Southern white is to be called "nigger-lover," and one of the worst to a Negro is to be called "white-folks nigger."

Genuine respect between whites and Negroes can be found in the South, though to a smaller degree than paternalistic affection and dependent gratefulness. It would be serious omission to fail to recognize undoubted services rendered by many white people, not in the spirit of "Christmas gift," but at the price of social ostracism, loss of preferment, and even physical violence. Sheriffs have braved mobs to protect their prisoners; women have leagued against lynching; preachers, editors, professional men, scholars and authors have spoken and acted against flagrant abuses; trade union organizers have risked life and limb in efforts to establish industrial democracy. Many people, less dramatically, have been generous and courageous in treating Negroes in the spirit of brotherhood. People like Frank Graham, Arthur Raper, Thomas Sancton, Lillian Smith, and Paul Snelling, to name a conspicuous few, are warrants that there are white Southerners who believe that a New South of justice is attainable, or at the least, worth fighting for.

These exceptions must be noted. Yet what I found most apparent among Southern Negroes—civilians and military men, upper and lower class, conservatives and radicals—was a sense of not belonging, and protest, sometimes not loud but always deeply felt. It is a mistake to believe that this protest in the South is instigated by Negroes from the North, or other "furriners," as Eugene Talmadge called them. I found a large degree of militancy in Negroes who were Southern born and bred, some of whom have never been out of the South. I talked with sharecroppers, union organizers, preachers, schoolteachers, newspapermen and bankers who spoke with bitter desperation and daring. Clinton Clark, certainly among the sturdiest fighters, was born in one of the back country parishes of Louisiana; when he was arrested for organizing in a parish nearby, the planters refused to believe him a native of the section. The protest I heard ranged from the quietly spoken aside, through twisted humor and sarcasm, to stridency. Time and time again I heard the anecdote, which spread like a folk tale, of the new sort of hero—the Negro soldier who having taken all he could stand, shed his coat, faced his persecutors and said: "If I've got to die for democracy, I might as well die for some of it right here and now." Some of the protest, undoubtedly, is chip-on-the-shoulder aggression, like that of the Negro woman who in a jammed bus lumbering through the Louisiana night, suddenly raised her voice, seemingly apropos of nothing, to say: "I had my Texas jack with me, and I told that white man I would cut him as long as I could see him."

At Columbus, Georgia, buses marked "K.O. for Tokyo" roared past Negro soldiers, who had to wait for special buses to take them to Fort Benning. It was not only the boys from Harlem or Jersey who griped. The Negro train passengers who, standing in the aisle, wise-cracked at the flushed conductor seated in his "office" in the Jim Crow coach, and then belabored the Negro porter for being a good man Friday, were not Northerners. It was not a Northern waiter who told the Negro sitting in the diner after lavish and ostentatious service: "Man, I was afraid you weren't coming back here." They were not Northern Negroes who repeated the refrain, whether called for or not, "That ain't no way to win the war."

I found this protest natural, since the Southern Negro is where the grip is tightest and the bite goes deepest and most often. The legend of Negro docility was always exaggerated. The novelists and poets, "befo' de war," wrote soothingly of contented slaves, but many of their readers lived in dread of insurrections, and applauded the politicians who, fuming about the loss of their property via the Underground Railroad, sought anxiously to put teeth into the fugitive slave bill, and to set up a code of *verbotens* to prevent slave uprisings. Printers, whose presses busily ran off stories of docile Mose and Dinah, kept handy the stereotype of a Negro with a bundle on a stick, loping towards free land. The image of docility was cherished as a dream, but the hard actuality of furtiveness, truculence, rebelliousness and desperation gave other images to the nightmares. The praises of old massa that white men wrote in "Negro" speech and "Negro" melody ring falsely when set beside "I been rebuked and I been scorned," "Go Down Moses, tell old Pharaoh, let my people go," and "I thank God, I'm free at last."

"When a man's got a gun in your face, ain't much to do but take low or die," a sharecropper in Macon County told Charles S. Johnson. In that setting he was talking sense, not docility. Southern Negroes too often have seen the gun in their faces; but many, all along, have asserted their manhood as far as they were able, walking as close to the danger line as they could and still survive. Some edged over, some were dragged over, and some found the line a shifting one; many of these last paid the penalty. This has been true through the long years, and now, when fine-sounding talk of freedom and democracy comes to them from the newspapers and sermons, tales swapped around the crackerbarrels of country stores, letters from their boys in camps, and speeches over the radio, Negroes begin putting in stronger, though still modest claims. Talk about freedom did not reveal a new discovery; true freedom was something they had long been hankering for. I do not believe that they were so naïve that they expected full values for all of the promissory notes. Freedom was a hard-bought thing, their tradition warned them; the great day of "jubilo" had been followed by gloomy days; but the talk sounded good and right, and perhaps a little more freedom *was* on its way. Through the radios—many of them the battery sets which fill needs in small shacks once filled only by phonographs and guitars—booming voices told them of the plans for a new world. Over the air-waves came the spark, lighting and nursing small fires of hope; the glow and the warmth were good in the darkness. "One of the worst things making for all this trouble," a Mississippi planter told me, with frank honesty, "is the radio. Those people up in Washington don't know what they're doing down here. They ought to shut up talking so much."

Evidence of the Negro's not belonging is readier at hand in the South. But the North is by no means blameless in its race relations. According to an alleged folk anecdote a Negro said he would prefer to be in a race riot in Detroit than in a camp meeting in Georgia. And orators repeatedly urge, "Come North, young man," as the only solution. Nevertheless, the folklore that the North is a refuge, a haven, has met up with the hard facts of unemployment, discrimination and tension. Paradise Valley, Detroit is as badly misnamed as Ideal, Georgia. The mobs that wrecked that Negro section of Detroit showed a crazed lust for bloodshed and destruction that was no Southern monopoly. Harlem has been fondly spoken of as a Mecca for Negroes; but the rioting Negroes who smashed the windows and looted the stores reveal that Negroes have found causes there for desperation and fury. In Northern cities that cradled abolitionism, Negroes are to be found cramped in ghettos, still denied a chance to earn decent livelihoods, to make use of their training, to develop into full men and women.

Though convinced that the Negro is "thoroughly Jim Crowed all over the North—considering Jim Crow in its deepest aspects," Thomas Sancton writes:

> And yet it is true that the main body of the race problem lies within the boundaries of the Southern states, because some three-fourths of America's 13,000,000 Negroes live there. . . . The Negro is oppressed in many ways in the North, and certainly economically, but the long anti-slavery tradition has at least given him some basic civil and social rights which the white South continues to deny him and would like to deny him forever.[3]

Since the problem of the Negro in America is of national scope, steps to integrate the Negro into American democracy must be taken everywhere. Nevertheless, it remains true that the gravest denial of democracy and the greatest opposition to it are in the South. It goes without saying that what happens to the Negro in the South has great bearing on what participation the Negro will attain in American democracy. If a Negro is allowed only second or third class citizenship in Tupelo, Mississippi, his Harlem brother's citizenship is less than first class. And if America has more than one class of citizenship, it is less than first class democracy.

NO TRESPASSING

What are the chances that freedom is really on its way; that the Negro may finally be "counted in"? Some signs are none too propitious. For instance, Negro soldiers are indoctrinated to believe that they are to fight for the four freedoms, but what they run up against daily is confusing, rather than reassuring. Fraternization between Negro soldiers and white soldiers is largely discouraged; it seems to be considered un-American for soldiers of different color, though fighting for the same cause, to be brothers-in-arms. A bulletin from headquarters may attack the subversiveness of race-hostility, but part of the bulletin will warn Negro soldiers that dissatisfaction with Jim Crow is tantamount to subversiveness. Democracy to many seems to be symbolized by this message, printed under a large red "V" on a bus in Charleston, South Carolina:

Victory Demands Your Co-operation

If the peoples of this country's races do not pull together, Victory is lost. We, therefore, respectfully direct your attention to the laws and

3. Thomas Sancton, "The South Needs Help," *Common Ground*, III (Winter, 1943), 12.

customs of the state in regard to segregation. Your cooperation in carrying them out will make the war shorter and Victory sooner. Avoid friction. Be patriotic. White passengers will be seated from front to rear; colored passengers from rear to front.

Looking about them, especially in the South but also in the North, Negroes see convincing proof of these implications: that patriotism means satisfaction with the *status quo ante* Pearl Harbor, that co-operation really does not mean pulling together but rather the Negro's acceptance of the subservient role; that otherwise friction threatens.

A current anecdote tells of a white officer who, seeing a Negro officer eating in the diner, exclaimed: "I'd rather see Hitler win the war than for niggers to get out of their place like that!" Negroes do not believe the attitude to be exceptional.

With all of the commendable efforts of the Army to improve the morale of Negro troops and to investigate and iron out the difficulties, Negro soldiers still find too many violations of democracy, ranging from petty irritations to rank injustices. Negroes may lose precious hours of leave because they can find no place to ride on the buses. Negro officers may find a studied refusal on the part of white soldiers to salute. Negro soldiers may be manhandled, cursed, and even killed by civilian officers of the law. Living the rough, exacting life on maneuvers, driving a jeep, manning a tank or machine gun, servicing or flying a fighter plane, the Negro soldier is expected to be a man doing a man-size job. In contact with civilian life, however, the Negro soldier is expected to be something else again.

There are signs elsewhere that do not reassure. That Negroes were given jobs at a steel plant "that have always been filled by white men," that Negro veterans of World War I were filing legal action "to force the American Legion in Alabama to charter Negro posts," that Tuskegee officials were demanding that pistols be restored to Negro military police in Tuskegee—these frightened and angered Horace Wilkinson of Bessemer, Alabama into urging the foundation of a "League to Maintain White Supremacy." He was shocked at the impertinence of the Fair Employment Practices Committee in coming to Birmingham and recording proof that Southern industrialists and labor unions discriminated against Negro labor and thereby hampered the war effort. Mr. Wilkinson's efforts have reached some success; the "League to Maintain White Supremacy" has been set up. A race-baiting sheet, *The Alabama Sun*, is being published. The first issue has a picture of Mrs. Roosevelt greeting a Negro Red Cross Worker, back from service in England, with the caption "Mrs. Roosevelt Greets Another Nigger."

Mr. Wilkinson is playing an old game, of course, and is a member of a large squad. Mrs. Roosevelt, because of her genuine and gracious democracy, has long been the target of abuse in the South. Years ago, in order to aid the election of Eugene Talmadge, the *Georgia Woman's World* published a picture of the first lady escorted by two Negro cadet officers on her visit to a Negro university. Recent rumormongering has built up a folklore of mythical Eleanor Clubs, dedicated to getting Negro women out of the kitchens, and white women into them. The smear campaign was indecently climaxed when a Mississippi editor, hardly concealing his satisfaction at the Detroit riots, blamed Mrs. Roosevelt for the massacre. The editorial impressed Representative Boykin of Alabama so favorably that he had it inserted in *The Congressional Record.* It closed:

> In Detroit, a city noted for the growing impudence and insolence of the Negro population, an attempt was made to put your preachments into practice . . . Blood on your hands, Mrs. Roosevelt, and the damned spots won't wash out, either.[4]

According to a Gallup Poll, many white Southerners believe that the Negro has been made "unruly and unmanageable" because "large scale reforms have been undertaken too swiftly."[5] Writing from his winter home in Florida, Roger Babson lectured his friends—"the several millions of colored people"—about their "lazy, wasteful, saucy moods." White workers may "strike when they shouldn't, but they are not lazy nor do they throw away money."

In all likelihood "sauciness," rather than laziness or wastefulness, is the chief cause of the present wide race-baiting. Any symbol of the Negro's getting out of "his place"—a lieutenant's shoulder bars, or even a buck private's uniform; a Negro worker at a machine, or a Negro girl at a typewriter, or a cook's throwing up her job—these can be as unbearable as an impudent retort, or a quarrel on a bus, or a fight.

The demagogues have had and are having a field day. Running for reelection as Governor in 1942 against strong opposition, Eugene Talmadge of Georgia preached race-prejudice from Rabun Gap to Tybee's shining light. He ordered his state constabulary to be vigilant against Northern

4. *The Congressional Record,* June 28, 1943.
5. George Gallup, "The Gallup Poll," *The Washington Post,* August 28, 1943.

Negroes and other "furriners" and warned Southern womanhood to arm. His opponent was not above race-baiting himself; it seemed that he had to do it to win. In neighboring states in the Deep South the demagogues may have been less spectacular, but they were busy. Results were soon forthcoming. Three Negroes, two of them boys, were lynched within a week in Mississippi. Negroes were beaten and thrown off buses and trains in all sections of the South. Crises have followed close on crises. A riot stopped work in a Mobile shipyard because Negroes were upgraded; a pogrom laid waste the Negro section of Beaumont, Texas, because of a rape charge, later discredited; and murder ran wild in Detroit.

Any concessions to Negroes—any guaranteeing of democratic rights—set the demagogues off full steam. Sometimes they cry "wolf," as in the instance of the voluminous report of the Office of Education which, among other recommendations, urged co-operation between Negro and white colleges "in the interest of national welfare." Congressman Brooks of Louisiana equated this co-operation to "forcible co-mingling of students of the two races in the South . . . unthinkable . . . leading to the producing of a mongrel race in the United States."

When two anthropologists published a pamphlet, *The Races of Mankind,* to give wide circulation to the scientific proof of the brotherhood of man, and to help bring it about that "victory in this war will be in the name, not of one race or another, but of the universal Human Race," Congressman May of Kentucky was enraged. He was especially irked to read that Northern Negroes scored higher on the A.E.F. Intelligence Test than Southern whites (of his native state, for instance), although the authors advised that the statistics meant only that "Negroes with better luck after they were born, got higher scores than whites with less luck." As Chairman of the House Military Affairs Committee, Congressman May decided that these scientific facts had "no place in the Army program," and promised to keep his eyes open lest the soldiers be contaminated with such doctrine. The pamphlets went to an Army warehouse.

Coincidental with the fight waged by the National Association for the Advancement of Colored People to equalize teachers' salaries in South Carolina, the South Carolina House of Representatives resolved:

> We reaffirm our belief in and our allegiance to establish white supremacy as now prevailing in the South and we solemnly pledge our lives and our sacred honor to maintaining it. Insofar as racial relations are concerned, we firmly and unequivocally demand that henceforth the damned agitators of the North leave the South alone.[6]

6. *The Washington Post,* March 7, 1944.

Shortly after the Negro teachers of South Carolina won the fight to equalize salaries, a Charleston judge stated that many Negroes "would be better off carrying a load of fertilizer rather than a bunch of school books. . . . I am going to break up some of this education."

The perennial demagogues of Mississippi, Senator Bilbo and Representative Rankin, hold the limelight. Senator Bilbo recently held up for the admiration of his constituents his old scheme for deporting Negroes to Africa. One of the first steps he planned as chairman of the Senate Committee for the District of Columbia was clearing Negroes out of the alleys of Washington. "I want them to get into the habit of moving so as to be ready for my movement to West Africa." Until the day of that migration, Senator Bilbo promises alley dwellers of Washington that they can find places to stay in the basements of city homes, and on farms in neighboring states, where the need for cooks and farm hands is acute. Senator Bilbo also threatens to repeat his record-making filibuster against the repeal of the poll tax.

Representative Rankin also stays busy: attacking the President's Committee on Fair Employment Practices as subversive of democracy, since white and Negro sailors in the National Maritime Union are assigned to the same ship; threatening with lynching "that gang of communistic Jews and Negroes that . . . tried to storm the House restaurants, and went around arm in arm with each other";[7] attacking the Federal ballot for soldiers; and raging at every specter of "social equality."

Both Senator Bilbo and Congressman Rankin, as so many other demagogues, protest that they act in the interests of the Negro. Senator Bilbo says, "I am the best friend the Negro has." And Representative Rankin blames "communistic Jews" for causing "the deaths of many good Negroes who never would have got into trouble if they had been left alone."

So run the warnings from the demagogues. But it is not only among the demagogues and their Gestapos—the frontier thugs, the state constabularies, the goon squads and the lynchers—that violent aversion to change is found. Many of the intellectuals speak lines that sound like Talmadge and Rankin. A decade ago, *The American Review,* now defunct, published their ideas. Donald Davidson viewed with dire misgivings "a general maneuver, the object of which is apparently to set the Negro up as an equal, or at least more than a subordinate member of society. The second, or unavowed, program was the new form of abolitionism, again proposing to emancipate the Negro from the handicap of race, color, and previous condition of servi-

7. *The Congressional Record,* July 1, 1943.

tude."[8] Mr. Davidson considered this program (he was talking chiefly of a program of ownership of small farms by Negroes) to be "unattainable as long as the South remains the South," and its sponsors he called ruthless. The only possible solution, he thought, is "to define a place for the American Negro as special as that which they [the American people] defined for the American Indian." Allen Tate, condemning the reformers "who are anxious to have Negroes sit by them on street cars," wrote:

> I argue it this way: the white race seems determined to rule the Negro race in its midst; I belong to the white race; therefore I intend to support the white rule. Lynching is a symptom of weak, inefficient rule; but you can't destroy lynching by *fiat* or social agitation; lynching will disappear when the white race is satisfied that its supremacy will not be questioned in social crises.[9]

Tempting the Negro to question this supremacy, he believes, is irresponsible behavior.

Frank Owsley called the agitation to free the Scottsboro boys the "third crusade."[10] More important to him than the defendants' innocence or guilt was the fact that some Negroes were going to get hurt: "The outside interference with the relationship of the whites and blacks in the South can result in nothing but organizations like the Ku Klux Klan and in violent retaliation against the Negroes—themselves often innocent."

It is to be expected that the die-hards should interpret Negro aspirations to democracy as incendiarism. But there are Southern liberals who do the same. Some congressmen, noted for their support of New Deal reforms, have been recently forced into race-baiting, in order to prove that they are not "nigger-lovers." Some of the liberals protest with David Cohn that they view the position of the American Negro with "a sore heart, a troubled conscience, and a deep compassion." A few of these have shown genuine sympathy with the Negro's progress. Nevertheless, by and large, they are defeatists. Mark Ethridge, one of the leaders of Southern white liberals, stated flatly: "There is no power in the world—not even in all the mechanized armies of the earth, Allied and Axis—which could now force

8. Donald Davidson, "A Sociologist in Eden," *The American Review*, VIII (December, 1936), 200 ff.

9. Allen Tate, "A View of the Whole South," *ibid.*, II (February, 1934), 424.

10. Frank L. Owsley, "Scottsboro: The Third Crusade," *ibid.*, I (Summer, 1933), 285.

the Southern white people to the abandonment of the principle of social segregation."[11]

Since the Negro hardly would count upon the armies of the Axis as friends in any case, the prophecy is all the more direful. Mr. Ethridge warns that "cruel disillusionment, bearing the germs of strife and perhaps tragedy" will result from exacting the abolition of social segregation as the price of participation in the war. It is inaccurate to say that the Negroes were exacting this: Negroes at the time of Mr. Ethridge's prophecy were in all likelihood participating as fully as they were allowed to participate.

It is the gravity of the fear, however, rather than the accurate description of its cause, that concerns us here. Howard Odum also sees the net results of outside agitation in the affairs of the South to be "tragedy of the highest order, tragedy of the Greek, as it were, because it was the innocent Negro who suffered."[12] Virginius Dabney sees the two races edging nearer and nearer "to the precipice," if the Negro continues his demands.

David Cohn echoes Mr. Ethridge. As so many Southern intellectuals do, he finds comfort in William Graham Sumner's adage that you cannot change the mores of a people by law. Segregation is "the most deep-seated and pervasive of the Southern mores"; Negroes and whites who would break it down by Federal fiat had therefore better beware. "I have no doubt," Mr. Cohn writes, "that in such an event every Southern white man would spring to arms and the country would be swept by Civil war." Patience, good will, and wisdom (wisdom meaning acceptance of segregation without protest) are needful, otherwise the question will be delivered out of the hands of decent whites and Negroes "into the talons of demagogues, fascists, and the Ku Kluxers, to the irreparable harm of the Negro."[13]

It is significant that Southern spokesmen, reactionaries and liberals alike, are exercised over the harm that may come to Negroes. Watch out, the warning goes, or *Negroes* will get hurt. This is an old refrain; over a century ago the first proslavery novelist threatened, when Garrison's blasts were sounding off from Boston, that the "mischievous interference of abolitionists would involve the negro in the rigor which it provokes." And the latest demagogue expresses this threat and this tenderness.

The whites and Negroes who hope for a democratic solution to the problem must learn that the problem is insoluble, warns Mr. Cohn: "It is

11. John Temple Graves, *The Fighting South* (New York, 1943), pp. 125 f.
12. Howard W. Odum, *Race and Rumors of Race* (Chapel Hill, 1943), p. 155.
13. David L. Cohn, "How the South Feels," *The Atlantic Monthly,* CLXXIII (January, 1944), 50 f.

at bottom a blood or sexual question." Southern whites are determined that "no white in their legal jurisdiction shall marry a Negro" and "white women shall not have physical relations with Negro men except, when discovered, upon pain of death or banishment inflicted upon one or both parties to the act."[14] And John Temple Graves takes his stand on two bed-rock "facts": "The unshakable belief of southern whites that the problem was peculiarly their own and that attempts to force settlement from outside were hateful and incompetent. The absolute determination that the blood of the two races should not be confused and a mulatto population emerge."[15]

Negroes have long recognized this as the hub of the argument opposing change in their status. A chief recruiting slogan for the Ku Klux Klan of Reconstruction, when Negroes were "getting out of their place" by voting, buying farms and homes, and attending schools, was that Southern white womanhood must be protected. "The closer the Negro got to the ballot-box, the more he looked like a rapist," is the quip of a Negro who has studied the period closely. Thomas Nelson Page wrote that the barbarities of Re-construction were based upon "the determination to put an end to the ravishing of their women by an inferior race, or by any race, no matter what the consequence."[16] Though a later Southern student, W. J. Cash, has estimated that "the chance [of the Southern white woman's being violated by a Negro] was much less . . . than the chance that she would be struck by lightning,"[17] it is Page rather than Cash whose opinions are most followed. Political campaigns still seem to be waged not so much to get into office as to protect women. In his last campaign, Eugene Talmadge reported "an unusual number of assault cases and attempts to assault white ladies" (though newspaper reporters could not find them), and he denounced the Rosenwald Fund, noted for its benefactions to the South, as being deter-mined to make a "mulatto South." Senator Ellender, in one of his attacks on an anti-lynching bill, revealed the train of thought of so many filibusters when he promised that if the bill should pass, he would propose three amendments all prohibiting intermarriage. If mobs were forbidden by Fed-eral law to lynch Negroes, white people were at least not going to be al-lowed to marry Negroes. Instances of such reasoning make up a sorry tale.

For all of their protesting of decency and good will, the intellectuals do not talk very differently from Gerald L. K. Smith, a spellbinder generally

14. *Ibid.*, p. 49.
15. Graves, *op. cit.*, p. 239.
16. Thomas Nelson Page, *The Negro: The Southerner's Problem* (New York, 1904), p. 100.
17. W. J. Cash, *The Mind of the South* (New York, 1941), p. 115.

considered to be of the native fascist variety. The Reverend Smith inherited one of Huey Long's mantles; he is certain that he knows what people want or at least that he can rouse them into wanting what he wants. Immediately after the Detroit riot, the Reverend Smith wrote in *The Cross and the Flag* that most white people would not agree to any of the following: intermarriage of blacks and whites; mixture of blacks and whites in hotels, restaurants; "intimate relationships" between blacks and whites in the school system; "wholesale mixture of blacks and whites in residential sections"; "promiscuous mixture" of blacks and whites in street cars and on trains, "especially when black men are permitted to sit down and crowd in close to white women and vice versa." The Reverend Smith added generously, "I have every reason to believe black women resent being crowded by white men." Mixture in factories was also offensive, "especially when black men are mixed with white women closely in daily work."

It is true that the Reverend Smith is no longer tilling Southern fields, but he learned his demagoguery in the South, and many of his audience were transplanted Southerners. It is also undeniable that his words struck responsive chords in many Northerners. But he expresses a cardinal tenet of the Southern creed that social mixture must be forbidden, or else as John Temple Graves puts it, "a mulatto population will emerge."

Negroes know well that that horse has been out of the stable too long a time for the lock to be put on the door now. Even the race purists must realize the large amount of mixture in the American Negro, that hybrid of African, Indian and Caucasian stock. And though, as the anthropologist Montague Cobb says, the Caucasian component is "the most apparent and the least documented," race purists must realize how the Negro got that way.

Fears that lowering the barriers of segregation will lower the level of civilization are often expressed. If these fears are not liars, one consequence might be that civilization in such Southern cities as Atlanta, Birmingham, Memphis, and Vicksburg will decline to the level of that in unsegregated Boston, New York, Iowa City, and Seattle. According to these fears, intermarriage will result when Negroes and whites eat in the same restaurants or in a diner without a little green curtain; when they stop in the same hotels, and ride the same street cars and buses without wooden screens, or other separating devices. Negroes laugh at the suggestion that crowded buses and street cars and cafeterias are marriage bureaus. They know that intermarriage is not widespread in the states where there are no segregation laws and no laws forbidding intermarriage. They believe with great reason that there is more illicit sexual relationship between the races in the states whose laws forbid intermarriage than there are mixed marriages elsewhere.

Intermarriage is hardly a goal that Negroes are contending for openly or yearning for secretly. It is certainly not a mental preoccupation with them and scarcely a matter of special concern. Nevertheless, they do not want laws on the statute books branding them as outcasts. They do not want governmental sanction of caste, however long they have seen it hardened about them. They know how prophetic were the words of the anguished heroine of George Washington Cable's story of the last century: "A lie, Père Jerome! Separate! No! They do not want to keep us [white men: colored women] separate: no, no! But they *do* want to keep us despised!"

It is likely of course that friendships will develop where Negroes and whites meet on a basis of respect and where people can be drawn together by kindred interests. It is likely that some of these friendships might ripen into love and marriage. That certainly should be left as a private matter, the affair of the persons involved, as it is now in most civilized lands. An individual's choice of a mate should hardly be considered as a chief cause of the downfall of western, or American, or even Southern civilization. A more grievous cause for alarm, a more dangerous omen of ruin, is the contempt for personality based on skin color and hair texture. Negroes laugh a bit ruefully at the dread that one-tenth of a nation's population will corner the marital market of the nine-tenths. They know to what a degree in the past the opposite has prevailed, though the market could not with accuracy be termed marital. They could scarcely consider laws banning intermarriage to be protective of their own women. And they do not share the Southern white man's fear that the white women of the South are so weak and easily misled that they cannot be trusted to select their own husbands. They agree instead with the numerous white women of the South who have publicly stated that they do not need lynching or special legislation to protect them.

The black herring of intermarriage has been dragged too often across the trail to justice. "Would you want your sister to marry a nigger?" is still the question that is supposed to stun any white man who sponsors rights for Negroes. It stirs Negroes to ironic laughter, although on all levels they recognize the white man's fear of intermarriage as deep-seated. From the jokes of the people—of Negroes talking to Negroes, where "Miss Annie's" name is changed to "Miss Rope" or "Miss Hemp"—to the satire of the publicists, this awareness is to be found. A Negro editor, fighting a covenant restricting housing, was asked point blank: "Do you believe in intermarriage?" to stop his guns of logic and facts. Some Negro public speakers, faced with the question, dodge behind statements like "Well, I'm married already myself." Some take refuge in Kipling's line, "Never the twain shall meet," without sharing Kipling's assurance or hope. The twain have met and the twain will meet. But Negroes are not convinced thereby that they must give up their struggle to share in American democracy.

Though David Cohn warns that irony and reason cannot answer what he calls "blood-thinking," the "biological" fear of "a chocolate-colored American people," Negroes wonder if that fear is as real among Southerners as the determination to keep the Negro in his place economically. Certain Southern liberals have stated their willingness for Negroes to have the rights of voting, good schools, sanitation, paved and lighted streets, justice in the courts, and equitable employment. But Negroes wonder if the possibilities of these—merely these without intermarriage—do not stir great and widespread fears, real instead of spectral. They wonder if the smokescreen of intermarriage is not raised to frighten Southerners from conceding any of these rights, which are fraught with more danger to privilege and exploitation. Some Negroes wonder if maintaining a cheap labor reservoir is not as important a motive as preventing Negroes from crowding whites on buses and proposing marriage to them. Pointing to a group of poor whites and poor Negroes, a planter said to Ira Reid and Arthur Raper: "As long as these whites keep those Negroes humble, we'll keep them both poor."[18]

Many Negroes are sardonic about the oddities of segregation. The white patron, who is willing to eat soup prepared in the kitchen by black hands and served by a black waiter who may get his thumb in it, but who nearly faints when he discovers a Negro eating at another table in the same restaurant; a man's fulsome worship of the black nurse in whose lap he was rocked to sleep, and his horror at sitting next to a black man on a street car (it might be the nurse's son); the preservation of white supremacy on a diner by a little green curtain, or on a street car by a screen or a rope, in a Jim Crow coach by a chalk line beyond which the overflow from the white coach may not roll, in a government office by setting a Negro's desk cater-cornered, slightly off the line of the other desks; these afford ribald amusement. They do not make sense; they do not add to respect for the rationality of Southern whites. Such instances are recognized as sprouting from deep roots, certainly; but other superstitions have been uprooted. Maybe these can be.

Some Negroes, of course, realize that a logic does lie behind the apparent oddities. This is the time-hallowed logic of dividing and ruling—the

18. Arthur Raper and Ira De A. Reid, *Sharecroppers All* (Chapel Hill, 1941), p. 78.

playing off of underprivileged whites against Negroes to prevent a real democratic union—a practice that has paid the oligarchs well. Northern industrialists in the South have done their full share of capitalizing on race hostility, exciting it by talk of Negroes "getting out of their places." Some Negroes, therefore, see segregation as more than a superstition; but they are convinced that it can, and must be uprooted.

Negroes are not contending for wholesale entree into drawing rooms. They see no contradiction in democracy that people shall select their own friends, cliques, husbands, and wives. They do see as contradictory that false fears of social intermingling should be raised to jeopardize honest aspirations to full citizenship. What segregationists denounce as "wanting to be with white folks," Negroes think of as participating in the duties and enjoying the privileges of democracy. This means being with white folks, undoubtedly, since whites have nearly monopolized these duties and privileges. But it means being with them in fields and factories, in the armed forces, at the voting booths, in schools and colleges, in all the areas of service to democracy.

COUNT US IN

Negroes want to be counted in. They want to belong. They want what other men have wanted deeply enough to fight and suffer for it. They want democracy. Wanting it so much, they disregard more and more the warnings: "This is not the time." "The time isn't ripe." "Take your time, take your time." Nearly a hundred years ago, in desperation at the plight of the slaves, Herman Melville wrote, "Time must befriend these thralls." And in crucial moments since, time has been pointed to as the solvent. Patience, urges David Cohn, rule out the emotional and irrational and then the burden will rest "upon the whites to do for the Negro what they have not done at all, or only in part." But the Negro has difficulty in finding the guaranties of this hope that so many Negro and white spokesmen have promised to him. Southern Negroes are not of one mind with Southern whites that "outside interference is hateful and incompetent." They do not see democracy as a commodity to be quarantined at the Potomac and Ohio Rivers; as a sort of a Japanese beetle to be hunted for in the luggage before travelers are allowed to go on. Negroes are glad whenever democratic ideas circulate through the South, whether by means of liberal weeklies, *PM*, the speeches of labor organizers, pamphlets, sermons, radio forums, books, Negro newspapers and magazines, or letters from the boys in service. They know, of course, that if democracy is to be achieved in the South, where it is least found, the greatest work must be done by Southerners, whites and Negroes together. But they welcome whatever help they can get from any sources.

And they know, furthermore, that the agencies working for democracy are not necessarily "outside agitators." The National Association for the Advancement of Colored People may have its headquarters in New York, but, as its name suggests, it is a *national* association. Many of its leaders are Southerners by birth and training. Many of its courageous workers are living in the South. The Negro teachers who risk their jobs and even worse in the struggle for equalization of salaries are Southern born and bred. Negro journalists in the deep South generally speak out uncompromisingly for justice. Southern Negroes have not needed Northern agitators to stir up dissatisfaction with discrimination and abuse. As pointed out earlier, they have learned the hard way, and the lessons have sunk in deeply.

They have heard the threats. Against their democratic aspirations they see a concerted line-up: college professors as well as hoodlums; congressmen as well as vigilantes; Rotarians as well as manual laborers; cotton planters as well as cotton hands. Negroes expect that some of them are going to get hurt before they get what they want. This is no new experience for them; the have been getting hurt in this country since 1619. But getting hurt in a stand-up struggle for justice is one thing; getting hurt merely because of the color of your skin, while lying down, is quite another.

On trips through the South, I have talked with several who had been hurt. With Roland Hayes, for example, shortly after he had been savagely beaten by the policemen of Rome, Georgia. With Hugh Gloster, a young college professor, who had been thrown off a train in Tupelo, Mississippi, because he asked the conductor to let Negroes who were standing in the aisles of the Jim Crow coach overflow into a white coach, only partly filled. With Clinton Clark, who had been beaten, arrested, jailed and threatened with the rope time and time again for organizing the cane-cutters and cotton hands of Louisiana into a union. Roland Hayes talked, broodingly; Hugh Gloster, sardonically; Clinton Clark, stoically, without any surprise: "You try to organize people to get out of slavery, may as well expect the big planters and their boys—the sheriffs and deputies—to get tough." But all of these, and others who told me their stories of abuse, knew the shock of the sudden oath, the blow, the murderous look in the eye.

They had been hurt, no doubt of that. But it is unlikely that they, or many other Negroes, merely because of the violence, will become reconciled to what caused it. Many Negroes are still going to protest rough language to their wives, as Roland Hayes did; or unfair travel accommodations, as Hugh Gloster did; or exploitation in the cane and cotton fields, as

Clinton Clark did. "Get out and stay out of this parish," the jailer in Natchitoches told Clark. "I'll be back," said Clark, "I'll have a stronger organization behind me the next time."

Some of the victims do not forget the lessons that the rubber hose, the fist, the long black hours in the smelly cell fix so deeply. But from as many other victims comes this: "And if I had it to do all over, I'd do the same thing again."

Negroes who profess faith, whether real or not, in passive waiting for decent whites to take up their burden, are losing that faith. Negroes who feared that asking for democracy would lead to some Negroes' getting hurt, are losing that fear. But losing the passive faith is not defeatism, and losing the fear is not bravado.

There are many Negroes who are not convinced, as some forlorn liberals are, that democracy is a doomed hope in the South. They see heartwarming signs. They see the opponents of the poll tax gathering strength. The filibusters may rant so long or maneuver so craftily that the repeal may not pass this year, but the struggle against the poll tax will continue. Negroes applaud the Supreme Court decisions outlawing the white primary as a private club's election. They see the FEPC holding on, a symbol of the hope to abolish discrimination in industry, though challenged on many sides, flouted occasionally, and hard beset. They hear native white South Carolinians disclaim the "white supremacy" resolution of their House of Representatives in humiliation "because it is white people who have thus held up the state to scorn. . . . The only white supremacy which is worthy of the name is that which exists because of virtue, not power." White supremacy is not the issue, they say, but that Negroes should serve on juries, that they should be allowed representation on boards which administer affairs involving Negro citizens and their property; that Negro policemen should be provided in Negro residential districts; that the disfranchisement of all Negroes in South Carolina cannot endure indefinitely; these are some of the pressing issues. Negroes are aware of the importance of such words from representative citizens, neither interracialists nor "radicals," in Cotton Ed Smith's bailiwick.

Of course, many Negroes keep their fingers crossed. They expected Congressman Rankin's blast at the Supreme Court vote, which ran true to form: "I see that the parlor pinks in the Department of Justice are already starting to harass the Southern states as a result of the blunder of the Supreme Court. The Negroes of the South are having their hope of peace and harmony with their white neighbors destroyed by these pinks." Canny through long experience with the politicos, Negroes realize that the road from outlawing white primaries and the poll tax to widespread voting may be long and rocky. "Let 'em try it," said the *Jackson Daily News;* "There are other ways of preserving southern tradition," the *Birmingham Post* said; "We will maintain white supremacy, let the chips fall where they may," said the Governor of South Carolina.

It may be a long and rocky road. But it is the right road. Some Negroes may remain lethargic about their rights and duties as citizens. Some Negroes may get hurt; some may be timorous; the overpraised "harmony" may go off-key. As a sign that they are being "counted in" Negroes see several Southern editors applauding the decision. One called it "a much-needed political safety valve" instead of a threat. Virginius Dabney writes that Tennessee, Kentucky, North Carolina, and Virginia, all of them without the white primary, have never seen white supremacy endangered. More significantly, he writes: "No society . . . is truly democratic . . . which shuts out anywhere from a quarter to a half of its people from all part in the choice of the officials under whom they must live and work."

Another cheering signpost, indicating that some mileage has been covered on the long journey, is the work of certain Southern white liberals. Virginius Dabney performed a historic act in advocating the abolition of Jim Crow on Virginia street cars and buses. It is true that he had to surrender his proposal; though numerous white Virginians applauded it, Mr. Dabney became convinced that the time was not right. But it was a first step that may count, and the proof that Virginia white opinion was not unanimous for Jim Crow is worth recording. Hoping that Negro leadership will rest in Atlanta (not so coincidentally Walter White's native city) rather than in New York, Mr. Dabney realizes that steps toward democracy must be taken *in the South.* This realization is quite as honest as his fear of trouble.

Southern white liberals deplore the demands of outsiders, and then come out themselves for many of the same reforms. The Atlanta Conference of representative white Southerners praised the Southern Negro Conference at Durham for frankness and courage. Among so much else the Atlanta Conference conclusions stated: "No Southerner can logically dispute the fact that the Negro, as an American citizen, is entitled to his civil rights and economic opportunities"; and "we agree . . . that it is 'unfortunate that the simple efforts to correct obvious social and economic injustices continue, with such considerable popular support, to be interpreted as the predatory ambition of irresponsible Negroes to invade the privacy of family life. . . .' We agree also that 'it is a wicked notion that the struggle by the

Negro for citizenship is a struggle against the best interest of the nation.' "[19]

Negroes look with hope to the continuing conference, composed of several Southern Negro leaders who met in Durham and Southern whites who met in Atlanta. The conference is "to covenant together for better co-operation, more positive and specific action, and for enduring ways and means for carrying out the recommendations." They have reason for confidence in the two co-chairmen, Guy Johnson of the University of North Carolina and Ira Reid of Atlanta University. Many Negroes deplore the isolation of the problem as a Southern regional affair, but they want the results that such a conference may achieve. They notice the stress on good manners and good will and on the absence of "any suggestion of threat and ultimatum," and may wonder just how these terms are defined; but they suspect that this forward step would not have been taken without the activity of organizations like the N.A.A.C.P. "We want those fellows to keep the heat on," a quiet Southern Negro preacher said to me.

On the national scene, wherever significant work is done to integrate the Negro into the war effort: in industry, in agriculture, in community planning, in the armed services, Negroes are cheered, and their morale rises accordingly. Sometimes discounted as drops in the bucket, these instances of integration might also be considered leaks in the levee, straws in the wind, or as the signposts I have frequently called them. If signposts, Negroes know that the longer, perhaps rougher journey lies ahead. They are therefore not in the mood for stopping, for laying over, for slowing up, or for detouring. And they do not want to be mere passengers, a sort of super-cargo, hitch-hikers being given a lift, guests being sped along. They want to do some of the map-reading and some of the driving. Thomas Sancton, a white Southerner who recognizes this truth, writes: "The real liberal knows that the Negro is never going to win any right he doesn't win for himself, by his own organization, courage, and articulation."[20]

The sticking point in the co-operation of Negro and Southern white liberals is segregation. The Atlanta Conference stepped gingerly about it: "We do not attempt to make here anything like a complete reply to the questions raised. . . . The only justification offered for [segregation] laws . . . is that they are intended to minister to the welfare and integrity of both races."[21]

19. Odum, *op. cit.*, p. 199.
20. Sancton, *op. cit.*, p. 15.
21. Odum, *op. cit.*, p. 197.

However segregation may be rationalized, it is essentially the denial of belonging. I believe that Negroes want segregation abolished. I realize that here, as so often elsewhere, it is presumptuous to talk of what *the* Negro wants. I understand that Negroes differ in their viewpoints toward segregation: the half-hand on a back county farm, the lost people on Arkansas plantations, the stevedore on Savannah docks, the coal miner in Birmingham, the cook-waitress-nurse in Charleston, the man-on-the-street in Waco, Los Angeles, New York, Boston, the government workers, the newspaper editors, the professional men, the spokesmen for pressure groups— all see segregation from different angles. An illiterate couple on Red River may differ greatly in attitude from their children on River Rouge. On the part of many there has been a long accommodation to segregation; but I believe that satisfaction with it has always been short.

An old railroad man in Birmingham, directing me to the FEPC hearings in the Federal Building, told me that whites and Negroes entered the court room by the same door (there was only one), but that they did not sit together. "No," he said. "They sits separate; whites on one side, the colored on the yother." Then he added, "And that's the way I'd ruther have it, too ef'n I had my druthers. Of course I don't believe in scorning nobody, but—" He might have had memories of whites and Negroes "mixing socially," where the gains had all fallen to the whites, or where insult or violence had followed. But he knew, in spite of his "druthers," that segregation and scorn were bedfellows.

During Mr. Talmadge's campaign against the co-education of the races, one Georgia Negro college president gave white folks the assurance that "Negroes didn't want to attend the University of Georgia; all they wanted was a little school of their own." I found a young Negro Army doctor who sharply opposed the setting up of mixed military units, especially a mixed hospital. Only in an all Negro hospital, according to his experience, could a Negro physician function to the best of his ability, realize his full development, and be free from insult. He was nevertheless violently opposed to Jim Crow in transportation and public services.

I heard varying defenses of segregation, but I still did not find many supporters of it, even in the South. Of the many who had gained from it in safety, comfort, wealth and prestige, I found some who were candid enough to admit that in segregated schools, churches, lodges, banks, and businesses, they had risen higher than they might have risen in competition with whites. Many were fighting to improve their side of the bi-racial fence, to equalize teachers' salaries, to obtain buses for students, and for similar ends. But the fighting was not to buttress bi-racialism, but to make the most of a bad thing, to lessen the inferiority that segregation always seemed to mean. The young flyers at the segregated Tuskegee base trained rigorously to become first-rate fighting men, to prove that Negroes should be piloting planes; but their most fervent admirers, however proud of their achievement, would not say that they would have made a poorer record at an unsegregated base. And they would not deny that there were indignities at the segregated base.

A sign in Atlanta read: "This line marks the separation of the races which were [sic] mutually agreed to by both." My friend, certainly no hothead but long "accommodated," interpreted it: "Mutual agreement. You know: a man puts his gun in your ribs and you put your pocketbook in his hands."

When the conference in Durham excluded Northern Negroes, many white Southerners (and Negroes, for that matter) were led to expect a conservative set of principles. As Benjamin Mays, an important member of the conference, states: "They were Negroes the whites of the South knew. They were not radicals. They were Negroes the South says it believes in and can trust." Yet the Durham charter went on record as fundamentally opposed to segregation, and Walter White considered the recommendations to be almost identical in language and spirit with those of the N.A.A.C.P. and the March-on-Washington movement.

A chief difference between Southern and Northern Negro spokesmen is not that one group defends and the other condemns segregation, but that Southern leaders, in daily contact with it, see it as deeply rooted; Northern leaders, not seeing it to be so widespread and knowing that occasionally it can be ripped out, do not see the long, sturdy tentacles. The dangers are that Southern Negroes will believe it ineradicable and that Northern Negroes will believe it can be easily uprooted by speeches and governmental decree.

At Negro mass meetings in the North, demands that racial segregation should be abolished, "that the Negro and the white must be placed on a plane of absolute political and social equality," have been roundly applauded. It is doubtful if even the orators themselves envisaged that their demands would be immediately or even soon forthcoming. Delegates from the South knew that on the return trip home, at St. Louis or Cincinnati or Washington, they would be herded into the inferior Jim Crow coach; that if they wished to travel by bus they would be lucky even to get on, into the rear seats; that once home, Jim Crow would be all about them wherever they turned. Even Northern delegates knew where Jim Crow had caught hold in their communities.

Negroes know that more than stirring speeches will be needed to re-move Jim Crow. But they also know another thing, on all levels and in all callings—whether an illiterate sharecropper comparing the one-room ramshackly school for his children with the brick consolidated school for the white children, or a college president who knows, in spite of the new brick buildings, how unequal a proportion of state funds has come to his school—Negroes recognize that Jim Crow, even under such high-sounding names as "bi-racial parallelism," means inferiority for Negroes. And most American whites know this too, and that is the way that many prefer it. As the beginning of one kind of wisdom, Negroes recognize that the phrase "equal but separate accommodations" is a myth. They have known Jim Crow a long time, and they know Jim Crow means scorn and not belonging.

What Negroes applauded from their orators, many recognized as a vision, the vision of a good thing. Though a dream, and difficult of achieving, it still was not wild and illogical. It made more sense than the reality: that in the world's leading democracy, democratic rights were withheld from one man out of every ten, not because he had forefeited his right to them, but because his skin was darker and his hair of a different texture from those of the other nine. The reality was that in a war against an enemy whose greatest crimes are based on spurious race thinking, this democracy indulged in injustice based on race thinking just as spurious.

This war is the Negro's war as much as it is anybody's. If the Axis were victorious, Negroes would be forced from the present second-class citizenship to slavery. Hitler's contempt for Negroes as apes and his sadistic treatment of Jews and all the conquered peoples, and Japan's brown Aryanism, similarly ruthless and arrogant, offer far less hope than America's system of democracy, bumbling though it may be, but still offering opportunity for protest and change. Even at the cost of the preservation of the *status quo,* this is still the Negro's war.

These are truisms. But they do not incite high morale. Indeed, they are somewhat like telling a man with a toothache that he should consider himself fortunate, since he might have a broken back. True, but his tooth still aches, and he wants something done for it.

This is even more the Negro's war, if it is truly a people's war, a war of liberation, aimed at establishing the Four Freedoms, ushering in the century of the common man, as the fine slogans have it. The Negro could do well with the Four Freedoms, especially the Freedoms from want and fear, for these two Freedoms have long been strangers to him. This is all the more the Negro's war if, as Michael Straight hopes, the peace will "guarantee to all of its citizens the right to constructive work at fair wages; to good low-cost housing; to minimum standards of nutrition, clothing, and medical care; to full opportunities for training and adult education; to real social security."

There is more cleverness than wisdom in the remark of John Temple Graves that asking for complete democracy at home is as logical as saying "that because America's house was on fire America must take the occasion for renovating the kitchen or putting Venetian blinds in the parlor." The trouble with the house is more serious than that; it really has much to do with the foundations. Wendell Willkie warns that:

> We cannot fight the forces and ideas of imperialism abroad and maintain any form of imperialism at home. . . . We must mean freedom for others as well as ourselves, and we must mean freedom for everyone inside our frontiers as well as outside.[22]

Pearl Buck points out:

> Our democracy does not allow for the present division between a white ruler race and a subject colored race. If the United States is to include subject and ruler peoples, then let us be honest about it and change the Constitution and make it plain that Negroes cannot share the privileges of the white people. True, we would then be totalitarian rather than democratic.[23]

Daily reports of the violations of democracy crowd upon the Negro, breeding cynicism. Nevertheless, while denouncing them, he does so in the framework of democracy. He continually relies on America's professions of democracy as having some validity; he has not yet descended to the hopeless view that America prefers totalitarianism.

As has been so often stated: If America is to indoctrinate the rest of the world with democracy, it is logical to expect that the American Negro will share it at home. It may take a long time, but segregation must be abolished before there will be true democracy at home. True democracy will mean the right and opportunity to win respect for human worth. It can have no truck with Nazi concepts of race-supremacy, with Nazi contempt for people because of race. Democracy will mean equal pay for equal labor, equal employment opportunities, opportunities to learn and use technical skills

22. Wendell Willkie, *One World* (New York, 1943), pp. 190 ff.
23. Pearl Buck, *American Unity and Asia* (New York, 1942), p. 15.

and to advance according to mastery of them, and the right to join and participate fully in trade unions. The tentative beginning made by FEPC must be developed. Democracy will mean equal educational opportunities, equalized salaries for teachers, equalized facilities in the schools. The spread of the segregated system of education must be checked and eventually abolished as wasteful and unjust. Democracy will mean that the Federal Government will go on record against mob violence, for, in spite of the decline in lynching, threats of mob-violence are still powerfully coercive. Democracy will mean the discouraging of police brutality, will mean justice in the courts rather than patronizing clemency or cruel intolerance. Negroes will serve on the police force, at the lawyers' bar, in the jury docks, and on the judges' bench. Democracy will mean the franchise, with elimination of the poll tax and the subterfuges and intimidations that keep qualified Negroes from the polls. It will mean training Negroes to fulfill the duties of free citizens. Democracy will mean the strengthening and extension of the social legislation begun by the New Deal in such agencies as the Farm Security Administration and the Federal Housing Authority; and the opportunity not only to share in the benefits of such agencies but also in their planning and operation. Democracy will mean the opportunity to qualify for service in the armed forces in all its branches; the opportunity for whites and Negroes to fight side by side in mixed commands. Democracy will mean simply the opportunities for all Americans to share to the full extent of their capacities in the defense of America in war and the development of America in peace.

This is not much to ask for, since it is essentially what America guarantees to every white citizen. Only when viewed from the angle that these opportunities are to be extended to Negro citizens, does the list seem staggering, outrageous to some, foolishly idealistic and unattainable to many.

I think that most Negroes are not so optimistic that they foresee the overnight arrival of these opportunities. No group should know better that perfectly functioning democracy in the United States has always been a hope, rather than an actuality. Even in those sections where one undemocratic practice—legal segregation—has been missing, democracy—to whites as well as to Negroes—has not been simon-pure. The poverty of the South would be oppressive on both whites and Negroes even if segregation laws were stricken from the books, and discrimination from the practices, tomorrow. The Negro's plight in the South will be lightened substantially only when the plight of the poor white is enlightened; when these cannot be pitted against each other in contempt and hatred; when genuine democracy replaces the fictitious (and fictitious not only in the matter of race relations). Nevertheless, however Herculean the task, Negroes are not so defeatist that they think democracy to be unattainable. They are good Americans in nothing more than in their faith that "democracy *can* happen here." Worth fighting for in Europe, it is worth working for here. But since time does not stand still, all America—black and white—had better start to work for it. President Roosevelt, speaking of the Four Freedoms, has said: "Magna Carta, the Declaration of Independence, the Constitution of the United States, the Emancipation Proclamation and every other milestone in human progress—all were ideals which seemed impossible of attainment—yet they were attained."[24]

Negroes should not want fundamental rights of citizenship donated to them as largesse, and should not consider them as barter for loyalty, or service. American whites should not consider Negroes as beneficiaries, being accorded gifts that to men of different complexion are rights. Nor should they think of Negroes as passive objects of humanitarianism, since Negroes can really be allies in a common struggle for democracy. Even after Hitler and Tojo are defeated, democracy is going to need all of its strength to solve grave problems. The strength of the Negro will be as much needed and as useful in the coming economic and political crises as it is needed and should be useful now.

I believe that many Negroes realize this, and wish to be allowed to share in the sacrifice and travail and danger necessary to attain genuine democracy. Wendell Willkie's world trip excited him with "fresh proof of the enormous power within human beings to change their environment, to fight for freedom with an instinctive awakened confidence that with freedom they can achieve anything."[25] In times of frustration, Negroes would do well to recognize that power, and to understand that it fights on their side.

Negroes know they have allies. There are the numerous colored peoples of the world, the millions of yellow, brown, and black men in China, India, the Philippines, Malaysia, Africa, South America, the Caribbean, all over the globe, where hope for democracy is stirring a mighty ferment. Almost all are concerned with their own perplexities, but they agree in their fight against color prejudice. The success of the Soviet Union in destroying race prejudice gives hope and courage. And there are other allies abroad, in the smaller as well as the larger, the conquered as well as the unconquered

24. Franklin D. Roosevelt, "The Four Freedoms," in Clayton Wheat, ed., *The Democratic Tradition in America* (Boston, 1943), p. 291.
25. Willkie, *op. cit.*, p. 163.

nations, who are tied, not by a common urge to abolish race prejudice, but by the determination to be free. And in America there are allies too. It does not seem over-optimistic to believe them on the increase, although still outnumbered by the indifferent or the hostile. Negroes must join with these American allies, in the North and in the South, in a truly interracial program, or better, a democratic program. The minority must work with the men of good will in the majority. Negroes recognize their allies here without difficulty, and their affection for them runs strong and deep.

Americans, Negroes and whites, may believe that to achieve full democracy is arduous. It may well take a slow pull for a long haul. But it can no longer be postponed. American dreams have been realized before this, however difficult they seemed to the faint-hearted and sceptical. Americans, Negro and white, have mustered the doggedness and courage and intelligence needed. I have confidence in my own people that they will help achieve and preserve democracy, and will prove worthy of sharing it. But we must be counted in.

Athletics and the Arts

◄═ THIS SUBJECT is a Goliath, and I am not sure that my slingshot can bring it down. The fields are numerous and their yield now at long last so abundant that thorough reckoning is out of the question. I should like to give something of the story of participation, some measure of the integration of the Negro athlete and of the Negro artist in the areas of music, the dance, the drama, moving pictures, the plastic and graphic arts, and literature. In some of the fields I have no business trespassing. I can plead only an active interest in all of them and in the general theme of integration.

The areas where integration is more solidly rooted are considered more fully; those where integration is only a promise are less considered. That, rather than the author's athletic and artistic preferences, is the factor governing the proportion of space devoted to each area. The respective stories of integration, however, have striking parallels, which should be pointed out. All of these stories are of significance to the student of American culture.

By integration I mean, in agreement with so many others at this conference, complete acceptance. I mean a parallel in the sports and the arts to what the political spokesmen call "first-class citizenship." The integration of the Negro athlete or artist means his acceptance as an individual to be judged on his own merits, with no favor granted, and no fault found, because of race. It means that, whether second-baseman or pugilist, jazz trumpeter or concert singer, poet or painter, the Negro will be judged evenly, neither over-rigorously nor over-gently, according to the standards of his calling. If his achievements warrant, he should receive the rewards as man, not as Negro; if they do not, he should be sent to the bush leagues (literal in the world of sports, figurative in the arts).

But the integrated man is a whole man, not a fractional. By integration in the arts I do not mean loss of artistic identity. The moot point of he Negro's distinctive gifts will of course be considered in this essay. While there is no Negro way to play shortstop, many believe that there is a distinctive Negro quality in arts derived from the folk, such as jazz and the popular dance. Integration does not have to mean the loss of such distinctiveness; it does not have to mean, for instance, the dilution of the deep blues into bluing-tinted water. Integration should mean fundamental respect for genuine quality, whatever its source, and acceptance of it in its wholeness.

In the arts, integration of the material of Negro life, as worthy of serious treatment, often preceded the integration of the Negro artist. This type of integration, therefore, certainly calls for consideration.

ATHLETICS

With the current success of Minoso with the Chicago White Sox; Jethroe with the Boston Braves; Suitcase Simpson, Doby, and Easter with the Cleveland Indians; Willie Mays and Monte Irvin with the New York Giants; Campanella, Newcombe, and Jackie Robinson with the Brooklyn Dodgers; and the ageless Satchel Paige with the St. Louis Browns, the integration of the Negro in baseball seems assured. But this integration, accepted easily now, was not achieved so easily. Many pressures were needed: the challenge of World War II and the postwar years that democracy should live up to its professions; the agitation for One World and for an FEPC; the Mayor's Anti-Discrimination Committee in New York City; continual insistence from fair-minded sports writers and fans, as well as from Negro organizations—all were needed before Jackie Robinson first donned a Montreal uniform to participate in our national game.

Only one other Negro before Robinson had broken into all-white professional baseball, and he had to pass as an Indian. A delegation of his racial fans, overproud of his achievement, waited upon him one day with flowers, gifts, and speeches, and cut short his major league career. This took place a half century ago.[1] Within the last decade it became more and more apparent that there were good Negro ballplayers in the Negro leagues. The long lines at the turnstiles, the sell-out crowds gathered to see the great Satchel Paige or Josh Gibson, certainly had their effect on major league club-owners, particularly when their average attendance was low.

1. "Folk" versions of this anecdote vary, but the most authenticated account seems to be in Roi Ottley's *Black Odyssey* (New York: Charles Scribner's Sons, 1948), p. 204.

In any consideration of integration, the saga of Jackie Robinson is instructive. Branch Rickey, who is responsible for his entry into major league baseball, was aware of many hurdles. Rickey had been manager of the St. Louis Cardinals in whose park no Negro had been allowed to sit in the grandstand. He knew how large a proportion of ballplayers are from the South. Therefore, in addition to finding a Negro ballplayer who could "deliver on the line in major league competition," he also had to select for his brave experiment "a Negro who would be the right man on the field" and one who would be most easily accepted by his teammates.[2] Robinson filled the bill in many respects. In the first interview, Rickey gave Jackie what he considered the crucial test. He warned him of insults, of "beanballs"; he acted out, with great realism, the roles of hot-headed players who came in with spikes and tempers flying high. Puzzled at first, Jackie asked, "Do you want a ballplayer who's afraid to fight back?" Rickey replied, "I want a ballplayer with guts enough not to fight back." Finally, after Rickey pretended to be a maddened player in the World Series who punched Robinson "right in the cheek," Jackie came up with, "I've got two cheeks . . . that it?," an answer that Rickey considered correct.[3]

Jackie Robinson's phenomenal success, as fielder, base-stealer, and hitter, as the spark plug of one of the finest teams of the last few years; his popularity with teammates, other ballplayers, and fans; his exemplary conduct on field and off; and his remarkable restraint when faced by the insults and crises that Rickey prophesied are widely known. It was no easy triumph, and the strain upon Robinson must have been severe. But his great pioneering succeeded. Today he can be less circumspect; he can participate in "rhubarbs," can argue with umpires and tangle with over-aggressive rivals as any other player can, and without its becoming a racial issue. He is still subject to a certain specialized criticism: sports writers have accused him of "popping-off" because of his pointed criticism of umpires, and even this last year he has received threatening letters from crackpots. But he is less symbol now than second-baseman; has been accepted by fans, fellow ballplayers, and sports writers as a great infielder. The American public seems willing now to recognize that on the baseball diamond a Negro ballplayer may well be temperamentally closer to Ty Cobb than to George Washington Carver.

A sports writer prophesied that once Jackie established himself as a

2. Arthur Mann, *The Jackie Robinson Story* (New York: F. J. Low Co., Inc., 1950), p. 6.

3. *Ibid.*, p. 60.

star, the fans would lose sight of his color. Established also as stars are Don Newcombe, selected as pitcher for the All-Star team; Campanella, Brooklyn's most valuable player of the year; Sam Jethroe, the leading base-stealer; Doby and Easter, Cleveland's sluggers; Mays and Minoso, two of the leading rookies of the year in their respective leagues; and Monte Irvin, the batting champion of the World Series.

Nevertheless, Walter White's belief that "within two years few persons thought of them as Negroes but only as good ballplayers,"[4] seems over-sanguine. It is hardly likely that the color of these players has been completely lost sight of. From exclusion to complete acceptance is not such a swift trip as all that. Certainly among Negroes the color of these stars is not forgotten. Negro ballplayers are nearer to integration than are Negro base-ball fans; Robinson and Campanella are more integrated in the Ebbetts Field clubhouse than Negroes are in the borough of Brooklyn. Reminded constantly and forcibly of race, Negro fans indulge in race pride instead of race obliviousness. In the box scores and long lists of batting averages Negroes zealously hunt out the records of the few Negro players. If their home clubs use no Negroes, they crowd the parks when teams with Negro players come to town; they boo rather than cheer the home team; local pride takes a back seat to racial. A cartoon by Ollie Harrington runs some-what in this way: an exasperated woman, just from the ball game, says, "And there was Campanella catching, and Newcombe pitching, and Jackie playing second base, and up comes Sam Jethroe. And there was 35,000 white folks looking at me to see what I was going to do!"

I once attended a game at Ebbetts Field with Ralph Bunche, who has been given a permanent pass by the Brooklyn club. He took along a couple of United Nations officials whom he was introducing to the great American game. In the first inning, Jackie Robinson parked a two-run homer. Ralph jumped up, yelling as frenziedly as any of the Dodgers' fans; the officials who knew Dr. Bunche best as a wise mediator, of established impartiality, seemed amazed. It was a good night for Ralph Bunche; Don Newcombe won his game; Campanella and Robinson for the Dodgers, and Thompson and Irvin for the Giants played flawless ball, and after the game Dr. Bunche went to the dressing room to get Jackie's autograph on a baseball.

A Gallup poll would probably register as one of the closest approaches to racial unanimity the hope of Negroes last season that Cleveland and Brooklyn should play in the World Series with the Giants a third choice.

4. Walter White, "Time for a Progress Report," *The Saturday Review of Literature*, September 22, 1951, p. 38.

When the Dodgers blew their chances and lost in the thrilling play-off, a stoical taxi driver philosophized thus to me: "Well, now we got television, it works out for the best. Campanella couldn't play nohow, and Newcombe couldn't pitch every day; but just think of all those million white folks looking in their screens and seeing three Negroes in the Giant outfield, left to right, right to left, all my folks." When Doby and Easter hit the long ball, when Jethroe steals a base (although one overly race-conscious lady deplores his stealing since it harks back to a stereotype), when Robinson and Campanella star and Newcombe hurls a fine game, Negro fans get a great lift. Even a racial bunt causes more noise than an Aryan homer (a poor thing but mine own). Therefore, for all of Robinson's Frank Merriwell home run in the last game of the season, there was no joy in Bronzeville when the Bums lost in the play-off. And the grief was compounded when the Giants lost the series.

But the Negro is in professional baseball to stay. Once the juke boxes had a record, "Did You See Jackie Robinson Hit That Ball?," and Jackie Robinson caps were the rage. But now Jackie has many allies in the majors; the minor leagues, including some Southern teams, are training Negroes; even the Washington Senators are flirting with the idea of hiring Negro players, and that is a real index of integration.

Once integration is begun in one area it seems to ease over into neighboring territory. The success of Negroes in baseball on the diamond and in the locker room, and their box-office appeal helped to break up the exclusion in professional football.

As amateurs, Negroes have for many years played on teams representing northern and western colleges, though the elections of Levi Jackson and of Bob Evans to the captaincy of the Yale and the University of Pennsylvania elevens, respectively, were new events of national moment. Early professional football in the North and West made use of a few Negro stars like Duke Slater, Fritz Pollard, and Paul Robeson; but when the National Football league was organized Negroes were excluded. The maverick league, the American Conference, kicked over the traces, however, in several ways; and one of the most important was the use of Negro players. Here again, the city of Cleveland was one of the pioneers. Of recent years, northern and western cities like Cleveland, Detroit, Los Angeles, and New York have signed up such stars as Kenny Washington, Motley, Gillom, Willis, Buddy Young, Taliaferro, Ford, Tunnell, and Deacon Towles, the ground-gaining rookie of the year. In the 1951 championship play-off, the teams included ten Negro stars.

In basketball two highly successful all-Negro teams, the Renaissance

Club and the Harlem Globe Trotters (who recently lived up to their name by conducting an international barnstorming tour against the Collegiate All Stars), have long acquainted the sports world with the prowess of Negroes. Negro collegiate teams have played a good brand of basketball; Negroes have increasingly made the teams of northern and western colleges. Though for a long time none played on the teams of the Big Ten of the Midwest, one of the busiest basketball centers, they have been numerous on the many collegiate teams of Metropolitan New York, another busy center. Some clubs of the professional leagues have Negro players on their rosters. The Washington Capitols Club was the first interracial team in the history of professional sports in the District of Columbia.

In professional football and basketball the competition for places on the comparatively few teams is fierce. It is likely, however, that outstanding Negro stars will continue to find places, particularly on the teams of northern cities. It is worth notice, moreover, that a Negro has played with the professional football team of Richmond, Virginia.

The integration in baseball, basketball, and football is significant as integration in team play. It is, of course, familiar that Negro athletes have long done well in sports involving individual against individual, such as boxing, and track and field athletics.

In the early nineteenth century a few Negroes—Tom Molineaux pre-eminently—were famed as pugilists, but they won their best purses in England. Since the turn of the century, when featherweight George Dixon, lightweight Joe Gans, and welterweight Joe Walcott (after whom the present heavyweight champion was named) held titles concurrently, Negro prize-fighters have more than maintained their own. The roll call is impressive with champions, near champions, good-enough to be champions, and dangerous contenders. (And, of course, a due share of club-house "stumble-bums.") The supremacy of Negro fighters has at times irked white America. Jack Johnson was a great stylist defensively and offensively in the ring, but his behavior outside the ring, while little different from that of other prizefighters of his time, was considered unfitting for a Negro. A frenzied hunt for a "white hope" to displace the unpopular Johnson came up with Willard and then Dempsey. Negro heavyweights, especially Harry Wills, were given the run-around. Barred from championship stakes, great Negro boxers like Sam Langford, Joe Jeannette, and Sam McVey fought each other so often that it became a habit.

When Joe Louis came along, his conduct, both in the ring and out, made him a most popular champion; Louis accelerated the change that was already coming over the sports public. In addition to Louis, Henry Armstrong, the only man to hold three titles at one time, and Ray Robinson, called the greatest living fighter "pound for pound"—to name the most brilliant of a long line of champions—have done much for the popularity of Negro fighters, and of course for the appeal of the sport itself. At the writing, five of the six major weight divisions have Negro champions, and at least four have Negroes as the outstanding challengers. The two heavyweight champions to follow Joe Louis are Ezzard Charles and Jersey Joe Walcott; and the man to whom Ray Robinson lost his middleweight championship, only to regain it soon after, was Randy Turpin, an English Negro.

Even on the managerial side Negroes are entering the picture, though for a long time Negro managers of Negro prizefighters were frozen out as money-makers. Truman Gibson, a Negro attorney, is an important figure in the International Boxing Club, a controlling power in pugilism. All in all, Negroes are in the foreground of the boxing picture. Any other picture is inconceivable.

In track and field athletics, where again it is man against man, Negro athletes have long-standing national prestige. From the early days of Howard Drew to the present, the record of Negro runners and jumpers has been brilliant. An incomplete listing would include champions of the recent past as Jesse Owens, Eulace Peacock, Eddie Tolan, Ralph Metcalfe in the sprints; Ned Gourdin, Ed Gordon, DeHart Hubbard in the broad jump; Cornelius Johnson and Dave Albritton in the high jump; Johnny Woodruff in the middle-distance runs; and John Borican, decathlon champion; and present stars such as Ewell in the sprints; Dillard in the hurdles, Reggie Pearmon, Mal Whitfield, McKinley, LaBeach, and Rhoden in the distance events. Nine of the eleven girls representing the United States in the 1948 Olympics were Negroes. Only in pole vaulting and the mile- and two-mile run are Negroes presently missing from the ranks of leading contenders.

When Jesse Owens, aided by such stars as Metcalfe, Woodruff, Archie Williams, and Cornelius Johnson, assured the United States of a clear-cut victory in the Olympic Games in Berlin in 1936, Hitler left the stadium in a huff, refusing to shake Owens's hand, thereby violating a time-honored custom. The Nazi press discounted the American victory as being won by "its black auxiliary force."

"Actually," *Der Angriff* contended, "the Yankees, . . . had been the great disappointment of the Games, for without these members of the black race—their 'auxiliary helpers'—the Germans won."[5]

5. Roi Ottley, *op. cit.*, p. 270.

This charge can be properly discounted as another of the Nazi "big lies." But it contained one grain of truth, symbolized by the fact that in spite of the outstanding achievement of Owens and his Negro teammates, they would not have been allowed, on their return to the United States, to race against white athletes in the nation's capital. This exclusion is now fortunately ended; Negroes participate in unsegregated track meets in the District of Columbia, and even, though still exceptionally, in the deeper South.

In such "leisure class" sports as tennis and golf, Negroes have had a much harder road. Almost all of the finest tennis players of the world can afford to play the game throughout the year. Many have received costly coaching. Promising young players who are not in the upper income brackets are in a measure subsidized by wealthy clubs and the National Tennis Association. Membership in the latter is restricted, and the tournaments under its auspices are open only to members of constituent clubs. Negroes founded the American Tennis Association, and sought unavailingly to have the bars lowered to the National Tennis Association. A few democratic individuals—Don Budge was one—played exhibition matches with Negroes. The first Negro to play in a "white" tournament was Reginald Weir, who had won the Negro national title several times. But no Negro has participated in the men's national tournament at Forest Hills. Through the courageous and determined sponsorship of former champion Alice Marble, Althea Gibson was invited to participate in the national tournaments at Forest Hills and the World's Championship at Wimbledon. The reigning champion of the Negro Association, Miss Gibson acquitted herself well. But tennis among Negroes—an after-work pastime—is of course less highly developed than among those whose wealth and leisure permit them to follow it as a vocation. Negroes lag behind the really great players just as whites who play the public courts lag behind the experts of the private clubs.

It is likely that integration of Negroes in tennis will take place, as it has started, in local open public court tournaments rather than in those of private clubs, which exclude on grounds additional to race. An interesting instance of integration, in reverse order, took place this summer at Wilberforce, where eleven white players from Dayton entered the Negro National Tournament. The American Tennis Association is, of course, without color bars.

The story repeats itself in golf. Many Negroes play the game well; it is a commonplace around many courses that Negro caddies shoot lower scores than the tired businessmen whose clubs they carry. A few public golf tournaments are "open" in the literal sense of the word, but most Negro golfers are segregated. Recently, Joe Louis, by threatening a suit, caused the Professional Golfers Association to loosen its ban on "non-whites." As in tennis, Negroes have their own association and hold a Negro National Championship.

In swimming, the story is about the same, with some participation in northern schools and colleges. In a few prestige sports—polo, the "millionaire's game," and rowing (with the exception of Joe Trigg at Syracuse)—Negroes have yet to make their marks. A few Negroes play professional hockey in Canada, but the first Negro to play organized hockey in the United States is Art Dorrington, a Nova Scotian who has wandered down to the southern clime to play with the Washington Lions. Cricket and soccer, British games, find many stars among the American Negroes from the West Indies and Africa, and occasionally visiting British teams are interracial. The long-standing racial bar in bowling has been lowered. The new integration extends even to such a social game as bridge—a few whites have competed in the Negro national championship, and a referendum is under way to allow Negro players to join the American Contract Bridge League.[6] I am uncertain whether to consider wrestling a sport or play-acting. Whichever it is, wrestling, in contrast to boxing, has seen few professional Negro participants. In amateur wrestling, Negroes have made the teams of northern colleges. The Howard University team has had matches with Gallaudet College, one of the first instances of integrated intercollegiate athletics in the District. But in the parade of races and nationalities on the television screen, Negro wrestlers are missing. Perhaps this is further proof of E. Franklin Frazier's dictum that "the Negro is being integrated first into those areas involving secondary contacts as opposed to primary contacts."[7] Be that as it may, from my experience with television I would say that the integration of the Negro in wrestling is one gain that I can contemplate without frenzy.

The acceptance of Negroes in American sports is now taken for granted to such a degree that it has posed a nice dilemma for integrationists. A letter written by E. B. Henderson, the leading historian of the Negro in sports, and for many years a staunch fighter against segregation, illustrates this:

6. This information was given me by Allen Woolridge, an authority on bridge and its organizations.

7. E. Franklin Frazier, *The Negro in the United States* (New York: The Macmillan Co., 1949), p. 693.

Certain sections of the American press still designate the racial association of criminals but seldom identify by race those who add to our prestige or culture. Too many Americans are ignorant of the fact that dozens of our Olympic athletes are colored boys and girls. . . . It is interesting to note how sports announcers fail to identify the great galaxy of football players on college and pro teams during the fall season. . . . Is this due to network policy that does not want to disturb the theory of the racists that there are innately inferior and superior racial groups?[8]

Ideally, the integrationist wants Negroes accepted on equal terms with all other men, to be judged strictly in terms of ability, without attention being given to such incidentals as race. Nevertheless, integration has not yet been achieved so fully that race pride is lost. Actually, many integrationists believe that the report of the death of "racism" in America has been greatly exaggerated, that it is not even moribund. As a counter-offensive they insist on publicizing facts proving the Negro to be worthy of integration. This seems a necessary immediate strategy to bring about inclusion. Achieving the ultimate ideal of completely ignoring race, of never even mentioning it, seems at this point of race relations in America to be a dim, far-off event.

JAZZ MUSIC

As in American sports, so in the arts, integration has gone apace. In American popular music the integration of the Negro composer and performer has been longest and most solid. As far back as 1855, an Austrian named Kurnberger wrote *Der Amerika müde (He Who Is Tired of America)*. One of the chief reasons for his hero's furious repudiation is that in the United States, "music is always left to the Negroes."[9] Though Kurnberger had never visited America, he was correct in stating the strong influence of the Negro on New World music.

A century later, the great influence of that hybrid, Afro-American music, is even more pervasive, whether in folk music, jazz, or concert music. It has reached European composers as well. Marshall Stearns, a close student of American music, is convinced that

8. E. B. Henderson, "Colored Boys in Sports," in "Letters to the *Star*," *The Washington Star*, December 6, 1948.
9. H. E. Jacob, *Johann Strauss, Father and Son* (New York: The Greystone Press, 1940), p. 365.

when the history of our folk and popular music is written, it will be found that—alongside the varying influence of every culture group in this country—an ever-increasing trend toward the incorporation of Negro musical characteristics in general and rhythm in particular has been taking place in our popular music.[10]

As far as jazz music is concerned, genuine integration of Negro material and of artists seems established. The recent histories of jazz have stressed the importance of the Negro idiom and musicians. The early accounts glorified Paul Whiteman, who usurped the title "King of Jazz" because of his semi-symphonic attempts to bring jazz closer to respectability. These books failed to mention the real king, Joe Oliver; the crown prince, Louis Armstrong; and the early, historically important hands of Fletcher Henderson and Duke Ellington. Present-day historians have toppled Whiteman from his throne as "King of Jazz," and look upon the "Whiteman Era" as a failure. They have traced jazz to its origins among Negroes in the South, especially in New Orleans; they have stressed its derivations from Negro folk music, sacred and secular, from ragtime and brass band marches; they have told how it emerged as collective polyrhythmic and polyphonic improvisation, a new kind of music that swept over America in the first decades of the century. Negro musicians Buddy Bolden, Bunk Johnson, King Oliver, Louis Armstrong, Sidney Bechet, Johnny Dodds, Jimmy Noone, Kid Ory, and Jelly Roll Morton—all from New Orleans—play prominent roles in the history. Negro composers Scott Joplin, W. C. Handy, Clarence Williams, and Spencer Williams were also important, and behind these a host of anonymous composers of blues and stomps that had become traditional.

Therefore, though a white band from New Orleans, The Original Dixieland Jass [sic] Band, was the first to make the new music commercially successful, the jazz musicians knew where the genuine source of the idiom and the best performers were to be found. Such prestige helped the Negro musician to integration. He might not be wanted or even allowed in the better-playing places, but he earned the respect, sometimes begrudged, of white fellow musicians who recognized his skill. Bix Beiderbecke, the brilliant young white cornetist, listened for hours to Bessie Smith, both in person and on records, rapt by her voice and delivery as she moaned the

10. Marshall W. Stearns, "American Popular Music," a paper read at the Conference on Music in Contemporary American Civilization held by the Committee on Musicology, American Council of Learned Societies, Library of Congress, December 13–14, 1951.

blues. The white musicians who form what is called the Chicago school have told the story of how they haunted the Southside to listen to Oliver and Armstrong and other Negro stars. Most came to worship, a few, alas! to steal; one Negro trumpet player, Freddie Keppard, refused to record lest his secrets of style be revealed, and another, King Oliver, regretted, in his declining years, the way the "educated cats" had stolen his stuff. Mezz Mezzrow, in his autobiography, *Really the Blues,* has revealed the fervent admiration shared by young Chicagoans for the great Negro jazz pioneers.

This respect for individual performers helped breach the wall of segregation. First instances of Negroes and whites playing together, except for private jam sessions, took place in recording studios. There was something of subterfuge in this: in those early days the companies did not list the personnel; the public did not have to know what went on inside the studio walls; and in order to make good records, good men on their instruments were sought, regardless of their color. So in the early years of recording, Fats Waller played piano for Ted Lewis, and Jelly Roll Morton for the New Orleans Rhythm Kings; and to switch around, Jack Teagarden and Joe Sullivan played with one of the bands Louis Armstrong picked up for a recording session. But these early instances involved single outstanding personalities. In the thirties the practice broadened: a notable free-and-easy come-and-go existed between the men in Teddy Wilson's and Benny Goodman's bands, and Lionel Hampton recorded many hits with thoroughly mingled groups.

Benny Goodman, who has done so much toward integrating Negro musicians, believes "one of the most important things that has happened musically in the last few years is the number of times good musicians have gotten together and played in mixed bands on records—something they don't get a chance to do in public."[11] Goodman points out that the first time that white and colored musicians played together for a paying audience in America was in 1936 when he and Gene Krupa sat in with Fletcher Henderson's orchestra at the Grand Terrace in Chicago.[12]

In the thirties, John Hammond planned to take to Europe an all-star band, "the first mixed band in jazz history." The interest of Europeans in jazz was then ardent, as it has remained, and the acceptance of a mixed band would be, of course, much easier than in America. The fine plan collapsed, however, probably because of labor difficulties in England. In

11. Benny Goodman and Irving Kolodin, *The Kingdom of Swing* (New York: Stackpole Sons, 1939), pp. 129–130.
12. *Ibid.,* p. 210.

the meanwhile, Goodman and Krupa had recorded with Teddy Wilson; the charming performances of this trio had won many enthusiasts around the country who wished to hear the group in person. A successful concert gave rise to "the thought of a white and colored group playing a hotel room . . . pretty revolutionary at the time."[13] At first Wilson played intermission piano while the band was off the stand, "and the trio was made a part of the floor show, spotted separately."[14] After a few days' trial, it was apparent that the thing was a natural from every standpoint.

After the trio and the quartette, with Lionel Hampton added, there was progress to Goodman's sextette, and soon Negroes were regular sidemen with the band. Other mixed bands were organized by Goodman's fellow Chicagoans, Joe Sullivan and Mezz Mezzrow. Such name band leaders as Tommy Dorsey, Artie Shaw, Harry James, and Gene Krupa made use of talented Negro stars, and a few white sidemen have played with Negro bands. But these bands are still exceptional; travelling and living accommodations still pose problems; and so integration in the large commercial bands remains token and not real. Negro bands, for all of their prestige in the jazz world, are still denied the most lucrative spots in hotel, theater, and radio work. Many of the famous Negro bands have broken up because of the current financial stress in band business.

In private jam sessions where fellow artists meet for relaxation on a basis of mutual respect—where a man is esteemed by his skill on trumpet, piano, trombone, or guitar—there integration is at its highest. In public jam sessions, in concerts such as the Jazz at the Philharmonic, there is complete acceptance. In the world of commercial jazz, however, integration is still unusual. The musicians may share mutual respect; but the magnates of commercial jazz seem to believe that the American public is not ready to see Negro and white musicians side by side.

Regardless of exclusions from the best-paying jobs both past and present, it is incontestable that Negroes have played an integral part in the history of jazz. The inventiveness of individual Negro artists, whether the "classic" blues stylists, Bessie Smith, Ma Rainey, and Lonnie Johnson; or the early New Orleans pioneers like Jelly Roll Morton, Oliver, and Bechet; or virtuosos on their instruments like Earl Hines and Coleman Hawkins; and of orchestra leaders such as Fletcher Henderson and Count Basie who were unique in their styles of swing music, and Duke Ellington, who introduced a new tone coloring, is fundamental in jazz history. Wherever a new

13. *Ibid.*, p. 214.
14. *Ibid.*

type of jazz becomes popular—whether boogie-woogie, which came from tenement flats of Chicago and Kansas City and swept America until there is now a hill-billy and cowboy boogie-woogie; or be-bop, of which cult Dizzy Gillespie and Charlie Parker are high priests—Negro performers will be found as originators. White bands pay Negro bands the flattery of imitation, the influence of Lunceford, Basie, and Ellington being easily apparent. Negro songstresses like Ivy Anderson, Ella Fitzgerald, Lena Horne, Billie Holiday, and Sarah Vaughan have set very definite singing styles and are widely imitated. Bing Crosby and other popular singers praise the singing of Louis Armstrong as influential in their formative years. The "jump" style of spiritual singing, widely popularized by the Golden Gates, has now influenced even the Grand Ole Opry in Nashville, the hill-billy musical capital. The give-and-take among barber shop quartettes has of course been strong; the jazz fillip added by the Mills Brothers helped to found a style. A logical outcome of the reciprocity is The Mariners, a quartette of two Negroes and two whites who learned integration in the Coast Guard and whom Arthur Godfrey uses on his programs, to the horror of Governor Herman Talmadge of Georgia, who suggests legislative action and economic boycott as a means to stop the new-fangled integration.

Despite the Negro's undoubted formative influence, jazz does not belong to the Negro. It is not an African music, though some analysts like Rudi Blesh stress the African survivals. It was never completely the American Negro's, or if so only briefly. Music rises over even the high walls of separation. As already pointed out, the first bands to popularize the new jazz were white bands out of New Orleans. In the dispersion and popularization white bands were of importance; in the preservation of the spirit of the older jazz when threatened by commercialism, the white musicians known as the Chicagoans (including Muggsy Spanier, Joe Sullivan, Jess Stacy, George Brunies, Pee Wee Russell, Wild Bill Davidson, Jack Teagarden, and Bud Freeman) struggled devotedly to keep the music from straying too far from its original qualities. In any type of contemporary jazz from New Orleans revival to be-bop, white musicians are among the best. One of the interesting aspects of jazz history is that young white bands are doing most now to keep alive the parent tradition of Oliver, Armstrong, and Jelly Roll Morton, whereas young Negro musicians, in revolt against the past, have gone in for the novelties of be-bop. To go further into that phenomenon would exceed the limits of this essay.

CONCERT MUSIC

The progress toward integration in serious music has been slower. In 1870, the ethnologist Dr. Van Evrie declared dogmatically: "Music is to the Negro an impossible art, and therefore such a thing as a Negro singer is unknown."[15] His statement was patently absurd even then when such a singer as Elizabeth Greenfield, "The Black Swan," had won acclaim in both the free states and England, and the Fisk Jubilee Singers were just about ready to make their triumphant musical tour. Yet even though the egregious belief might be disowned, America by and large held out no great welcome to the serious Negro musician.

Even before the Civil War, and of course increasingly after, many Negroes seriously studied classical music. Though the first concert artists were too often considered by the rest of America as curiosities, the desire to perform concert music was strong. Negro singers, violinists, pianists, and concert orchestras of outstanding ability and advanced training emerged, but they performed largely for their own. Many barriers had to be breached before the Negro was accepted as a concert artist. Despite international recognition, Roland Hayes was unrecorded by major phonograph companies for many years. Hayes's undaunted will, however, had much to do with weakening the barriers, and his success on the concert stage and on phonograph records together with that of Marian Anderson, Dorothy Maynor, Paul Robeson, Todd Duncan, Carol Brice and others proves that the individual concert singer has arrived. Yet, as Howard Taubman has pointed out:

> You cannot name more than a handful who have reached the top in the field of serious music. . . . It is because they do not have the educational opportunities. If they have the chance to study, they have even less chance of using their talents in public. A Negro must have an exceptional gift to crash through to distinction. . . . There are no Negroes in symphony or opera orchestras. . . . Nor are there any in theater pit orchestras, radio house bands, hotels, or on sustaining or commercial radio programs. . . . The situation is grim. It is not peculiar to music and the remedy will come only when the entire nation begins to live up to the letter and spirit of the thirteenth, fourteenth, and fifteenth amendments of our Constitution as well as the dictates of an enlightened humanity.[16]

Mr. Taubman wrote this over a decade ago. In the meanwhile it seems that the "dictates of an enlightened humanity" have not appreciably

15. C. J. Van Evrie, *White Supremacy and Negro Subordination* (New York: Van Evrie, Horton & Co., 1870), p. 102.
16. Howard Taubman, *Music as a Profession* (New York: Charles Scribner's Sons, 1939), pp. 143–144.

strengthened. But a few swallows point to the looked-for summer. Whereas Madam Evanti sang her operatic roles only in Europe and South America, Camilla Williams, Todd Duncan, and Larry Winters have appeared with the New York City Center Opera Company; and the dancer, Janet Collins, has joined the Metropolitan Opera Company. Adele Addison, a promising young soprano, the featured soloist at the Berkshire Music Festival of 1951, has sung two seasons with the New England Opera Company. The early "native opera" *Deep River* by Harling and Stallings and the experimental *Four Saints in Three Acts*, starring Edward Matthews, acquainted Americans with the rich potentialities of the Negro in musical drama. The "folk-opera" *Porgy and Bess;* the various swing Mikados; *Carmen Jones*, whose book was Harlemized by Oscar Hammerstein, but whose score remained Bizet's; and the more recent *Lost in the Stars* and *The Barrier*, an interracial venture uniting the talents of Langston Hughes, Jan Meyerowitz, Muriel Rahn, and Lawrence Tibbett, all bore witness to training, precision in a more sophisticated art-form, and dramatic ability that in all likelihood will pave the way for genuine integration. Excluded from grand opera for so long, Negroes formed their own local opera groups. But they were training themselves for inclusion. Mary Cardwell Dawson, director of the ten-year-old National Negro Opera Company, states, "By its repeated successes . . . the company has gained the respect and recognition of other races, and doors are now being opened to colored artists which have never before been open."[17]

The Hall Johnson, Eva Jessye, and other choruses have served not only as first-rate singing groups but also as training and proving grounds. To this group must be added Leonard de Paur's Infantry Chorus, which according to Virgil Thomson "could, without half trying, raise the whole level of our current taste in semi-popular music."[18] Using a wide range of material from Palestrina to contemporary American composers, Conductor de Paur clarifies his aims:

> When we sing a Cossack song, we're as near to being Cossacks as we can get; when we sing the Jewish chant Eli Eli, we're as close to being Jews with their whole history of oppression and religious faith as is possible for us.[19]

17. *The Washington Afro-American,* December 25, 1951, p. 6.
18. *Time,* January 12, 1948, LI, No. 2, p. 38.
19. *Ibid.*

More and more Negro singers and instrumentalists are being accepted as American, as world artists, without limitation upon repertoires. A few Negroes, Louis Vaughn Jones, the violinist, for instance, have played in local symphonic orchestras, and Dean Dixon is widely known as a symphonic conductor. Negro composers, notably William Grant Still and Howard Swanson, whose *Short Symphony* the New York Critics Circle called the best new orchestral work of the last season, have won national acceptance. A worthy instance of integration is interracial choral singing, directed by Warner Lawson and others.

By and large, however, the truth remains: individual Negro concert singers are warmly acclaimed, but in operatic and symphonic music the Negro musician is far from integrated. The tabu on Negro artists at Constitution Hall, though its stringency has recently been released, is still uncomfortably symbolic.

DANCE

The story of the dance repeats that of music, to which it is so closely related. The material, the idiom of the Negro dance, has been assimilated into American dancing, especially to the ballroom and theatrical varieties. As James Weldon Johnson often quipped, "Where music and dancing are concerned, Americans are always doing their best to pass for colored." The influence on America's ballroom dancing of the folk dancing of the American Negro, of dances with such names as the Turkey Trot, the Fox Trot, the Bunny Hug, and the Grizzly Bear, is indisputable. Vernon and Irene Castle, who taught a generation of American dancers to break away from the old European waltzes, polkas, and schottisches, really took the dances out of the barnyards, out of denims and ginghams, and put them in ballrooms in tuxedos and evening gowns. An important guide to the Castles was James Reese Europe, their favored band leader, whose music was grounded on the traditional Negro idiom. The later dances—the Big Apple, trucking, the boogie, the Susie Que, the various types of jitterbugging—all stem from the same folk sources. Like the earlier dances, these later dances

> . . . will be toned down and formalized by the dancing masters when [they reach] the pupils. There will be nothing left of the uncouth jive jamming, but all the basic steps will be there, carefully lifted out of the groove, analyzed and arranged in neat routines guaranteed to disturb nobody but your Aunt Caroline who still clings to the cotillion.

That is the way this particular clash between propriety and freedom of the dance has been ending for the past five hundred years.[20]

From Latin America, and chiefly of Negro origin, have come the tango, the conga, the rhumba, the samba, and the latest mamba. The inventiveness of such famous dance teachers as Billy Pierce, of such masters as Bill Bojangles Robinson, Eddie Rector, and the Nicholas Brothers, has influenced current tap dancing. According to John Martin again:

> The Negro has certainly given us at least the basis for all our popular dances. . . . His dance brings a certain vitality . . . to what would otherwise be a distinctly anemic field. The Negro, indeed, has discovered for himself a rich and admirable recreational dance and his contribution to [American] development along these lines has far greater potentialities than have been realized.[21]

Admirable study into the roots of American Negro dancing has been made by Katherine Dunham, stressing the West Indian backgrounds, and Pearl Primus, stressing the African. Together with Belle Rosette and Josephine Premice, who dance in the Caribbean tradition, these are accepted as American dancers and choreographers of significant achievement and promise. Haitian, West Indian, and African dance groups (especially that of Asadata Dafora) have met with high esteem. As far as integration goes, however, the building on these origins, the folding of these styles into major American choreography is still in the future. Tamiris has founded dances on Negro spirituals and set a group work, "How Long Brethren," to Negro songs of protest. Occasionally a bold producer has sponsored a chorus of white and Negro dancers, but this remains an exception. Janet Collins's inclusion with the Metropolitan Opera is certainly a striking step to integration. John Martin has written:

> A development that is destined to have great significance in the post-war dance world is the emergence of a number of highly gifted Negro artists. As a direct result of the old minstrel tradition, the Negro has heretofore been confined almost exclusively to the inertias of the entertainment field, but with the advent of the modern dance, in which he has found a medium for expressing himself in forms of his own

20. John Martin, "From Minuet to Jitterbug," *The New York Times Magazine*, November 7, 1943, p. 17.

21. John Martin, *Introduction to the Dance* (New York: W. W. Norton, 1939), p. 163.

devising, he has begun to find his rightful place in the creative arts and to do so with impressive results. . . . Eventually, no doubt, the purely objective racial approach to the art will give place to a more universal attitude in which the artist dances simply as an individual human being, allowing his racial heritage to voice itself freely through him but not to limit his range of subject and content.[22]

ART

Important in the culture of Africa and the West Indies, dancing could thrive as a folk-art in American slavery, since all that was needed was the voice to sing and the hands and feet to beat out the vigorous rhythms. For the similarly important plastic arts of Africa, there could be no such survival. Alain Locke has written:

We will never know and cannot estimate how much technical African skill was blotted out in America. The hardships of cotton and rice-field labor, the crudities of the hoe, the ax, and the plow reduced the typical Negro hand to a gnarled stump, incapable of the fine craftsmanship even if materials, patterns and artistic incentives had been available.[23]

The story of the Negro artist in America runs parallel to the stories already told in this essay. Historians have recorded earlier Negro painters, even in Colonial days, but the first really noteworthy Negro artist is Henry O. Tanner. Like Roland Hayes and Marian Anderson, Tanner received his first great recognition from Europe. Tanner found it difficult to obey the injunction of his teacher, Thomas Eakins, to remain in America.[24] An expatriate like so many artists of his generation, he sought refuge and inspiration in France from an America disdainful of artists in general, and of a Negro artist in particular. There he remained, seeking finer artistic training and criticism, painting Biblical subjects chiefly in Europeanized style. The New Negro movement, sharing in the awakened interest in African art, was more congenial to aspiring artists than Tanner's time was to him. Many of the younger artists discovered the African tradition, stimulated by the

22. John Martin, *The Dance* (New York: Tudor Publishing Co., 1946), p. 145.
23. Alain Locke, *Negro Art, Past and Present* (Washington, D.C.: Associates in Negro Folk Education, 1936), pp. 2–3.
24. Oliver W. Larkin, *Art and Life in America* (New York: Rinehart & Co., Inc., 1949), p. 279.

vogue among advance guard artists and critics in Europe and America. But the tradition was a discovery, not an old land revisited.

From the time of the New Negro movement, Negro artists have increased in numbers and ability. Several artists have achieved strikingly. But there is no single school, no dominant stylist; eclecticism, as might be expected, marks their work, as it does that of other American artists. Painters as various as Aaron Douglass, Archibald Motley, Hale Woodruff, James Porter, J. Lesesne Wells, Lois Jones, Charles Alston, Horace Pippin, Jacob Lawrence, Romare Bearden, Elton Fax, and Charles Sebree and the sculptors Sargent Johnson, Augusta Savage, and Richmond Barthé range the gamut of styles from realism to abstractionism. These artists are not confined to racial themes; some find rich inspiration in Negro experience, and some do not. A sculptor like Richmond Barthé is equally at home in his carving of a Harlem dancer or of a bust of Katherine Cornell. Jacob Lawrence is drawn to stirring epochs in the life of his people; Lois Jones is drawn to the landscape of her deeply loved France; both are exercising an artistic right. Certainly the plastic and graphic artist's freedom has been so hardly won that he should not be constrained within racial bonds. The quality of the painting or sculpture is what matters.

In black-and-white, and cartooning generally, Charles Alston, Ollie Harrington, and E. Simms Campbell rank with America's most popular artists. Campbell has been one of the steadiest cartoonists for *Esquire* since its start, and his bevy of harem beauties is more widely known than his hilarious cartoons of Negro life.

The controversy over the use of subject matter from Negro life has become less of a pressing issue: like all American artists, Negro artists now join opposing sides in such controversies as regionalism versus internationalism. In a recent debate, Thomas Benton rephrased his old objections to "Parisian esthetics which was more and more turning art away from the living world of active men and women into an academic world of empty pattern . . ."[25] and took his stand by "meaningful subject matter—in our cases specifically American subject matter."[26] James Thrall Soby believes that American art must "find its way into the international mainstream where it . . . must now take an upright, strong course," and while not ruling out regionalism, takes his stand that form, "whether abstract or realistic, remains a central part of [the artist's] business."[27]

25. Thomas Hart Benton, "What's Holding Back American Art," *The Saturday Review of Literature*, December 15, 1951, p. 9.

26. *Ibid.*

27. James Thrall Soby, "A Reply to Mr. Benton," *loc. cit*, p. 14.

What James Porter wrote in 1943 has even more support today:

> The future of the Negro painter is promising. No longer does he find himself handicapped by poor facilities for study. Moreover, the public attitude toward the Negro painter is changing rapidly from indifference to active encouragement.[28]

An instance in point is the recent award of prizes in the Corcoran Art Show to Richard Dempsey. No fanfare was made of his being a Negro; race was incidental or unmentioned in accounts of his achievement; he was an artist living in Washington whose paintings were judged as prize worthy.

As far as the treatment of Negro life and character by white artists goes, the caricature and the overstress of the sentimental or the exotic belong to the past. The advent of the realists at the turn of the century has made for a recognition of the artistic possibilities of Negro life and character, worthy of sincere and dignified presentation.

DRAMA

This recognition also marks the recent history of the drama. Negro oldtimers of the theatre remember ruefully the old cry, "Never let a nigger speak a line," i.e., confine him to singing and dancing roles. It was only after a quarter century of fabulous success for *Uncle Tom's Cabin* that a genuine Negro played the title role; even as late as the 1930's, a revival of *Uncle Tom's Cabin* called *Sweet River* had a white girl in the role of Eliza, pronouncing the "disses" and "dats" with the precision of elocution school. In black-face minstrelsy, Negro performers were not accepted for half a century; in serious drama the actor Ira Aldridge, like the painter Tanner, had to go to Europe to make his reputation.

The segregated Negro theatre became chiefly a theatre of vaudeville comedy and song and dance. Such star performers as Bert Williams, George Walker, Flo Mills, Josephine Baker, Ethel Waters, and Bojangles Robinson were noted for drollery, pantomime, or singing and dancing ability. It was only at the end of his career that the acting ability of Richard Harrison was discovered; the same story is true of Rose McLendon. Ethel Waters had a long apprenticeship as singer and dancer in honkytonks and cabarets and in musical shows before Broadway discovered her potentialities as actress in *Mamba's Daughters*.

28. James A. Porter, *Modern Negro Art* (New York: The Dryden Press, 1943), p. 133.

Before Eugene O'Neill, the Negro character in drama was minor, most often a servant for comic relief. Whenever serious attention was given to him, he was a pawn to be battled over, or a "tragic mulatto" waking up to discover the woe of being a Negro, as in Sheldon's *The Nigger*. But in the 1920's and 30's *The Emperor Jones, All God's Chillun Got Shoes, Porgy and Bess, In Abraham's Bosom, The Green Pastures, Run, Little Chillun*, and *Stevedore* brought more revelatory material to the stage. Negro actors, whether trained in Negro vaudeville in such rare companies as the Lafayette Players, or in college dramatic and little theatre groups, were found ready to step into the roles.

Negro actors came into their first large opportunities in these dramas of social realism, concerned with the tragic aspects of Negro life in America. With the Federal Theatre's *Haitian Macbeth*, a trend of adapting famous plays and operas to a "Negro" (or Harlemized) style began. Louis Armstrong's trumpet was called upon to aid Shakespeare in *A Midsummer Night's Dream; Carmen* became *Carmen Jones* of Harlem; *The Mikado* was presented in two versions, one "Hot" and one "Swing"; even *Lysistrata* introduced a king of swing into ancient Athens.

This fusion of unlike traditions, of Negro song and dance with theatrical masterpieces, often leaves unsatisfied not only the devotees of each tradition but also the fewer admirers of both. But it seems to please Broadway impresarios more than the experiment of having Negroes play the masterpieces straight.

A few brave experiments have cast individual Negro performers in famous dramas of the past. Reversing the historical procedure, Canada Lee, with the aid of white make-up, acted the role of Bosola in Webster's *The Duchess of Malfi*; he also acted Caliban in *The Tempest*. Mr. Lee, in all likelihood, owed his selection to his acting verve, but the roles—of villain and of grotesque brute—smacked of earlier casting practices. More to be cheered was the casting of Paul Robeson as Othello, the first instance of a Negro in the role in a professional Broadway production. This did not take place, however, until Robeson's Othello had been most favorably received in England; after glowing reports, Broadway was finally prepared to see a real Negro playing opposite a white Desdemona. The tremendous box-office success on Broadway and the road is indicative of a great change in audience and critical response. In 1924, against *All God's Chillun Got Wings*, Eugene O'Neill's drama of an interracial marriage, there were dire threats of violence, especially when it was learned that the white wife was called upon to kiss the hand of her husband (played by Paul Robeson). But this *Othello*, with Robeson, Uta Hagen, and Jose Ferrer in the leading roles, ran consecutively longer than any Shakespearean drama has done. A different kind of achievement, still a prime instance of integration, was the Scandinavian tour of the Howard Players, whose presentation of *The Wild Duck* interested the Norwegian ambassador so much that he had the government of Norway invite the troupe to play before Ibsen's countrymen.

Instances of individual Negro stars in dramas not based on Negro life are the stellar appearances in Menotti's *The Medium* of Leo Coleman, throughout the long run, and of Zelda Duke George in the leading role. Integration of whites and Negroes in choruses of musical shows was featured in the Federal Theatre *Sing for Your Supper* (1939), *Call Me Mister* (1946), *Bloomer Girl* (1944), and especially *Finian's Rainbow*, a fine spoof of racism, where Negroes shared major and minor roles. *Beggar's Holiday*, an adaptation of Gay's *Beggar's Opera*, united the talents of two Negroes—the composer Duke Ellington and the co-producer and designer Perry Watkins—with those of two whites—lyric writer John LaTouche and co-producer John R. Sheppard; and the cast was thoroughly interracial.

The all-Negro musical comedies, *Cabin in the Sky* by Lynn Root, Vernon Duke, and John LaTouche; and *St. Louis Woman*, with book by two Negroes, Arna Bontemps and Countee Cullen, with music by the white song writers, Harold Arlen and Johnny Mercer, and directed by Rouben Mamoulian, were star-studded extravaganzas, but they did not create the furor on Broadway caused by those high-hearted shows of the twenties, such as *Shuffle Along* and *Running Wild*. Revivals of the earlier musical shows also did not last long, nor did the revival of *The Green Pastures*; the theatrical fashion has changed.

Most fundamental in integration have been such realistic plays of the last decade as *Native Son*, *Strange Fruit*, *Deep Are the Roots*, *Jeb*, and *On Whitman Avenue*, which set forth with honesty and insight certain tragic aspects of race relations in America. The success of *Anna Lucasta* is significant: written originally about Polish life, it was adapted to a Harlem setting, and thereby revealed that the fundamental humanity was the same. The play also demonstrated the good work that was being done by the American Negro Theatre, and introduced Broadway to some promising young actors. Though commercially unsuccessful, Theodore Ward's *Our Lan'* and Paul Peter's *Nat Turner* have interpreted the Negro's militant role in American history in new fashion. At present, however, no realistic plays of Negro life are on Broadway.

The Negro playwright is still missing from the picture. As one of the signposts to integration, Langston Hughes wrote the lyrics for *Street Scene*, collaborating with Elmer Rice and Kurt Weill in an able production; he also prepared an operatic version, *The Barrier* from his play *Mulatto*. Richard Wright collaborated with Paul Green on *Native Son*. Theodore Ward's *Our Lan'* was the first play by a Negro to be sponsored by the Theatre Guild. But Negro playwrights still have little chance to serve the apprenticeship *in the theatre* so necessary for learning the exacting, technical craft.

Integration of the Negro playwright is therefore far behind that of the material and that of the actor. Edith J. R. Isaacs sees Broadway as "too hurried and harried and too expensive" to offer much to any playwrights. Where, then, is the hope for Negro playwrights? The answer, she states, is simple, and has little to do with race. "The answer will apply if playwrights—all playwrights—will learn to take their time; if they will stop looking with over-eager eyes at the fortunes rolled up by half-a-dozen hit plays a year, and count the money and time and the talents and the courage that are squandered every year on Broadway failures. . . ."[29] She concludes that Negro dramatists must, like any other dramatists, learn their craft *before* they head for Broadway. "Among the Negro actors who have made good, those that were well trained have had the best results and . . . they got their training before they met the tough professional competition of Broadway."[30]

The tributary theatre, then, is still the Negro playwright's best hope. Even there the outlook is dubious, for Randolph Edmonds, one of the sturdiest workers in that field, writes ruefully that if anybody knows where to locate good scripts of Negro life "he knows more than the writer who is going into his twenty-fifth year in the educational theatre."[31]

MOVING PICTURES

The lag of the moving pictures behind legitimate drama is nowhere more apparent than in the treatment of Negro life. The earlier story is familiar: in lighter pictures Negroes were inevitably shown as pop-eyed, quaking, terror-stricken at ghosts, or as slow-drawling, indolent nitwits; in "serious" pictures such as *The Birth of the Nation* they were shown as threatening beasts, if they were not slaphappy slaves and buffoons. Hollywood's most successful *Gone With the Wind* merely perpetuated these stereotypes. All-Negro shows like *Hallelujah* and *Hearts of Dixie* did little

29. Edith J. R. Isaacs, *The Negro in the American Theatre* (New York: Theatre Arts, Inc., 1947), p. 134.

30. *Ibid.*, p. 138.

31. Randolph Edmonds, "The NAACP Program and Negro Theatrical and Musical Artists," *The Pittsburgh Courier*, November 3, 1951.

more than add a kind of local color and exotic quaintness. *Imitation of Life* was sentimental, without understanding. Only an occasional bit character, like the Negro doctor in *Arrowsmith*, came anywhere close to authenticity and sincerity. The filming of such dramatic successes as *The Emperor Jones* and *The Green Pastures* were high-water marks in the period before World War II, but neither was based on the common experience of Negro life in America.

During and after World War II, efforts to bring the treatment of Negro life closer to reality came to a head. Negro and trade union organizations, film writers and artists, such political figures as Walter White and Wendell Willkie brought promises from Eric Johnston and other powers in Holly-wood that better and truer roles would be forthcoming. The first ventures, however, were merely such superior musical shows as *Stormy Weather* and *Cabin in the Sky*. These were lavishly produced in the tradition of Holly-wood extravaganza; there was an abundance—perhaps a superabun-dance—of song and dance talent; artists like Lena Horne, Katherine Dunham, and Ethel Waters and musicians like Fats Waller, Duke Elling-ton, and Cab Calloway got fuller opportunities on the screen. Occasionally Negro performers were given better spots in films not concerned primarily with Negro life, but even some of these newer pictures were *verboten* in certain areas of the South, where shots of Negro and white actors sharing the scene had to be cut out by orders of the local censors.

Serious social commentary was still missing. One of the oddities of the history of moving pictures in America was that for a long time the best treatment of convict labor, of sharecropping, and of lynching were to be found respectively in *I Was a Fugitive From a Georgia Chain-Gang*, *The Grapes of Wrath*, and *They Won't Forget*. In each of these the central char-acter was white, and the injustices, certainly marked in the experience of American Negroes, were in all cases directed against whites. In *They Won't Forget*, a film depicting the lynching of a white Northerner, a Negro janitor has a minor role. A historian of the moving pictures calls his portrayal "one of the few instances in American films in which the fear and oppression that fill the life of the Negro is strikingly told."[32]

In the last few years serious realism has strengthened in Hollywood. The causes of the franker recognition of social ills are several. One is the present need for national unity and for counteracting divisive forces. More than ever Americans feel that the moral leadership of world democracy,

32. Lewis Jacobs, *The Rise of the American Film* (New York: Harcourt, Brace and Co., 1939), p. 486.

which they have assumed, must be firmly grounded. The Negro's determined struggle for full citizenship is slowly gaining in Hollywood as elsewhere. Authors are growing more aware of the Negro's status in, and importance to America; and audiences have a maturity of outlook, which, if not recently developed, is only recently being taken into consideration by Hollywood moguls.

Of the pictures in the new trend, *Intruder in the Dust* showed a Negro of stiff-necked pride, shrewdness, and courage set against the vicious mob-spirit of the South. *Lost Boundaries* showed a more genteel but still searing race prejudice in a small New Hampshire town when a family's Negro blood was discovered. *Pinky* showed the dilemma, familiar in fiction but not in moving pictures, of the very fair Negro torn between service to "her" people and an interracial marriage (service and marriage being mutually exclusive according to this version). *Home of the Brave* stressed the fundamental sameness of Negro and white troops. *No Way Out* dealt with the pathological roots of race hatred and the difficulties confronting a young Negro doctor, against which he pitted great doggedness. *The Quiet One* is a powerful documentary on the impoverished lives of Negro children.[33]

All of these were marked by sympathy and sincerity; all presented serious aspects of Negro life in America. From the young GI in *Home of the Brave*, the young doctor in *No Way Out*, and Lucas Beauchamp in *Intruder in the Dust*, the reach is very far back to Stepin Fetchit and Amos and Andy. One can be grateful for these favors, which are by no means small, yet feel it a critical duty to point out that the pictures contained grave weaknesses.

Two of the pictures handle the book-worn theme of "passing" and the "woebegone mulatto," with little insight and too many clichés. That the doctor in *Lost Boundaries* was "forced" to buy a white practice in a New England town because he was too light to join the staff of a Negro hospital in the South, is certainly news to the Negro medical profession, or to anybody else with 20/200 vision. The Inferno of Harlem in contrast to the Paradise of the New England small town is too pat for credence. The solution in *Pinky*, brought about by the largesse of an old aristocratic lady who rose above the crass prejudices of her area, is as unconvincing as the initial dilemma of the heroine. The attack on prejudice in *No Way Out* was two-fisted, but also wild-swinging in places; the psychotic villain showed his race-hatred so violently that the audience might be forgiven for overlooking

33. Later pictures, especially *The Well*, continue this social realism, but the writer has not yet seen them.

its own less violent but no less sinister prejudices. *Home of the Brave*, taken from a play in which the central figure is Jewish, stressed the theme that Negroes and whites are not different, psychologically, but underplayed the acutely different social factors. The close of *Home of the Brave* with the one-armed white veteran and the chastened Negro going off to start an interracial restaurant reminds one of Dickens's London more than of Harlem or Southside Chicago or Cicero, Illinois.

Ralph Ellison sees a danger in these films:

> For the temptation toward self-congratulation which comes from seeing these films and sharing in their emotional release is apt to blind us to the true nature of what is unfolding—or failing to unfold— before our eyes. As an antidote to the sentimentality of these films, I suggest that they be seen in predominantly Negro audiences. For here, when the action goes phony, one will hear derisive laughter, not sobs. Seriously, *Intruder in the Dust* is the only film that could be shown in Harlem without arousing unintended laughter. For it is the only one of four in which Negroes can make complete identification with their screen image. Interestingly, the factors that make this identification possible lie in its depiction not of racial, but of human, qualities.[34]

Nevertheless the treatment of the Negro in these films goes far beyond what might have been envisioned a decade ago. The integration of material, and even of actors is certainly far ahead of the integration of technicians, authors, and directors in Hollywood. Here there is still almost complete exclusion. This is not solely a matter of integration of employment. Before Negroes will be integrated fully in Hollywood they must be allowed to enter into the manifold processes that go into the making of pictures. Before films of Negro life can reach truthfulness and significance and revelation, Negro authors and consultants must be integrated into the industry.

LITERATURE

In American literature, Negro life and character have been considered worthy material for well over a century. Concerned with what differentiated the American experience from the European, early novelists turned

34. Ralph Ellison, "The Shadow and the Act." *The Reporter* (December 6, 1949), I, 19. *No Way Out* was not included in his review.

to the Negro in America as a fertile source. Less wary than when writing about the Indian, these authors delivered *obiter dicta* on the basis of brief and superficial acquaintance. The slavery controversy produced stereotypes; proslavery authors concentrated on contented and comical slaves; antislavery authors on victims—either submissive like Uncle Tom, or militant like George Harris, or the tragic octoroon like Eliza. True to the prevailing literary fashion, both sides shrouded reality with sentimental idealization. To buttress social policy in the Reconstruction and after, authors created the stereotype of the brute Negro, insulting and swaggering (and incidentally wanting to vote). The "tragic mulatto" stereotype was further developed, in order to dramatize the evils of miscegenation.

It was only with the development of realism that characterization of the Negro broke some of the shackles of stereotyping. It was only then that genuine integration of the material began. Before this, treatment of Negro life and character was set apart in an alcove of special pleading. Paul Laurence Dunbar, part of the local color movement, and Charles Waddell Chesnutt, both a local colorist and a problem novelist, presented Negro characters who were more than walking arguments or exotic oddities. W. E. B. Du Bois in *The Souls of Black Folk* revealed the depth of Negro experience rather than the surface. Like the writers of the Irish Renaissance, these authors were beginning to uncover the essential dignity of their material.

The Negro author, however, was less integrated than the material of Negro life. Though highly praised by the leading critic, William Dean Howells, Dunbar expressed resentment at the groove to which his audience relegated him. Chesnutt's racial identification was concealed by his publishers, who feared that knowledge that he was a Negro would injure his reception in a market where there was a high premium on books *about* Negroes but not by Negroes.

In the 1920's, interest in Negro life reached a new high. It was stimulated by southern white authors like Stribling, Du Bose Heyward, Julia Peterkin, E. C. L. Adams, Roark Bradford, and Howard Odum, all of whom had studied Negro folk life carefully; and by Carl Van Vechten, who took Harlem for his province. Coincidentally, the New Negro movement, centered in Harlem but drawing recruits from many sections, began reporting Negro life from the inside. Influential mentors of this "Renaissance" were Alain Locke and Charles S. Johnson, then editor of *Opportunity*. In both theory and practice, James Weldon Johnson taught younger Negro authors to respect the material of Negro life.

The poets Claude McKay, Countee Cullen, and Langston Hughes and the fiction writers Jean Toomer, Rudolph Fisher, and Eric Walrond won nationwide recognition. Walter White and Jessie Fauset wrote of the hitherto neglected Negro middle class. Though there was exploitation as well as exploration of Negro life, the New Negro movement turned out a body of intrinsically sound work, and most definitely opened publishers' offices to Negro authors. Previously, a Negro appearing in a publisher's office was likely to be considered (rightly) as a messenger with a package.

From the New Deal '30's to the present, the deepening regionalism and the social awareness in American fiction have naturally influenced novels and poetry of Negro life. Novelists such as Arna Bontemps, Zora Hurston, Richard Wright, Chester Himes, and Ann Petry joined with such white novelists as Erskine Caldwell, William Faulkner, Lillian Smith, and Bucklin Moon in presenting Negro life with a new fullness and depth. Negro life in the back country, in small southern towns, in industrial cities, and in Harlem, lodestone of so many novelists, received a fairly thorough coverage. Negro personalities of many types are now in the picture: illiterate farm hands, frustrated intellectuals, the long-suffering accommodator, the bad Negro run amok, the hat-in-hand race leader, the militant returning veteran, the run-of-the-mill "little man" wanting happiness and no trouble—the list is very long.

As far as representation of Negro life is concerned, then, there has been increasing integration in American literature. Though plays of Negro life are now scarce, novels and biographies of Negro life, by both white and Negro authors, appear steadily. A few of these books become best-sellers; many are good-sellers. That the pocket-size reprint editions include many books of Negro life is warrant that canny publishers find the material to have the requisite vitality to reach a large public. This, in turn, is part guarantee of integration into the economics of literature, an important matter since professional Negro authors, i.e., those making a living from their writings, are still few.

The amazing career of Frank Yerby in the field of the historical romance, where he has turned out novel after novel, all best-sellers; the high esteem of Willard Motley, among both the critical and the wider reading public, for his novel of an Italian gangster in Chicago; the experiments of such authors as Zora Neale Hurston, Ann Petry, and William Gardner Smith who have turned from writing chiefly of Negroes to writing of whites; all of these have caused many literary commentators to speak of the integration of the Negro author as something near at hand. The majority of the critics in the valuable *Phylon* Symposium of the Negro in Literature (Fourth Quarter, 1950) are of this opinion.

What is meant by the integration of the author is not always made clear, however. To some it seems to mean "the making of cake and Cadillac money by free lancing for the pulps." The opening of the larger magazines to Negro authors is another sign, one of undue optimism from where I sit, for I can see only a few swallows to indicate *that* summer. Others seem to equate integration with avoidance of Negro life; the thesis seems to run that writers, in order to escape the personal perplexities and the artistic distractions of race, should turn from writing about American Negroes to writing about American whites. Those exploiting this thesis the farthest make integration into a literary "passing for white." A young artist once told me plaintively, "I don't want to paint Negroes; I want to paint human beings." I should have thought his ambition estimable, if I had not learned that for him the groups were mutually exclusive.

The freedom of the Negro author has long been a debated subject. Dunbar ruefully believed that his audience turned from his "deeper" poetry to praise "a jingle in a broken tongue." Cullen rightfully insisted on being considered poet, rather than "Negro poet":

> What shepherd heart would keep its fill
> For only the darker lamb?

From Fisk University recently a group of young writers issued a brave manifesto, in opposition to chauvinism, special pleading, and

> . . . to having our work viewed, as the custom is, entirely in the light of sociology and politics, to having it overpraised on the one hand by those with an axe to grind or with a conscience to salve . . . to having it misinterpreted on the other hand by coterie editors, reviewers, anthologists . . . because we deal with realities we find it neither possible nor desirable to ignore. . . .[35]

Hugh Gloster deplores "the limiting and crippling effects of racial hypersensitivity and Jim-Crow esthetics."[36] And J. Saunders Redding has spoken a valedictory, *On Being Negro in America:*

> I hope this piece will stand as the epilogue to whatever contribution I have made to the "literature of race." I want to get on to other

35. Robert Hayden, Myron O'Higgins, *et al., Counterpoise* (Nashville [Tenn.], 1948).

36. Hugh Gloster, "Race and the Negro Writer," *Phylon* (Fourth Quarter, 1950), XI, 4, p. 369.

things. . . . The obligations imposed by race on the average educated or talented Negro (if this sounds immodest, it must) are vast and become at last onerous. I am tired of giving up my creative initiative to these demands.[37]

White critics have also noticed the limitations forced upon Negro writers. Bucklin Moon, a novelist and publishing editor, believes that "the whole of Negro life has a richness, in spite of second-degree citizenship, which seems made to order for the writer."[38] The Negro writer, however, "under the existing American mores, . . . is always, in essence, telling the same story."[39]

Our racial mores are changing, but so slowly that it seems unlikely that any immediate solution of this creative frustration is likely to come from that direction. . . . There will always be a place for the Negro protest novel, but until it becomes the exception, rather than the rule, American literature will suffer along with the Negro artist.[40]

Jean Paul Sartre believes that, faced with disfranchisement and other evils, the Negro writer cannot "pass his life in the contemplation of the eternal True, Good, and Beautiful." "Thus, if an American Negro finds that he has a vocation as a writer, he discovers his subject at the same time." Whether "pamphleteer, blues writer, or the Jeremiah of the Southern Negroes," the Negro writer "sees the whites from the outside, assimilates the white culture from the outside," and will show the alienation of the black race within American society, "not objectively, like the realists, but passionately."[41] Unlike Bucklin Moon, Sartre sees this absorption, an instance of the "engagement" of the author, as a good thing.

Bernard Wolfe sees the Negro as similar to the pariah in a caste society; an "interplay of image, reflex, and masquerade" goes on constantly; the Negro artist for long has been passively enslaved by the "white man's tyrant image." Now, however, the caste system is "losing its hold on the

37. J. Saunders Redding, *On Being Negro in America* (Indianapolis: The Bobbs-Merrill Co., 1951), p. 26.

38. Bucklin Moon, "A Literature of Protest," *The Reporter*, I, 17 (December 6, 1949), p. 36.

39. *Ibid.*

40. *Ibid.*, p. 37.

41. Jean Paul Sartre, *What Is Literature?* (New York: Philosophical Library, 1949), pp. 77–78.

Negro's inner life," and here and there something new is being added: "a rebellion against both reflex and false face, a disowning of the white man's image entirely."[42]

According to Cedric Dover, his fellow Eurasian writers and colored writers generally exist in an arid and lonely atmosphere, with an audience small and "poorly schooled, priest-ridden, socially and intellectually imitative, limited in its attitudes."[43]

> We have allowed our creativeness to be crushed not only by oppression and exploitation, but by our own sycophancy, bigotry, Uncle Tomism, and desire to equal and excel our masters in the culture they have allowed us to sniff.[44]

From a position on the extreme left, Lloyd Brown argues that the Negro writer is still in a Jim-Crow ghetto, excluded from general avenues of expression; but he adds that the Negro writer, far from being preoccupied with Negro material, "has not been Negro enough—that is, has not fully reflected the real life and character of the people."[45]

Diametrically opposite, a swing of the pendulum from the usual protest against the publishers' unwillingness to take forthright work about Negro life, Richard Gibson tells of liberal publishers who rejected a novel because it did not deal topically with a race theme. He also attacks the Professional Liberal as a bane to the Negro writer:

> The Professional Liberal will not fail to remind him that he cannot possibly know anything else but Jim Crow, sharecropping, slum-ghettos, Georgia crackers, and the sting of his humiliation, his unending ordeal, his blackness.[46]

And so the war rages. Several of the battlers are "either-or" extremists. Echoes resound of battles long ago: propaganda versus pure art; the ivory tower versus the arena of action; the sociological versus the belle-lettristic;

42. Bernard Wolfe, "Ecstatic in Blackface," *The Modern Review*, III (January, 1950), pp. 201ff.

43. Cedric Dover, *Feathers in the Arrow* (Bombay: Padma Publications, Ltd., 1947), p. 17.

44. *Ibid,.* p. 21.

45. Lloyd Brown, "Which Way for the Negro Writer?," *Masses and Mainstream*, 4 (April, 1951), p. 54.

46. Richard Gibson, "Is the Negro Writer Free?," reprinted from *The Kenyon Review*, Spring, 1951, in *The Negro Digest*, XX, 11 (September, 1951), pp. 43ff.

the radical versus the conservative; the conscious avoidance of racial material versus the exclusive use. But these extreme positions confuse, it seems to me, the real battle line.

Even if the status of Negroes in America did not make the propaganda novel a natural expectancy, such mentors as Zola, Dreiser, Steinbeck, and Farrell in uncovering the lower depths would certainly have been potent influences. It cannot be gainsaid, however, that concentration on the problem has narrowed and hardened creative writing among Negroes. True to the tactics of pressure groups, characters have too often been villains or victims. Mob violence and lynching have become the hackneyed climaxes to dramatize the Negro's wrong; apparently easy, apparently sure-fire "big scenes," they are often ineptly handled artistically and misfire. But all of this is not the fault of "race material"; it is rather bad characterization, weak dramatization of the theme, and often fails just because the writer is not being true to the type of Negro life that he feels and has absorbed most deeply. An example of different use of "race material" is such a novel as Owen Dodson's *Boy in the Window*. Its achievement is the sensitive, painstaking account of a Negro boy's growing up in Brooklyn and Washington, obviously set firmly in the author's experience. Race impinges on the plot, but fundamentally the novel gives the picture of childhood. It cannot be said that the boy's being a Negro is incidental; in most of the experience it is central. But the novel sets out to solve no problem, to denounce no wrongs, only to reveal personality and a way of life, which it does with great skill. And critics generally have considered it an American, not a Negro, novel, revealing a significant American, not Negro, talent.

That way, it seems to me, true integration lies. It does not lie in default, in letting the treatment of Negro life go by forfeit. On examination, what most of the sponsors of the exodus from Negro materials really are attacking is not race material, but its treatment. The real *bête noire* is not so much the Negro as it is the Negro Problem, handled in crude, ungainly fashion.

There is nothing new in the belief that Negro artists can only be free when they write about white people. Dunbar, believing that "we must write like the white men . . . our life is now the same,"[47] concentrated on white characters in three of his four novels, and the results were negligible. Before the present vogue, Chesnutt, Arna Bontemps, and William Attaway wrote fiction about white characters, but their fiction about Negroes is superior.

47. Benjamin Brawley, *Paul Laurence Dunbar* (Chapel Hill, N.C.: University of North Carolina Press, 1936), p. 77.

The best-selling successes of Yerby and Motley are pointed to as signs of an artistic maturity and emancipation, refuting the theory that the artist writes best about what he knows best. But such instances do not really refute. As far as Yerby is concerned, escapist romance we always have with us, and the industrious novelist can find historical material galore to deck out in glamour and excitement; his success does not depend upon how deeply he has absorbed his material and how significantly he communicates it. Yerby's canny skill as a plot contriver, not his illumination of history, has built up his immense following. Motley's success in an opposite direction, that of social protest on a naturalistic base, is an exception proving the rule. Granted Motley's undoubted talents, there is no reason why a Negro brought up in a polyglot, fringe community should not render its life vividly and movingly.

But Negro writers, by and large, do not have similar experience to levy upon; too often, in the words of Sartre, they see "the whites from the outside." Ann Petry, making use of her experience as the daughter of a druggist in a Connecticut small town, writes a novel about whites in such a community; Zora Hurston, from her copious knowledge of folklore, writes a novel about crackers in the Florida scrub. To a degree they are drawing from experience, but this is not what they *fully* know, only what they *half* know. As a consequence, Miss Petry's *County Place* does not measure up to her earlier *The Street,* and Miss Hurston's *Seraph on the Suwanee* falls far below her *Mules and Men* and *Their Eyes Were Watching God.*

The new freedom (if it is new) is good, in that freedom is better than forced confinement (if it was forced). But the proof must be in the caliber of the work produced, instead of in the fact that Negroes are no longer writing about Negroes. Much of the hostility to the treatment of Negro life in art is summed up in James Weldon Johnson's phrase, "second generation respectability." "A man climbing a steep hill does not like to stop and look back down," a friend once said to me. Many Negroes to whom integration in America can be symbolized by fish-tail Cadillacs and mink coats (which are certainly *one* kind of Americanization) are hurt to the quick by such characters as Porgy and Bigger Thomas; their ears are jarred by even God's trombones. They do not want art to deal with Negro life, whether truly or falsely, with revelation or caricature; they just want out. All of the critics counseling flight, of course, are not afflicted by this anti-Negro feeling, which is as pronounced in many Negroes as anti-Semitism is in many Jews. Some readers and critics, with greater literary pretensions, are just offended by modern realism, whether of Oakies or Shanty Irish or Ghetto Jews or Tobacco Road Anglo-Saxons or Reservation Navahos. But whether anti-Negro or anti-realistic, or both, such readers and critics hail as the only integration the fact that a few Negroes, with varying success, have written novels about white characters.

But Phillis Wheatley, writing her heroic couplets in the manner of Pope for the matter of Puritan Boston, is less integrated in American culture than Frederick Douglass, writing *My Bondage and My Freedom* and treading the anti-slavery platforms, a peer among peers, with Wendell Phillips and Theodore Parker. W. E. B. Du Bois's *Souls of Black Folk* is more integrally American literature than Dunbar's novels about white people. Countee Cullen's poems on Keats are no more integrated in American poetry than his "Shroud of Color," and Cullen, who disliked the term "Negro poet," is no more and no less an American poet than Langston Hughes. Braithwaite's biography of the Bronte sisters stands no better chance of integration, merely because of the stature of the subjects, than his autobiography, *House Under Arcturus.* Frank Yerby's romances of the Old South are no more integrated in American historical fiction than Arna Bontemps's *Black Thunder,* which is about a slave insurrection. James Weldon Johnson's *Along This Way* and short stories by Jean Toomer, Eric Walrond, and Rudolph Fisher are as integral to American literature as the new, "emancipated" fiction is, even though new types of publishers' promotion have raised this fiction to best-selling prestige.

> What [asks David Daiches] is a great work of fiction? . . . We shall probably find that the greatest works are those which, while fulfilling all the formal requirements, most adequately reflect the civilization of which they are a product. This does not conflict with the traditional view that great art presents the universal through the particular. . . .[48]

For the most serious and important modern fiction, it is a truism that the artist must have fullest comprehension of his material in order to achieve the "solidity of specification" that is basic. Before he can attain to the universal he must have absorbed those particulars which come from his deepest experience, those that he understands best and to which his imagination is most responsive.

Though telling of Irish writers, Sean O'Faolain says good things for Negro writers, or those of any minority, to heed:

48. David Daiches, *The Novel and the Modern World* (Chicago: The University of Chicago Press, 1939), p. 219.

The Irish writer was a provincial while he imitated slavishly and tried to write beyond his talents; he ceased to be a provincial when he wrote of what he knew and could describe better than anybody else. . . . It was an entirely new thing for men to realise the full and complete dignity of the simplest life of the simplest people. Once they had acknowledged that, then they were free to do anything they liked with it in literature—treat it naturalistically, fantastically, romantically, see it in any light they chose. They had conquered their material by accepting it.[49]

Two historians of American poetry praise the elder generation of Dunbar, Johnson, and Braithwaite, who "not without wisdom . . . saw the figure of the Russian poet, Alexander Pushkin, as a distant end in view for their accomplishment."[50] The careers of Alexander Dumas, *père* and *fils*, in nineteenth century drama and fiction are also held up by many as beacons to the American Negro writer. But these men were accepted to a degree almost unknown by American Negroes even today. For the elder Dumas, at home on Parisian boulevards and in the salons; for the younger, equally at home in the Parisian theatre world; and for Pushkin, the brilliant courtier and poet of St. Petersburg, race was unquestionably meaningless. For resemblances to such social situations, one must go to certain Latin-American countries (Cuba and Brazil, for instance) and even here the situations are not parallel. To envisage the future of the Negro writer in the United States in terms of the acceptance and achievement of Alexander Dumas and Alexander Pushkin seems to overlook too many complicating factors.

It is easy to agree with Charles Glicksberg that contemporary Negro authors suffer from "psychological repression and cultural frustration," and that an "exacerbated racial motif" results. But, as he points out, that does not end the story. The motif is justified and fruitful:

The Negro writers in the United States know what they are about. Their ultimate goal is not to accentuate differences of color and race, not to deepen the cleavage and render inevitable the sense of cultural alienation. Their objective is nothing less than complete assimilation, not in the sense of discarding whatever belongs properly to him as a

49. Sean O'Faolain, *The Irish* (New York: The Devin-Adair Co., 1942), pp. 162ff.
50. Horace Gregory and Marya Zaturenska, *A History of American Poetry* (New York: Harcourt, Brace and Co., 1946), p. 397.

man and as a member of his group, but in the sense of being an integral part of the life of the nation.[51]

Signs of integration are heart-warming. On one—certainly not negligible—level, the reissue in the cheap editions of books by Negro authors and by white authors on Negro life is a good sign. On a higher level are the Book-of-the-Month selections of Richard Wright and the Pulitzer Prize award in poetry to Gwendolyn Brooks. A few anthologies and textbooks include a sprinkling of Negro names and works. More and more frequently literary fellowships are won by Negroes; literary groups receive Negroes on the basis of equality; Negro authors share the hospitality and stimulation of Yaddo and summer schools of writing. Another good sign is the Negro author's surrender of his missionary fervor, the conscious struggle to overcome his alienation, to secure as much objectivity as possible, to see and render not whites and Negroes, but men (which is not the same as "conscious avoidance of race"). There are also good signs that an audience is increasing in America and abroad, and that the Negro audience is losing some of its hypersensitivity, and learning something of the respect due to its artistic interpreters. Most important of all, are the signs that the Negro writer is gaining in craftsmanship and understanding.

When Negro authors emerge worthy to tell the story, the stories, of the Negro in America, they will write with authenticity and power, not because of any racial *mystique*, but because they have lived the story so fully, brooded upon it so deeply, and fashioned it with loving and informed care. And that will mean not only that the Negro author is integrated into American literature, but even more that he will be given passport to enter the Republic of Letters of the world.

But that is the dim hope for the far-off time. The present fact weighs heavily: that, despite all the multiplied signs of integration, the Negro author, like the Negro athlete and the Negro artist in any field, is not likely to achieve full integration in American culture until American Negroes, by and large, are themselves integrated into all the rights and responsibilities of full American citizenship.

51. Charles I. Glicksberg, "Eurasian Racialism," *Phylon*, XII (First Quarter, 1951), p. 18.

American Literature

Our Literary Audience

❦ WE HAVE HEARD in recent years a great deal about the Negro artist. We have heard excoriations from one side, and flattery from the other. In some instances we have heard valuable honest criticism. One vital determinant of the Negro artist's achievement or mediocrity has not been so much discussed. I refer to the Negro artist's audience, within his own group. About this audience a great deal might be said.

I submit for consideration this statement, probably no startling discovery: that those who might be, who should be a fit audience for the Negro artist are, taken by and large, fundamentally out of sympathy with his aims and his genuine development.

I am holding no brief for any writer, or any coterie of writers, or any racial credo. I have as yet no logs to roll, and no brickbats to heave. I have however a deep concern with the development of a literature worthy of our past, and of our destiny; without which literature certainly, we can never come to much. I have a deep concern with the development of an audience worthy of such a literature.

"Without great audiences we cannot have great poets." Whitman's trenchant commentary needs stressing today, universally. But particularly do we as a racial group need it. There is a great harm that we can do our incipient literature. With a few noteworthy exceptions, we are doing that harm, most effectually. It is hardly because of malice; it has its natural causes; but it is none the less destructive.

We are not a reading folk (present company of course forever excepted). There are reasons, of course, but even with those considered, it remains true that we do not read nearly so much as we should. I imagine our magazine editors and our authors if they chose, could bear this out. A young friend, on a book-selling project, filling in questionnaires on the reason

why people did not buy books, wrote down often, with a touch of malice—
"Too much bridge." Her questionnaires are scientific with a vengeance.

When we do condescend to read books about Negroes, we seem to read
in order to confute. These are sample ejaculations: *"But we're not all like
that." "Why does he show such a level of society? We have better Negroes
than that to write about." "What effect will this have on the opinions of
white people."* (Alas, for the ofay, forever ensconced in the lumber yard!)
. . . *"More dialect. Negroes don't use dialect anymore."* Or if that sin is too
patent against the Holy Ghost of Truth—*"Negroes of my class don't use
dialect anyway."* (Which *mought* be so, and then again, which *moughtn't*.)

Our criticism is vitiated therefore in many ways. Certain fallacies I
have detected within at least the last six years are these:

> We look upon Negro books regardless of the author's intention,
> as representative of all Negroes, i.e., as sociological documents.
>
> We insist that Negro books must be idealistic, optimistic tracts
> for race advertisement.
>
> We are afraid of truth telling, of satire.
>
> We criticize from the point of view of bourgeois America, of racial
> apologists.

In this division there are, of course, overlappings. Moreover all of these
fallacies might be attributed to a single cause, such as an apologistic chip
on the shoulder attitude, imposed by circumstance; an arising snobbishness; a delayed Victorianism; or a following of the wrong lead. Whatever
may be the primary impulse, the fact remains that if these standards of
criticism are perpetuated, and our authors are forced to heed them, we
thereby dwarf their stature as interpreters.

One of the most chronic complaints concerns this matter of Representativeness. An author, to these sufferers, never intends to show a man who happens to be a Negro, but rather to make a blanket charge against the race.
The syllogism follows: Mr. A. shows a Negro who steals; he means by this
that all Negroes steal; all Negroes do not steal; Q.E.D. Mr. A. is a liar, and
his book is another libel on the race.

For instance, *Emperor Jones* is considered as sociology rather than
drama; as a study of the superstition, and bestiality, and charlatanry of the
group, rather than as a brilliant study of a hard-boiled pragmatist, far more
"American" than "African," and a better man in courage and resourceful-
ness than those ranged in opposition to him. To the charge that I have

misunderstood the symbolism of Brutus Jones's visions, let me submit that superstition is a human heritage, not peculiar to the Negro, and that the beat to the tom-tom, as heard even in a metropolitan theater, can be a terrifying experience to many regardless of race, if we are to believe testimonies. But no, O'Neill is "showing us the Negro race," not a shrewd Pullman Porter, who had for a space, a run of luck. By the same token, is Smithers a picture of the white race? If so, O'Neill is definitely propagandizing against the Caucasian. O'Neill must be an East Indian.

All God's Chillun Got Wings is a tract, say critics of this stamp, against intermarriage; a proof of the inferiority of the Negro (why he even uses the word Nigger!!! when he could have said Nubian or Ethiopian!); a libel stating that Negro law students all wish to marry white prostitutes. (The word prostitute, by the way, is cast around rather loosely, with a careless respect for the Dictionary, as will be seen later.) This for as humane an observation of the wreck that prejudice can bring to two poor children, who whatever their frailties, certainly deserve no such disaster!

This is not intended for any defense of O'Neill, who stands in no need of any weak defense I might urge. It is to show to what absurdity we may sink in our determination to consider anything said of Negroes as a wholesale indictment or exaltation of all Negroes. We are as bad as Schuyler says many of "our white folks" are; we can't admit that there are individuals in the group, or at least we can't believe that men of genius whether white or colored can see those individuals.

Of course, one knows the reason for much of this. Books galore have been written, still are written with a definite inclusive thesis, purposing generally to discredit us. We have seen so much of the razor-toting, gin-guzzling, chicken-stealing Negro; or the pompous walking dictionary spouting malapropisms; we have heard so much of "learned" tomes, establishing our characteristics, "appropriativeness," short memory for joys and griefs, imitativeness, and general inferiority. We are certainly fed up.

This has been so much our experience that by now it seems we should be able to distinguish between individual and race portraiture, i.e., between literature on the one hand and pseudo-science and propaganda on the other. These last we have with us always. From Dixon's melodramas down to Roark Bradford's funny stories, from Thomas Nelson Page's "Ole Virginny retainers" to Bowyer Campbell's *Black Sadie* the list is long and notorious. One doesn't wish to underestimate this prejudice. It is ubiquitous and dangerous. When it raises its head it is up to us to strike, and strike hard. But when it doesn't exist, there is no need of tilting at windmills.

In some cases the author's design to deal with the entire race is explicit, as in Vachel Lindsay's *The Congo*, subtitled "A Study of the Negro Race"; in other cases, implicit. But an effort at understanding the work should enable us to detect whether his aim is to show one of ours, or all of us (in the latter case, whatever his freedom from bias, doomed to failure). We have had such practice that we should be rather able at this detection.

We have had so much practice that we are thin-skinned. Anybody would be. And it is natural that when pictures of us were almost entirely concerned with making us out to be either brutes or docile housedogs, i.e., infra-human, we should have replied by making ourselves out superhuman. It is natural that we should insist that the pendulum be swung back to its other extreme. Life and letters follow the law of the pendulum. Yet, for the lover of the truth, neither extreme is desirable. And now, if we are coming of age, the truth should be our major concern.

This is not a disagreement with the apologistic belief in propaganda. Propaganda must be counterchecked by propaganda. But let it be found where it should be found, in books explicitly propagandistic, in our newspapers, which perhaps must balance white playing up of crime with our own playing up of achievement; in the teaching of our youth that there is a great deal in our racial heritage of which we may be justly proud. Even so, it must be artistic, based on truth, not on exaggeration.

Propaganda, however legitimate, can speak no louder than the truth. Such a cause as ours needs no dressing up. The honest, unvarnished truth, presented as it is, is plea enough for us, in the unbiased courts of mankind. But such courts do not exist? Then what avails thumping the tub? Will that call them into being? Let the truth speak. There has never been a better persuader.

Since we need truthful delineation, let us not add every artist whose picture of us may not be flattering to our long list of traducers. We stand in no need today of such a defense mechanism. If a white audience today needs assurance that we are not all thievish or cowardly or vicious, it is composed of half wits, and can never be convinced anyway. Certainly we can never expect to justify ourselves by heated denials of charges which perhaps have not even been suggested in the work we are denouncing.

To take a comparison at random, Ellen Glasgow has two recent novels on the Virginia gentry. In one she shows an aging aristocrat, a self-appointed lady killer, egocentric, slightly ridiculous. In another she shows three lovely ladies who stooped to "folly." It would be a rash commentator who would say that Ellen Glasgow, unflinching observer though she is, means these pictures to be understood as ensemble pictures of all white

Virginians. But the same kind of logic that some of us use on our books would go farther; it would make these books discussions of *all* white Americans.

Such reasoning would be certainly more ingenuous than intelligent.

The best rejoinder to the fuming criticism "But all Negroes aren't like that" should be "Well, what of it. Who said so?" or better, "Why bring that up?" ... But if alas we must go out of our group for authority, let this be said, "All Frenchwomen aren't like Emma Bovary but *Madame Bovary* is a great book; all Russians aren't like Vronsky, but *Ann Karenina* is a great book; all Norwegians aren't like Oswald but *Ghosts* is a great play." Books about us may not be true of all of us; but that has nothing to do with their worth.

As a corollary to the charge that certain books "aiming at representativeness" have missed their mark, comes the demand that our books must show our "best." Those who criticize thus want literature to be "idealistic"; to show them what we should be like, or more probably, what we should like to be. There's a great difference. It is sadly significant also, that by "best" Negroes, these idealists mean generally the upper reaches of society; i.e., those with money.

Porgy, because it deals with Catfish Row, is a poor book for this audience; *Green Thursday*, dealing with cornfield rustics, is a poor book; the *Walls of Jericho*, where it deals with a piano mover, is a poor book. In proportion as a book deals with our "better" class it is a better book.

According to this scale of values, a book about a Negro and a mule would be, because of the mule, a better book than one about a muleless Negro; about a Negro and a horse and buggy a better book than about the mule owner; about a Negro and a Ford, better than about the buggy rider; and a book about a Negro and a Rolls Royce better than one about a Negro and a Ford. All that it seems our writers need to do, to guarantee a perfect book and deathless reputation, is to write about a Negro and an aeroplane. Unfortunately, this economic hierarchy does not hold in literature. It would rule out most of the Nobel prize winners.

Now Porgy in his goat cart, Kildee at his ploughing, Shine in a Harlem poolroom may not be as valuable members of the body economic and politic as "more financial" brethren. (Of course, the point is debatable.) But that books about them are less interesting, less truthful, and less meritorious as works of art, is an unwarranted assumption.

Some of us look upon this prevailing treatment of the lowly negro as a concerted attack upon us. But an even cursory examination of modern literature would reveal that the major authors everywhere have dealt and are dealing with the lowly. A random ten, coming to mind, are Masefield, Hardy, Galsworthy in England; Synge and Joyce in Ireland; Hamsun in Norway; O'Neill, Willa Cather, Sherwood Anderson, Ernest Hemingway in America. Not to go back to Burns, Crabbe, Wordsworth. The dominance of the lowly as subject matter is a natural concomitant to the progress of democracy.

This does not mean that our books must deal with the plantation or lowly Negro. Each artist to his taste. Assuredly let a writer deal with that to which he can best give convincing embodiment and significant interpretation. To insist otherwise is to hamper the artist, and to add to the stereotyping which has unfortunately been too apparent in books about us. To demand on the other hand that our books exclude treatment of any character other than the "successful Negro" is a death warrant to literature.

Linked with this is the distaste for dialect. This was manifested in our much earlier thrice told denial of the spirituals. James Weldon Johnson aptly calls this "Second Generation Respectability."

Mr. Johnson is likewise responsible for a very acute criticism of dialect, from a literary point of view, rather than from that of "respectability." Now much of what he said was deserved. From Lowell's *Bigelow Papers* through the local colorists, dialect, for all of its rather eminent practitioners, has been a bit too consciously *"quaint,"* too *condescending.* Even in Maristan Chapman's studies of Tennessee mountainers there is a hint of "outlandishness" being shown for its novelty, not for its universality.

Negro dialect, however, as recorded by the most talented of our observers today, such as Julia Peterkin, Howard Odum, and Langston Hughes, has shown itself capable of much more than the "limited two stops, pathos and humor." Of course, Akers and Octavus Roy Cohen still clown, and show us Negroes who never were, on land or sea, and unreconstructed Southrons show us the pathetic old mammy weeping over vanished antebellum glories. But when we attack these, we do not attack the medium of expression. The fault is not with the material. If Daniel Webster Davis can see in the Negro "peasant" only a comic feeder on hog meat and greens, the fault is in Davis's vision, not in his subject.

Lines like these transcend humor and pathos:

> "I told dem people if you was to come home cold an' stiff in a box, I could look at you same as a stranger an' not a water wouldn' drean out my eye."

Or this:

"Death, ain't yuh got no shame?"

Or this:

"Life for me ain't been no crystal stair."

Or:

"She walked down the track, an' she never looked back,
I'm goin' whah John Henry feel dead."

Julia Peterkin, Heyward, the many other honest artists have shown us what is to be seen, if we have eyes and can use them.

There is nothing "degraded" about dialect. Dialectical peculiarities are universal. There is something about Negro dialect, in the idiom, the turn of the phrase, the music of the vowels and consonants that is worth treasuring.

Are we to descend to the level of the lady who wanted "Swing Low, Sweet Chariot" metamorphosed into "Descend, welcome vehicle, approaching for the purpose of conveying me to my residence"?

Those who are used only to the evasions and reticences of Victorian books or of Hollywood (!) (i.e., the products of Hollywood, not the city as it actually is) are.or pretend to be shocked by the frankness of modern books on the Negro. That the "low" rather than the "lowly" may often be shown, that there is pornography I do not doubt. But that every book showing frankly aspects of life is thereby salacious, I do stoutly deny. More than this, the notions that white authors show only the worst in Negro life and the best in theirs; that Negro authors show the worst to sell out to whites, are silly, and reveal woeful ignorance about modern literature.

Mamba and Hagar are libellous portraits say some; *Scarlet Sister Mary* is a showing up of a "prostitute" say others. "Our womanhood is defamed." Nay, rather, our intelligence is defamed, by urging such nonsense. For these who must have glittering falsifications of life, the movie houses exist in great plenty.

The moving picture, with its enforced happy ending, may account for our distaste for tragedy; with its idylls of the leisure class, may account for our distaste for Negro portraiture in the theatre. Maybe a shrinking optimism causes this. Whatever the reason, we do not want to see Negro plays.

Our youngsters, with some Little Theatre Movements the honorable exceptions, want to be English dukes and duchesses, and wear tuxedoes and evening gowns. Our "best" society leaders want to be mannequins.

Especially taboo is tragedy. Into these tragedies, such as *In Abraham's Bosom*, we read all kinds of fantastic lessons. "Intended to show that the Negro never wins out, but always loses." "Intended to impress upon us the futility of effort on our part." Some dramatic "critics" say in substance that the only value of plays like *Porgy* and *In Abraham's Bosom* is that they give our actors parts. "Worthwhile," "elevating" shows do not get a chance. They are pleading, one has reason to suspect, for musical comedy which may have scenes in cabarets, and wouldn't be confined to Catfish Row. With beautiful girls in gorgeous "costumes," rather than Negroes in more but tattered clothing.

"These plays are depressing," say some. Alas, the most depressing thing is such criticism. Should one insist that *In Abraham's Bosom* is invigorating, inspiring; showing a man's heroic struggle against great odds, showing the finest virtue a man can show in the face of harsh realities—enduring courage; should one insist upon that, he would belong to a very small minority, condemned as treasonous. We seem to forget that for the Negro to be conceived as a tragic figure is a great advance in American Literature. The aristocratic concept of the lowly as clowns is not so far back. That the tragedy of this "clown" meets sympathetic reception is a step forward in race relations.

I sincerely hope that I have not been crashing in open doors. I realize that there are many readers who do not fit into the audience I have attempted to depict. But these exceptions seem to me to fortify the rule. There are wise leaders who are attempting to combat supersensitive criticism. The remarks I have seen so much danger in are not generally written. But they are prevalent and powerful.

One hopes that they come more from a misunderstanding of what literature should be, than from a more harmful source. But from many indications it seems that one very dangerous state of mind produces them. It may be named—lack of mental bravery. It may be considered as a cowardly denial of our own.

It seems to acute observers that many of us, who have leisure for reading, are ashamed of being Negroes. This shame makes us harsher to the shortcomings of some perhaps not so fortunate economically. There seems to be among us a more fundamental lack of sympathy with the Negro farthest down, than there is in other groups with the same Negro.

To recapitulate. It is admitted that some books about us are definite propaganda; that in the books about us, the great diversity of our life has not been shown (which should not be surprising when we consider how recent is this movement toward realistic portraiture), that dramas about the Negro character are even yet few and far between. It *is* insisted that these books should be judged as works of literature; i.e., by their fidelity to the truth of their particular characters, not as representative pictures of all Negroes; that they should not be judged at all by the level of society shown, not at all as good or bad according to the "morality" of the characters; should not be judged as propaganda when there is no evidence, explicit or implicit, that propaganda was intended. Furthermore those who go to literature as an entertaining building up of dream worlds, purely for idle amusement, should not pass judgment at all on books which aim at fidelity to truth.

One doesn't wish to be pontifical about this matter of truth. "What is truth, asked Pontius Pilate, and would not stay for an answer." The answer would have been difficult. But it surely is not presumptuous for a Negro, in Twentieth Century America, to say that showing the world in idealistic rose colors is not fidelity to truth. We have got to look at our times and at ourselves searchingly and honestly; surely there is nothing of the far-fetched in that injunction.

But we are reluctant about heeding this injunction. We resent what doesn't flatter us. One young man, Allison Davis, who spoke courageously and capably his honest observation about our life, has been the target of second-rate attacks ever since. George Schuyler's letter bag seems to fill up whenever he states that even the slightest something may be rotten on Beale Street or Seventh Avenue. Because of their candor, Langston Hughes and Jean Toomer, humane, fine-grained artists both of them, have been received in a manner that should shame us. This is natural, perhaps, but unfortunate. Says J. S. Collis in a book about Bernard Shaw, "The Irish cannot bear criticism; for like all races who have been oppressed they are still *without mental bravery*. They are afraid to see themselves exposed to what they imagine to be adverse criticism. . . . But the future of Ireland largely depends upon *how much she is prepared to listen to criticism* and how far she is capable of preserving peace between able men." These last words are worthy of our deepest attention.

We are cowed. We have become typically bourgeois. Natural though such an evolution is, if we are *all* content with evasion of life, with personal complacency, we as a group are doomed. If we pass by on the other side, despising our brothers, we have no right to call ourselves men.

Crime, squalor, ugliness there are in abundance in our Catfish Rows, in our Memphis dives, in our Southwest Washington. But rushing away from them surely isn't the way to change them. And if we refuse to pay them any attention, through unwillingness to be depressed, we shall eventually be dragged down to their level. We, or our children. And that is true "depression."

But there is more to lowliness than "lowness." If we have eyes to see, and willingness to see, we might be able to find in Mamba an astute heroism, in Hagar a heartbreaking courage, in Porgy, a nobility, and in E. C. L. Adams's Scrip and Tad, a shrewd, philosophical irony. And all of these qualities we need, just now, to see in our group.

Because perhaps we are not so far from these characters, being identified racially with them, at least, we are revolted by Porgy's crapshooting, by Hagar's drinking, by Scarlet Sister Mary's scarletness. We want to get as far away as the end of the world. We do not see that Porgy's crapshooting is of the same fabric, fundamentally, psychologically, as a society lady's bridge playing. And upon honest investigation it conceivably might be found that it is not moral lapses that offend, so much as the showing of them, and most of all, the fact that the characters belong to a low stratum of society. Economically low, that is. No stratum has monopoly on other "lowness."

If one is concerned only with the matter of morality he could possibly remember that there is no literature which is not proud of books that treat of characters no better "morally" than Crown's Bess and Scarlet Sister Mary. But what mature audience would judge a book by the morality of its protagonist? Is *Rollo* a greater book than *Tom Jones* or even than *Tom Sawyer?*

Negro artists have enough to contend with in getting a hearing, in isolation, in the peculiar problems that beset all artists, in the mastery of form and in the understanding of life. It would be no less disastrous to demand of them that they shall evade truth, that they shall present us a Pollyanna philosophy of life, that, to suit our prejudices, they shall lie. It would mean that as self-respecting artists they could no longer exist.

The question might be asked, why should they exist? Such a question deserves no reply. It merely serves to bring us, alas, to the point at which I started.

Without great audiences we cannot have great literature.

Negro Character As Seen by White Authors

INTRODUCTION

❧ THERE ARE three types of Negroes, says Roark Bradford, in his sprightly manner: "the nigger, the 'colored person,' and the Negro—upper case N." In his foreword to *Ol' Man Adam an' His Chillun,* the source from which Marc Connelly drew *The Green Pastures,* and a book causing the author to be considered, in some circles, a valid interpreter of *the* Negro, Roark Bradford defines *the* Negro's character and potentialities. The Negro, he says, is the race leader, not too militant, concerned more with economic independence than with civil equality. The colored person, "frequently of mixed blood, loathes the blacks and despises the whites. . . . Generally he inherits the weaknesses of both races and seldom inherits the strength of either. He has the black man's emotions and the white man's inhibitions."[1] Together with the "poor white trash" it is the "colored persons" who perpetuate racial hatreds and incite race riots and lynchings. "The nigger" interests Mr. Bradford more than the rest. He is indolent, entirely irresponsible, shiftless, the bugaboo of Anglo-Saxon ideals, a poor fighter and a poor hater, primitively emotional and uproariously funny.

Such are the "original" contributions of Mr. Bradford, who states modestly that, in spite of the Negro's penchant to lying:

> I believe I know them pretty well. I was born on a plantation that was worked by them; I was nursed by one as an infant and I played with one when I was growing up. I have watched them at work in the fields,

1. Roark Bradford, *Ol' Man Adam an' His Chillun.* New York: Harper and Bros., 1928, p. xi.

in the levee camps, and on the river. I have watched them at home, in church, at their picnics and their funerals.[2]

All of this, he believes, gives him license to step forth as their interpreter and repeat stereotypes time-hallowed in the South. It doesn't. Mr. Bradford's stories remain highly amusing; his generalizations about *the* Negro remain a far better analysis of a white man than of *the* Negro. We see that, even in pontifical moments, one white Southerner cannot escape being influenced by current folk-beliefs.

Mr. Bradford's views have been restated at some length to show how obviously dangerous it is to rely upon literary artists when they advance themselves as sociologists and ethnologists. Mr. Bradford's easy pigeonholing of an entire race into three small compartments is a familiar phenomenon in American literature, where the Indian, the Mexican, the Irishman, and the Jew have been similarly treated. Authors are too anxious to have it said, "Here is *the* Negro," rather than here are a few Negroes whom I have seen. If one wishes to learn of Negro individuals observed from very specialized points of view, American literature can help him out. Some books will shed a great deal of light upon Negro experience. But if one wishes to learn of *the* Negro, it would be best to study *the* Negro himself; a study that might result in the discovery that *the* Negro is more difficult to find than the countless human beings called Negroes.

The Negro has met with as great injustice in American literature as he has in American life. The majority of books about Negroes merely stereotype Negro character. It is the purpose of this paper to point out the prevalence and history of these stereotypes. Those considered important enough for separate classification, although overlappings *do* occur, are seven in number: (1) The Contented Slave, (2) The Wretched Freeman, (3) The Comic Negro, (4) The Brute Negro, (5) The Tragic Mulatto, (6) The Local Color Negro, and (7) The Exotic Primitive.

A detailed evaluation of each of these is impracticable because of limitations of space. It can be said, however, that all of these stereotypes are marked either by exaggeration or omissions; that they all agree in stressing the Negro's divergence from an Anglo-Saxon norm to the flattery of the latter; they could all be used, as they probably are, as justification of racial proscription; they all illustrate dangerous specious generalizing from a few particulars recorded by a single observer from a restricted point of view— which is itself generally dictated by the desire to perpetuate a stereotype.

2. *Ibid.*, p. ix.

All of these stereotypes are abundantly to be found in American literature, and are generally accepted as contributions to true racial understanding. Thus one critic, setting out imposingly to discuss "the Negro character" in American literature, can still say, unabashedly, that *"The whole range of the Negro character is revealed thoroughly,"*[3] in one twenty-six-line sketch by Joel Chandler Harris of Br'er Fox and Br'er Mud Turtle.

The writer of this essay does not consider everything a stereotype that shows up the weaknesses of Negro character; sometimes the stereotype makes the Negro appear too virtuous. Nor does he believe the stereotypes of contented slaves and buffoons are to be successfully balanced by pictures of Negroes who are unbelievably intellectual, noble, self-sacrificial, and faultless. Any stereotyping is fatal to great, or even to convincing literature. Furthermore, he believes that he has considered to be stereotypes only those patterns whose frequent and tedious recurrence can be demonstrably proved by even a cursory acquaintance with the literature of the subject.

THE CONTENTED SLAVE

"Massa make de darkies lub him
'Case he was so kind. . . ."
(Stephen Foster)

The first lukewarm stirrings of abolitionary sentiment in the South were chilled with Eli Whitney's invention of the cotton gin at the close of the 18th Century. Up until this time the *raison d'être* of slavery had not been so powerful. But now there was a way open to quick wealth; Cotton was crowned King, and a huge army of black servitors was necessary to keep him upon the throne; considerations of abstract justice had to give way before economic expediency. A complete rationale of slavery was evolved.

One of the most influential of the authorities defending slavery was President Dew of William and Mary College, who stated, in 1832,

> . . . slavery had been the condition of all ancient culture, that Christianity approved servitude, and that the law of Moses had both assumed and positively established slavery. . . . It is the order of nature and of God that the being of superior faculties and knowledge, and therefore of superior power, should control and dispose of those who

3. John Herbert Nelson, *The Negro Character in American Literature.* Lawrence, Kansas: The Department of Journalism Press, 1926, p. 118.

are inferior. It is as much in the order of nature that men should enslave each other as that other animals should prey upon each other.[4]

The pamphlet of this young teacher was extensively circulated, and was substantiated by Chancellor Harper of the University of South Carolina in 1838:

> Man is born to subjection. . . . The proclivity of the natural man is to domineer or to be subservient. . . . If there are sordid, servile, and laborious offices to be performed, is it not better that there should be sordid, servile, and laborious beings to perform them?[5]

The economic argument had frequent proponents; an ex-governor of Virginia showed that, although Virginia was denied the tremendous prosperity accruing from cotton raising, it was still granted the opportunity to profit from selling Negroes to the far South. Sociologists and anthropologists hastened forward with proof of the Negro's three-fold inferiority: physically (except for his adaptability to cotton fields and rice swamps), mentally, and morally. Theologists advanced the invulnerable arguments from the Bible; in one of the "Bible Defences of Slavery" we read: "The curse of Noah upon *Ham*, had a *general* and *interminable* application to the whole Hamite race, in placing them under a *peculiar* liability of being enslaved by the races of the two other brothers."[6]

The expressions of these dominant ideas in the fiction and poetry of the period did not lag far behind. In fact, one influential novel was among the leaders of the van, for in 1832, the year in which Professor Dew stated the argument that was to elevate him to the presidency of William and Mary College, John P. Kennedy published a work that was to make him one of the most widely read and praised authors of the Southland. His ideas of the character of the Negro and of slavery are in fundamental agreement with those of Dew and Harper. According to F. P. Gaines, in *The Southern Plantation*, Kennedy's *Swallow Barn* has the historical significance of starting the plantation tradition, a tradition hoary and mildewed in our own day, but by no means moribund.

Swallow Barn is an idyllic picture of slavery on a tidewater plantation.

4. William E. Dodd, *The Cotton Kingdom*, Chapter III, Philosophy of the Cotton Planter, p. 53.

5. *Ibid.*, p. 57.

6. Josiah Priest, *Bible Defence of Slavery*. Glasgow, Ky.: W. S. Brown, 1851, p. 52.

The narrator, imagined to be from the North (Kennedy himself was from Tidewater Maryland), comes to Virginia, expecting to see a drastic state of affairs. Instead, he finds a kindly patriarchy and grateful, happy slaves. After vignettes of the Negro's laziness, mirth, vanity, improvidence, done with some charm and, for a Southern audience, considerable persuasiveness, the "Northern" narrator concludes:

> I am quite sure they never could become a happier people than I find them here. . . . No tribe of people has ever passed from barbarism to civilization whose . . . progress has been more secure from harm, more genial to their character, or better supplied with mild and beneficent guardianship, adapted to the actual state of their intellectual feebleness, than the Negroes of *Swallow Barn*. And, from what I can gather, it is pretty much the same on the other estates in this region.[7]

Shortly after the publication of *Swallow Barn*, Edgar Allan Poe wrote:

> . . . we must take into consideration the peculiar character (I may say the peculiar nature) of the Negro. . . . [Some believe that Negroes] are, like ourselves, the sons of Adam and must, therefore, have like passions and wants and feelings and tempers in all respects. This we deny and appeal to the knowledge of all who know. . . . We shall take leave to speak as of things *in esse*, in a degree of loyal devotion on the part of the slave to which the white man's heart is a stranger, and of the master's reciprocal feeling of parental attachment to his humble dependent. . . . That these sentiments in the breast of the Negro and his master are stronger than they would be under like circumstances between individuals of the white race, we believe.[8]

In *The Gold-Bug*, Poe shows this reciprocal relationship between Jupiter, a slave, and his master. Southern fiction of the thirties and forties supported the thesis of Kennedy and Poe without being so explicit. The mutual affection of the races, the slave's happiness with his status, and his refusal to accept freedom appear here and there, but the books were dedicated less to the defense of the peculiar institution than to entertainment. William Gilmore Simms, for instance, includes in *The Yemassee*, a novel

7. John P. Kennedy, *Swallow Barn*, p. 453.
8. Edgar Allan Poe, *Literary Criticism*, Vol. 1, "Slavery in the United States," p. 271.

published in the same year as *Swallow Barn*, the typical pro-slavery situation of a slave's refusing freedom: "I d—n to h—ll, maussa, ef I guine to be free!" roared the *adhesive* black, in a tone of unrestrainable determination.[9] But the burden of this book is not pro-slavery; Hector earns his freedom by the unslavish qualities of physical prowess, foresight, and courage in battle.

In 1853, Simms, in joining forces with Dew and Harper in the *Pro-Slavery Argument*, writes: "Slavery has elevated the Negro from savagery. The black man's finer traits of fidelity and docility were encouraged in his servile position. . . ."[10] Simms turned from cursory references to slavery to ardent pro-slavery defense, in company with other novelists of the South, for a perfectly definite reason. The abolitionary attacks made by men like Garrison had taken the form of pamphlets, and these had been answered in kind. The publication of *Uncle Tom's Cabin* in 1851, however, showed that the abolitionists had converted the novel into a powerful weapon. Pro-slavery authors were quick to take up this weapon, although their wielding of it was without the power of Harriet Beecher Stowe. *Swallow Barn* was reissued in 1851, and "besides the numerous controversial pamphlets and articles in periodicals there were no fewer than fourteen pro-slavery novels and one long poem published in the three years (1852–54) following the appearance of *Uncle Tom's Cabin*."[11]

These novels are all cut out of the same cloth. Like *Swallow Barn*, they omit the economic basis of slavery, and minimize "the sordid, servile and laborious offices" which Chancellor Harper had considered the due of "sordid, servile, and laborious beings." The pro-slavery authors use the first adjective only in considering free Negroes, or those who, by some quirk of nature, are disobedient; admit the second completely; and deny the third. Slavery to all of them is a beneficent guardianship, the natural and inevitable state for a childish people.

There is very little reference to Negroes working in the fields; even then they are assigned to easy tasks which they lazily perform to the tune of slave melodies. They are generally described as "leaving the fields." They are allowed to have, for additional provisions and huckstering, their own garden-plots, which they attend in their abundant leisure. Their holi-

9. William Gilmore Simms, *The Yemassee*. Richmond: B. F. Johnson Publishing Co., 1911, p. 423. The italics are mine but not the omissions.
10. Jeanette Reid Tandy, "Pro-Slavery Propaganda in American Fiction of the Fifties," *South Atlantic Quarterly*, Vol. XXI, No. 1, p. 41.
11. *Ibid.*

days are described at full length: the corn huskings, barbecuing, Yuletide parties, and hunting the possom by the light of a kindly moon.

In *Life at the South, or Uncle Tom's Cabin As It Is* (1852), Uncle Tom, out of hurt vanity, but not for any more grievous cause, runs away. His wife, Aunt Dinah, although loving Tom, realizes that her greater loyalty is due to her master, and not to her errant spouse, and refuses to escape with him. Tom, after experiencing the harshness of the unfeeling North, begs to return to slavery. In *The Planter's Northern Bride*, the bride, having come to the slave South with misgivings, is quickly converted to an enthusiast for slavery, since it presents "an aspect so tender and affectionate." One fears that the bride is not unpartisan, however, since her appearance on the plantation elicited wild cries of worship, and her beloved husband is a great ethnologist, proving that the Negro's peculiar skull and skin were decreed by the divine fiat so that he could pick cotton. In *The Yankee Slave Dealer*, the meddling abolitionist cannot persuade any slaves to run off with him except a half-witted rogue. One slave recited to him *verbatim* a minia-ture *Bible Defence of Slavery*, citing the book of the Bible, the chapter, and the verse. In *The Hireling and the Slave*, William J. Grayson, "poet laure-ate" of South Carolina, contrasts the lot of the industrial worker of the North with that of the slave. Gems of this widely read poetical disquisition follow:

> And yet the life, so unassailed by care,
> So blessed with moderate work, with ample fare,
> With all the good the starving pauper needs,
> The happier slave on each plantation leads. . . . (p. 50)

> And Christian slaves may challenge as their own,
> The blessings claimed in fabled states alone. . . . (p. 50)

This pattern of the joyous contentment of the slave in a paradisiacal bondage persisted and was strongly reenforced in Reconstruction days. If it was no longer needed for the defense of a tottering institution, it was needed for reasons nearly as exigent. Ancestor worshippers, the sons of a fighting generation, remembering bitterly the deaths or sufferings of their fathers, became elegists of a lost cause and cast a golden glow over the plantation past; unreconstructed "fire-eaters," determined to resurrect slavery as far as they were able, needed as a cardinal principle the belief that Negroes were happy as slaves, and hopelessly unequipped for freedom. Both types were persuasive, the first because the romantic idealizing of the past will always be seductive to a certain large group of readers, and the second because the sincere unremitting harping upon one argument will finally make it seem plausible. We find, therefore, that whereas *Uncle Tom's Cabin* had triumphed in the antebellum controversy, the pro-slavery works of Page, Russell, and Harris swept the field in Reconstruction days. It is from these last skillful authors, undeniably acquainted with Negro folk-life, and affectionate toward certain aspects of it, that the American reading public as a whole has accepted the delusion of the Negro as contented slave, entertaining child, and docile ward.

Mutual affection between the races is a dominant theme. Thus, Irwin Russell, the first American poet to treat Negro life in folk speech, has his ex-slave rhapsodizing about his "Mahsr John." "Washintum an' Franklum . . . wuzn't nar a one . . . come up to Mahsr John":

> Well times is changed. De war it come an' sot de nigger free
> An' now ol' Mahsr John ain't hardly wuf as much as me;
> He had to pay his debts, an' so his lan' is mos'ly gone—
> An' I declar' I's sorry for my pore ol' Mahsr John.[12]

The volume has many other references to the slave's docility toward, and worship of his master.

Irwin Russell implies throughout that the Southern white best understands how to treat the Negro. Perhaps this is one reason for Joel Chandler Harris' praise:

> But the most wonderful thing about the dialect poetry of Irwin Russell is his accurate conception of the negro character. . . . I do not know where could be found today a happier or a more perfect representation of negro character.

On reading Russell's few poems, one is struck by the limited gamut of characteristics allowed to Negroes. Inclined to the peccadilloes of cheating, lying easily; a good teller of comic stories, a child of mirth, his greatest hardship that of being kicked about by refractory mules, and his deepest emotion, compassion for his master's lost estate—surely this is hardly a "perfect" representation of even Negro folk character?

Thomas Nelson Page followed Russell's lead in poetry. In the poems of

12. Irwin Russell, *Christmas Night in the Quarters*. New York: The Century Co., 1917, pp. 63 ff.

Befo' De War, Page puts into the mouths of his Negroes yearnings for the old days and expressions of the greatest love for old marster. One old slave welcomes death if it will replace him in old "Marster's service." Old Jack entrusts his life-earnings to his son to give to young "Marster," since the latter can't work and needs them more.[13]

In most of Page's widely influential stories, there is the stock situation of the lifelong devotion of master and body-servant. In *Marse Chan*, old "Marse" is blinded in rescuing a slave from a burning barn. Sam accompanies his young Marse Chan to the war, his devotion overcoming "racial cowardice" to such a degree that he rides to the very cannon's mouth with him, and brings back his master's body. Of slavery, Sam speaks thus:

> Dem wuz good old times, marster—de bes' Sam ever see! Dey wuz, in fac'! Niggers didn't hed nothin 't all to do—jes' hed to 'ten to de feedin' an' cleanin' de hosses, an' doin' what de marster tell 'em to do; an' when dey wuz sick, dey had things sont 'em out de house, an' de same doctor come to see 'em whar ten' do de white folks when dey wuz po'ly. D'yar warn' no trouble nor nothin.[14]

Over all his fiction there is the reminiscent melancholy of an exiled Adam, banished by a flaming sword—wielded not by Michael but by a Yankee devil, from what was truly an Eden. In *The Negro: The Southerner's Problem*, we read:

> In fact, the ties of pride were such that it was often remarked that the affection of the slaves was stronger toward the whites than toward their own offspring.[15]

And in the same book there is an apostrophe to the "mammy" that is a worthy forerunner of the bids so many orators make for interracial goodwill, and of the many remunerative songs that emerge from Tin Pan Alley.

Joel Chandler Harris is better known for his valuable contribution to literature and folk-lore in recording the Uncle Remus stories than for his aid in perpetuation of the "plantation Negro" stereotype. Nevertheless, a merely cursory study of Uncle Remus' character would reveal his close

13. Thomas Nelson Page, *Befo' De War*. New York: Chas. Scribner's Sons, 1906, "Little Jack."

14. Thomas Nelson Page, *In Ole Virginia*. New York: Chas. Scribner's Sons, 1889.

15. Thomas Nelson Page, *The Negro: The Southerner's Problem*. New York: Chas. Scribner's Sons, 1904, p. 174.

relationship to the "Caesars," "Hectors," "Pompeys," *et al.* of the pro-slavery novel, and to Page's "Uncle Jack" and "Uncle Billy." In Uncle Remus's philosophizing about the old days of slavery there is still the wistful nostalgia. Harris comments, "In Middle Georgia the relations between master and slave were as perfect as they could be under the circumstances." This might mean a great deal, or nothing, but it is obvious from other words of Harris that, fundamentally, slavery was to him a kindly institution, and the Negro was contented. Slavery was:

> . . . in some of its aspects far more beautiful and inspiring than *any* of the relations between employers and the employed in this day.[16]

George Washington Cable, although more liberal in his views upon the Negro than his Southern contemporaries, gives an example of the self-abnegating servant in *Posson Jone'*. This slave uses his wits to safeguard his master. A goodly proportion of the Negro servants are used to solve the complications of their "white-folks." They are in a long literacy tradition—that of the faithful, clever servant—and they probably are just as true to Latin prototypes as to real Negroes. In the works of F. Hopkinson Smith, Harry Stilwell Edwards, and in Maurice Thompson's *Balance of Power*, we have this appearance of a black *deus ex machina*.

To deal adequately with the numerous books of elegiac reminiscence of days "befo' de war" would be beyond the scope and purpose of this essay. The tone of them all is to be found in such sad sentences as these:

> Aunt Phebe, Uncle Tom, Black Mammy, Uncle Gus, Aunt Jonas,
> Uncle Isom, and all the rest—who shall speak all your virtues or
> enshrine your simple faith and fidelity? It is as impossible as it is to
> describe the affection showered upon you by those whom you called
> "Marster" and "Mistis."[17]

Ambrose Gonzales grieves that "the old black folk are going fast" with the passing of the "strict but kindly discipline of slavery," yearning, in Tennysonian accents, "for the tender grace of a day that is dead."[18]

16. Julia Collier Harris, *Joel Chandler Harris, Editor and Essayist*. Chapel Hill: University of North Carolina Press, 1931, "The Old-Time Darky," p. 129.
17. Essie Collins Matthews, *Aunt Phebe, Uncle Tom and Others*. Columbus, Ohio: The Champlin Press, 1915, p. 13.
18. Ambrose Gonzales, *With Aesop Along the Black Border*. Columbia, S.C.: The State Co., 1924, p. xiv.

Although the realism of today is successfully discounting the sentimentalizing of the Old South, there are still many contemporary manifestations of the tradition. Hergesheimer, arch-romanticist that he is, writes that he would be happy to pay with everything the wasted presence holds for the return of the pastoral civilization based on slavery.[19]

Donald Davidson, a Tennessee poet, has written this:

> Black man, when you and I were young together,
> We knew each other's hearts. Though I am no longer
> A child, and you perhaps unfortunately
> Are no longer a child, we still understand
> Better maybe than others. There is the wall
> Between us, anciently erected. Once
> It might have been crossed, men say. But now I cannot
> Forget that I was master, and you can hardly
> Forget that you were slave. We did not build
> The ancient wall, but there it painfully is.
> Let us not bruise our foreheads on the wall.[20]

Ol' Massa's People, by Orlando Kay Armstrong, is one of the most recent of the books in which ex-slaves speak—as in Page apparently with their master's voice—their praise of slavery. The theme seems inexhaustible; in the February issue of the *Atlantic Monthly* it is restated in nearly the words that have already been quoted. Designed originally to defend slavery, it is now a convenient argument for those wishing to keep "the Negro in his place"—out of great love for him, naturally—believing that he will be happier so.

THE WRETCHED FREEMAN

"Go tell Marse Linkum, to tek his freedom back."

As a foil to the contented slave, pro-slavery authors set up another puppet—the wretched free Negro. He was necessary for the argument. Most of the pro-slavery novels paid a good deal of attention to his degradation. Either the novelist interpolated a long disquisition on the disadvantages of his state both to the country and to himself, or had his happy slaves fear contact with him as with a plague.

19. Joseph Hergesheimer, *Quiet Cities.* New York: Alfred A. Knopf, 1928, pp. 14 ff.
20. Donald Davidson, *The Tall Men.* New York: Houghton Mifflin Co., 1927, p. 39.

In *Life at the South, or Uncle Tom's Cabin As It Is,* Uncle Tom experiences harsh treatment from unfeeling Northern employers, sees Negroes frozen to death in snow storms, and all in all learns that the North and freedom is no stopping place for him. In *The Yankee Slave Dealer,* the slaves are insistent upon the poor lot of free Negroes. In *The Planter's Northern Bride,* Crissy runs away from freedom in order to be happy again in servitude. Grayson in *The Hireling and the Slave* prophesies thus:

> Such, too, the fate the Negro must deplore
> If slavery guards his subject race no more,
> If by weak friends or vicious counsels led
> To change his blessings for the hireling's bread. . . .
> There in the North in surburban dens and human sties,
> In foul excesses sung, the Negro lies;
> A moral pestilence to taint and stain.
> His life a curse, his death a social gain,
> Debased, despised, the Northern pariah knows
> He shares no good that liberty bestows;
> Spurned from her gifts, with each successive year.
> In drunken want his numbers disappear.[21]

There was a carry-over of these ideas in the Reconstruction. Harris, in one of his most moving stories, *Free Joe,* showed the tragedy of a free Negro in a slave-holding South, where he was considered a bad model by slave-owners, an economic rival by poor whites, and something to be avoided by the slaves. The story might be considered as a condemnation of a system, but in all probability was taken to be another proof of the Negro's incapacity for freedom. Although Harris wrote generously of Negro advancement since emancipation, there is little doubt that the implications of many passages furthered the stereotype under consideration.

Page, a bourbon "fire-eater," for all his yearnings for his old mammy, saw nothing of good for Negroes in emancipation:

> Universally, they [Southerners] will tell you that while the old-time Negroes were industrious, saving, and, when not misled, well-behaved, kindly, respectful, and self-respecting, and while the remnant of them who remain still retain generally these characteristics, the

21. William J. Grayson, *The Hireling and the Slave.* Charleston, S.C.: McCarter and Co., 1856, pp. 68 ff.

"new issue," for the most part, are lazy, thriftless, intemperate, inso-
lent, dishonest, and without the most rudimentary elements of morality. . . . Universally, they report a general depravity and retrogression
of the Negroes at large, in sections in which they are left to themselves, closely resembling a reversion to barbarism.[22]

The notion of the Negro's being doomed to extinction was sounded by a
chorus of pseudo-scientists, bringing forth a formidable (?) array of proofs.
Lafcadio Hearn yielded to the lure of posing as a prophet:

As for the black man, he must disappear with the years. Dependent
like the ivy, he needs some strong oak-like friend to cling to. His
support has been cut from him, and his life must wither in its pros-
trate helplessness. Will he leave no trace of his past? . . . Ah, yes!
. . . the weird and beautiful melodies born in the hearts of the poor,
child-like people to whom freedom was destruction.[23]

Many were the stories ringing changes on the theme: "Go tell Marse Lin-
kum, to tek his freedom back." Thus, in *The Carolina Low Country*, Mr.
Sass writes of Old Aleck, who, on being freed, spoke his little piece: "Miss,
I don't want no wagis." "God bless you, old Aleck," signs Mr. Sass.

Modern neo-confederates repeat the stereotype. Allen Tate, co-member
with Donald Davidson of the Nashville saviors of the South, implies in
Jefferson Davis, His Rise and Fall, that to educate a Negro beyond his
station brings him unhappiness. One of the chief points of agreement in
the Neo-Confederate *I'll Take My Stand* by Davidson, Tate and ten others
is that freedom has proved to be a perilous state for the Negro. Joseph
Hergesheimer agrees: "A free Negro is more often wretched than not."[24]
"Slavery was gone, the old serene days were gone. Negroes were bad because they were neither slave nor free."[25] And finally, a modern illustration
must suffice. Eleanor Mercein Kelly in an elegy for the vanishing South,
called *Monkey Motions*, pities "the helplessness of a simple jungle folk, a
bandar-log, set down in the life of cities and expected to be men."[26]

22. Thomas Nelson Page, *The Negro: The Southerner's Problem, op. cit.*, p. 80.
23. Lafcadio Hearn, *Letters from the Raven*. New York: A. & C. Boni, 1930, p. 168.
24. Joseph Hergesheimer, *op. cit.*, p. 137.
25. *Ibid.*, p. 293.
26. Blanche Colton Williams, *O. Henry Memorial Award Prize Stories of 1927*. Garden City: Doubleday, Doran & Co., p. 207.

It is, all in all, a sad picture that these savants give. What concerns us here, however, is its persistence, a thing inexpressibly more sad.

THE COMIC NEGRO

"That Reminds Me of a Story. There Were Once Two Ethiopians, Sambo and Rastus. . . ."

(1,001 After-Dinner Speakers.)

The stereotype of the "comic Negro" is about as ancient as the "contented slave." Indeed, they might be considered complementary, since, if the Negro could be shown as perpetually mirthful, his state could not be so wretched. This is, of course, the familiar procedure when conquerors depict a subject people. English authors at the time of Ireland's greatest persecution built up the stereotype of the comic Irishman, who fascinated English audiences, and unfortunately, in a manner known to literary historians, influenced even Irish authors.[27] Thus, we find, in a melodrama about Irish life, an English officer soliloquizing:

> I swear, the Irish nature is beyond my comprehension. A strange people!—merry 'mid their misery—laughing through their tears, like the sun shining through the rain. Yet what simple philosophers they! They tread life's path as if 'twere strewn with roses devoid of thorns, and make the most of life with natures of sunshine and song.[28]

Any American not reading the words "Irish nature" could be forgiven for taking the characterization to refer to American Negroes. Natures of sunshine and song, whose wretchedness becomes nothing since theirs is a simple philosophy of mirth! So runs the pattern.

In her excellent book, *American Humor,* Constance Rourke points out the Negro as one of the chief ingredients of the potpourri of American humor. She traces him as far back as the early '20's when Edwin Forrest made up as a Southern plantation Negro to excite the risibilities of Cincinnati. In *The Spy,* Cooper belabors the grotesqueness of Caesar's appearance, although Caesar is not purely and simply the buffoon:

27. *Vide:* George Bernard Shaw's *John Bull's Other Island,* Daniel Corkery's *Synge and Anglo-Irish Literature,* Yeats's *Plays and Controversies,* Lady Gregory's *Our Irish Theatre,* for attacks upon the "comic" Irishman stereotype.

28. John Fitzgerald Murphy, *The Shamrock and the Rose.* Boston: Walter H. Baker Co., n.d., p. 25.

. . . But it was in his legs that nature had indulged her most capricious humor. There was an abundance of material injudiciously used. The calves were neither before nor behind, but rather on the outer side of the limb, inclining forward. . . . The leg was placed so near the center (of the foot) as to make it sometimes a matter of dispute whether he was not walking backward.[29]

Kennedy in his *Swallow Barn* not only reveals the Negro as delighted by the master's benevolence, but also as delighting the master by his ludicrous departure from the Anglo-Saxon norm. Kennedy revels in such descriptions as the following:

His face . . . was principally composed of a pair of protuberant lips, whose luxuriance seemed intended as an indemnity for a pair of crushed nostrils. . . . Two bony feet occupied shoes, each of the superfices and figure of a hoe. . . . Wrinkled, decrepit old men, with faces shortened as if with drawing strings, noses that seemed to have run all to nostril, and with feet of the configuration of a mattock. . . . [30]

It was in the early '30's, however, that T. D. Rice first jumped "Jim Crow" in the theatres along the Ohio River and set upon the stage the "minstrel Negro." Apparently immortal, this stereotype was to involve in its perpetuation such famous actors as Joseph Jefferson and David Belasco, to make Amos 'n' Andy as essential to American domesticity as a car in every garage, and to mean affluence for a Jewish comedian of whom only one gesture was asked: that he sink upon one knee, extend his white-gloved hands, and cry out "Mammy."

In pro-slavery fiction the authors seemed to agree on the two aspects of the comic Negro—that he was ludicrous to others, and forever laughing himself. Grayson writes in *The Hireling and the Slave:*

The long, loud laugh, that freemen seldom share,
Heaven's boon to bosoms unapproached by care;
And boisterous jest and humor unrefined. . . .[31]

To introduce comic relief, perhaps, in stories that might defeat their own purposes if confined only to the harrowing details of slavery, anti-slavery

29. James Fenimore Cooper, *The Spy.* New York: Scott, Foresman Co., 1927, p. 45.
30. Kennedy, *op. cit., passim.*
31. Grayson, *op. cit.,* p. 51.

authors had their comic characters. Topsy is the classic example; it is noteworthy that in contemporary acting versions of "Uncle Tom's Cabin," Topsy and the minstrel show note, if not dominant, are at least of equal importance to the melodrama of Eliza and the bloodhounds.

Reconstruction literature developed the stereotype. Russell's Negroes give side-splitting versions of the Biblical story (foreshadowing Bradford's *Ol' Man Adam an' His Chillun*), or have a fatal fondness for propinquity to a mule's rear end. Page's Negroes punctuate their worship of "ole Marse" with "Kyah-kyahs," generally directed at themselves. The humor of Uncle Remus is nearer to genuine folk-humor, which—it might be said in passing—is *not* the same as the "comic Negro" humor. Negroes in general, in the Reconstruction stories, are seen as creatures of mirth—who wouldn't suffer from hardship, even if they had to undergo it. Thus a Negro, sentenced to the chain-gang for stealing a pair of breeches, is made the theme of a comic poem.[32] This is illustrative. There may be random jokes in Southern court rooms, but joking about the Negroes' experiences with Southern "justice" and with the chain-gang is rather ghastly—like laughter at the mouth of hell. Creatures of sunshine and of song!

The "comic Negro" came into his own in the present century, and brought his creators into theirs. Octavius Cohen, who looks upon the idea of Negro doctors and lawyers and society belles as the height of the ridiculous, served such clienteles as that of *The Saturday Evening Post* for a long time with the antics of Florian Slappey. His work is amusing at its best, but is pseudo-Negro. Instead of being a handicap, however, that seems a recommendation to his audience. Trusting to most moth-eaten devices of farce, and interlarding a Negro dialect never heard on land or sea— compounded more of Dogberry and Mrs. Malaprop than of Birmingham Negroes,[33] he has proved to the whites that all along they have known the real Negro—"Isn't he funny, now!"—and has shown to Negroes what whites wanted them to resemble. Mrs. Octavius Roy Cohen follows in the wake of her illustrious husband in *Our Darktown Press*, a gleaning of "boners" from Aframerican newspapers. Editorial carelessness is sadly enough familiar in race journals; every item in the book is vouched for, but the

32. Belle Richardson Harrison, *Poetry of the Southern States*, edited by Clement Wood. Girard, Kansas: Haldeman-Julius Co., 1924, p. 36.

33. "Yeh, an' was he to git one good bite at a cullud man like me, he'd exterminate me so quick I wouldn't even have a chance to notrify my heirs," "I ain't hahdly sawn her right recent," are examples of his inimitable (fortunately so, although Amos an' Andy try it in "I'se regusted," etc.) dialect; "Drastic" "Unit" "Quinine" "Midnight," and "Sons and Daughters of I Will Arise" are examples of his nomenclature.

total effect is the reenforcing of a stereotype that America loves to believe in.

Arthur E. Akers, with a following in another widely read magazine, is another farceur. He uses the situation of the domestic difficulty, as old as medieval fabliaux and farces—and places it in a Southern Negro community, and has his characters speak an approximation to Negro dialect—but too slick and 'literary' for conviction. Irate shrews and "Milquetoast" husbands, with razors wielded at departing parts of the anatomy, are Akers' stock-in-trade. Hugh Wiley with his Wildcat, inseparable from his goat, Lady Luck, unsavory but a talisman, is another creator of the farce that Negro life is too generally believed to be. E. K. Means, with obvious knowledge of Southern Negro life, is concerned to show in the main its ludicrous side, and Irvin Cobb, with a reputation of after-dinner wit to uphold, is similarly confined.

The case of Roark Bradford is different. An undoubted humorist, in the great line of Twain and the tall tales of the Southwest, he gleans from a rich store of Negro speech and folk-ways undeniably amusing tales. But as his belief about the Negro (cf. Introduction) might attest, he has a definite attitude to the Negro to uphold. His stories of the easy loves of the levee (frequently found in *Collier's*) concentrate upon the comic aspect of Negro life, although another observer might well see the tragic. In *Ol' Man Adam an' His Chillun* we have farce manufactured out of the Negro's religious beliefs. It seems to the writer that the weakest sections of *Green Pastures* stick closest to Bradford's stories, and that the majesty and reverence that can be found in the play must come from Marc Connelly. In *John Henry*, Bradford has definitely weakened his material by making over a folk-hero into a clown.

Although the situations in which the comic Negro finds himself range from the fantastic as in Cohen, to the possible as in "The Two Black Crows" and in "Amos 'n' Andy," his characteristics are fairly stable. The "comic Negro" is created for the delectation of a white audience, condescending and convinced that any departure from the Anglo-Saxon norm is amusing, and that any attempt to enter the special provinces of whites, such as wearing a dress suit, is doubly so. The "comic Negro" with certain physical attributes exaggerated—with his razor (generally harmless), his love for watermelon and gin, for craps, his haunting of chicken roosts, use of big words he doesn't understand, grandiloquent names and titles, "loud" clothes, bluster, hysterical cowardice, and manufactured word-play—has pranced his way by means of books, vaudeville skits, shows, radio programs, advertisements, and after-dinner speeches, into the folklore of the nation. As Guy B. Johnson urges there is a sort of—

> . . . folk attitude of the white man toward the Negro. . . . One cannot help noticing that the white man must have his fun out of the Negro, even when writing serious novels about him. This is partly conscious, indeed a necessity, if one is to portray Negro life as it is, for Negroes are human and behave like other human beings. Sometimes it is unconscious, rising out of our old habit of associating the Negro with the comical.[34]

In pointing out the stereotype, one does not deny the rich comedy to be found in Negro life. One is insisting, however, that any picture concentrating upon this to the exclusion of all else is entirely inadequate, that many of the most popular creators of the "comic Negro," "doctor" their material, and are far from accurate in depicting even the small area of Negro experience they select, and that too often they exceed the prerogative of comedy by making copy out of persecution and injustice.

THE BRUTE NEGRO

"All Scientific Investigation of the Subject Proves the Negro to Be An Ape."

(Chas. Carroll, *The Negro a Beast.*)

Because the pro-slavery authors were anxious to prove that slavery had been a benefit to the Negro in removing him from savagery to Christianity, the stereotype of the "brute Negro" was relatively insignificant in antebellum days. There were references to vicious criminal Negroes in fiction (vicious and criminal being synonymous to discontented and refractory), but these were considered as exceptional cases of half-wits led astray by abolitionists. *The Bible Defence of Slavery*, however, in which the Rev. Priest in a most unclerical manner waxes wrathful at abolitionists, sets forth with a great array of theological argument and as much ridiculousness, proofs of the Negro's extreme lewdness. Sodom and Gomorrah were destroyed because these were strongholds of *Negro* vice. The book of Leviticus proved that *Negroes*

34. Guy B. Johnson, "Folk Values in Recent Literature on the Negro" in *Folk-Say*, edited by B. A. Botkin, Norman, Oklahoma, 1930, p. 371.

outraged all order and decency of human society. Lewdness of the most hideous description was the crime of which they were guilty, blended with idolatry in their adoration of the gods, who were carved out of wood, painted and otherwise made, so as to represent the wild passions of lascivious desires. . . . The baleful fire of unchaste amour rages through the negro's blood more fiercely than in the blood of any other people . . . on which account they are a people who are suspected of being but little acquainted with the virtue of chastity, and of regarding very little the marriage oath. . . .[35]

H. R. Helper, foe of slavery, was no friend of the Negro, writing, in 1867, *Nojoque*, a lurid condemnation of the Negro, setting up black and beastly as exact synonyms. Van Evrie's *White Supremacy and Negro Subordination, or Negroes A Subordinate Race, and (so-called) Slavery Its Normal Condition* gave "anthropological" support to the figment of the "beastly Negro," and *The Negro a Beast* (1900) gave theological support. The title page of this book runs:

> The Reasoner of the Age, the Revelator of the Century! The Bible As It Is! The Negro and his Relation to the Human Family! The Negro a beast, but created with articulate speech, and hands, that he may be of service to his master—the White Man. . . . by Chas. Carroll, who has spent 15 years of his life and $20,000.00 in its compilation. . . .

Who could ask for anything more?

Authors stressing the mutual affection between the races looked upon the Negro as a docile mastiff. In the Reconstruction this mastiff turned into a mad dog. "Damyanks," carpetbaggers, scalawags, and New England schoolmarms affected him with the rabies. The works of Thomas Nelson Page are good examples of this metamorphosis. When his Negro characters are in their place, loyally serving and worshipping ole Marse, they are admirable creatures, but in freedom they are beasts, as his novel *Red Rock* attests. *The Negro: The Southerner's Problem* says that the state of the Negro since emancipation is one of minimum progress and maximum regress.

> [This] is borne out by the increase of crime among them, by the increase of superstition, with its black trail of unamable immorality

35. Josiah Priest, *op. cit.*, Eighth Section, *passim.*

and vice; by the homicides and murders, and by the outbreak and growth of that brutal crime which has chiefly brought about the frightful crime of lynching which stains the *good name of the South* and has spread northward with the spread of the ravisher. . . . The crime of rape . . . is the fatal product of new conditions. . . . The Negro's passion, always his controlling force, is now, since the new teaching, for the white woman. [Lynching is justifiable] for it has its root deep in the basic passions of humanity; the determination to put an end to the *ravishing of their women by an inferior race,* or by any race, no matter what the consequence. . . . A crusade has been preached against lynching, even as far as England; but none has been attempted against the ravishing and tearing to pieces of white women and children.[36]

The best known author of Ku Klux Klan fiction after Page is Thomas Dixon. Such works as *The Clansman,* and *The Leopard's Spots,* because of their sensationalism and chapter titles (e.g., "The Black Peril," "The Unspoken Terror," "A Thousand Legged Beast," "The Hunt for the Animal"), seemed just made for the mentality of Hollywood, where D. W. Griffith's in *The Birth of a Nation* made for Thomas Dixon a dubious sort of immortality, and finally fixed the stereotype in the mass-mind. The stock Negro in Dixon's books, unless the shuffling hat-in-hand servitor, is a gorilla-like imbecile, who "springs like a tiger" and has the "black claws of a beast." In both books there is a terrible rape, and a glorious ride of the Knights on a Holy Crusade to avenge Southern civilization. Dixon enables his white geniuses to discover the identity of the rapist by using "a microscope of sufficient power [to] reveal on the retina of the dead eyes the image of this devil as if etched there by fire." . . . The doctor sees "The bestial figure of a negro—his huge black hand plainly defined. . . . It was Gus." Will the wonders of science never cease? But, perhaps, after all, Negroes have been convicted on even flimsier evidence. Fortunately for the self-respect of American authors, this kind of writing is in abeyance today. Perhaps it fell because of the weight of its own absurdity. But it would be unwise to underestimate this stereotype. It is probably of great potency in certain benighted sections where Dixon, if he could be read, would be applauded—and it certainly serves as a convenient self-justification for a mob about to uphold white supremacy by a lynching.

36. Page, *The Negro: The Southerner's Problem, passim* (italics mine).

THE TRAGIC MULATTO

"The gods bestow on me
A life of hate,
The white man's gift to see
A nigger's fate."
("The Mulatto Addresses His Savior
on Christmas Morning," Seymour
Gordden Link.)

Stereotyping was by no means the monopoly of pro-slavery authors defending their type of commerce, or justifying their ancestors. Anti-slavery
authors, too, fell into the easy habit, but with a striking difference. Where
pro-slavery authors had predicated a different set of characteristics for the
Negroes, a distinctive sub-human nature, and had stereotyped in accordance with such a comforting hypothesis, anti-slavery authors insisted that
the Negro had a common humanity with the whites, that in given circumstances a typically human type of response was to be expected, unless
certain other powerful influences were present. The stereotyping in abolitionary literature, therefore, is not stereotyping of *character*, but of *situation*. Since the novels were propagandistic, they concentrated upon abuses:
floggings, the slave mart, the domestic slave trade, forced concubinage,
runaways, slave hunts, and persecuted freemen—all of these were frequently repeated. Stereotyped or not, heightened if you will, the anti-slavery novel has been supported by the verdict of history—whether recorded
by Southern or Northern historians. Facts, after all, are abolitionist. Especially the fact that the Colonel's lady and old Aunt Dinah are sisters under
the skin.

Anti-slavery authors did at times help to perpetuate certain pro-slavery
stereotypes. Probably the novelists knew that harping upon the gruesome,
to the exclusion of all else, would repel readers, who—like their present-
day descendants—yearn for happy endings and do not wish their quick
consciences to be harrowed. At any rate, comic relief, kindly masters (in
contrast to the many brutes), loyal and submissive slaves (to accentuate
the wrongs inflicted upon them) were scattered throughout the books. Such
tempering of the attacks was turned to pro-slavery uses. Thus, Harris
writes:

It seems to me to be impossible for any unprejudiced person to read
Mrs. Stowe's book and fail to see in it a defence of American slavery

as she found it in Kentucky. . . . The real moral that Mrs. Stowe's book teaches is that the possibilities of slavery . . . are shocking to the imagination, while the realities, under the best and happiest conditions, possess a romantic beauty and a tenderness all their own. . . .[37]

Anti-slavery fiction did proffer one stereotype, doomed to unfortunate longevity. This is the tragic mulatto. Pro-slavery apologists had almost entirely omitted (with so many other omissions) mention of concubinage. If anti-slavery authors, in accordance with Victorian gentility, were wary of illustrating the practice, they made great use nevertheless of the offspring of illicit unions. Generally the heroes and heroines of their books are near-whites. These are the intransigent, the resentful, the mentally alert, the proofs of the Negro's possibilities. John Herbert Nelson says with some point:

Abolitionists tried, by making many of their characters almost white, to work on racial feeling as well. This was a curious piece of inconsistency on their part, an indirect admission that a white man in chains was more pitiful to behold than the African similarly placed. Their most impassioned plea was in behalf of a person little resembling their swarthy protegés, the quadroon or octoroon.[38]

Nelson himself, however, shows similar inconsistency, as he infers that the "true African—essentially gay, happy-go-lucky, rarely ambitious or idealistic, the eternal child of the present moment, able to leave trouble behind—is unsuited for such portrayal. . . . Only the mulattoes and others of mixed blood have, so far, furnished us with material for convincing tragedy."[39]

The tragic mulatto appears in both of Mrs. Stowe's abolitionary novels. In *Uncle Tom's Cabin*, the fugitives Liza and George Harris and the rebellious Cassy are mulattoes. Uncle Tom, the pure black, remains the paragon of Christian submissiveness. In *Dred*, Harry Gordon and his wife are nearly white. Harry is an excellent manager, and a proud, unsubmissive type:

Mr. Jekyl, that humbug don't go down with me! I'm no more of the race of Ham than you are! I'm Colonel Gordon's oldest son—as white

37. Julia Collier Harris, *op. cit.*, p. 117.
38. John Herbert Nelson, *op. cit.*, p. 84.
39. *Ibid.*, p. 136.

as my brother, who you say owns me! Look at my eyes, and my hair, and say if any of the rules about Ham pertain to me.[40]

The implication that there are "rules about Ham" that do pertain to blacks is to be found in other works. Richard Hildreth's *Archy Moore, or The White Slave,* has as its leading character a fearless, educated mulatto, indistinguishable from whites; Boucicault's *The Octoroon* sentimentalizes the hardships of a slave girl; both make the mixed blood the chief victim of slavery.

Cable, in the *Grandissimes,* shows a Creole mulatto educated beyond his means, and suffering ignominy, but he likewise shows in the character of Bras-Coupé that he does not consider intrepidity and vindictiveness the monopoly of mixed-bloods. In *Old Creole Days,* however, he discusses the beautiful octoroons, whose best fortune in life was to become the mistress of some New Orleans dandy. He shows the tragedy of their lives, but undoubtedly contributed to the modern stereotype that the greatest yearning of the girl of mixed life is for a white lover. Harriet Martineau, giving a contemporary portrait of old New Orleans, wrote:

> The quadroon girls . . . are brought up by their mothers to be what they have been; the mistresses of white gentlemen. The boys are some of them sent to France; some placed on land in the back of the State. . . . The women of their own color object to them, *"ils sont si degoutants!"*[41]

Lyle Saxon says that "the free men of color are always in the background; to use the Southern phrase, 'they know their place.' "

The novelists have kept them in the background. Many recent novels show this: *White Girl, The No-Nation Girl, A Study in Bronze, Gulf Stream, Dark Lustre*—all of these show luridly the melodrama of the lovely octoroon girl. Indeed "octoroon" has come to be a feminine noun in popular usage.

The stereotype that demands attention, however, is the notion of mulatto character, whether shown in male or female. This character works itself out with mathematical symmetry. The older theses ran: First, the mulatto inherits the vices of both races and none of the virtues; second, any achievement of a Negro is to be attributed to the white blood in his

40. Harriet Beecher Stowe, *Nina Gordon, or Dred.* Boston: Houghton, Mifflin and Co., 1881, p. 142.
41. Quoted in Lyle Saxon, *Fabulous New Orleans.* New York: The Century Co., 1928, p. 182.

veins. The logic runs that even inheriting the worst from whites is sufficient for achieving among Negroes. The present theses are based upon these: The mulatto is a victim of a divided inheritance; from his white blood come his intellectual strivings, his unwillingness to be a slave; from his Negro blood come his baser emotional urges, his indolence, his savagery.

Thus, in *The No-Nation Girl*, Evans Wall writes of his tragic heroine, Précieuse:

> Her dual nature had not developed its points of difference. The warring qualities, her double inheritance of Caucasian and black mingled in her blood, had not yet begun to disturb, and torture, and set her apart from either race. . . .
>
> [As a child,] Précieuse had learned to dance as soon as she could toddle about on her shapely little legs; half-savage little steps with strange movements of her body, exotic gestures and movements that had originated among the remote ancestors of her mother's people in some hot African jungle.
>
> . . . the wailing cry of the guitar was as primitive and disturbing as the beat of a tom-tom to dusky savages gathered for an orgy of dancing and passion in some moon-flooded jungle. . . . Self-control reached its limit. The girl's half-heritage of savagery rose in a flood that washed away all trace of her father's people except the supersensitiveness imparted to her taut nerves. She must dance or scream to relieve the rising torrent of response to the wild, monotonous rhythm.

It is not long before the girl is unable to repress, what Wall calls, the lust inherited from her mother's people; the environment of debauchery, violence, and rapine is exchanged for concubinage with a white paragon, which ends, of course, in the inevitable tragedy. The girl "had no right to be born."

Dark Lustre, by Geoffrey Barnes, transfers the main essentials of the foregoing plot to Harlem. Aline, of the darkly lustrous body, thus analyzes herself in accordance with the old clichés: "The black half of me is ashamed of itself for being there, and every now and then crawls back into itself and tries to let the white go ahead and pass. . . ." Says the author: "There was too much of the nigger in her to let her follow a line of reasoning when the black cloud of her emotions settled over it." Half-white equals reason; half-black equals emotion. She too finds her ideal knight in a white man, and death comes again to the tragic octoroon who should never have been born. *White Girl, Gulf Stream, A Study in Bronze* are in substance very similar to these.

Roark Bradford in *This Side of Jordan* gives an unconscious *reductio ad absurdum* of this stereotype.

> The blade of a razor flashed through the air. Scrap has concealed it in the folds of her dress. Her Negro blood sent it unerringly between two ribs. Her Indian blood sent it back for an unnecessary second and third slash.

It might be advanced that Esquimaux blood probably would have kept her from being chilled with horror. The strangest items are attributed to different racial strains: In *No-Nation Girl* a woman cries out in childbirth because of her Negro expressiveness; from the back of Précieuse's "ankles down to her heels, the flesh was slightly thicker"—due to her Negro blood; Lessie in Welbourn Kelley's *Inchin' Along* "strongly felt the urge to see people, to talk to people. . . . That was the white in her maybe. Or maybe it was the mixture of white and black."

This kind of writing should be discredited by its patent absurdity. It is generalizing of the wildest sort, without support from scientific authorities. And yet it has set these *idées fixés* in the mob mind: The Negro of unmixed blood is no theme for tragedy; rebellion and vindictiveness are to be expected only from the mulatto; the mulatto is victim of a divided inheritance and therefore miserable; he is a "man without a race" worshipping the whites and despised by them, despising and despised by Negroes, perplexed by his struggle to unite a white intellect with black sensuousness. The fate of the octoroon girl is intensified—the whole desire of her life is to find a white lover, and then go down, accompanied by slow music, to a tragic end. Her fate is so severe that in some works disclosure of "the single drop of midnight" in her veins makes her commit suicide.

The stereotype is very flattering to a race which, for all its self-assurance, seems to stand in great need of flattery. But merely looking at one of its particulars—that white blood means asceticism and Negro blood means unbridled lust—will reveal how flimsy the whole structure is. It is ingenuous that mathematical computation of the amount of white blood in a mulatto's veins will explain his character. And it is a widely held belief. But it is nonsense, all the same.

THE LOCAL COLOR NEGRO

"The defects of local color inhere in the constitution of the cult itself, which, as its name suggests, thought . . . first of the piquant surfaces and then—if at all—of the stubborn deeps of human life."
(Carl Van Doren, *Contemporary American Novelists.*)

Local color stresses the quaint, the odd, the picturesque, the different. It is an attempt to convey the peculiar quality of a locality. Good realistic practice would insist upon the localizing of speech, garb, and customs; great art upon the revelation of the universal beneath these local characteristics. Local color is now in disrepute because of its being contented with merely the peculiarity of dialect and manners. As B. A. Botkin, editor of *Folk-Say*, has stated: "In the past [local consciousness] has been narrowly sectional rather than broadly human, superficially picturesque rather than deeply interpretative, provincial without being indigenous."[42]

The "local color Negro" is important in any study of the Negro character in American literature. But, since the local colorists of the Negro were more concerned with fidelity to speech and custom, with revelation of his difference in song and dance and story, than with revelation of Negro character, they accepted at face valuation the current moulds into which Negro character had been forced. Therefore, local colorists have been and will be considered under other heads. Page and Russell were local colorists in that they paid close attention to Negro speech, but the Negro they portrayed was the same old contented slave. Their study of Negro speech, however, was fruitful and needed—for pro-slavery authors had been as false in recording Negro speech as they were in picturing Negro experience. Kennedy, for instance, forces a confessedly wretched dialect into the mouths of poor Negroes, and W. L. G. Smith has his Shenandoah Negroes speak Gullah, because his master, Simms, had written of South Carolina Negroes.

Cable, one of the best of the local colorists, in *The Grandissimes*, goes a step beyond the mere local color formula; *Old Creole Days* is local color, but has been considered under the "Tragic Mulatto." The Negroes in Lyle Saxon's old and new New Orleans, E. Larocque Tinker's old New Orleans, R. Emmett Kennedy's Gretna Green, are in the main kinsfolk to the contented slave; in Evans Wall's Mississippi canebrakes are exotic primitives, or tragic mulattoes; on Roark Bradford's levees are primitives; and those on Julia Peterkin's Blue Brook plantation, in Heyward's Catfish Row, and in John Vandercook's Surinam, Liberia, and Haiti, usually surmount, in the writer's opinion, the deficiencies of local color. Stereotyped, or genuinely interpreted, however, they all agree in one respect: they show the peculiar differences of certain Negroes in well-defined localities.

John B. Sale in *The Tree Named John* records with sympathy the dialect, superstitions, folk-ways of Mississippi Negroes. He is meticulous, per-

42. B. A. Botkin, *Folk-Say, A Regional Miscellany*. Norman: The Oklahoma Folk-Lore Society, 1929, p. 12.

haps to a fault, in his dialectal accuracy; the milieu is correspondingly convincing. His Negroes do carry on the pattern of mutual affection between the races—and yet they are far nearer flesh and blood than those of Page. Samuel Stoney and Gertrude Shelby, in *Black Genesis*, give the peculiarities of the Gullah Negro's cosmogony. Care is paid to fidelity in recording the dialect, but the authors' comments reveal a certain condescension toward quaintness which is the usual bane of local colorists. In *Po' Buckra* the authors reveal the localized tragedy of the "brass-ankle"— the Croatan-Negro-near-white caste. Much of the "tragic mulatto" theme is in this book, as well as the purely local color interest. Ambrose Gonzales in his Gullah renditions of Aesop, and in his tales of the "black border," reveals for the curious the intricacies of a little known Negro dialect, following the lead of Harris, and C. C. Jones, who recorded the Br'er Rabbit tales in the dialect of the Georgia coast.

Although most of these authors who dwell upon quaint and picturesque divergencies are discussed under other headings, it will not do to underestimate this local color Negro. The showing of Negro peculiarities in speech, superstitions, and customs has been popular for many years, and is likely to be for a long while yet. It undoubtedly has its artistic uses; but being an end in itself is surely not the chief of them.

THE EXOTIC PRIMITIVE

"Then I saw the Congo, cutting through the black. . . ."
—(Vachel Lindsay)

This stereotype grew up with America's post-war revolt against Puritanism and Babbittry. Literary critics urged a return to spontaneity, to unrestrained emotions; American literature had been too long conventional, drab, without music and color. Human nature had been viewed with too great a reticence. Sex, which the Victorians had considered unmentionable, was pronounced by the school of Freud to have an overwhelming importance in motivating our conduct. So the pendulum swung from the extreme of Victorian prudishness to that of modern expressiveness.

To authors searching "for life in the raw," Negro life and character seemed to beg for exploitation. There was the Negro's savage inheritance, as they conceived it: hot jungle nights, the tom-tom calling to esoteric orgies. There were the frankness and violence to be found in any underprivileged group, or on any frontier. There were the traditional beliefs of the Negro being a creature of his appetites, and although pro-slavery fiction had usually (because of Victorianism) limited these to his yearnings for hog meat and greens, 'possum and yams, and for whiskey on holidays, Reconstruction fiction had stressed his lustfulness. He seemed to be cut out for the hands of certain authors. They promptly rushed to Harlem for color. In Harlem dives and cabarets they found what they believed to be *the* Negro, *au naturel.*

The figure who emerges from their pages is a Negro synchronized to a savage rhythm, living a life of ecstasy, superinduced by jazz (repetition of the tom-tom, awakening vestigial memories of Africa) and gin, that lifted him over antebellum slavery, and contemporary economic slavery, and placed him in the comforting fastnesses of their "mother-land." A kinship exists between this stereotype and that of the contented slave; one is merely a "jazzed-up" version of the other, with cabarets supplanting cabins, and Harlemized "blues," instead of the spirituals and slave reels. Few were the observers who saw in the Negroes' abandon a release from the troubles of this world similar to that afforded in slavery by their singing. Many there were, however, who urged that the Harlem Negro's state was that of an inexhaustible *joie de vivre.*

Carl Van Vechten was one of the pioneers of the hegira from downtown to Harlem; he was one of the early discoverers of the cabaret; and his novel, *Nigger Heaven,* is to the exotic pattern what *Swallow Barn* was to the contented slave. All of the possibilities of the development of the type are inherent in the book. In the prologue, we have the portrait of the "creeper," Don Juan of Seventh Avenue, whose amatory prowess causes him to be sought by women unknown to him. We feel that this prologue sets the tone of the work: we are going to see the Harlem of gin mills and cabarets, of kept men and loose ladies, of all-day sleepers and all-night roisterers. Van Vechten, who was already famed as a sophisticated romantic novelist, writes graphically of this Harlem. His style invited emulation from young men desiring to be men-about-town first and then novelists, just as Kennedy invited emulation from young Southerners desiring to defend slavery first. Van Vechten's novel does more than present the local color of Harlem; there is as well the character study of a young Negro intellectual who cannot withstand the dissipations of the "greatest Negro city." But the Bohemian life in Harlem is the main thing, even in this youngster's life. According to the publisher's blurb, "Herein is caught the fascination and tortured ecstasies of Harlem. . . . The author tells the story of modern Negro life." The blurb claims too much. There is another, there are many other Harlems. And *the* story of modern Negro life will never be found in one volume, or in a thousand.

Lasca Sartoris, exquisite, gorgeous, golden-brown Messalina of Seventh Avenue, is one of the chief characters of the book. On seeing her one of the characters comments: "Whew! She'll make a dent in Harlem." She does. She causes the young hero, Byron, in a drunken rage, to empty his gun in the body of one of her lovers, although the man was already dead, and a policeman was approaching.

Van Vechten has a noted magazine editor comment pontifically on the possibilities of Negro literature:

> Nobody has yet written a good gambling story; nobody has gone into the curious subject of the divers tribes of the region. . . . There's the servant-girl, for instance. Nobody has ever done the Negro servant-girl, who refuses to 'live in.' Washing dishes in the day-time, she returns at night to her home in Harlem where she smacks her daddy in the jaw or else dances and makes love. On the whole I should say she has the best time of any domestic servant in the world. . . . The Negro fast set does everything the Long Island fast set does, plays bridge, keeps the bootlegger busy, drives around in Rolls-Royces and commits adultery, but it is vastly more amusing than the Long Island set for the simple reason that it is *amused*. . . . Why, Roy McKain visited Harlem just once and then brought me in a cabaret yarn about a Negro pimp. I don't suppose he even saw the fellow. Probably just made him up, imagined him, but his imagination was based on a background of observation. The milieu is correct. . . .[43]

Although these are merely the offhand comments of an editor, and not to be taken too seriously as final critical pronouncements on *the* Negro, still certain implications are obvious. The best Negro characters for literary purposes are suggested: gamblers, fast set, servant-girl-sweet-mamma, etc. All are similar in their great capacity for enjoyment—and it is that side that must be shown. The eternal playboys of the Western hemisphere! Why even one trip to Harlem will reveal the secret of their mystery. The connection of all of this to the contented slave, comic, local color Negro is patent. Another thing to be noticed is the statement issued by the literary market: Stereotypes wanted.

In *Black Sadie*, T. Bowyer Campbell, whose preference is for the stereotype of the contended slave of the South, ironically accounts for the Harlem

---

43. Carl Van Vechten, *Nigger Heaven*. New York: Grosset and Dunlap, 1928, pp. 225 ff.

fad by the desire of jaded sophisticates for a new thrill. But Campbell does agree in some degree with the Harlem stereotype: "Colored people demand nothing but easy happiness, good nature." Black Sadie, child of a man hanged for raping an old white woman, having become the toast of artistic New York, remaining a kleptomaniac—"it was in her blood"—even in affluence, causing a murder, returns—in the best tradition of minstrel songs—to happy Virginia. "Easy come, easy go, niggers," Campbell closes his book, philosophically.

Sherwood Anderson, in *Dark Laughter*, expresses a genuine Rousseau-ism. Hostile toward the routine of industrialism and Puritanism, Anderson sets up as a foil the happy-go-lucky sensuality of river-front Negroes, who laugh, with genial cynicism, at the self-lacerations of hypersensitive Nordics. His "dark laughter" lacks the sinister undertone of Llwellyn Powys' "black laughter" heard in Africa. Anderson's Negroes are too formalized a chorus, however, for conviction, and are more the dream-children of a romanticist than actual flesh-and-blood creations. Anderson has drawn some excellent Negro characters; in *Dark Laughter*, however, he character-izes the Negroes too straitly. That the chief response of the Negro to his experience is a series of deep rounds of laughter at white sex-tangles is difficult of credence.

William Seabrook in *Magic Island* and *Jungle Ways* writes sensational travel tales—according to some, in the tradition of Munchausen and Marco Polo. He exploits the exotic and primitive, recording voodoo rites, black magic, strange sexual practices, weird superstitions, and cannibalism. His work brings a sort of vicarious satisfaction to Main Street, and advances the stereotype. He traces back to original sources what downtown playboys come up to Harlem to see.

The stereotype of the exotic-primitive would require more than a dog-matic refutation. Not so patently a "wish-fulfillment," as the "contented slave" stereotype was, nor an expression of unreasoning hatred, as the "brute Negro," it is advanced by novelists realistic in technique and rather convincing, although demonstrably "romantic" in their choice of the sensa-tional. But it would be pertinent to question the three basic assumptions—either insinuated or expressed—underlying the stereotype: that the "natural" Negro is to be found in Harlem cabarets; that the life and charac-ter depicted there are representative of Negro life in general; and that the Negro is "himself," and startlingly different in the sensational aspects of his life.

It is strange that the "natural" Negro should be looked for in the most sophisticated of environment. Even the names "Cotton Club," "Plantation

Revue," the lavish, though inaccurate, cotton bolls decorating the walls, the choruses in silken overalls and bandanas do not disguise but rather enforce the fact that Negro entertainers, like entertainers everywhere, give the public what clever managers, generally Caucasian, believe the public wants. Unwise as it is to generalize about America, or New York State, or even Queens from the Great White Way, it is no less unwise to generalize about Negro life and character from Harlem. It is even unwise to generalize about Harlem, from *the* Harlem shown in books. Strange to say, there is a Harlem that can be observed by the cold glare of daylight.

The exotic primitives of Mississippi levees and cane-brakes, of Catfish Row and Blue Brook Plantation are more convincing, as examples of frontier communities, and of underprivileged groups who are known to live violent lives. It is surely not impossible, however, to believe that observers with an eye for environmental factors might see an entirely different picture from the one presented by searchers for exotic-primitive innate tendencies.

Harvey Wickham in *The Impuritans* writes:

> On Pacific Street, San Francisco, there used to be, and probably still is, a Negro dance hall called the So-Different Cafe. The name was deceptive. It was not so different from any other slum-hole. [A slum hole] is tediously the same, whether it be in Harlem, lower Manhattan, London, Paris, Berlin, Rome, Athens, Pekin, or Timbuctoo. There is no possible variety in degradation. . . .[44]

Such a comment surely deserves as careful attention as the stereotype of the exotic-primitive.

ATTEMPTS AT REALIZATION

"John Henry said to his captain,
A man ain't nothin' but a man. . . ."
                (Ballad of John Henry.)

It would be a mistake to believe that the works of all white authors bear out these stereotypes. Some of the best attacks upon stereotyping have come from white authors, and from Southerners, just as some of the strongest upholding of the stereotypes has come from Negroes. Moreover, the writer of this essay hopes that he will not be accused of calling everything a stereotype that does not flatter Negro character, or of insisting that the

44. Harvey Wickham, *The Impuritans.* New York: The Dial Press, 1929, p. 284.

stereotypes have no basis in reality. Few of the most apologistic of "race" orators could deny the presence of contented slaves, of wretched freemen, in our past; nor of comic Negroes (even in the joke-book tradition), of self-pitying mulattoes, of brutes, of exotic primitives in our present. Negro life does have its local color, and a rich, glowing color it can be at times. What this essay has aimed to point out is the obvious unfairness of hardening racial character into fixed moulds. True in some particulars, each of these popular generalizations is dangerous when applied to the entire group. Furthermore, most of these generalizations spring from a desire to support what is considered social expediency rather than from a sincere attempt at interpretation, and are therefore bad art.

Attempts at sincere "realization" rather than imitation of set patterns can be found in the early works of Eugene O'Neill, whose plays first brought a tragic Negro to Broadway. Ridgeley Torrence saw another side to the familiar guitar playing clown—showing him to be a dreamer of dreams like the other Playboy of the Western World—and saw dignity in his long suffering, hard-working wife. *The Rider of Dreams*, in its quiet way, did much to demolish the old stereotypes.

Julia Peterkin, for all of her tendency to local color (*Bright April* is a storehouse of Negro superstitions and folk customs) and her emphasis on sex and violence,[45] is still of importance in her departure from the stereotypes.

In a simple, effective manner, she reveals the winning humanity of the Gullah people, whom she obviously loves and respects. If critics would refuse to call her the interpreter of *the* Negro, and realize that she writes of a very limited segment of life from a very personal point of view, they would do a service to her and to their own reputations. She has well-nigh surmounted the difficulty of being a plantation owner.

Du Bose Heyward has given us some of the best Negro characterizations in *Porgy* and *Mamba's Daughters*. Though the first is naturalistic with a flair for the exotic-primitive, Heyward does show in it essential humanity: Porgy reveals himself as capable of essential fineness, and even Bess is not completely past reclaiming. *Mamba's Daughters* reveals that Negroes, too, can be provident as Mamba was, or heroic as Hagar was, for the sake of the young. The travesty of Southern justice toward the Negro, the difficulties of the aspiring Negro, the artistic potentialities and actualities of Negroes, receive ample attention. Except for certain forgivable slips into the

45. *Vide: Black April, Scarlet Sister Mary* for examples of extreme promiscuity, and *Bright Skin* for violent deaths.

"comic," the book is an excellent illustration of the dignity and beauty than can be found in some aspects of lowly Negro life.

E. C. L. Adams, because he seems to let Negro characters speak for themselves, in their own idiom, and as if no white man was overhearing, has been very successful in his interpretation of Negro folk-life. Here the humor expressed by the Negro is miles away from Cohen's buffoonery. There is a sharp, acid flavor to it; in the Negroes' condemnation of the Ben Bess case there is the bitterness that has been stored up for so very long. These folk are not happy-go-lucky, nor contented; they are shrewd, realistic philosophers, viewing white pretense and injustice with cynicism— though not with Sherwood Anderson's "Dark Laughter." Illiterate they may be, but they are not being fooled.

Howard Odum, by letting the Negro speak for himself, presents a similarly convincing folk-Negro, in this case, the rambling man, who has been everywhere, and seen everybody. Many of the stereotypes are overthrown in *Rainbow Round My Shoulder,* although comic, and brutal, and submissive Negroes may be seen there. These are viewed, however, "in the round," not as walking generalizations about *the* Negro, and Odum is intent on making us understand how they got to be what they are.

Evelyn Scott and T. S. Stribling, historical novelists of the Civil War, as different as may be in technique, agree in giving us rounded pictures of antebellum Negroes. Slavery is not a perpetual Mardi Gras in their novels, nor are Negroes cast in the old, rigid moulds. They are characterized as human beings, not as representatives of a peculiar species. Paul Green's *In Abraham's Bosom* shows the Negro's handicapped struggles for education during the Reconstruction; Green has brought great dramatic power to bear upon revealing that the Negro is a figure worthy of tragic dignity. In *The House of Connelly* he has disclosed aspects of the so-called "contented slave" that antebellum authors were either ignorant of, or afraid to show.

Erskine Caldwell, George Milburn, William Faulkner, and Thomas Wolfe, while their metier is the portraiture of poor whites, help in undermining the stereotypes by showing that what have been considered Negro characteristics, such as dialect, illiteracy, superstitions, sexual looseness, violence, etc., are to be found as frequently among poor whites. When they do show Negro characters, they frequently show them to be burdened by economic pressure, the playthings of Southern justice, and the catspaws for sadistic "superiors."

A recent novel, *Amber Satyr,* shows a lynching that follows a white woman's relentless and frenzied pursuit of her hired man, a good-looking Negro. Welbourne Kelley's *Inchin' Along,* although influenced by some stereotypes (his mulatto wife, true to type, is the easy prey of the first white man who rides along), does show the hard-working, provident, stoical Negro. James Knox Millen wrote a powerful attack upon lynching in *Never No More*, showing the precarious hold the Southern Negro has upon peace and happiness. Scott Nearing, with a proletarian emphasis, has presented graphically the new slavery, peonage, in the South, with its horrible concomitant lynchings, and the bitter prejudice of organized labor in the North. And finally, John L. Spivak, in *Georgia Nigger*, has written a second *Uncle Tom's Cabin*, an indictment of peonage, and convict-labor in Georgia, powerful enough to put to shame all the rhapsodists of the folk Negro's happy state.

To trace the frequency with which the Negro author has stepped out of his conventional picture frame, from the spirituals and satiric folk-rhymes down to Langston Hughes, would exceed the bounds of this paper, and for present purposes is not needed. A reading of only a few of the white authors just mentioned (many of whom are from the South) would effectively illustrate the inadequacy of the familiar stereotypes.

It is likely that, in spite of the willingness of some Negro authors to accept at face value some of these stereotypes, the exploration of Negro life and character rather than its exploitation must come from Negro authors themselves. This, of course, runs counter to the American conviction that the Southern white man knows the Negro best, and can best interpret him. Nan Bagby Stephens states what other Southern authors have insinuated:

> Maybe it was because my slave-owning ancestors were fond of their darkies and treated them as individuals that I see them like that. It seems to me that no one, not even the negroes themselves, can get the perspective reached through generations of understanding such as we inherited.[46]

The writer of this essay holds to the contrary opinion, agreeing with another Southerner, F. P. Gaines,[47] that when a white man says that he knows the Negro he generally means that he knows the Negro of the joke-book tradition. Stephen Vincent Benet has written:

> Oh, blackskinned epic, epic with the black spear,
> I cannot sing you, having too white a heart,

46. *Contempo*, Volume II, No. 2, p. 3.
47. F. P. Gaines, *op. cit.*, p. 17.

And yet, some day a poet will rise to sing you
And sing you with such truth and mellowness . . .
That you will be a match for any song. . . .[48]

But whether Negro life and character are to be best interpreted from
without or within is an interesting by-path that we had better not enter
here. One manifest truth, however, is this: the sincere, sensitive artist,
willing to go beneath the clichés of popular belief to get at an underlying
reality, will be wary of confining a race's entire character to a half-dozen
narrow grooves. He will hardly have the temerity to say that his necessarily
limited observation of a few Negroes in a restricted environment can be
taken as the last word about some mythical *the* Negro. He will hesitate to
do this, even though he had a Negro mammy, or spent a night in Harlem,
or has been a Negro all his life. The writer submits that such an artist is
the only one worth listening to, although the rest are legion.

48. Stephen Vincent Benet, *John Brown's Body*. Garden City, N.Y.: Doubleday,
Doran and Co., 1928, p. 347.

The New Negro in Literature
(1925–1955)

❧ I AM GRATEFUL for the chance to participate in this symposium, dedicated to the memory of Alain LeRoy Locke. My acquaintance with Alain Locke dates back to his appearance at this university when, together with the other "Young Howards," a gang of boys that infested the campus, I stood in awe of the dapper man with a cane who had been a Rhodes Scholar at Oxford. Young barbarians on the brink of an unknown world, we thrilled at those magic words and wondered how so much learning could be stored in so slight a frame. When years later I joined the faculty here, I was struck by his incisive and wide ranging mind and by his devotedness to the university; I soon learned how firm a respect he enjoyed from such peers as Kelly Miller, Ernest Just, Charles Burch, Abram Harris, and Ralph Bunche, all stalwarts who have now left us. I have collaborated with him on articles, I was one of his associates in the Bronze Booklet Series, and although our critical views did not always coincide, I have profited from his wise counsel. I should like here to salute him as benefactor, colleague, and friend.

This conference, assessing the achievements of the New Negro movement and paying tribute to one of its prime launchers and sponsors, fills a need. Official biographers of eminent Negroes have commented only scantily on Alain Locke; in Embree's *Brown America* (1943) Locke's name is in neither bibliography nor index; in Embree's *Thirteen Against the Odds* he gets part of a sentence. In Brawley's *The Negro Genius*, he is merely called the "*maestro* of the New Negro performance" and is solely praised for "a fine sense of the value of words"—this of a man whose essays in *The New Negro* said more about the "Negro genius" than Brawley's entire book. It is true that, though little recorded, his place as mentor and interpreter is established. But it is good for this conference, in memoirs and elucidations, to make that place even clearer.

THE TWENTIES

My colleagues have ably filled in the social and historical backgrounds of the New Negro movement. It is my task to trace and evaluate the literature by and about Negroes from 1925 to the present. Because of the exigencies of time and space, drama must be excluded.[1] The divisions of this essay are natural, corresponding roughly with decades which had distinct cultural characteristics: they are (1) The Harlem Vogue, 1920–1930; (2) The Depression Thirties, and (3) World War II and Its Aftermath. I have hesitated to use the term Negro Renaissance for several reasons: one is that the five or eight years generally allotted are short for the lifespan of any "renaissance." The New Negro is not to me a group of writers centered in Harlem during the second half of the twenties. Most of the writers were not Harlemites; much of the best writing was not about Harlem, which was the show-window, the cashier's till, but no more Negro America than New York is America. The New Negro movement had temporal roots in the past and spatial roots elsewhere in America, and the term has validity, it seems to me, only when considered to be a continuing tradition.

The rise of the New Negro movement coincided with increased interest in Negro life and character in the twenties. American literature was in revolt against the squeamishness and repression of Victorianism, and the philistinism of an acquisitive society. Carl Van Doren wrote: "What American literature decidedly needs at the moment is color, music, gusto, the free expression of gay or desperate moods. If the Negroes are not in a position to contribute these items, I do not know what Americans are." The decade was ushered in by Eugene O'Neill's *The Emperor Jones* (1920), an undoubted theatrical success, significant in placing the Negro at the tragic

---

1. The treatment of the Negro in drama is of course significant, but complete coverage of three decades of a fairly abundant literature is impossible for an essay of this length. The major plays, *In Abraham's Bosom* (1924); *The Green Pastures* (1930); *Porgy and Bess*, the "folk opera" (1935); *Stevedore* (1934); *Native Son* (1941); *Strange Fruit* (1945); *Deep Are the Roots* (1945), and the recent Louis Peterson's *Take a Giant Step* (1953), and Charles Sebree's and Greer Johnson's *Mrs. Patterson* (1954), conform to the trends that will be discussed. In 1927 Alain Locke saw on the near horizon great tragedy and comedy of Negro life, "universal even in sounding its most racial notes." ("Introduction," *Plays of Negro Life*, edited by Locke and Montgomery Gregory, New York and London, 1927, p. vi.) But that hope has yet to be fulfilled.

center instead of in comic relief, but overly reliant on tom-toms, superstition, and atavism. Waldo Frank's *Holiday* (1923), along with a humanitarian's dismay at injustice, defined white and Negro "consciousness" too schematically. Sherwood Anderson's *Dark Laughter* (1925) protests his fondness for the "Negro way of life," but when he equates this with self-satisfied satire of white neuroticism he shows how fondness could use a little knowledge. In his harrying of Puritanism, Carl Van Vechten made excursions to Harlem; despite his defenders' claim that he discovered the Negro élite, *Nigger Heaven* (1926) emphasizes the flamboyant and erotic. The influence of Europe was strong on the new sophisticates. Picasso's admiration for African sculpture, Gide's interest in the Congo, and the award of the *Prix Goncourt* to René Maran's naturalistic *Batouala* (1921) indicated France's turning to vital, genuine sources. But Paul Morand is merely a cynical camp follower in *Magie Noire* (1929), in which he includes absurd fantasies of American Negroes reverting at slightest provocation to ancestral savagery. Several British books seasoned Kipling's white man's burden with Mayfair ridicule; Ronald Firbank's *Prancing Nigger* (1925) is such sophisticated racist burlesque. Americans found the West Indies to be a treasure trove for authors, but where John Vandercook brought back from Haiti the stirring epic of Henri Christophe, W. B. Seabrook could find there little more than the weird, the voodooistic, the orgiastic, which he exploited in *The Magic Island* (1929).

Written with some distinction, these widely selling books by white authors enforced a tradition of exotic primitivism. Healthier interest in Negro life, of the here and now in America, was manifested in the liberal periodicals, the *Nation*, the *New Republic*, and the *American Mercury*. Alerted by James Weldon Johnson, Charles S. Johnson, and Alain Locke to the growing expression of Negro life by Negroes themselves, the *Survey Graphic* issued a Harlem number in March, 1925. This afforded the nucleus of an epochal collection of the work of young and old, aspiring and established, fledgling poet and established racial statesman, which, under the creative editing of Alain Locke, appeared a few months later as *The New Negro: An Interpretation*.

Alain Locke introduced the volume confidently: The New Negro "wishes to be known for what he is, even in his faults and shortcomings, and scorns a craven and precarious survival at the price of seeming to be what he is not."[2] The already published *Cane* (1923) by Jean Toomer de-

2. Locke, "The New Negro," in Locke, ed., *The New Negro: An Interpretation* (New York, 1925), p. 11.

serves such praise. Apprenticeship to experimental writing had helped Toomer develop a revelatory prose; deep pondering over Negro life in border cities and Georgia had supplied him with rich material; the resultant book, *Cane*, expressed Negro life with insight, beauty, and power. Eric Walrond's *Tropic Death* (1926), brilliant impressionism about the tragedies of his native Caribbean, was unapologetically naturalistic, and firmly controlled in style.

Neither wrote another work of fiction, however, and their pioneering was not followed. Negro writers instead trooped off to join Van Vechten's band and share in the discovery of Harlem as a new African colony. Wawa trumpets, trap drums (doubling for tom-toms), and shapely dancers with bunches of bananas girdling their middles in Bamboo Inns and Jungle Cabarets nurtured tourists' delusions of "the Congo cutting through the black." Claude McKay's *Home to Harlem* (1926) concentrates on the primitive, which McKay defiantly glorifies in *Banjo* (1929), whose hero decides to "let intellect go to hell and live instinct." *Joie de vivre* was acclimated to Harlem especially, to Negroes generally. It was all rhythm, rhythm; jazzbands swung out on "That's Why Darkies Were Born;" pent-houses sprouted miraculously atop Lenox Avenue tenements; the cabin was exchanged for the cabaret but the old mirth was still inside. Even Countee Cullen in *One Way to Heaven* (1932) proclaims "Enjoyment isn't across the [racial] line." The whites have only money, privilege, power; Negroes have cornered the joy.

Gay with youth, heady from attention, caught up along with much of America in ballyhoo, flattered by influential creators, critics, and publishers who had suddenly discovered the dark world at their doorstep, many Negroes helped to make a cult of Harlem. They set up their own Bohemia, sharing in the nationwide rebellion from family, church, small town, and business civilization, but revolt from racial restrictions was sporadic. Rash in the spurt for sophistication (wisdom was too slow and did not pay off), grafting primitivism on decadence, they typified one phase of American literary life in the twenties. A few magazines such as *Fire* and *Harlem* flared like rockets; good experiments jostled against much that was falsely atavistic and wilfully shocking.

But several writers were uncomfortable at the racial mystique that seemed the price of the new freedom. Wallace Thurman illustrates their ambivalence in *Blacker the Berry* (1929), which counterposes lurid descriptions of Harlem with a somber account of a dark heroine who is defeated by color snobbishness among Negroes themselves. All was certainly not joy in Thurman's heaven. Alain Locke warned that "too many of our younger writers . . . are pot-plants seeking a forced growth according to the exotic tastes of a pampered and decadent public."[3] Rudolph Fisher rose above this ruck. Kin to O. Henry with his quick eyes and ears and curiosity, Fisher wrote insouciant fiction that tells more about Harlem than is in all of *Nigger Heaven* and its brood.

The obvious preference for low-life Harlem was chided by W. E. B. Du Bois, who wished creative literature to enlist in his trenchant crusade for equal rights. His novels, *The Quest of the Silver Fleece* (1911) and *The Dark Princess* (1928), have undoubted social wisdom and prophetic vision, but their virtues are those of pamphleteering. The fiction by the officers of the NAACP is programmatic, fighting Nordicism, disfranchisement, segregation, mob violence, and other racial evils. Walter White's *Fire in the Flint* (1924) has strength chiefly as an anti-lynching tract. Alert against the obvious stereotypes, White lent his support in *Flight* (1926) to the stereotype of the heroine who passes for white until she gets a mystical revelation that happiness belongs on the darker side of the racial boundary. Passing, in novels, became an inordinate preoccupation of leisure class Negro women. Such is true of Nella Larsen's heroine in *Passing* (1930); and in *Quicksand* (1928) her heroine is torn between pulls of race and caste. Jessie Fauset's novels also have an undue amount of passing, but her chief purpose is to exhibit the Negro world of education, substance, and breeding. Like most novels of the Negro middle class, however, these have little penetration; they record a class (idealized) in order to praise a race (imperfectly understood).

Whether licentious Harlem or sedate brown Babbittry, the most frequent setting for New Negro fiction was the urban North. Great segments of Negro life obviously remained unrecorded. Agreeing with the wag who would rather be "a lamppost on Lenox Avenue than the mayor of Atlanta," most Negro novelists left the South to white authors. Julia Peterkin's absorption in the plantation life of coastal South Carolina and Du Bose Heyward's poetic use of the lives of Charleston Negroes, at its best in *Porgy*, showed unusual grasp of folkspeech and folkways, an unfeigned sympathy different from the old cozy condescension. There remained some stress on the exotic and violent, some traces of the plantation tradition, some failure or unwillingness to comprehend. But regionalism drew close to reality. Howard Odum's Left Wing Gordon is as authentic as countless conversations with footloose working-men and minstrels could make him. The little-

3. Locke, "Art or Propaganda?" *Harlem, A Forum of Negro Life*, I (November, 1928), 12.

heralded books of E. C. L. Adams contained dialogues of folk Negro talking to folk Negro, which were unsurpassed in their ironic awareness and added dimensions to people who had long been considered quaint, artless children. John Sale and R. Emmett Kennedy wrote of Mississippi and Louisiana Negroes from long and loving study; even Roark Bradford, of the same region, knew much about the folk Negro. But, for all of his grasp of idiom and mannerism, he saw little in folk-life beyond the ludicrous and wasted his knowledge on burlesque.

Thorough collection and study of Negro folksong accompanied the growing regionalism. Howard Odum and Guy Johnson turned up the valuable ore in *The Negro and His Songs* (1925) and *Negro Workaday Songs* (1926). The researches of Guy Johnson and Louis Chappell set John Henry deservedly in the pantheon of American folk heroes. Abbe Niles and W. C. Handy, in *Blues: An Anthology* (1926), pioneered in the analysis and history of this original music, which Mamie and Bessie Smith and Ma Rainey were popularizing. James Weldon Johnson and J. Rosamond Johnson edited collections of spirituals in 1925 and 1926, for which the former wrote valuable introductions. These together with Alain Locke's perceptive appreciation in *The New Negro* and the appealing voices of Roland Hayes, Paul Robeson, Taylor Gordon, Marian Anderson, and the Hall Johnson choir, made the spirituals, in the words of one enthusiast, "the finest medium for interpreting to the whites some of the best qualities of the Negroes."[4]

Claude McKay's *Harlem Shadows* signalled the new movement in poetry. The substance of McKay's poems was different; nostalgic recreations of early Jamaica life alternated with harsh pictures of America. The poet's manly anger and militant self-assurance were properly influential. Countee Cullen, a precocious disciple of the romantic tradition, produced gifted lyrics on love and death as brown youth coped with them. For all of his disclaimers, race pride and defense hovered over his verse. Cullen sought a tradition to glorify, turning, as in "Heritage," to story-book Africa, or to romantic heroes such as Christophe and Simon the Cyrenian. When he turned to American Negro experience the result was the unconvincing *Black Christ*. Langston Hughes felt Negro life more sincerely and portrayed it more movingly. *Weary Blues* (1926) and *Fine Clothes to the Jew* (1927) presented blues singers, honky-tonk dancers, lonely piano players, wastrels, and others of the urban folk with sympathy and authenticity. Hughes learned from Lindsay and Sandburg, but wisely also studied the rhythms

4. "In the Driftway," *Nation*, CXXXI (September 3, 1920), 245.

of jazz, the spirituals, and the blues. Deceptively simple, these poems often contain real insight. James Weldon Johnson was influenced by the new regionalism to discard his older rhetorical approach; *God's Trombones* (1927) dramatically resurrects the eloquence of the bard-like folk preacher. These seven poetized sermons, wrought with loving care, showed as did some of Toomer's lyrics, how folkstuff could be invested with dignity. These were the more important poets; lyrics of merit were written conventionally by Georgia Douglas Johnson and Angelina Grimke, and unconventionally by Anne Spencer and Fenton Johnson, who bitterly echoed *Spoon River Anthology*. Helene Johnson, Frank Horne, Arna Bontemps, and Waring Cuney won prizes in the annual contests held by the *Crisis* and *Opportunity* magazines.

What was the critical standing of the literature of Negro life in the twenties? Reviewers were generous, but in later accounts of the period omit books once praised. Opposition critics included Wyndham Lewis, whose *Paleface* (1929) railed at sentimental primitivism, which he felt was swelling the fearful tide of color. Harvey Wickham, deploring the degradation of much fiction about Negroes, still counseled the Negro to be "engagingly different" and to create "the romance of Africa espoused to our own South, the savage's sense of the nearness of the spiritual world."[5] Present day literary historians of the decade are silent about the New Negro movement. The latest and fullest coverage mentions only Van Vechten, Sherwood Anderson, and Waldo Frank, and summarizes the interest in the Negro as simplification, distortion, and exploitation of primitivism.[6]

Such easy dismissal is injustice, however; primitivism is not the only trend of early New Negro writing. When one realizes that since Chesnutt's pioneering, no fiction by Negroes had tapped the rich materials except James Weldon Johnson's *Autobiography of an Ex-Colored Man* (1912) and since Dunbar, little poetry except genre sentimentality and race rhetoric, one sees in fresh perspective the positive achievements of the earliest New Negroes. The fiction of Toomer, Walrond, Fisher, and of McKay at his uncontroversial best; the poetry of *God's Trombones*, McKay, Cullen, and Hughes; the winning of real respect for Negro spirituals, seculars, and

5. Harvey Wickham, *The Impuritans* (New York, 1929), p. 283.
6. Frederick J. Hoffman, *The Twenties: American Writing in the Postwar Decade* (New York, 1955), p. 269. Edmund Wilson's *The Shores of Light* (1952) touched only on Frank and Toomer; John K. Hutchen's *The American Twenties* anthologizes no work about Negro life; William Hodapp's *The Pleasures of the Jazz Age* (1948) anthologizes only a dithyramb by Sherwood Anderson to Negro easy living as an instance of the period's interest in The Race Question!

folkstuff generally; all of these had solid merit. New publishing houses—Knopf, Harcourt Brace, Viking, Liveright and the Bonis—welcomed Negro talents, who opened doors that have stayed open.

Langston Hughes's credo expressed proud independence: "We younger Negro artists intend to express our individual dark-skinned selves without fear or shame." In not caring whether white people or Negroes were pleased, these artists stand "on the top of the mountain, free within ourselves." But the fine idealism runs up hard against the reality that white critics were constantly looking over the writers' shoulders and, even when well-meaning, often counseled amiss.[7] There were few Negro critics for guidance. One of the best equipped, Allison Davis, keenly analyzed the opportunism of the rampant primitivism, cynicism, and luridity. He found in the experience of Negroes here in America, both past and present, qualities better worth attention; these were "fortitude, irony, and a relative absence of self pity"[8]—a broader human nature available for the imagination that could grasp it, and a higher potential for truer and more universal literature. But such trust and such prescription point forward to the thirties.

THE THIRTIES

Those who nostalgically recall the Harlem boom include in their memoirs far more of the good time parties and big contacts than of the writing. Alain Locke was troubled by the feckless irresponsibility of a fad produced "by a period of inflation and overproduction."[9] Langston Hughes dated its end "when the crash came in 1929 and the white people had much less money to spend on themselves and practically none to spend on Negroes."[10] For all of its positive services in encouraging racial respect and self reliance, a large number of Negroes were ignorant of, indifferent or ill disposed toward the new literature of Negro life.

The current literary fashion in America is to make the thirties a whipping boy, while pampering the glamorous twenties. Nevertheless a period which saw the maturing of Dos Passos, Farrell, Wolfe, Hemingway, Steinbeck, Caldwell, and Faulkner cannot be cavalierly dismissed as stodgily

7. See, for example, Dorothy Van Doren's review of Schuyler's *Black No More*, which says, "The Negro will never write great literature while he tries to write white literature. It may be that he can express himself only by music and rhythm and not by words." "Black, Alas, No More!" *Nation*, CXXXII (February 25, 1931), 219.

8. Allison Davis, "Our Intellectuals," *Crisis*, XXXV (August, 1928), 285.

9. Locke, "This Year of Grace," *Opportunity*, IX (February, 1931), 48.

10. Langston Hughes, *The Big Sea* (New York, 1940), p. 247.

naturalistic or proletarian. The central characteristic of the period is its grave reappraisal of American life and positive affirmation of democracy. When Black Friday ushered in the Depression, American writers were shocked by the unfamiliar sights of bread lines, unemployed workers, closed factories, farm evictions, hunger, and loss of human decency. It *had* happened here, and America wanted to know why. American writers, sensitive and dismayed, assumed serious social responsibilities.

Negro authors of the thirties, like their compatriots, faced reality more squarely. For the older lightheartedness they substituted sober self searching; for the bravado of false Africanism and Bohemianism they substituted attempts to understand Negro life in its workaday aspects in the here and now. Clear-eyed and forthright social scientists—Charles S. Johnson, E. Franklin Frazier, and Abram Harris—supplied needed documentation, analysis, and synthesis. Alert to the changing times, a few critics—Alain Locke among them—charted new directions.

The first books by Negroes in the thirties continued the preoccupations of the twenties, when they were conceived. Taylor Gordon's bawdy autobiography *Born to Be* (1930) was sponsored as usual by Van Vechten, who praised the author's six-foot lankiness, "falsetto voice, and molasses laugh," but neglected to point out his literary distinctions; one of which—a murderous way with grammar—charmed several aesthetes. George Schuyler's swashbuckling *Black No More* (1931), a fantasy about the dire results of the discovery of a treatment to whiten dark complexions, indiscriminately lampooned Dixie racists and professional race-men. Wallace Thurman's *Infants of the Spring* (1932) exposes the Harlem literati, whom he calls Niggerati, in their dissipation. Seven years after their brave beginning Thurman is grieving over the New Negroes as a lost generation, pandering to tourists on the safari for queer dives in Harlem.

More engagingly written, Arna Bontemp's *God Sends Sunday* (1931) belongs with the earlier school in its evocation of the life of jockeys, rounders, and demi-mondaines of the gaudy Negro tenderloin at the turn of the century. His second novel illustrates the change: now involved with the Negro's struggle for freedom, Bontemps chose a new sort of history for *Black Thunder* (1936). Based on a little-known slave revolt, written with imaginative identification, *Black Thunder* is one of America's better historical novels.[11] Langston Hughes, a barometer of this decade as of others,

---

11. Historical fiction about slavery, the Civil War, and Reconstruction has been plentiful. Despite the phenomenal success of *Gone with the Wind*, the plantation tradition is in decline. More satisfying artistically and historically has been the recreation of the past by regionalists whose documentation and honesty draw them far from the moonlight and magnolia school.

turned to semi-autobiographic fiction in *Not Without Laughter* (1930), a quietly moving novel of boyhood in a Kansas town. *The Ways of White Folks* (1934), a collection of Hughes's short stories, contains fondness for underprivileged people and shrewd, sometimes exasperated irony at patronage. Zora Neale Hurston showed a ripeness worth waiting for in the tales she contributed to *Story Magazine* in the thirties, and in the folk-based *Jonah's Gourd Vine* (1934) and *Their Eyes Were Watching God* (1937), a superior regional novel about the rural Negroes of Miss Hurston's native Florida. Miss Hurston's *Mules and Men* (1935) is a first class collection of Negro yarns, gaining from the author's being both insider and trained folklorist. Inside intimacy is also in George Wylie Henderson's *Ollie Miss* (1935); George Lee's combination of river legend, sharecropping realism and protest in *River George* (1937); and the promising beginnings of a family saga in E. Waters Turpin's *These Low Grounds* (1937) and *O Canaan* (1939). But, not staying with their material, these authors forfeited the slow maturation so apparent in the best of American regionalist writing.

The nation's Economic Problem Number One—The South—strongly attracted the social conscience. The poor white sharecropper—America's forgotten man—written of definitively by William Faulkner in *As I Lay Dying* (1930) and by Erskine Caldwell in *Tobacco Road* (1932) was shown as having much the same characteristics—improvidence, shiftlessness, promiscuity, superstition—that had been superficially considered Negro traits. "Kneel to the Rising Sun," Caldwell's most striking story, showed a Negro who has grit denied to his white fellow in misery, and humanity denied to the sadistic landlord. Novels by white authors aware of the harshness of Negro life include Roy Flannagan's *Amber Satyr* (1932), and Robert Rylee's *Deep Dark River* (1935). William March's *Come In at the Door* (1934) and Hamilton Basso's *Courthouse Square* (1936) go even farther, portraying Negroes of education and ambition with sympathy hitherto reserved for peasant types.

Left-wing authors, among them Scott Nearing, John Spivak, and Myra Page, attacked the rampant injustices—wholesale discrimination, peonage, the chain gang, unjust employment practices, and lynching—in a catalogue too true in its tragic particulars, with veracity as a *J'accuse*, but with less verisimilitude as literature. Grace Lumpkin's *A Sign for Cain* (1935), the best "proletarian" novel about Negro life, springs from wide knowledge and deep feeling. A schematic conclusion to most of the proletarian fiction was the union of white and Negro workers, which at this point of history, not only in the deep South, was more wishful than realizable.

In 1938 Richard Wright's *Uncle Tom's Children* won *Story Magazine's* contest for the best book of fiction by a member of the Federal Writers' Project. Comprising four novellas, this book showed intense militancy and a power to present the starkest of tragedies. Largely self-trained, a brooding, lonely seeker for decency, rasped by constant racial rebuffs in the South, Wright poured more anger and terror into his fiction than any other Negro author had done. He made his people vivid and convincing in their full humanity, courage, and wisdom, their frustration and fortitude. In 1939 Wright added to the volume "The Ethics of Living Jim Crow," which was an early draft of *Black Boy*, and "Bright and Morning Star," which, though as bleak as the first novellas, nourished the hope for brotherhood of the oppressed, which for a short while Wright believed that Communism was to achieve.

Most of the poetry of the decade is regionalism or social protest. Welborn V. Jenkins's *Trumpet in the New Moon* (1934) is rhapsodic but vivid cataloguing of Negro experience; Frank Marshall Davis is likewise panoramic in *Black Man's Verse* (1935) and *I Am the American Negro* (1937) which mingle sharp etchings with irony and belligerence. Richard Wright's occasional poems were farthest to the left. In the early thirties, Langston Hughes suddenly rebelled from a white patron who believed that Negroes had "mystery and mysticism and spontaneous harmony in their souls" when not polluted by whites. He responded that he did not feel the primitive surging through him. He admitted a love for the surface and the rhythms of Africa, but said, "I was not Africa. I was Chicago and Kansas City and Broadway and Harlem."[12] "Advertisement for the Waldorf Astoria," contrasting luxury with down-and-out Harlem, signalized Hughes's revolt, which extended to praise of revolutionary heroes, attacks upon false Negro leadership, and heated defense of the Scottsboro boys.

Negro, an anthology edited by Nancy Cunard in 1934, struck insistently the chord of protest against colonialism in Africa and the Caribbean and second-class citizenship at home; the numerous contributors included whites as well as Negroes. The "united front" against Fascism partly broke down the isolation of the Negro author. The Federal Writers' Project gave even fuller participation to Negroes, employing Bontemps, McKay, Roi Ottley, Ted Poston, Henry Lee Moon, Wright, William Attaway, Ellison, Margaret Walker, Willard Motley, Frank Yerby, and Zora Neale Hurston. The Writers' Project aided Negro authors as well as white by exploring the American past and encouraging a sound, unchauvinistic regionalism. Of the planned series of books on Negro life, only the *Negro in Virginia* (1940)

12. Hughes, *op. cit.*, pp. 316 ff.

prepared by Roscoe Lewis from materials amassed by Negroes on the Virginia Project was completed, but this book is earnest of what might have developed had not the solons at the Capitol killed the Project so soon. In December, 1940, as a sort of climax to the New Deal interest in Negro life, the seventy-fifth anniversary of the Thirteenth Amendment was commemorated at the Library of Congress by an exhibit of paintings, books, and manuscripts, and a festival of music in which Dorothy Maynor and Roland Hayes sang, and the Budapest Quartet played music on Negro themes. On the evening devoted to Negro folk music, Alain Locke was commentator on the Spirituals, Sterling Brown on the Blues and Ballads, and Alan Lomax on the Reels and Worksongs. Locke repeated his proud faith in the survival of the spirituals, and believed them at last safe "under the protection of the skilful folklorist."[13] He was correct: around the hall in the Folk-Archives were thousands of records of Negro folk music of all types, needing interpretation and creative shaping certainly, but available to any honest searcher for truth.

FROM THE FORTIES TO THE PRESENT

The rediscovery of the American past in the thirties deepened into passionate affirmation of democracy in the early forties when Fascism menaced the entire world. American Negroes shared as always the determination that democracy should survive. But they knew bitterly that democracy had never been simon-pure for them; that, as Langston Hughes wrote: "America never was America to me." Fighting against Hitlerism abroad, they found nothing contradictory in fighting against injustice at home. The democracy they endorsed was of the future; they were lukewarm at the slogan that victory would restore American life exactly as it had been. Exclusion from complete service in factory and on firing line was galling. The irony of rejecting one tenth of the nation from an all-out defense of democracy was apparent both at home and among our allies.

In Richard Wright's significant *Native Son* (1940), Bigger Thomas was native born, but an exploited ghetto was his home, and a straight course from delinquency to crime was his doom. *Native Son* was composed in great anger, but except for excessive melodrama and the Marxist lawyer's harangue explaining what Wright's powerful dramatic scenes had already

13. *Seventy Years of Freedom* (Commemoration of the 75th Anniversary of the Proclamation of the 13th Amendment to the Constitution of the United States) (Washington, 1940), p. 15.

left clear, the anger was disciplined by craft. A large audience, prepared by Dreiser and Farrell and depression naturalists, acclaimed *Native Son;* the Book-of-the-Month and The Modern Library selected it (the first choice in both instances of a book by a Negro). Wright's impressionist "folk history," *Twelve Million Black Voices* (1941), excellently illustrated by Edwin Rosskam, stresses exploitation and revolt. *Black Boy* (1945), the autobiography of Wright's early years, is also violent and outspoken. Hatred of racial injustice made Wright seek France as refuge. Here, having broken with the Communist Party, he wrote fiction of the Underground Man, Wright's new symbol for the American Negro. Influenced by existentialism, *The Outsider* (1953) lacks roots in the American scene that Wright knew so well, and suffers in the transplanting.

William Attaway's *Blood on the Forge* (1941), another unapologetic novel, is based on unused material—the experiences of three brothers who give up sharecropping for work in the steel mills; its style, veering from naturalistic to symbolic, is mature; the ideas are perceptive. Chester Himes in his shorter fiction had drawn his characters from the lower depths; his novels are concerned with the lonely and frustrated who, no more than Bigger Thomas, can find a home in America. Himes's *If He Hollers* (1945) portrays a Negro whose neuroticism is tormented by wartime experiences; *Lonely Crusade* (1947) shows a labor organizer's disillusionment with fellow Negroes, organized labor, and the Communist Party. The white world is blamed by Himes for most of the dead-ends of his characters; in *Third Generation* (1954), however, a family is ruined by a mulatto mother's pathologic worship of color and upper-class striving.

The intra-racial problem of color has now ousted the once favorite problem of passing. Dorothy West's *Living Is Easy* (1948), written from long familiarity with Boston, satirizes convincingly the snobbishness based on color and social prestige. Willard Savoy's *Alien Land* (1949) probes anew the dilemmas of a fair-skinned Negro confronted by race loyalty and racial rebuffs. J. Saunders Redding's *Stranger and Alone* (1950) uses a new milieu, Negro college life,—about which Redding certainly has an insider's knowledge—, but revelation is sacrificed for embittered exposure of two mulatto misleaders who exhaust the vices of Uncle Tomism.

Tribulations of the slum-shocked filled most of the decade's novels of Negro life. Best of these is Ann Petry's *The Street* (1946), the winner of the Houghton Mifflin Literary Fellowship. Miss Petry's crowded tenements, delinquent youngsters, hunted women, and predatory men inhabit a city drastically different from the joy-filled playground of the Harlem Vogue. A skilled and thoughtful novelist, Miss Petry has also written *Narrows* (1953), which tells of a doomed interracial affair in Connecticut. Carl Offord's *White Face* (1943) about Harlem, Philip Kaye's *Taffy* (1950) about Harlem and Brooklyn, Alden Bland's *Behold a Cry* (1947) about Chicago, and Curtis Lucas's *Third Ward Newark* (1946) are typical of the sociological fiction where poverty, family disorganization, alcoholism, unemployment, police brutality, and other urban evils are rendered better than the characters. Case studies at their best, literary slumming at their worst, they are exposures of the obvious rather than illumination of the hidden. Too often hopelessness palls; the course of the neurotic pawns is disastrous instead of tragic; the protagonists are victims, not heroes, because they struggle half-heartedly if at all. In the soft-back publishing bonanza, however, such novels sell well; it is likely that the four S's of sex, sadism, sensationalism, and sentimentality pay off better than the justified racial indignation.

William Gardner Smith's *South Street* (1954) seeks a wider scope than the slums, but his handling of an interracial romance lacks the biting reality of his earlier *The Last of the Conquerors* (1948). This novel, one of the few to tap the Negro's rich war experience, tells much about the Negro G.I. in Europe, where the lack of color prejudice among the defeated Hitlerites contrasts ironically with its presence among white soldiers of the American occupation. John O. Killen's novel *Youngblood* (1954) departs from the futility of the slum exposures, and sets its major sections in Crossroads, Georgia, where slow improvements are brought about by militant unionists, teachers, and preachers, who learn to organize their strength. *Have You Been to the River* (1952) by Chancellor Williams is also solidly documentary, this time on the cult religions and their zealots, with a social scientist expounding the meanings.

White authors did not neglect the dramatic life of Negroes in the changing South. Lillian Smith's *Strange Fruit* (1944) with sharp and deep understanding shows race-crossed lovers in a mean-spirited Georgia town. Insight into the many types, Negro and white, a cross-section of the South, helps *Strange Fruit* disclose hitherto concealed truths. Bucklin Moon's *Without Magnolias* (1949) gives another cross-section: its delineations of a Southern Negro college under white control, the Uncle Toms, courageous labor leaders, working folk, and intellectuals, are authentic and sincere. Hodding Carter, alarmed by war tensions, wrote *Winds of Fear* (1944), a middle-of-the-road novel recognizing the Negro's growing and justified militancy. William Russell's *A Wind Is Rising* (1950), Arthur Gordon's *Reprisal* (1950), and Earl Conrad's fiction are protests against lynching and exploitation, as are several of Caldwell's sardonic later novels. The incidental Negro characters in the fiction of Carson McCullers and Peter

Taylor reveal aspects of race relations unrecorded earlier. Without stressing violence, Jefferson Young's *A Good Man* (1953), Lonnie Coleman's *Clara* (1952), and Hubert Creekmore's family saga *The Chain in the Heart* (1953) tell of Negroes whose essential dignity is firmly respected. William Faulkner has grown in wisdom about Negroes; after early stereotyping and groping, he created in *Go Down Moses* (1942) Negro characters of complexity and depth. Sometimes, as in *Intruder in the Dust* (1948), Faulkner yields to fierce anti-yankeeism, but when he lets Negroes do their own talking and acting, they refute his political tirades, and join the company of his best characterizations.

The most recent fiction by Negro authors is personal, not social; psychological more than sociological; it attacks no problems but wrestles with philosophical meanings. It shares the current distrust of liberalism and naturalism. One young critic denounces the "professionally liberal" publishers who insist that the Negro writer "cannot possibly know anything else but Jim Crow, sharecropping, slum-ghettoes, Georgia crackers, and the sting of his humiliation, his unending ordeal, his blackness."[14] This swing of the pendulum from the publishers of the Van Vechten vogue with their demands for the exotic is striking. Nevertheless, some publishers still take risks with Negro fiction not burdened with the conventional problem. William Demby's *Beetle Creek* (1950) presents a stifling small town where an old white eccentric seeking friendship from Negroes is rejected with cruel barbarity. Owen Dodson's *Boy at the Window* (1951) focuses steadily on a Negro boy's growing up in Brooklyn and Washington; the problems are those of youth and adolescence, not race. James Baldwin considers the problem novel to be the cage of Negro writing. Of his novel, *Go Tell It on the Mountain* (1953), Baldwin says: "I wanted my people to be people first, Negroes almost incidentally. . . . I hoped by refusing to take a special, embattled tone, to involve the reader in their lives [so that] he would close the book knowing more about himself, and therefore more about Negroes, than he had known before." Baldwin's depiction of a Negro family and of the religion of Harlem storefront churches has rich insight. Ralph Ellison's *Invisible Man* (1952) is by any reckoning a major novel. Its theme is time-honored—the education of a provincial; its manner ranges from naturalistic to surrealistic. Its hero—humiliated as a boy in the South, disillusioned by a Southern college, catspaw of Communists, quarry of frenzied Negro nationalists, rejected and harassed, denied identity as a person—pays ex-

14. Richard Gibson, "A No to Nothing," *Kenyon Review* (Spring, 1951), reprinted in *Perspectives USA* (Winter, 1953), p. 92.

orbitantly for his education. But Ellison has humor as well as starkness. His swarming gallery of characters: Negroes, whites; folk illiterates, Park Avenue sophisticates; menials and mad messiahs; all have the ring of truth. Saying more about Negro life than any preceding novelist, Ellison claims universality for his novel. "Who knows, but that on the lower frequencies, I speak for you," his protagonist asks all other men who are perplexed by the tensions of modern civilization.

Because of the phenomenal sales of Frank Yerby's historical romances and the critical esteem accorded Willard Motley's novels, certain critics now counsel Negro novelists to stop writing about Negro life. But Yerby's period pieces are hardly pertinent to such counsel. Escapist fiction, shrewdly concocted of sex and sadism, sensationalizing rather than illuminating history, has never invalidated the time-proven truth that in representational literature an artist does best with what he knows best and feels most deeply. Motley's *Knock on Any Door* (1947) about an Italian gangster, and his *We Fished All Night* (1952) about perplexed veterans, support the axiom; this polyglot, fringe world is precisely the world that Motley knows best. Most Negroes, however, have not shared such experiences. The pragmatic proof is still the quality of the book; the "white novels" of Zora Neale Hurston, Ann Petry, Chester Himes, William Gardner Smith are inferior in significance and skill to their novels centered in Negro experience. That Negro novelists should not be confined to Negro characters goes without saying. Even if said, bold imaginations would always be found to disobey; Negroes will write of whites with as much knowledge and sympathetic identification as they can muster. But this does not mean the forfeiture of the life that perforce they know best. Negro life is called a prison by certain critics who equate civic disabilities with artistic, but for the artist of imagination it is no more imprisoning than the worlds of Zola, Dostoevsky, Joyce, O'Casey, or Faulkner.

Negro poets of the last fifteen years have followed the course of modern poetry, from "public" verse to private symbolism. Poetry of the early forties was social: Waring Cuney turned from elegiac lyrics to harsh blues, which the folk singer, Joshua White, recorded as *Southern Exposure*. Langston Hughes continued his racial indignation in *Jim Crow's Last Stand* (1943) and his quizzical portraiture in several books, from *Shakespeare in Harlem* (1942) to *One Way Ticket* (1949). *Montage of a Dream Deferred* (1951), experimenting with counterparts of jazz forms—from swing through boogie-woogie to bebop—shows Hughes at his mature best in revealing the complexity of his beloved Harlem. Frank Marshall Davis's *47th Street* (1948) has vigor and bite and the same kind of knowingness about Chicago that

Hughes has about Harlem. Margaret Walker's *For My People*, which won the Yale University Younger Poets award in 1942, expressed strong racial pride and faith in both dithyrambs and ballads. Quite different is the carefully disciplined poetry of Gwendolyn Brooks's *A Street in Bronzeville* (1945); frankness, insight, and increasingly intricate symbolism mark her *Annie Allen* (1949), which won the Pulitzer Prize. *Powerful Long Ladder* (1946), by Owen Dodson, another highly trained poet, includes sincerely felt poetry on race experience; his later poems, in step with *avant-gardism*, explore a private mystical world.

Robert Hayden's earliest *Heart Shapes in the Dust* (1940) contained deft lyrics of clarity and melody; the poems of his second phase explored the heroic and tragic in the history of the Negro; his latest poems in *The Lion and the Archer* (1948) and *Figure of Time* (1955) are densely symbolic. Hayden is the leading spirit in a group that issued a manifesto, "Counterpoise," which opposed the "chauvinistic, the cultist, the special pleading" of Negro writing, and its evaluation "entirely in the light of sociology and politics."[15] Myron O'Higgins, whose poems comprised the second part of *The Lion and the Archer*, Bruce McWright, May Miller, and Carl Holman are also skilful modernist poets. M. Beaunorus Tolson's poetic career extends from the rhapsodic poetry of *Rendezvous with America* (1944) to the *Libretto for the Republic of Liberia* (1955), where Whitman's influence is exchanged for those of Hart Crane, Pound, and Eliot. Tolson's praise of the Liberian experiment is not perfunctory; *Libretto* grew out of long antagonism to imperialism, a wide-reaching intelligence, and a vigorous vocabulary. Allen Tate has called this poem the Negro's first complete assimilation of the "language of the Anglo-American poetic tradition," i.e., the tradition of Allen Tate. With great respect for Tolson's gifts, one may still say of his latest sponsor, to paraphrase one of his favorite poets: *Timeo Tateos, donas ferentes*. The *Libretto* has a *succès d'estime* and is to be studied over the land in college classes; for this explication Tolson has supplied sixteen pages of notes for twenty-nine sparsely printed pages of text, but for one reader these are not yet enough.[16]

The discovery of America, encouraged by the Writers' Project, stimulated Roi Ottley's *New World A-Comin'* (1943), which gave an up-to-date, guardedly optimistic account of the changes of the racial front. Ottley's *Black Odyssey* (1948) is sprightly, journalistic history; his *No Green Pas-*

15. "Counterpoise" (Nashville, 1948), n.p.
16. "Introduction," Tolson, *Libretto for the Republic of Liberia* (New York, 1955), n.p.

tures (1951) records disillusionment with Europe, concluding that despite the disabilities, America still offers the greatest promises to Negroes. J. Saunders Redding's *No Day of Triumph* (1942) is one of the best examples of the reportage of the forties, telling much about Negro America with keenness and perceptiveness. These qualities also mark *They Came in Chains* (1950), a volume in Louis Adamic's People of America Series. Redding's *On Being Negro in America* (1951), baring the exasperations of a Negro intellectual, was supposed to be his last word on "race," but in *An American in India* (1954) race confronts him constantly and he is forced to spend much of his mission defending America from Communist hecklers. Carl Rowan's *South of Freedom* (1954) is the discovery by a Negro veteran of a few changes in his native South, slowed down by prevailing and dangerous inertia. Langston Hughes's *Simple Speaks His Mind* (1950) and *Simple Takes a Wife* (1954) are a concoction of reportage, satire and fiction. The chats of the author and his sharp witted buddy center about race in a new kind of crackerbox philosophizing transferred to Harlem juke joints, with no loss of the old pith and pungency. Two books on Africa contrast: Era Bell Thompson has written a breezy, journalistic travelogue in *Africa: Land of My Fathers* (1954); and Richard Wright has written an angry and troubled account of a visit to the Gold Coast in *Black Power* (1954); both books are based on short trips, to which Africa proverbially yields up few secrets.

At the start of the twenties, the only books available on the folk Negro were the Uncle Remus Tales, a few collections of spirituals, and Talley's *Negro Folk Rhymes*. Today materials abound. B. A. Botkin's *Lay My Burden Down* (1945), edited from the thousands of ex-slave narratives collected by the Writer's Project, is valuable "folk history," helping to lay the ghosts of the plantation tradition. The vast collection of discs in the Library of Congress Archives, started by the Lomaxes, has discovered unknown songs and singers; among these was the dynamic Leadbelly, who, together with Josh White, brought unadulterated folk music to thousands of Americans. The record companies have responded to the appeal of this music. It is significant that whereas even an artist like Roland Hayes found the recording studios closed to him in his early years, today not only are the voices of Marian Anderson, Dorothy Maynor, and other concert singers everywhere available on records, but staid companies issue long-play volumes of folk singers such as Bessie Smith and Mahalia Jackson, with their strong faces gracing the colorful album jackets. Frederick Ramsey's *Music from the South* in ten long-play volumes, from field recordings in areas hitherto untouched, crowns Ramsey's tireless search for the roots of jazz.

Together with Charles Smith, Ramsey pioneered in the historical and critical study of jazz; today a long bibliography by many authors shows the wisdom of such pioneering. Most of the above collectors and interpreters are white; Negro collectors of folk material have been rare, but second-generation respectability is declining: J. Mason Brewer has enthusiastically collected yarns; Lorenzo Turner has studied Gullah with scientific linguistic techniques; and William H. Pipes, with sociological interest, has recorded old-time sermons in backwoods churches. The interest in Negro folk expression is not a momentary fad; the collection and interpretation are the work of both white and Negro folklorists, united in respect for material which, no longer set in isolation, is becoming recognized as integral part of the American experience.

But with folk culture corresponding less and less to Negro experience in America, it is of course to the conscious literature that we turn for fullest expression. The New Critics find such a literature negligible, unworthy of anthologizing or evaluation. To a young white critic, John W. Aldridge, literature about Negroes has a "specialness" that works against universality;[17] to a young Negro critic, Richard Gibson, literature by American Negroes is a dismaying spectacle because no single work "stands out as a masterpiece."[18] But universality and masterpieces are never called out of the vasty deep by critics' incantations or debarred by their proscriptions. That they are hard-won and rare in whatever time or place is not likely to stop the vigorous contemporary writing. The Negro writer's task is that of his fellows in England, France, Italy, and America; to do as honest, truthful, well-designed, and revelatory work as his powers and insight permit; the rest he must leave to the future. Some signs confute the Cassandras who decry the possibilities of a sound literature of Negro life: the growing craftsmanship, learned from the best models; the waning provincialism, self-pity, and denunciation; the increasing integration in American literary life; the leisure for creative maturing, more possible because of new publishing conditions; the loss, on the part of Negro readers, of their hypersensitivity and, on the part of white readers, of their superficial preconceptions. In one of the last essays he wrote, Alain Locke looked with serenity

17. John W. Aldridge, *After the Lost Generation* (New York, 1953), pp. 102 ff. Aldridge is sound in hoping that "problems of race" will be treated as human problems, not as "forced polemics journalistically presented." But, though he categorizes the Negro and the Jew with the homosexual (p. 103) as the last remaining tragic types, he considers their problems minor issues, not "central to the meaning of this age." Such lofty dismissal divulges the narrowness of much current academic criticism.

18. Gibson, *op. cit.*, p. 92.

upon the future of the literature to which he had given such support and guidance. He saw how improving race relations have relaxed the Negro writer's tensions, and made possible deeper human understanding on his part; on the part of whites he saw growing fraternal acceptance. Should this cultural recognition and acceptance be realized, he wrote,

> the history of the Negro's strange and tortuous career in American literature may also become the story of America's hard-won but easily endured attainment of cultural democracy.[19]

19. Locke, "The Negro in American Literature," Arabel J. Porter, ed., *New World Writing* (New York, 1952), p. 33.

African American
Music and Folk Culture

Folk Literature

THE SPIRITUALS

~ TRAVELERS through the antebellum South were struck by the singing and dancing of the slaves. Some dismissed these as uncouth barbarism, others were stirred by the vigor of the dancing and the weird sadness of the songs. Report of these reached the North in travelers' accounts, published journals, novels, and the narratives of fugitive slaves. Southern authors, in the main, did not consider the songs and dances worth mentioning, except, strangely, as proofs of the slave's contentment.

It was not until the Civil War that any of these songs were collected. In 1864, Charlotte Forten wrote down a few songs that she heard the new freedmen sing on Saint Helena Island. Thomas Wentworth Higginson, moved greatly as the black soldiers of his regiment sang in the evenings about the campfires, recorded several spirituals for an article in *The Atlantic Monthly* (1867) and included a chapter on them in his *Army Life in a Black Regiment* (1870). The first systematic collection was made by three Northerners, William F. Allen, Charles P. Ware, and Lucy McKim Garrison, in their *Slave Songs of the United States* (1867). This book, sympathetically edited, is an important landmark in American musical history.

The wider introduction of these songs to the world came a few years later in 1871, when a group of Fisk University students, under the leadership of George White, started on tour, singing the songs that they had learned from their slave parents. They had to struggle for a hearing. One tavern keeper, astounded that real Negroes and not burnt-cork singers were advertised to sing Negro songs, drove them out of his tavern. In Brooklyn they were scoffed at as Beecher's Nigger Minstrels. But they packed churches there and in New York and went on to Europe on a truly triumphal tour. When they left Fisk, the school was in straitened circumstances; when they returned, they had enough money to construct a new building, Jubilee Hall. Their example has been followed even until the present by a large number of colleges that send out choral groups that specialize in spirituals.

Fisk University's part in establishing the spirituals is definite. The origins of the type of songs that the young college group sang is less definite. Whether they are of individual or group authorship, for instance, is one problem. An early collector heard a slave tell how the songs were made:

> I'll tell you, it's dis way. My master call me up and order me a short peck of corn and a hundred lash. My friends see it, and is sorry for me. When dey come to de praise-meeting dat night dey sing about it. Some's very good singers and know how; and dey work it in—work it in, you know, till they get it right; and dat's de way.

Higginson found a young oarsman who boasted that

> Once we boys went for tote some rice, and de nigger-driver, he keep a-callin' on us, and I say, "O de ole nigger-driver." Den anudder said, "Fust ting my mammy told me was, nothin' so bad as nigger-drivers." Den I made a sing, just puttin' a word, and den anudder word.

When this poet started singing, however, the other oarsmen, after listening a moment joined in the chorus "as if it were an old acquaintance though they evidently had never heard it before."

James Weldon Johnson, who called the makers of spirituals "black and unknown bards of long ago," believed that many spring from highly gifted individuals. Robert W. Gordon, according to his *Folk Songs of America*, discovered in the isolated Low Country of South Carolina a type of spiritual that in its primitive structure (single line of recitative alternating with simple line refrain) is probably closest to the earliest spirituals sung. For their "recitative" these spirituals demanded a highly special sort of singer:

> He was not an "author" in the ordinary sense, for he did not himself create new lines. He merely put together traditional lines in new forms, adding nothing of his own. . . . He gathered together and held in his memory countless scraps and fragments, and had the ability to sew or patch them together as occasion demanded.

One of the present groups most productive of new spirituals, The Golden Gate Quartet, works similarly, according to report. Willie Johnson, their talented poet and leader, with an enormous stock of folk idioms and lines, reworks these into new and original patterns. Yet the songs that this quartet sings, though obviously showing a creative gift, are not so "original" that the folk would not recognize them as theirs. "Composers" of the best of present-day blues likewise levy upon the folk storehouse, turning out products that are close to authentic folk stuff.

Something of this sort is meant by the folk origin of the spirituals. It is unlikely that any group of worshipers and singers, as a group, composed spirituals. Single individuals with poetic ingenuity, a rhyming gift, or a good memory "composed" or "remembered" lines, couplets, or even quatrains out of a common storehouse. The group would join in with the refrain or the longer chorus. When one leader's ingenuity or memory was exhausted, another might take up the "composition." About two matters of origin, however, there is more certainty than about method of composition. The first is that stories purporting to tell the circumstances and dates of individual spirituals are more fanciful than accurate. This is true of all folk song. The claims of ex-slaves that they were present at the creation of well-known spirituals are to be trusted no more than the claims of many yarn-spinners that they worked side by side with John Henry or were shot at by Stackalee. The second is that the spirituals are genuinely folk products, regardless of the fact that gifted individuals may have played leading roles in their composition. From the folk storehouse came the ideas, the vocabulary, the idioms, the images. The folk approved the song or rejected it, as it squared with folk knowledge, memory, and vision. The folk changed lines that were not easily understood, inserted new stanzas, sometimes bringing the songs up to date, and transmitted them orally to the next generation. In the long journey, stanzas were lost or imperfectly remembered; and new and often incoherent interpolations took their places. But the folk kept a very large number of the songs alive and in a rather sound condition.

A second problem of origin: whether the spirituals were derived from African music or European music, whether they were "original" with the Negro or imitations, started its controversial course at the end of the nineteenth century. In a period when the glorification of the Aryan by Gobineau and Houston Stewart Chamberlain was popular, the attribution of artistic capacity to the Negro seemed presumptuous. In 1893 Richard Wallaschek, a German musicologist, attacked the songs of the Negro as "very much overrated," "mere imitations of European compositions," "ignorantly borrowed." Certain musical critics, irritated by the praise of the spirituals, and especially by Dvořák's use of Negro melodies in his symphony *From the New World,* gladly made use of Wallaschek's dicta. In 1915, Henry E. Krehbiel, an American musical critic of high repute, answered Wallaschek's charges. This was not difficult, since Wallaschek had included many spurious minstrel melodies in the "Negro" songs he studied. Krehbiel set out to prove, in a discriminating analysis, that the Negro songs were the only indigenous body of folk songs in America, and that these songs were the Negro's own.

John W. Work, James Weldon Johnson, R. Nathaniel Dett, N. Ballanta-Taylor, and several other Negroes allied themselves with Krehbiel. Naturally sensitive about the aspersion on the originality of their race, some of these at times overstated their argument and stressed not only the complete originality of the songs, but also their Africanism.

A cogent attack on the Africanism of the songs came from Guy B. Johnson, one of the most sympathetic and informed students of Negro folklore. In *Folk Culture on St. Helena Island* (1930) Johnson approached the Negro spiritual as a problem in anthropology: "What happened when the Negro slave, possessing a system of music admittedly different from European or Western music, came into contact with the American white man's music?" Johnson established definite points of contact between the slave and "white music," which the defenders of the originality of the spirituals had scouted. He found both musical and textual similarities in white revival hymns and Negro spirituals. Newman White in *American Negro Folk Songs* (1928) adduced proof of the slaves' participation in the camp meetings of the South, and of the similarity of white and Negro religious primitivism. He found a large number of close textual resemblances in white revival hymns and the spirituals. George Pullen Jackson in *White Spirituals of the Southern Uplands* (1934) illustrates melodic and textual similarities between white and Negro spirituals. A large school of commentators now accepts the conclusions of these scholars.

Extremists have set up the controversy as between Africanism, or complete originality, and white camp-meeting derivation, or complete unoriginality. This oversimplification does injustice to the careful scholarship of some of the men on both sides.

As far as the music is concerned, this is not the place to enter the controversy, since the spirituals have to be represented in this anthology solely as folk literature. Certain observations, however, may be useful, since they pertain to the whole picture of the Negro in American culture. Few of the disputants know all three of the musics involved: African music (if the music of an entire continent of different peoples can be so simply categorized); Southern white music of the slavery period with which the slave might have come into contact; and the spirituals themselves. Collections of slave songs were made very late; they are at best only approximations, in a system of notation that is admittedly skeletal. Analyzing the songs collected by Allen, Ware, and Garrison is a long way from analyzing the songs as sung by folk Negroes, either then or now. That the slave had contact with white religious folk and minstrel music is no less undebatable than that whites had contact with Negro music. A give-and-take seems logical to expect. Correspondences between white and Negro melodies have been established. The complete Africanism of the spirituals was never tenable. The spirituals are obviously not in an African musical idiom, not even so much as the music of Haiti, Cuba, and Brazil. But all of this does not establish the Negro spiritual, and most certainly not hot jazz, the blues, and boogie-woogie, as imitative of white music, or as unoriginal, or as devoid of traces of the African idiom. Believing one's ears, especially where folk-music is concerned, is probably better than believing the conventional notation of that music; believing phonograph records, as recent scholars are doing, is even better. The obstinate fact of a great difference between Negro folk-songs and the white camp-meeting hymns exists. Even the strongest adherents of the view that the origin of the Negro spirituals is in white music, agree that now the spiritual is definitely the Negro's own and, regardless of birthplace, is stamped with originality. The conclusions of Milton Metfessel, derived from a use of "phonophotography" in music, are that

> In bridging the gap between civilized and primitive music, the Negro sings some songs in which the analyzed elements are probably more often European than African, others in which the two are equally present, and others still in which the African element predominates. In our present group, the work songs seem to have more of the latter elements, the blues and workaday religious songs partake of both, while the formal spirituals appear to lean toward Europe.

The present state of scholarship on the subject is summarized by George Herzog:

> It becomes more and more clear that Southern Negro folk music does not furnish a chapter in the rigid survival of original musical features, but an equally fascinating chapter in the recreation of musical forms. European folk song, in the hands of the Negro, achieved special forms

and idiosyncrasies, one step further removed from the European prototypes and from the old European background.

To many this step is a good long one. Lovers of Negro folks songs need not fear either its detractors or the students of origins. Neither European nor African, but partaking of elements of both, the result is a new kind of music, certainly not mere imitation, but more creative and original than any other American music.

The resemblance of words and ideas in white hymns and Negro spirituals is not of such great moment. The slaves, accepting Christianity, naturally accepted the vocabulary and subject matter of Christianity; and, liking a good song wherever they heard it, they sang church hymns as well as spirituals. Jupiter Hammon used the common evangelical currency. Exact correspondences between lines in white hymns and spirituals have been discovered; Guy Johnson found such lines as "Ride on, Jesus"; "O, Lord, remember me"; "I am bound for the land of Canaan"; "O, could I hear some sinner pray"; "Lay this body down"; and "You will see the graves a-bursting" in a single white songbook, *The Millennial Harp* (published in 1843). Both Negro and white religious songs tell of "poor, wayfaring strangers," "a union band," on "a pilgrimage to heaven."

But, as Guy Johnson states, the line, or at most the stanza, seems to be the unit of transfer; there are not many instances (though more than generally suspected) "in which a white song was taken over in its entirety by Negroes." This fact should be considered with the fact that some of the correspondences are forced. For instance, George Pullen Jackson cites the following lines:

> At his table we'll sit down,
> Christ will gird himself and serve us with sweet
>   manna all around. (white)

as parallel with

> Gwine to sit down at the welcome table,
> Gwine to feast off milk and honey. (Negro)

and

> To hide yourself in the mountaintop
> To hide yourself from God. (white)

as parallel with

> Went down to the rocks to hide my face,
> The rocks cried out no hiding place. (Negro)

These are similar only in general idea, certainly not in the poetry. Newman White believes that white songs in "crossing over" are greatly transformed. Samuel Asbury believes "the words of the best white spirituals," cannot compare as poetry with the words of the best Negro spirituals and Carl Engel sees the spirituals as amazingly profound and beautiful verse, unlike anything in "the Bay Psalm Book or its numerous successors," though both men deny "complete originality" to the music. Louis Untermeyer writes that the slaves, having absorbed the Christianity to which they were exposed, repeated it in a highly original way:

> Only those who have heard the *cadences* can appreciate the originality of the Negro's contribution. . . . The magic emanates from the unaffected nobility of the themes, the teasing-shifting rhythms, so simple on the surface, so intricately varied beneath; it rises from a deep emotional sincerity in every beat.

Where suspicions of the new scholarship were justified was in the interpretation of the spirituals, based on the verbal similarities between white hymns and Negro spirituals. Finding that white camp-meeting hymns spoke of "freedom" and of "hard trials," Newman White argued against the "abolitionist use of the spirituals as an instrument of propaganda," as sorrow songs produced by the oppression of slavery. He bases his argument upon the paucity of songs containing "unequivocal references to the desire for freedom," and upon his assumption that the Negro "seldom contemplated his low estate in slavery." According to White, the spirituals of the slaves, when referring to freedom mean exactly what the camp-meeting hymns of slaveholders mean by their references to freedom: namely, freedom from the oppression of sin. This is ingenious but unconvincing reasoning.

There are not many spirituals that speak openly of a love for freedom and a determination to be free. The slaves were not so naïve as that; they knew, better than several of their historians, how close to hysteria the slaveholders really were, how rigid the control could be. The very fact of a group of slaves meeting and singing and praying together was cause of anxiety to many masters, even if the slaves were singing of Jordan or Jericho.

If we can believe several fugitive slave autobiographies, however, there were many not so indirect references to physical bondage and freedom. It required no stretch of imagination to see the trials of the Israelites as paralleling the trials of the slaves, Pharaoh and his army as oppressors, and Egyptland as the South. "Go Down, Moses" was a censored song, according to fugitive slaves. "O Mary don't you weep, don't you mourn; Pharaoh's army got drowned, O Mary don't you weep" is less direct, but expresses the same central idea. Douglass tells us not only of the double-talk of the slaves' songs, but also sees the whole body of spirituals as reflecting a desire for freedom.

Nevertheless, the spirituals which without ingenious forcing are seen to have double meanings: "Didn't my Lord deliver Daniel, and why not every man?" "Rich man Dives, he lived so well—When he died he found a home in hell"; the challenging "Go Down, Moses"; the shouts of jubilee possible under the banners of a liberating army: "O Freedom, befo' I'd be a slave, I'd be buried in my grave!" are numerically in the minority. The slaves sang songs expressing Christianity, and then not as "Christian sol-diers, marching on to war," but as lost sheep, all crying for a shepherd.

Yet Newman White goes too far in stating that the slave "never contem-plated his low estate," and that because few outspoken abolitionist spiritu-als can be found, the slave's references to freedom connote only freedom from sin, from the bonds of the flesh and the world. Analysis of the body of white camp-meeting "spirituals" reveals fairly perfunctory references to heaven as freedom; but in Negro spirituals references to trouble here below are far more numerous, and are poignant rather than perfunctory, springing from a deep need, not from an article of faith. Such lines as

Bye and bye, I'm gonna lay down dis heavy load.

———

De blind man stood on de road, and cried
Crying Lord, my Lord, save-a po' me.

———

Keep a-inchin' along, lak a po' inchworm.

———

I don't know what my mother wants to stay here
fuh,
Dis ole worl' ain't been no friend to huh.

———

I'm rolling through an unfriendly worl'.

———

Lord, keep me from sinking down.

surely reflect the slave's awareness of his bitter plight more than his consciousness of the oppression of sin.

The spirituals tell of hard trials, great tribulations; or wanderings in
some lonesome valley, or down some unknown road, a long ways from
home, with brother, sister, father, mother gone. It is only a half-truth to see
the spirituals as otherworldly. "You take dis worl', and give me Jesus" is
certainly one of the least of the refrains. In the spirituals the slave took a
clear-eyed look at this world, and he revealed in tragic poetry what he saw:

O I been rebuked, and I been scorned,
Done had a hard time sho's you born.

There are spirituals, many of them well known, that spring with joy.
The convert shouts when he gets out of the wilderness. The true believer
sees heaven as a welcome table, a feasting place; quite as often, significantly, as a place of rest where the worn out ones can sit down, for once at
their ease. The saved dilate on the activities of that great "gittin' up morning" with greater zeal and trust than that with which Michael Wigglesworth
foresaw his Day of Doom. But even in heaven, life on earth is not forgotten:

I'm gonna tell God all my troubles,
    When I get home. . . .

I'm gonna tell Him the road was rocky
    When I get home. . . .

I'm gonna tell Him I had hard trials
    When I get home. . . .

I'm gonna tell God how you're doing
    When I get home.

If the spirituals that talk about heaven are often joyful, it should be remembered that the joy is a joy at escape.

The spirituals were born of suffering. Yet Zora Neale Hurston is right
when, thinking of their rendition, she refuses the inclusive title "Sorrow
Songs." Negro folk singers, certainly today, sing spirituals with great gusto.
There is much more than melancholy in their singing; there is a robustness,
vitality, a fused strength. The singing serves as a release; the fervor of the

release indicates something of the confining pressure that folk Negroes know too well and have known too long.

Musicologists find in the spiritual singing of today a musical relative of the wild free improvisations of hot jazz. The resemblance is seen especially in the singing of such groups as the Golden Gate Quartet and the Mitchell Christian Singers. The spirituals that they sing are often of recent origin, frequently narratives of Biblical characters, and their arrangements of the older spirituals are probably more dynamic and less restrained than their forefathers' singing in the old brush arbors. With some pronounced exceptions, the new spirituals seem more evangelical in nature and less the outpourings of "a troubled sperrit." Besides the new spirituals springing up in the rural churches of the South, evangelists sell hymns, printed as broadsides, as their own compositions, though many of the lines seem lifted from hymnbooks.

Newman White states that there was a time "when most of the literate and semi-literate members of the Negro race were desirous of forgetting [the spiritual]." This is only a half-truth. Many Negroes in the upper strata did so, some because of what James Weldon Johnson calls "second-generation respectability," some because of the dubious uses to which spirituals were put, some because of the interpretations of them as plantation songs, reminiscent of the good ole days befo' de war, which is exactly what they are not. Some Negro college students have refused to sing them, but more colleges have stressed them in the repertoires of their choral groups, not only because of their value in gaining finances and prestige. Most of the leading race interpreters: Frederick Douglass, Booker T. Washington, Paul Laurence Dunbar, W. E. B. Du Bois, Kelly Miller, Carter G. Woodson, and Alain Locke have paid honor to them. Leading musical scholars such as those mentioned earlier have praised them even extremely; leading musicians like Harry T. Burleigh, R. Nathaniel Dett, Hall Johnson, Eva Jessye, W. C. Handy, Charles Cooke, William Grant Still, and William Dawson have interpreted and arranged them; leading artists like Marian Anderson, Dorothy Maynor, Roland Hayes, and Paul Robeson sing them with utmost respect.

For nearly a century, articulate Negroes have recognized the spirituals as the Negro's first important cultural gift to America. Folk Negroes have nourished them for longer than that, and are still creating new ones, hoarding a treasure though unconscious of its value.

SLAVE SECULARS

The first collectors of Negro folk song were New Englanders, of abolitionist background, seriously concerned with the grave problems facing the newly freed. The first use of the folk songs in the colleges was to foster race pride. Naturally, therefore, the secular songs of the slaves were considered least worthy of collection. Their appropriation by blackface minstrelsy, the ribaldry of some of the verses, their overuse by writers to show the Negro's carefree nature, were other forces militating against them. One early commentator, John Mason Brown in *Lippincott's Magazine* (1868), included a few secular songs, but collectors generally neglected them.

But slaves did not sing sorrow songs only. There were many dance songs, children's play songs, humorous songs. These are by no means merely nonsense songs of giddy clowns. American counterparts to the stylized Calypso songs of Trinidad were to be found chiefly in New Orleans, but there were many satiric songs elsewhere. In terse stanzas the folk Negro carries his irony as far as he can:

> Naught's a naught, figger's a figger,
> All for de white man, an' none fo' de nigger.

> ——————

> When dey gits old and gray,
> When dey gits old and gray,
> White folks looks like monkeys,
> When dey gits old and gray.

Many seculars were good-humoredly irreverent of religion. These songs, called "upstart crows" by Newman White, and other "fiddle-sings," "cornfield hollers," and "jig-tunes" were considered "devil tunes." Though well known by many true-believing Negroes, they are not easily surrendered to collectors.

> Our Father, who art in heaven
> White man owe me 'leven, and pay me seven,
> Thy kingdom come, thy will be done
> And ef I hadn't tuck that, I wouldn't a got none.

The slave seculars afford many realistic glimpses of slavery:

> Old master bought a yaller gal,
> He bought her from the South.

The tussles with "pattyrollers," the contempt for "po' white trash," the complaints at short rations and tough masters, appear in swift biting lines.

There is very little in the seculars like Stephen Foster's gentle "Massa's in de Cold, Cold Ground." The spirit is closer to Louis Armstrong's "I'll Be Glad When You're Dead, You Rascal, You."

J. A. Macon and Joel Chandler Harris collected several slave songs, but in rendering them to the public, they forced them into patterns of standard versifying. Thomas W. Talley's *Negro Folk Rhymes* (1922) was the first collection of the secular songs of the Negro, a valuable pioneering work. Odum and Johnson, Newman White, John and Alan Lomax, Carl Sandburg, and Zora Neale Hurston are recent collectors of seculars. But the songs they collect are not chiefly slave seculars, many of which must be lost beyond recovery.

APHORISMS

Like all folk groups, the folk Negro has a store of aphorisms or proverbs expressing his weather lore, love lore, medicinal lore, and general wisdom about life. In the early years of the discovery of the Negro folk, Joel Chandler Harris and J. A. Macon collected many of these pithy sayings. The folk Negro's gift of compressing much into a little space is found in the spirituals:

Better mind dat sun, and see how she run,
And don't let him catch you wid yo' work undone.

Better look out, sister, how you walk on de cross
Yo' foot might slip and yo' soul git lost.

See dat sister, dressed so fine,
She ain't got Jesus on her mind.

in the blues:

Every shut-eye ain't sleep, every good-bye ain't gone.

My mammy tole me, my pappy tole me too,
Everybody grin in yo' face, son, ain't no friend to you.

You never miss de water till de well goes dry
You'll never miss yo' baby till she says good-bye.

and in the ballads:

> Never drive a stranger from your do'
> He may be yo' best friend; you never know.

Not the concern of collectors today, aphorisms are still abundantly used by the old folk to hand down to the young ones what they have learned of life by the hard way:

> De ole sheep dey knows de road
> Young lambs gotta find de way.

BALLADS

Ballad collectors have found many variants of English and Scotch ballads among folk Negroes. This is not so strange as it may seem. The social isolation of southern folk Negroes, like the physical isolation of the mountain folk in Kentucky, Tennessee, North Carolina, and the Ozarks, has made for the preservation of older English dialects, lore, and songs. "Barbara Allen," "The Briary Bush," "Lady Isabel and the Elf Knight," and "Lord Lovell" are examples of traditional ballads that the Negro has helped to preserve.

The charming lullaby that has been sung by so many Negroes, with such lines as:

> Mister Frog went a-courting, he did ride
>   Unh-hunh, unh-hunh,
> Mister Frog went a-courting, he did ride,
>   Sword and pistol by his side
>   Unh-hunh, unh-hunh.
>
> Said Miss Mousie, will you marry me?
>   Unh-hunh, unh-hunh, [etc.]
>
> Not without Uncle Rat's consent
>   Unh-hunh, unh-hunh
> Not without Uncle Rat's consent
>   Would I marry de President,
>   Unh-hunh, unh-hunh.

first appeared in London in 1580 as "A Moste Strange Weddinge of the Frogge and the Mouse." Stanzas like

> There was a tall an' handsome man,
>   Who came a-courtin' me,
> He said "Steal out atter dark tonight,
>   An' come a-ridin' with me,
>   An' come a-ridin' with me;"

from "Lady Isabel and the Elf Knight," and

> Hangman, hangman, slack on the line,
>   Slack on the line a little while;
> For I think I see my brother coming
>   With money to pay my fine.

from "The Briary Bush," show that the stuff of the old ballads was not too remote from Negro folk experience. The question

> Who's gonna shoes yo' little feet
> Who's gonna glove yo' hand

which is asked of John Henry's little woman has come down the long years from the old Scottish ballad called "The Lass of Roch Royal."

Native American ballads also have been altered in Negro versions. Among these are "Casey Jones," of sure appeal to working-class Negroes because of its railroading heroism, and "Frankie and Johnnie," not certainly of white or Negro origin, and probably partaking of both. An interesting example of how a Negro guitar player builds up a "symphonic drama" out of Frankie and Johnnie is given in John and Alan Lomax's *Negro Folk Songs As Sung by Leadbelly.* "Careless Love," originally a mountain ballad, has been added to so often by Negro troubadours that there is now a new song, definitely Negro.

But preserving traditional ballads or altering other American ballads that strike their fancy are not the chief pursuits of Negro balladeers. They create ballads narrating the exploits of their own heroes and lives. They have contributed some of the finest ballads to America's "songbag," such as "John Henry," "Stackalee," "Uncle Bud," "Railroad Bill," and "Po' Lazarus." The corrupt condition of some of these leads to the fear that ballad making and singing are on the decline. Yet the assiduous efforts of such collectors as the Lomaxes are uncovering fine ballads still—as their versions of "Poor Lazarus" and of "De Grey Goose" indicate. Like all folk ballads, Negro ballads celebrate the outlaw as in "Railroad Bill" and "Stackalee," or the swift fugitive as in "Long Gone Lost John" and "The Travellin' Man," or the hero of strength, courage, and endurance as in "John Henry." Spectacular events like the sinking of the Titanic, the death of Floyd Collins in the cave, the Mississippi River on a grand rampage, and a tornado's "busting loose" call for ballads. Negro folk ballads tell a story with economy, without sentimentality, and very often with the tragic sense of life characteristic of the best ballads of all lands.

WORK SONGS, SOCIAL SONGS, SONGS OF PROTEST

On many jobs—chopping cotton, roustabouting on the levees, "coonjining" on the gangplank, laying ties and rails on the railroad, driving spikes, swinging picks—the working-class Negro sings in rhythm with his labor. Higginson found examples of rowing songs in South Carolina. These work-songs are generally remembered or improvised stanzas strung together on the thread of melody, not of narrative. Timed with the swinging of his pick, a Negro laborer may sing

Lawdy, lawdy,—hunh—
Think I will—hunh—
Make my home—hunh—
In Jacksonville.

Many of the stanzas are thrusts at the captain or boss, sometimes good-humored, sometimes—when he is far enough away—frankly rebellious:

If I'd had—hunh—
My weight in lime—
I'd a-whupped my captain—
Till he went stone-blind.

There are also a large number of social songs, differing from the ballads in that they deal with personal emotions and differing from the blues in their stanzaic form.

The Lomaxes, Lawrence Gellert, and Joshua White have recently brought to light many songs of strong social protest. These are censored songs, to be discovered in prison construction camps and on chain gangs only by collectors who have won the confidence of the singers. They express a bitterness, not new to the Negro folk, but fairly new in song collections. Lawrence Gellert, who has garnered the richest yield of such songs in *Negro Songs of Protest* and *Me and My Captain*, realized the need of "cultivating and cementing confidences with individual Negroes" in order to get to the "core of living folklore." At that core he found an "otherwise inarticulate resentment against injustice, a part of the unrest stirring the South." Joshua White's "Silicosis Blues" is the creation of an individual folk singer who phrases the bitter awareness of many industrial workers.

THE BLUES

Among Negro folk songs the blues are second in importance only to the spirituals. In contrast to the spirituals, which were originally intended for group singing, the blues are sung by a single person. They express his feelings and ideas about his experience, but they do this so fundamentally, in an idiom so recognizable to his audience, that his emotion is shared as theirs. The mood is generally a sorrowful one; the word "blues" is part of the American vocabulary now as a synonym for melancholy, for unhappy moodiness.

Most blues use a fairly strict form: a leading line, repeated (sometimes with slight variations), and generally a rhyming third line. Sometimes the first line is repeated twice; in the less developed blues, sometimes the last line does not rhyme. The form is simple, but well adapted to express the laments of folk Negroes over hard luck, "careless" or unrequited love, broken family life, or general dissatisfaction with a cold and trouble-filled world. The standard form of the blues stanza is as follows:

> I went down to the depot; I looked upon the board;
> It say: There's good times here, they's better up the road.

The blues go far back in time probably in their most rudimentary form to slavery. John and Alan Lomax trace them to the "hollers," the mournful line sung over and over again by a man or woman at work, the brief phrasing of some line sharply meaningful:

> Oh I ain't gonna stay here no mo!

or

> Sometimes I think my woman, she too sweet to die;
> Den sometimes I think she ought to be buried alive.

"Jelly Roll" Morton, while playing piano in the sporting houses of New Orleans, heard Mamie Desdunes play and sing the "first blues I no doubt heard in my life":

De 219 took my baby away
219 took my babe away
217 bring her back someday.

"Ma" Rainey heard the blues while trouping up and down her native southland, and started singing them herself to audiences that were spellbound as her deep husky voice gave them back their songs. W. C. Handy's quick ear heard them on the levees, outside of country railroad depots, and in the streets of southern towns. He recognized their value, and in 1909 wrote "Memphis Blues," and in 1912, the most widely known blues of all, "St. Louis Blues." Handy is called the "Father of the Blues." As "the first musician of creative and analytical powers to appreciate the possibilities of the blues, and the writer of the first published blues," Handy is credited by Abbe Niles with "commencing a revolution in the popular tunes of this land comparable only to that brought about by the introduction of ragtime."

The blues are recognized as indubitably the Negro's. Many songs that have come out of Tin Pan Alley are called blues with very dubious warrant. Irving Berlin's "Schoolhouse Blues," Jerome Kern's "Left All Alone Again Blues," Braham's "Limehouse Blues," Hess's "Homesickness Blues," and "Blues My Naughty Sweetie Gave to Me" are examples of these pseudo blues. As one critic summarizes it, in the blues by Tin Pan Alley composers the grief is feigned, but in genuine Negro blues the gayety is feigned. The musical influence upon jazz of the genuine blues is great; the "blue note" is one of the most significant developments in jazz, and it is entering "serious" American music. Certain bands are advertised as bands that play the blues as they should be played; certain white singers, such as Dinah Shore and Jack Teagarden, are famous for the way they sing the blues. One music critic points to a hillbilly's singing of a Negro blues with Swiss yodeling added, as a good instance of the hybridization of American popular music. The blues are now an inseparable part of that music. But they are still, almost entirely, of Negro origin, and at their best are close to folk sources.

Because of the enormous popularity on phonograph records of women blues singers such as Ma Rainey, Mamie Smith, Bessie Smith (the "Blues Empress"), Clara Smith, Trixie Smith, Ida Cox, and Billy Holiday, the blues are frequently thought of as a woman's plaint for her departed or departing lover. Not so widely known to America are the many male blues singers such as Jim Jackson, Lonnie Johnson, Leroy Carr, Leroy's Buddy (Bill Gaither), Peetie Wheatstraw, Hound Head Henry, Big Bill, and Huddie Ledbetter (Leadbelly), but they are enthusiastically received by the Negro masses.

The commercial recording companies issue more blues about love than any other kind. Love is looked upon with shrewd cynicism or irony or self-pity or sincere despair:

> Love is like a faucet, you can turn it off or on,
> But when you think you've got it, done turned off and gone.

> All you men, sho' do make me tired,
> You gotta hand full of gimme, mouthful of much obliged.

> Soon dis morning, 'bout de break of day,
> Laid my head on de pillow, where my mamma used to lay.

> If you don't want me, you don't have to carry no stall,
> I can git mo' women than a passenger train can haul.

> If you don't want me, why don't you tell me so,
> I'm little and low, can get a man anywhere I go.

> I stay drunk so much, I cain't tell night from day,
> But the woman I love, she treat me any way.

> If you don't think I'm sinking, look what a hole I'm in,
> If you don't think I love you, look what a fool I've been.

> I hear my daddy calling some other woman's name
> I know he don't mean me; I'm gonna answer jes' de same.

> Many a long day I sit and watch de sun,
> Thinking about de good things you and I have done.

Some blues celebrate the charms of the loved one, in imagery related to that of the American tall tale:

> De train I ride is sixteen coaches long,
> De gal I love is chocolate to de bone.

Big fat mamma wid de meat shaking on her bones,
Everytime she shakes, some skinny gal done lost her home.

My gal's got teeth like a lighthouse on de sea,
Everytime she smile, she throw a light on me.

A good-looking woman make a cow forget her calf.

A good-looking woman make a rabbit chase a hound.

A good-looking woman make a bulldog gnaw his chain.

But love is not the sole subject of the blues. A general vague dissatisfaction, romantic longing for other people and places, fills many of them. The road, the train, and recently the bus are the metaphors of escape, or sometimes of forces of separation:

I'd rather drink muddy water, sleep in a hollow log,
Dan to stay in dis town, treated like a dirty dog.

Going to Chicago where de water drinks like cherry wine,
Cause dis Birmingham water drinks like turpentine.

I'm going to leave here tomorrow, if I have to ride de blinds.

I'm got a mind to ramble, a mind for to leave dis town.

How long, how long, has dat evenin' train been gone?

Sitting here wondering would a matchbox hold my clothes,
I ain't got so many, and I got so far to go.

I'd rather be a catfish swimming in dat deep blue sea,
Dan to stayed in Texas, treated like dey wanted to do po' me.

I'm going where the Southern cross de Yellow Dog.

Did you ever ride on dat Mobile Central Line?
Dat's the road to ride to ease yo' troublin' mind.

I went down to de depot, I looked up on de board,
Couldn't see no train, couldn't hear no whistle blow.

———————

Greyhound, Greyhound, I heard you when you blowed yo' horn,
Well, I knew it was yo' warning that my baby was long gone.

Many blues deal with the social life of "folk" Negroes. Not so commercially rewarding as the love blues, they still exist in large numbers, as the
large Library of Congress collection bears witness. Blues have sprung up
in the wake of such disasters as the boll-weevil plague, the Mississippi in
flood, tornadoes, and fires. "Backwater Blues," composed during the tragic
flood of 1927, and the "St. Louis Cyclone Blues" are examples. Several
WPA blues have been recorded; the "Pink Slip Blues" and the "304
Blues" tell of the hardships of WPA cuts.

The examples already given show something of the poetic imagery of
the blues, which is often of a high order. Honest, elemental, sometimes
frank to the point of starkness, the blues are welcome to many because of
their contrast to the saccharine and insincere lyrics too often produced in
Tin Pan Alley. The blues are valuable, also, as shedding a great deal of
light on the social experience of the Negro masses. The smutty variants
sung in cabarets and on best-selling records should not be allowed to blur
the real qualities of this important folk poetry.

FOLK TALES

The most widely known examples of the folk tales of slavery are the
Brer Rabbit stories of Joel Chandler Harris. A good listener to the taletell-
ers of the slave quarters, friendly to plantation Negroes and artistically
sensitive, Harris was well fitted to become what Alain Locke calls him: "a
kindly amanuensis for the illiterate Negro peasant." Harris deserves great
credit for recognizing the worth of the Negro fables about Brer Rabbit, Brer
Terrapin, Brer Bear, Brer Fox, Brer Wolf, and the others of that fine company. His handling of southern Negro speech was superior to that of any
writer preceding him. Yet, as Arthur Huff Fauset points out in *The New
Negro*, his Uncle Remus stories are not folk tales, but adaptations:

In true folk tales, the story teller himself was inconsequential. . . .
The Uncle Remus stories break this tradition, however; instead the
story teller plays an important, a too important role. By that very fact,
this type of story ceases to be a folk tale and becomes in reality a

product of the imagination of the author. . . . These stories cannot present Negro folk life and feeling seen and felt on its own level. Enough has been said, perhaps, to show, without in any way detracting from the true service and real charm of the Harris stories, that there are enough incongruous elements insinuated into the situation to make it impossible to accept them as a final rendering of American Negro folklore.

Fauset blames the Harris variety of the Negro folk tale for assuming to interpret Negro character instead of simply telling stories. Harris shows Uncle Remus telling the stories for the entertainment of his little white master, and Uncle Remus too often conforms to the plantation tradition. Finally, the Uncle Remus stories are considered children's classics; the stark and almost cynical qualities of genuine folklore, especially that of rural Negroes, are deleted in favor of gentility and sentiment. A whole school of reminiscent writers gave stories as told by faithful uncles and aunties. But their purpose was more to cast a golden glow over the antebellum South than to set forth authentic Negro folklore.

Of the numerous collectors of folklore essentially in the Uncle Remus tradition, the following did work interesting to the general reader and of some usefulness for the student: C. C. Jones, Jr., whose *Negro Myths from the Georgia Coast* (1888) are renderings of Negro tales, closer than Harris' to the genuine, in the Gullah dialect of the coast; and Virginia Frazer Boyle, whose *Devil Tales* (1900) are able transcripts of superstitions.

William Wells Brown, as he was the first Negro in so many fields, was the first to publish folk anecdotes, in *My Southern Home* (1880). Much more informed and artistically handled are the tales in *The Conjure Woman* (1899) by Charles W. Chesnutt. These seven tales, rich in folklore, were compared favorably with the work of Harris and Thomas Nelson Page. The dialect is meticulous, almost to a fault. The narrator of the tales is Uncle Julius, an ex-slave Munchausen, who differs from Harris' and Page's Uncles by being sarcastic about the "good ole days." Uncle Julius tells his stories with cunning, leading up to morals that benefit his designs.

For a long time, Brown and Chesnutt were the only Negroes to publish folktales. But white folklorists have been assiduous. Ambrose Gonzales' *With Aesop Along the Black Border* (1922) is a rendering of fables in carefully phonetic dialect. Here is a sample from "The Fox and the Grapes":

Bumbye 'e git up 'en 'e walk off, 'en 'e walk berry sedate. Attu-while 'e biggin fuh grin. 'E suck 'e teet, en' 'e say to 'eself, 'e say, "Me yent hab time fuh w'ary me bone en' t'ing fuh jump attuh no sour grape lukkuh dem. Soon as Uh smell 'um Uh know dem *done* fuh sour! No, suh! Ef Uh haffuh chaw t'ing lukkuh dat, Uh gwine hunt green possimun. . . ." Buh Fox sma'at!

Other collections from South Carolina are Elsie Clews Parson's *Folklore of the Sea Islands, South Carolina* (1923); Stoney and Shelby's *Black Genesis* (1930), a collection of what are said to be Negro biblical tales; and Guy Johnson's *Folk Culture on St. Helena Island* (1930), which includes typical folk tales, riddles, and superstitions. Guy Johnson takes the common-sense approach of the observer of social reality, rather than that of the seeker for the picturesque and quaint:

> To the student of folklore, this vast body of stories is something to be collected, preserved, studied, compared, analyzed, something which it would be a shame to let die out. But to the Negroes these stories are like any other stories. They lie tucked away in memory most of the time. . . . New stories, perhaps cheap stories, are constantly crowding in upon them, and if some of the old-time ones which go back almost to Adam slip out of memory through disuse, no tears are shed. Finding a rare tale may thrill the collector, but the islander may think something else is far more valuable. To them the story of a stuttering slave's being beaten up by a stuttering Irish patrol because the Irishman thought the Negro was mocking him may be more attractive than Buh Rabbit's victory over Buh Lion.

Julia Peterkin, in *Roll, Jordan, Roll* (1933) and Carl Carmer in *Stars Fell on Alabama* (1934) include good Negro yarns. John Sale's *The Tree Named John* (1929) is a valuable collection of Mississippi lore and tales. Howard Odum's trilogy about Left Wing Gordon: *Rainbow Round My Shoulder* (1928); *Wings on My Feet* (1929); and *Cold Blue Moon* (1930) are a sociologist's collections of living folklore rendered almost as creative literature. E. C. L. Adams in *Congaree Sketches* (1927) and *Nigger to Nigger* (1928) combines the abilities of folklorist and short-story writer. More than anyone else he catches the truth about folk Negroes when talking to each other. The humor of some of Adams' sketches is uproarious, but the bitter irony of some goes deeper than any other treatment of the Negro folk had ever gone before. B. A. Botkin's critical articles sponsoring the new regionalism as opposed to the old local color, and his creative editing of

Folk-Say from 1929 to 1932, were spurs to understanding studies and re-creations of Negro folk stuff.

Whether familiarity has bred contempt, or whether there has been too great a sensitivity toward folk expression, Negroes have lagged behind whites in the gathering of folk tales. Without Joel Chandler Harris, it is likely that the Uncle Remus stories, which now belong with the minor masterpieces of American literature, would have been lost. Awareness of the importance of a study of the folk is increasing among Negroes, but still slowly. Under the auspices of the American Folk Lore Society, Arthur Huff Fauset studied Nova Scotian folklore in 1923 and the Mississippi Delta folklore in 1925. In 1932 J. Mason Brewer made a small collection of slave tales under the title *Juneteenth.* The first substantial collection of folk tales by a Negro scholar is *Mules and Men* (1935) by Zora Neale Hurston. Miss Hurston is a trained anthropologist, who brings a great zest to both the collecting and the rendering of the "big old lies" of her native South. Onah L. Spencer's tales of John Henry and Stackalee are the first ventures of a new writer in the field. Charles S. Johnson has amassed a large collection of folklore, as yet unpublished, at Fisk University.

Whether laughing at the mishaps of his master or of a fellow slave; whether siding with Brer Rabbit while he checkmates stronger opponents with cunning and deceit, or with the Tar-Baby while he foils Brer Rabbit; whether telling about John Henry defeating the steam drill, or Railroad Bill outshooting the sheriff and his deputies, oral telling of tales has been a favorite occupation of American Negroes. Down by the big gate, at the store or cotton gin, at the end of the row at lunch time, in poolroom, barbershop, fraternal lodge, college dormitory, railroad depot, railroad coach, the Negro has told his tall tales and anecdotes, now sidesplitting, now ironic, now tragic. Though it is an art not likely to die out, it certainly deserves more serious attention that it has received.

FOLK SERMONS

The Negro folk preacher has long been burlesqued; Roark Bradford's *Ol' Man Adam an' His Chillun,* from which *The Green Pastures* was derived, is a well known example. Beginning with James Weldon Johnson's "The Creation," to which Johnson added the other sermons that went to make up *God's Trombones,* a different attitude to "folk" sermons has developed. Vachel Lindsay and E. C. L. Adams, white authors, and Arthur Huff Fauset and Zora Neale Hurston, Negro authors, in their recreations of

Negro folk sermons, have definitely caught something of their eloquence, essential dignity, and poetic picturesqueness.

SPIRITUALS

(The following spirituals are derived from the *Book of American Negro Spirituals* by James Weldon Johnson and J. Rosamond Johnson, *Religious Folk-Songs of the American Negro* by R. Nathaniel Dett, *Slave Songs of the United States* by Allen, Ware, and Garrison, *American Folk Songs* by John Lomax and Alan Lomax, *Songs of Our Fathers* by Willis James, the repertory of the Golden Gate Quartette, and from the collections of the editors of *The Negro Caravan*.)

Sometimes I Feel Like a Motherless Child

Sometimes I feel like a motherless child,
Sometimes I feel like a motherless child,
Sometimes I feel like a motherless child,
A long ways from home;
A long ways from home.

Sometimes I feel like I'm almost gone,
Sometimes I feel like I'm almost gone,
Sometimes I feel like I'm almost gone,
A long ways from home;
A long ways from home.

Swing Low, Sweet Chariot

Swing low, sweet chariot,
Coming for to carry me home,
Swing low, sweet chariot,
Coming for to carry me home.

I looked over Jordan and what did I see
Coming for to carry me home,
A band of angels, coming after me,
Coming for to carry me home.

If you get there before I do,
Coming for to carry me home,
Tell all my friends I'm coming too,
Coming for to carry me home.

Swing low, sweet chariot,
Coming for to carry me home,
Swing low, sweet chariot,
Coming for to carry me home.

Steal Away

Steal away, steal away, steal away to Jesus,
Steal away, steal away home,
I ain't got long to stay here.

My Lord, He calls me,
He calls me by the thunder,
The trumpet sounds within-a my soul,
I ain't got long to stay here.

Steal away, steal away, steal away to Jesus,
Steal away, steal away home,
I ain't got long to stay here.

Green trees a-bending,
Po' sinner stands a-trembling
The trumpet sounds within-a my soul,
I ain't got long to stay here.

Steal away, steal away, steal away to Jesus,
Steal away, steal away home,
I ain't got long to stay here.

Deep River

Deep river, my home is over Jordan,
Deep river, Lord; I want to cross over into camp ground.

O children, O, don't you want to go to that gospel feast,
That promised land, that land, where all is peace?

Deep river, my home is over Jordan,
Deep river, Lord; I want to cross over into camp ground.

I Got a Home in Dat Rock

I got a home in dat rock,
Don't you see?
I got a home in dat rock,
Don't you see?

Negro Folk Expression

꽃 FOR A LONG TIME Uncle Remus and his Brer Rabbit tales stood for the Negro folk and their lore. One thing made clear by the resurrection of Uncle Remus in Walt Disney's *Song of the South* is the degree to which he belonged to white people rather than to the Negro folk. A striking contrast to the favored house servant is such a folk character as Huddie Ledbetter, better known as Leadbelly, whose knowingness is stark rather than soft, and whose audience (certainly in his formative years) was his own kind of people, not the white quality. The bitter brew that Leadbelly concocted in the levee camps and jooks and prisons differs from the sugary potions that Remus and the other "uncles" dispensed. Both Uncle Remus and Leadbelly portray sides of the Negro folk, but to round out the portraiture Bessie Smith, Josh White, the Gospel Singing Two Keys, and such big old liars as those heard by E. C. L. Adams in the Congaree swamps and by Zora Neale Hurston in Central Florida are also needed. In any consideration of American Negro folk expression it is important to realize that even before Joel Chandler Harris revealed the antics of Brer Rabbit to America, John Henry was swinging his hammer in the Big Bend Tunnel on the C. & O. Road.

There is rich material on hand for a revaluation of the Negro folk. Out of penitentiaries in the deep South, John and Alan Lomax have brought the musical memories of singers with such names as Iron Head, Clear Rock, and Lightning. From what is more truly folk culture these men and others like John Hammond, Willis James, and John Work have brought hidden singers and songs. The Library of Congress Archives of Folk Music are crammed with solid stuff; the large recording companies are following the lead of small companies like Disc, Folkways and Circle in issuing albums of Negro folk music. Ten years after her tragic death in the Delta, Bessie

Smith has been honored in a Town Hall Concert (even now I can hear her surprised cry: "Lord, Lord, Lord!"). And in Carnegie Hall Big Bill has sung blues from the sharecropping country, and Josh White has sung both mellow-blues and sardonic mockery, and Blind Sonny Terry has blown on his wild harmonica the joys of the fox hunt, of a high-balling train, and the wailing fear of a lost wanderer in a southern swamp. Folk singers of the spirituals, unknown yesterday, have their names placarded now; Harlemites pass around the name of Mahalia Jackson as they used to do that of Mamie Smith; and in the Harlem dance-halls where jazz bands "cut" each other on Saturday nights, spiritual singers battle each other on Sundays to cheering crowds. This commercializing will affect the genuineness of the stuff, but it is getting a hearing for folk material. And an audience for the authentic is growing.

All of this is part of the generally awakened interest in American folk culture, indicated by the diligence and popularity of collectors, anthologists, musicologists, and interpreters. Before its demise the WPA Federal Projects laid in a fine backlog of American folkstuff and World War II, of course, quickened interest in the American past. Though the furore may have something of the faddish about it, American folklore stands to gain more from enthusiasm and careful study than from the earlier disdain and neglect. The Negro creators of an important segment of American folklore should no longer be subjected to the condescension of the "oh so quaint," "so folksy," school. Looking on Negro lore as exotic *curiosa* becomes almost impossible if the body of available material is thoughtfully considered. Outmoded now are those collectors who could or would find only ingratiating aunties and uncles, most of whose lore consisted in telling how good their white folks were.

With the discarding of the old simplifications, the study of the Negro folk becomes complicated. The field of folklore in general is known to be a battle area, and the Negro front is one of the hottest sectors. One sharply contested point is the problem of definition of the folk; another that of origins. Allies are known to have fallen out and skirmished behind the lines over such minor matters as identifying John Hardy with John Henry. But this is not a battle piece. In general the vexed problems of origin are left for others, more competent in that area; strict delimitation of the concepts "folk," "folk literature" and "folk music" is not the purpose here. This essay aims instead to tell what the "folk Negro" (as most students understand the term)[1] has expressed in story and proverb and song. It is

1. That is, as a rural people, living in a kind of isolation, without easy contact with

well known that folk culture among Negroes is breaking up. Some of the material (in discussing the blues, for instance) has been transplanted in the cities, but, though inexactly folk, it is used because its roots drew first sustenance from the folk culture.

I: FOLK TALES AND APHORISMS

Collectors, both scholarly and amateur, have long paid tribute to the richness of Negro folk expression. Enthusiasts like Roark Bradford and Zora Hurston overpraise Negro folk speech at the expense of the speech of white Americans. According to Bradford, "The most ignorant Negro can get more said with a half-dozen words than the average United States Senator can say in a two-hour speech."[2] But folk should be compared with folk; and considering the speech of white America to be barren and bleak does injustice to a large part of American folklore, to the gusto of the tall tale, for instance. The folk Negro's imaginativeness and pith can easily be recognized; they stand in no need of dubious comparisons.

In Africa the telling of tales is a time honored custom. The slaves brought the custom with them to the New World. According to the latest scholarship of Melville Herskovits, the body of tales they brought has been retained in relatively undisturbed fashion.[3] These tales were not dangerous; they were a way to ease the time; they could entertain the master class, especially the children. So they were not weeded out as were many of the practices of sorcery, or discouraged as were the tribal languages. In the African cycles the heroes were the jackal or fox, the hare, the tortoise, and the spider. The last, a sort of hairy tarantula, is little used in the lore of the southern Negro, but is hero of the Anansi tales of Jamaica. The African fox, more like our jackal, has become the American fox; the African hare, "Cunnie Rabbit," really a chevrotain, water deerlet, or gazelle, has become the American rabbit with the word cunnie Englished into cunning, and the African tortoise has become the American dry-land turtle or terrapin. In America, Brer Terrapin is a hero second only to Brer Rabbit whom he bests occasionally. Of the hero's victims the African hyena has become the

---

the outside world. Sometimes they are cut off from progress geographically (especially the sea-islanders or swamp dwellers or the people on back-county plantations). But even rural Negroes with better communication and transportation facilities are socially isolated by segregation and lack of educational and economic advantages. Unlettered, folk Negroes have a local culture transmitted orally rather than by the printed page.

2. Roark Bradford, *Ol' Man Adam an' His Chillun* (New York, 1928), p. xiv.
3. Melville Herskovits, *The Myth of the Negro Past* (New York, 1941), p. 275.

American wolf, and the American fox and bear have joined the losing side. African animals—lions, leopards, tigers, and monkeys are still in the cast of characters.

Close parallels to American Negro tales have been found extensively in Africa and the Caribbeans. Nevertheless, folklorists are wary of finding Africa the place of ultimate origin of all of the tales. Many of the basic plots are of great age and spread. Oddly enough, the three stories that Joel Chandler Harris considered unquestionably African, namely: "How the Rabbit Makes a Riding-horse of the Fox," "Why the Alligator's Back Is Rough," and "The Tar Baby Story," have close European counterparts, dating back hundreds of years. "The Tar Baby Story" has been traced to India through a study of nearly three hundred versions. According to Stith Thompson, it reached the Negroes and Indians of America by several paths, the main one being "from India to Africa, where it is a favorite and where it received some characteristic modifications before being taken by slaves to America."[4] In the Congo version a jackal is stuck to a tortoise covered with beeswax; among the Pueblo Indians a coyote catches a rabbit with a gum-covered wooden image.

To indicate the problems facing source-hunters, one of the most popular European stories might be considered here. In the Reynard cycle, and reappearing in Grimm's *Fairy Tales*, is the plot of the fox who played godfather in order to sneak away and eat food that he and the bear have stored in common. Asked the name of his godchildren (for he leaves three times) he answers Well Begun, Half Done and Done. Several collectors found the story in South Carolina, with Brer Rabbit cheating Brer Wolf, and the children variously named: "Fus' Beginnin'," "Half-Way" and "Scrapin' de Bottom," or "Buh Start-um," "Buh Half-um" and "Buh Done-Um." Easy attribution to American slaveowners, however, comes up sharp against the numerous African versions in one of which the rabbit fools his working partner, the antelope, with non-existent children named Uncompleted One, Half-completed One, and Completed One.

All of this illustrates the underlying unity of Old World culture. Africa then, is not the starting place of all the favorite Negro tales, but was a way-station where they had an extended stop-over. The long association with Asiatic Moslems in East Africa and the penetration of European powers into West Africa beginning with the slave trade affected the native tradition of tale telling. According to Stith Thompson, "The African finds enjoyment in nearly every kind of European folktale. He may do some queer things

4. Stith Thompson, *The Folk Tale* (New York, 1947), pp. 225ff.

with them and change them around so that little more than a skeleton of the original remains and so that it takes the expert eye to discover that they are not actually native. On the other hand he may take the tale over completely with all its foreign trappings." Nevertheless Thompson believes that "the great majority of their [African] tales have certainly had their origin on the soil of central or southern Africa."[5] Regardless of original source, whether in Europe or Africa, American Negro fables have been so modified with new beasts and local color added, different themes, and different experiences, that an almost new, certainly a quite different thing results. Such is the way of written literature where authors took "their own where they found it," and such is even more the way of folktales.

"Den Br' Hoss, an' Br' Jack-ass, an' Br' Cow an' all dem, crowd close roun' Br' Dog, for dem was like yard-chillen, dey is peaceable an' sort o' scary. An' all de creeters what stan' up for Br' Gator scatter out wide away from dere, for dem was woods-chillen, rovin' an' wild."[6] Thus, according to a South Carolina tale, started the big row in the world between the tame and the wild creatures that is never going to stop.

This illustrates the process. The basic incident, the war between domestic and wild animals, is widely used in folktales, from the Orient to the Reynard cycle. But the details, the "entrimmins," according to Uncle Remus, the phrases "yard chillen," and "woods chillen," and the naming of their traits, give the flavor of the low country, where Samuel Stoney and Gertrude Shelby heard the above yarn.

Public recognition of the wealth of American Negro stories came in the late eighties with the appearance of Joel Chandler Harris's Uncle Remus Tales. A few animal tales had seen print earlier, but Harris was the first to give a substantial number. Soon he was besieged with correspondents who told him new tales or variants that they had heard from Negroes. Harris deserves the credit of a pioneer. He insisted that he gave the tales "uncooked," but there is too much evidence of his alterations to accept his word. The tales are not genuine folktales, in the sense of by the folk for the folk, for they are told by an old Uncle to entertain Young Marster. In line with literary trends of the time, Harris made them more sentimental and genteel and less racy than the folk tell them; he gives much about Negro life and character, valuable for purposes of local color but likely to be taken for granted by the folk; and he uses the devices of a skillful short

5. *Ibid.*, pp. 284–286.
6. Samuel Gaillard Stoney and Gertrude Mathews Shelby, *Black Genesis* (New York, 1930), p. 21.

story writer. Simpler and starker tales, with fewer alterations, have been taken from their native habitat by collectors such as C. C. Jones, Jr. (a contemporary of Harris), Ambrose Gonzales, Elsie Clews Parsons, Guy Johnson, and A. W. Eddins. Negro collectors are few and far between; Charles W. Chesnutt fashioned skillful short stories out of folk beliefs in *The Conjure Woman* (1889); and Thomas Talley, pioneer folk-collector, Arthur Huff Fauset, Zora Neale Hurston and J. Mason Brewer have published collections. Stella Brewer Brooks has written the best study of Joel Chandler Harris as folklorist. But educated Negroes by and large have not been greatly interested. From Harris's day to the present, collectors, being of different race or class or both, have been viewed by the folk with natural distrust.

Nevertheless, a considerable number of tales has been recorded. Many are animal tales; of these all are not strictly fables, which convey an ostensible moral, though some are. Whereas the more efficient Fox, crafty and cruel, hypocritical and scheming, amused the European peasantry, the American Negro slave took Brer Rabbit for hero. The harmless scary creature he invested with a second nature, and made him a practical joker with a streak of cruelty, a daring hunter of devilment, a braggart, a pert wit, a glutton, a lady's man, a wily trickster, knowing most of the answers, and retaining of his true characteristics only his speed on the getaway. Animals noted for greater strength and ferocity are his meat. Brer Fox has degenerated from crafty Reynard into something of a fool, though still a worthy opponent, but Brer Wolf and Brer Bear are numskulls. Commentators have long considered these tales of cunning overcoming strength, of the weakling out-smarting the bully, as a compensatory mechanism, a kind of oblique revenge, the wish fulfillment of an ironic people who could see few ways out of oppression.[7] It might be pointed out that none of the hero-animals in Africa are quite so helpless as the American rabbit. It is unlikely that the slaves did not see pertinence to their own experiences in these tales. Outsmarting was one of the few devices left them. So they made heroes out of the physically powerless who by good sense and quick wit overcame animals of brute strength who were not right bright. "You ain't got no cause to be bigger in de body, but you sho' is got cause to be bigger in de brain."

With his pardonable fondness for the creature, Joel Chandler Harris placed Brer Rabbit in the limelight. He is less focused on in other collections, though still the star performer. The theme of weakness overcoming

7. For a very suggestive essay on this point, F. Bernard Wolfe, "Uncle Remus and the Malevolent Rabbit," in *Commentary*, July, 1949 (Vol. 8, No. 1), 31–41.

strength through cunning remains uppermost. Brer Squirrel escapes from Brer Fox by reminding him to say grace; when the fox closes his eyes, the squirrel is treetop high. Brer Goat foils Brer Wolf, never trusting him from that day to this. Brer Rooster outeats Brer Elephant: "it ain't de man wid de bigges' belly what kin eat de longest." Animals and birds of everyday observation swell the company: the officious yard dog, the fierce bulldog, the hound, another fall-guy for the rabbit; the horse, the mule, the jackass, the bull, the stupid ox; the deer, the raccoon, possum and squirrel; the frog, the crawfish, and many kinds of snakes; the turkey buzzard, the partridge, the blue-jay, the marsh-hen; the mosquito, the hornet, the gnat.

Many tales drive home a point about mankind based on the animals' observed traits. The gnat, riding the bull's horn, says: "I gwine now. Ain't you glad you don't have to tote me puntop yo' horn no more?" The bull answers: "I never know when you come, and I ain't gonna miss you when you gone." The possum tells the raccoon that he can't fight because he is ticklish and has to laugh when in the clutch of his enemy, but the raccoon sees through the rationalization. With his belly full, running in the pasture, Brer Mule dreams that his father was a race-horse, but harnassed to a heavy cart and hungry, he recalls that his father was only a jackass. The ox rebukes the axle wheels for groaning; *he* is the one pulling the load, though he refuses to cry out. "Some men holler if briar scratch his foot, and some men lock their jaws if a knife is sticking in their heart."[8]

Ingenious explanations of animal characteristics and behavior occur in many tales. You never see a blue-jay on Friday because that is the day for his weekly trip to hell; the woodpecker's head is red because Noah caught him pecking holes in the ark and whipped his head with a hammer; the possum's tail is bare because, wanting music on the ark, Ham used the hairs to string a banjo; the alligator's mouth is all out of whack because the dog, God's apprentice helper, was either careless or cruel while wielding the knife in the week of creation, making the alligator and dog eternal foes; the porpoise's tail is set crossways because with his tail straight up and down the porpoise was too fast, he outsped the sun; Sis Nanny Goat, self sacrificing, allowed all of the other animals to get their tails first, hence, "Kind heart give Sis Nanny Goat a short tail"; the wasp is so short-patienced because he thinks everybody is laughing at his tiny stomach (he can't laugh himself because he would "bust spang in two").

8. The quoted lines in the above paragraph are taken from Ambrose E. Gonzales, *With Æsop Along the Black Border* (Columbia [South Carolina]: The State Company, 1924), *passim.*

Though performing other functions in the Old World, animal tales are often considered by American Negroes as "stories for the young uns." Animal stories were by no means the only stock, even in slavery. More realistic tales made direct use of unallegorized human experience. In coastal Georgia the folk still remember the tale of the Eboes who, hating slavery, marched singing into the tidal river and were drowned. The name of Ebo's Landing gives historic color to the tradition. The same folk tell also of the magic hoe that worked itself, and of the flying Africans who changed into birds and soared away to their homeland rather than take the overseer's whipping. Modelled on tales in African folklore, in the New World they take on the quality of dreams of escape.

More widespread in Negro folklore are the tales of the trickster Jack or John. In slavery days he outwits not only the devil but Ole Marster, Ole Miss, and the "patterollers." More recently his competitors have been the grasping landlord, the browbeating tough, and the highhanded sheriff, deputy, and policeman. Sometimes Jack, like Brer Rabbit, comes to grief himself, but oftener he outsmarts the opposition or makes his dare and is long gone. Jack schemes to get out of a whipping or to obtain freedom. Sometimes he is in cahoots with a sharp witted master to take advantage of gullible neighbors. Sometimes the repartee is sharp; a master tells that he dreamt of a heaven set aside for Negroes and found it to be run-down and generally messed-up; Jack retorts with his dream of white folk's heaven, all gleaming and glittering, with streets of gold, but without a solitary person in the place! The tellers aim at comedy, often richly satiric; the hardships of slavery are casually mentioned as if taken for granted by teller and audience; but Ole Marster and Ole Miss and the slaves themselves are ribbed with gusto, with toughminded humor. Pretentiousness and boasting ride for a fall; sentimentality is pricked; all the characters, white and black, master and slave, come "under the same gourd-vine," all are "made out of meat."

A favorite object of lampooning, familiar in general folklore, was the old maid, the master's sister. One of the fanciful plots has her turning into a squinch owl, her long-drawn wails voicing her yearning for a husband, but other tales satirize her bossiness and silliness in down-to-earth situations. The Irish were also satirized. Comparative newcomers with their own brogues and dirty jobs, the Irish were characterized as big dunces. Here, of course, the American Negro shares an Anglo-Saxon tradition. The "po' buckra," the "poor white trash," the "cracker," came in for contempt and hostility in Negro tales, but the stories about them were not often funny.

Exaggeration in the hearty tradition of American tall talk is pervasive. In Zora Hurston's recording, mosquitoes sing like alligators, eat up the cow and then ring the bell for the calf. The plague of the boll-weevil is graphically symbolized: "Old Man Boll Weevil whipped little Willie Boll Weevil 'cause he couldn't carry two rows at a time." Land is so rich that the next morning after a mule is buried, "he had done sprouted li'l jackasses"; it is so poor that "it took nine partridges to holler Bob White" or needed "ten sacks of fertilizer before a church congregation could raise a tune on it." A snail is sent for a doctor. After seven years his sick wife heard a scuffling at the door and cries out her relief. The snail says, "Don't try to rush me—ah' ain't gone yet." He had taken all that time to get to the door. Weather is so hot "till two cakes of ice left the icehouse and went down the streets and fainted."[9]

Quite common are the "why" stories; jocular explanation of the creation of the world, the position of woman, the origin of the races. One teller informed Zora Hurston: "And dats why de man makes and de woman takes. You men is still braggin' about yo' strength and de women is sitting on de keys [to kitchen, bedroom, and cradle] and lettin' you blow off 'til she git ready to put de bridle on you." But another informant explains why "de sister in black works harder than anybody else in the world. De white man tells de nigger to work and he takes and tells his wife."[10]

Mythological tales explain the origin of the ocean, where the hurricane comes from, why the wind and waters are at war, why the moon's face is smutty. Others enlarge material from the Bible. Ingenuity is especially exercised on filling in gaps in the creation story. Up in heaven a newcomer tells of the havoc of the Johnstown flood to a bored listener who turns out to be Noah. Peter is humanized more than the other apostles: famished, he brings a huge rock to the Lord to turn into bread and is nonplussed when he hears the pronouncement: "And upon this rock will I found my church." Religion is treated freely, even irreverently, but not to the degree of Roark Bradford's *Ol' Man Adam an' His Chillun*, which is synthetic, not genuine folk-stuff.

Tales about the origin of the races leave little room for chauvinism about a chosen people. The slaves knew at first hand that the black man had a hard road to travel and they tell of the mistakes of creation with sardonic fatalism. Uncle Remus tells how all men were once Negroes, "en 'cordin' ter all de counts w'at I years fokes 'uz gittin' long 'bout ez well in dem days as dey is now." One of Zora Hurston's informants told her that

9. The quoted lines in the above paragraph are taken from Zora Neale Hurston, *Mules and Men* (Philadelphia, 1935), *passim*.
10. *Ibid., passim.*

"God made de world and de white folks made work." Another said that the Negro outraced the white man and took the larger of two bundles that God had let down in the road. But the smaller bundle had a writing-pen and ink in it, while the larger bundle had a pick and shovel and hoe and plow and cop-axe in it. "So ever since then de nigger been out in de hot sun, usin' his tools and de white man been sittin' up figgerin', ought's a ought, figger's a figger; all for de white man, none for de nigger."[11]

Irony has been in the stories from the earliest recorded versions, but recent collectors have found it less veiled. Zora Hurston retells the yarn of the dogs' convention where a law was passed not to run rabbits any more. But Brer Rabbit stayed cautious: "All de dogs ain't been to no convention and anyhow some of dese fool dogs ain't got no better sense than to run all over dat law and break it up. De rabbit didn't go to school much and he didn't learn but three letters and that trust no mistake. Run every time de bush shake."[12] She tells another of the slave who saved his master's children from drowning. Old Master sets him free. As he walks off, old master calls to him: "John, de children love yuh." . . . "John, I love yuh." . . . "And Missy *like* yuh!" . . . "But 'member, John, youse a nigger." John kept right on stepping to Canada, answering his master "every time he called 'im, but he consumed on with his bag."

The age-old tale of the deceptive bargain gets added point down in the Brazos Bottom. Brer Rabbit, father of a large, hungry family, is sharecropping for Brer Bear who has him in his power. Brer Rabbit is forced to promise Brer Bear everything that grows above the ground. But that year he planted potatoes. The second year, Brer Bear settles for root crops, but Brer Rabbit planted oats. The third year, Brer Bear claimed both tops and roots, leaving Brer Rabbit only the middles. As a fine climax, Brer Rabbit planted corn. Another old tale of the goose that the fox threatened to kill for swimming on "his" lake, now ends with Sis Goose taking her just cause to court. "When dey got dere, de sheriff, he was a fox, and de judge, he was a fox, and de attorneys, dey was foxes, and all de jurymen, dey was foxes, too. An' dey tried ole sis goose, and dey convicted her and dey executed her, and dey picked her bones."[13]

There is similar edge in numerous jokes about sharecropping and the law. Landlords who "figure with a crooked pencil" are derided. One sharecropper held back a couple of bales from the reckoning. When told, after

11. *Ibid.*, pp. 101–102.
12. *Ibid.*, p. 147.
13. A. W. Eddins, "Brazos Bottom Philosophy," *Publications of the Texas Folk Lore Society*, No. II, 1923, edited by J. Frank Dobie. Austin, Texas: Texas Folk-Lore Society, pp. 50–51.

elaborate figuring, that he had come out even, he expressed his happiness that he could sell his extra bales. The landlord then cursed him to hell and back, telling him that he had to do all that hard figuring over again. When another sharecropper was told that his return was zero after making a bumper crop, he shut up like a clam. The landlord, distrusting his silence, insisted that he tell him what he was thinking. The sharecropper finally said: "I was just thinking, Mister Charlie, that the next time I say 'Giddap' to a mule again, he's gonna be setting on my lap." Yarnspinners weep in mimicry of the landlord who, in the early days of the New Deal, had to give government checks to his tenants, crying: "After all I've done for you, you so ungrateful that you cashed those checks."

Negroes borrow, of course, from the teeming storehouse of American jokes. Jokes about Negroes are of three types. The first includes those told by whites generally to whites (the kind collected by Irvin Cobb, for instance, and the stand-bys for after-dinner speakers, with such black face minstrelsy props as watermelon, chicken, razors, excessive fright, murder of the English language, etc.). Some of these may be found among Negroes who will belittle their own for a laugh as quickly as any other people will, but they are not the most popular. The white man's mark on a Negro joke often does not help it. A second type is told by Negroes to whites to gain a point. Sometimes verging on sarcasm, they use the license of the court fool. Then there are jokes strictly for a Negro audience, what John Dollard calls "part of the arsenal of reprisal against white people."[14]

Often too, the joke lays bare what the tellers consider a racial weakness and the outsider must not be let into the family secrets, as it were. Sometimes it pleads the racial cause. Jokes ridicule the myth of "separate but equal"; a Negro gets off free in traffic court by telling the judge that he saw whites drive on the green light so he knew the red light was for him. Hat-in-hand Negroes and workers too zealous on the job are satirized. During the war the jokes, or more truly anecdotes, took on a grimmer tone. One folk hero became the soldier who after being badgered on a bus, faced his tormentors and said, "Well, if I am going to die for democracy, I might as well die for some of it down here in Georgia." One repeated line concerned an epitaph: "Here lies a black man killed by a yellow man while fighting to save democracy for the white man." Many of these anecdotes are bitter; some, dealing with sadistic sheriffs and mobs are gruesome; yet they produce laughter, a sort of laughter out of hell. But they are shared by educated as well as uneducated and though passed along by word of mouth, they take us somewhat afield from the folk.

14. John Dollard, *Caste and Class in Southern Town* (New Haven, 1937), p. 308.

Negro Folk Expression: Spirituals, Seculars, Ballads and Work Songs

THE SPIRITUALS

❧ THOMAS WENTWORTH HIGGINSON, one of the very first to pay respectful attention to the Negro spiritual, called it a startling flower growing in dark soil. Using his figure, we might think of this flower as a hybrid, as the American Negro is a hybrid. And though flowers of its family grew in Africa, Europe, and other parts of America, this hybrid bloom is uniquely beautiful.

A large amount of recent scholarship has proved that the spirituals are not African, either in music or meaning (a claim made once with partisan zeal), that the American Negro was influenced by the religious music of rural America from the Great Awakening on, that at the frontier camp meetings he found to his liking many tunes both doleful and brisk, and that he took over both tunes and texts and refashioned them more to his taste. But careful musicologists, from studying phonograph records of folk singing rather than, as earlier, inadequate, conventional notations of "art" spirituals, are coming around to the verdict of Alan Lomax that "no amount of scholarly analysis and discussion can ever make a Negro spiritual sound like a white spiritual."

A new music, yes. But what of the poetry? Scholars have discovered that many phrases, lines, couplets, and even whole stanzas and songs, once thought to be Negro spirituals, were popular in white camp meetings. A full comparison of the words of white and Negro spirituals is out of the question here. It might be said that some of the parallels turn out to be tangents. Thus, "At his table we'll sit down, Christ will gird himself and serve us with sweet manna all around" is supposed to be the white source of "Gwine to sit down at the welcome table, gwine to feast off milk and honey," and "To hide yourself in the mountain top, to hide yourself from

God" is supposed to have become "Went down to the rocks to hide my face, the rocks cried out no hiding place." Even when single lines were identical, the Negro made telling changes in the stanza. Briefly, the differences seem to result from a looser line, less tyrannized over by meter and rhyme, with the accent shifted unpredictably, from a more liberal use of refrains, and from imagery that is terser and starker. The improvising imagination seems freer. Some of the changes of words arose from confusion: "Paul and Silas bound in jail" has been sung: "bounded Cyrus born in jail;" and "I want to cross over into camp-ground" has been sung as "I want to cross over in a calm time." Some of the changes, however, result from the truly poetic imagination at work on material deeply felt and pondered: "Tone de bell easy, Jesus gonna make up my dying bed." "I'll lie in de grave and stretch out my arms, when I lay dis body down." "Steal away, steal away, steal away to Jesus. Steal away, steal away home; I ain't got long to stay here."

Many spirituals tell of the joys of Christian fellowship. "Ain't you glad you got out de wilderness?" "I been bawn of God, no condemnation; no condemnation in my soul." "I been down in the valley; Never turn back no mo'."

> I went down in the valley to pray
> My soul got happy and I stayed all day.

"Just like a tree, planted by the waters, I shall not be moved." Belonging to the glorious company, the slaves found comfort, protection. Sinners would find no hole in the ground, but those of the true faith had "a hiding place, around the throne of God." "I got a home in that rock, don't you see?" "In God's bosom gonna be my pillow." Their souls were witnesses for their Lord. "Done done my duty; Got on my travelin' shoes." "I done crossed the separatin' line; I done left the world behind."

The world could be left behind in visions.

> I've got two wings for to veil my face
> I've got two wings for to fly away. . . .

Gabriel and his trumpet caught the imagination. "Where will you be when the first trumpet sounds; sounds so loud its gonna wake up the dead?" "O My Lord, what a morning, when the stars begin to fall!" "When the sun refuse to shine, when the moon goes down in blood!" In that great getting up morning, "you see the stars a falling, the forked lightning, the coffins bursting, the righteous marching." "The blind will see, the dumb will talk; the deaf will hear; the lame will walk." This apocalyptic imagery, clear to the initiated, is a release, a flight, a message in code, frequently used by oppressed people.

> Then they'll cry out for cold water
> While the Christians shout in glory
> Saying Amen to their damnation
> Fare you well, fare you well.

It was not only to the far-off future of Revelations that the dreams turned. Heaven was a refuge too. In contrast to the shacks of slave row and the slums of the cities, to the work clothes and the unsavory victuals, would be the throne of God, the streets of gold, the harps, the robes, the milk and honey.

> A-settin' down with Jesus
> Eatin' honey and drinkin' wine
> Marchin' round de throne
> Wid Peter, James, and John. . . .

But the dream was not always so extravagant. Heaven promised simple satisfactions, but they were of great import to the slaves. Shoes for instance, as well as a harp. Heaven meant home: "I'm gonna feast at de welcome table." Heaven meant rest: just sitting down was one of the high privileges often mentioned. And acceptance as a person: "I'm going to walk and talk with Jesus." Moreover, the Heaven of escape is not a Heaven bringing forgetfulness of the past. The River Jordan is not Lethe.

> I'm gonna tell God all my troubles,
> When I get home . . .
> I'm gonna tell him the road was rocky
> When I get home.

The makers of the spirituals, looking toward heaven, found their triumphs there. But they did not blink their eyes to the troubles here. As the best expression of the slaves' deepest thoughts and yearnings, they speak with convincing finality against the legend of contented slavery. This world was not their home. "Swing low, sweet chariot, coming for to carry me home." They never tell of joy in the "good old days." The only joy in the spirituals is in dreams of escape.

That the spirituals were otherworldly, then, is less than half-truth. In more exact truth, they tell of this life, of "rollin' through an unfriendly world." "Oh, bye and bye, bye and bye, I'm going to lay down this heavy load." "My way is cloudy." "Oh, stand the storm, it won't be long, we'll anchor by and by." "Lord keep me from sinking down." And there is that couplet of tragic intensity:

> Don't know what my mother wants to stay here fuh,
> Dis ole world ain't been no friend to huh.

Out of the workaday life came figures of speech: "Keep a-inchin' along lak a po' inch-worm"; such a couplet as:

> Better mind that sun and see how she run
> And mind! Don't let her catch you wid yo' work undone.

And such an allegory: "You hear de lambs a-crying; oh, shepherd, feed-a my sheep." Out of folk wisdom came: "Oh de ole sheep, they know de road; young lambs gotta find de way," and "Ole Satan is like a snake in the grass."

> Sister, you better watch how you walk on the cross
> Yo' foot might slip, and' yo' soul git lost.

The spirituals make an anthology of Biblical heroes and tales, from Genesis where Adam and Eve are in the Garden, picking up leaves, to John's calling the roll in Revelations. There are numerous gaps, of course, and many repetitions. Certain figures are seen in an unusual light; Paul, for instance, is generally bound in jail with Silas, to the exclusion of the rest of his busy career. Favored heroes are Noah, chosen of God to ride down the flood; Samson, who tore those buildings down; Joshua, who caused the walls of Jericho to fall (when the rams' lambs' sheephorns began to blow); Jonah, symbol of hard luck changed at last; and Job, the man of tribulation who still would not curse his God. These are victors over odds. But losers, the wretched and despised, also serve as symbols. There is Lazarus, "poor as I, don't you see?" who went to heaven, in contrast to "Rich man Dives, who lived so well; when he died he found a home in hell." And finally there is Blind Barnabas, whose tormented cry found echoes in slave cabins down through the long, dark years:

> Oh de blind man stood on de road an' cried
> Cried, "Lord, oh, Lord, save-a po' me!"

In telling the story of Jesus, spirituals range from the tender "Mary had a little baby" and "Little Boy, how old are you" to the awe-inspiring "Were You There" and "He Never Said A Mumbalin' Word." Jesus is friend and brother, loving counselor, redeemer, Lord and King. The Negro slave's picturing of Calvary in such lines as

> Dey whupped him up de hill . . .
> Dey crowned his head with thorns . . .
> Dey pierced him in de side,
> An' de blood come a-twinklin' down;
> But he never said a mumbalin' word;
> Not a word; not a word.

belongs with the greatest Christian poetry. It fused belief and experience; it surged up from most passionate sympathy and understanding.

Some scholars who have found parallels between the words of Negro and white spirituals would have us believe that when the Negro sang of freedom, he meant only what the whites meant, namely freedom from sin. Free, individualistic whites on the make in a prospering civilization, nursing the American dream, could well have felt their only bondage to be that of sin, and freedom to be religious salvation. But with the drudgery, the hardships, the auction-block, the slave-mart, the shackles, and the lash so literally present in the Negro's experience, it is hard to imagine why for the Negro they would remain figurative. The scholars certainly do not make it clear, but rather take refuge in such dicta as: "The slave did not contemplate his low condition." Are we to believe that the slave singing "I been rebuked, I been scorned; done had a hard time sho's you bawn," referred to his being outside of the true religion? Ex-slaves, of course, inform us differently. The spirituals speak up strongly for freedom not only from sin (dear as that freedom was to the true believer) but from physical bondage. Those attacking slavery as such had to be as rare as anti-Hitler marching songs in occupied France. But there were oblique references. Frederick Douglass has told us of the double-talk of the spirituals: Canaan, for instance, stood for Canada; and over and beyond hidden satire the songs also were grapevines for communications. Harriet Tubman, herself called the Moses of her people, has told us that *Go Down Moses* was tabu in the slave states, but the people sang it nonetheless.

Fairly easy allegories identified Egypt-land with the South, Pharaoh with the masters, the Israelites with themselves and Moses with their leader. "So Moses smote de water and the children all passed over; Children, ain't you glad that they drowned that sinful army?"

> Oh, Mary don't you weep, don't you moan;
> Pharaoh's army got drownded,
> Oh, Mary, don't you weep.

Some of the references were more direct:

> Didn't my Lord deliver Daniel,
> And why not every man?

In the wake of the Union army and in the contraband camps spirituals of freedom sprang up suddenly. The dry grass was ready for the quickening flame. Some celebrated the days of Jubilo: "O Freedom; O Freedom!, And before I'll be a slave, I'll be buried in my grave! And go home to my Lord and be free." Some summed up slavery starkly: "No more driver's lash for me, no more, no more. . . . No more peck of corn for me; Many thousand go." "Slavery's chain done broke at last; gonna praise God till I die." And in all likelihood old spirituals got new meanings: "Ain't you glad you got out the wilderness?" "In That Great Gittin' Up Morning!" "And the moon went down in blood."

The best of the spirituals are, in W. E. B. Du Bois's phrase, "the sorrow-songs of slavery." In spite of indifference and resentment from many educated and middle class Negroes, the spirituals are still sung, circulated, altered and created by folk Negroes. Some of the new ones, started in the backwoods, have a crude charm; for instance Joseph and Mary in Jerusalem "to pay their poll-taxes," find the little boy Jesus in the temple confounding with his questions the county doctor, lawyer, and judge. Some of them mix in more recent imagery: "Death's little black train is coming!" "If I have my ticket, Lord, can I ride?" and a chant of death in which the refrain "Same train. Same train" is repeated with vivid effect:

> Same train took my mother.
> Same train. Same train.

Some use modern inventions with strained incongruity: "Jus' call up Central in Heaven, tell Jesus to come to the phone," and "Jesus is my aeroplane, He holds the whole world in his hands"; and "Standing in the Safety Zone." But there is power in some of the new phrasing:

> God's got your number; He knows where you live;
> Death's got a warrant for you.

Instead of college choirs, as earlier, today it is groups closer to the folk like the Golden Gates, the Silver Echoes, the Mitchell Christian Singers, the Coleman Brothers, the Thrasher Wonders and the Original Harmony Kings, who carry the spirituals over the land. These groups and soloists like the Georgia Peach, Mahalia Jackson, Marie Knight and Sister Rosetta Tharpe, once churched for worldly ways but now redeemed, are extremely popular in churches, concert halls, and on records. They swing the spirituals, using a more pronounced rhythm and jazz voicing (some show-groups, alas, imitate even the Mills Brothers and the Ink Spots). Even the more sincere singers, however, fight the devil by using what have been considered the devil's weapons. Tambourines, cymbals, trumpets and even trombones and bass fiddles are now accepted in some churches. The devil has no right to all that fine rhythm, so a joyful noise is made unto the Lord with bounce and swing.

The Gospel Songs, sung "out of the book" as signs of "progress," are displacing the spirituals among the people. These are even more heavily influenced by jazz and the blues. One of the most popular composers of Gospel Songs is Thomas Dorsey, who once played barrelhouse piano under the alias of Georgia Tom. Many lovers of the older spirituals disdain the Gospel Songs as cheap and obvious. But this new urban religious folk music should not be dismissed too lightly. It is vigorously alive with its own musical values, and America turns no unwilling ear to it. And to hear some fervent congregations sing "Just a Closer Walk with Thee," "He Knows How Much You Can Bear," and "We Sure Do Need Him Now" can be unforgettable musical experiences. In sincerity, musical manner, and spirit, they are probably not so remote from the old prayer songs in the brush arbors.

SECULARS AND BALLADS

The slaves had many other moods and concerns than the religious; indeed some of these ran counter to the spirituals. Irreverent parodies of religious songs, whether coming from the black-face minstrelsy or from tough-minded cynical slaves, passed current in the quarters. Other-worldliness was mocked: "I don't want to ride no golden chariot; I don't want no golden crown; I want to stay down here and be, Just as I am without one plea." "Live a humble to the Lord" was changed to "Live a humbug." Bible stories, especially the creation, the fall of Man, and the flood, were spoofed. "Reign, Master Jesus, reign" became "Rain, Mosser, rain hard! Rain flour and lard and a big hog head, Down in my back yard." After couplets of nonsense and ribaldry, slaves sang with their fingers crossed, or hopeless in defeat: "Po' mourner, you shall be free, when de good Lord set you free."

Even without the sacrilege, many secular songs were considered "devil-tunes." Especially so were the briskly syncopated lines which, with the clapping of hands and the patting of feet, set the beat for swift, gay dancing. "Juba dis, Juba dat; Juba skin a yeller cat; Juba, Juba!" Remnants of this syncopation are today in such children's play songs as

> "Did you feed my cow?" "Yes, Maam."
> "Will you tell-a me how?" "Yes, Maam."
> "Oh, what did you give her?" "Cawn and hay."
> "Oh, what did you give her?" "Cawn and hay."

Verses for reels made use of the favorite animals of the fables. "Brer Rabbit, Brer Rabbit, yo' eare mighty long; Yes, My Lord, they're put on wrong; Every little soul gonna shine; every little soul gonna shine!" Often power and pomp in the guise of the bullfrog and bulldog have the tables turned on them by the sassy blue-jay and crow:

> A bullfrog dressed in soldier's clothes
> Went in de field to shoot some crows,
> De crows smell powder and fly away,
> De bullfrog mighty mad dat day.

Even the easy going ox or sheep or hog acquired characteristics:

> De ole sow say to de boar
> I'll tell you what let's do,
> Let's go and git dat broad-axe
> And die in de pig-pen too.
> Die in de pig-pen fighting,
> Die wid a bitin' jaw!

Unlike Stephen Foster's sweet and sad[1] songs such as "Massa's in the Cold, Cold Ground," the folk seculars looked at slavery ironically. And where Foster saw comic nonsense, they added satiric point. Short comments flash us back to social reality: "Ole Master bought a yaller gal, He bought her from the South"; "My name's Ran, I wuks in de sand, I'd rather be a nigger dan a po' white man." Frederick Douglass remembers his fellow slaves singing "We raise de wheat, dey gib us de corn; We sift de meal, de gib us de huss; We peel de meat, dey gib us de skin; An dat's de way dey take us in."[2] Grousing about food is common: "Milk in the dairy getting mighty old, Skippers and the mice working mighty bold. . . . A long-tailed rat an' a bowl of souse, Jes' come down from de white folk's house." With robust humor, they laughed even at the dread patrollers:

> Run, nigger, run, de patterollers will ketch you
> Run, nigger, run; its almost day.
> Dat nigger run, dat nigger flew;
> Dat nigger tore his shirt in two.

The bitterest secular begins:

> My ole Mistis promise me
> Fo' she died, she'd set me free;
> She lived so long dat her head got bald,
> And she give out de notion dyin' at all.

Ole marster also failed his promise. Then, with the sharp surprise of the best balladry: "A dose of poison helped him along, May de devil preach his funeral song!"

Under a certain kind of protection the new freedmen took to heart the songs of such an abolitionist as Henry C. Work, and sang exultantly of jubilo. They sang his lines lampooning ole master, and turned out their own:

> Missus and mosser a-walkin' de street,
> Deir hands in deir pockets and nothin' to eat.
> She'd better be home a-washin' up de dishes,
> An' a-cleanin' up de ole man's raggity britches. . . .[3]

1. Thomas Talley, *Negro Folk Rhymes* (New York, 1922), p. 39.
2. Frederick Douglass, *Life and Times* (Hartford, Conn., 1882), p. 39.
3. Talley, *op. cit.*, p. 97.

But when the protection ran out, the freedmen found the following parody too true:

> Our father, who is in heaven,
> White man owe me eleven and pay me seven,
> They kingdom come, thy will be done,
> And if I hadn't took that, I wouldn't had none.

Toward the end of the century, there was interplay between the folk-seculars and the vaudeville stage, and the accepted stereotypes appeared. "Ain't no use my working so hard, I got a gal in the white folks yard." From tent shows and roving guitar players, the folks accepted such hits as the "Bully Song" and the "coon-songs." "Bill Bailey, Won't You Please Come Home," and "Alabama Bound" shuttled back and forth between the folk and vaudeville. In the honky-tonks ribald songs grew up to become standbys of the early jazz: "Make Me a Pallet on the Floor," "Bucket Got a Hole in It," "Don't you leave me here; if you must go, baby, leave me a dime for beer." "Jerry Roll" Morton's autobiography, now released from the Library of Congress Archives, proves this close connection between the rising jazz and the old folk seculars. In the honky-tonks, songs handled sex freely, even licentiously; and obscenity and vituperation ran rampant in songs called the "dirty dozens."

One of the heroes of secular balladry is Uncle Bud, who was noted for his sexual prowess, a combination Don Juan and John Henry. His song is perhaps as uncollected as it is unprintable. Appreciative tales are told of railroading, of crack trains like The Cannon Ball and The Dixie Flyer, and The Rock Island Line, which is praised in rattling good verses. Such folk delights as hunting with the yipping and baying of the hounds and the yells and cheering of the hunters are vividly recreated. "Old Dog Blue" has been memorialized over all of his lop-eared kindred. The greatest trailer on earth, Old Blue keeps his unerring sense in heaven; there he treed a possum in Noah's ark. When Old Dog Blue died,

> I dug his grave wid a silver spade
> I let him down wid a golden chain
> And every link I called his name;
> Go on Blue, you good dog, you!

The above lines illustrate a feature of Negro folksong worth remarking. Coming from an old sea-chantey "Stormalong," their presence in a song about a hunting dog shows the folk habit of lifting what they want and using it how they will. Like southern white groups, the Negro has retained many of the old Scotch-English ballads. Still to be found are Negroes singing "In London town where I was born" and going on to tell of hard-hearted Barbara Allen. John Lomax found a Negro mixing up "Bobby Allen" with the cowboy song "The Streets of Laredo," burying "Miss Allen in a desert of New Mexico with six pretty maidens all dressed in white for her pallbearers."[4] But Negroes hand down fairly straight versions of "Lord Lovel," "Pretty Polly," and "The Hangman's Tree," which has special point for them with its repetend: "Hangman, hangman, slack on the line." The Elizabethan broadside "The Frog Went A-Courtin'" has long been a favorite Negro lullaby. From "The Lass of Roch Royal" two stanzas beginning "Who's gonna shoe yo' little feet" have found their way into the ballad of John Henry. The famous Irish racehorse Stewball reappears in Negro balladry as Skewball and Kimball. English nonsense refrains appear in songs like "Keemo-Kimo" and "Old Bangum." Even the Gaelic "Schule Aroon" has been found among Negroes, though the collector unwarily surmises it to be Guinea or Ebo. Similarly the Negro folk singer lends to and borrows from American balladry. "Casey Jones," though about an engineer, is part of the repertory; it has been established that a Negro engine-wiper was the first author of it. "Frankie and Johnnie," the most widely known tragedy in America, is attributed to both white and Negro authorship. It could come from either; it probably comes from both; the tenderloin cuts across both sections. Current singers continue the trading of songs: Leadbelly sings cowboy songs, yelling "Ki-yi-yippy-yippy-yay" with his own zest; and Josh White sings "Molly Malone" and "Randall, My Son" with telling power. But it is in narratives of their own heroes that Negro ballad makers have done best.

Prominent among such heroes are fugitives who outtrick and outspeed the law. "Travelin' Man" is more of a coon-song than authentically folk, but the hero whom the cops chased from six in the morning till seven the next afternoon has been warmly adopted by the people. Aboard the Titanic he spied the iceberg and dove off, and "When the old Titanic ship went down, he was shooting crap in Liverpool." More genuine is "Long Gone, Lost John" in which the hero outmatches the sheriff, the police, and the bloodhounds: "The hounds ain't caught me and they never will." Fast enough to hop the Dixie Flyer—"he missed the cowcatcher but he caught the blind"—Lost John can even dally briefly with a girl friend, like Brer

4. John Lomax, *Adventure of a Ballad Hunter* (New York, 1947), p. 179.

Rabbit waiting for Brer Tortoise. But when he travels, he goes far: "the funniest thing I ever seen, was Lost John comin' through Bowlin' Green," but "the last time I seed him he was jumping into Mexico."

When Lost John "doubled up his fist and knocked the police down" his deed wins approval from the audience as much as his winged heels do. With bitter memories and suspicion of the law, many Negroes admire outlaws. Some are just tough killers; one is "a bad, bad man from bad, bad land"; another is going to start "a graveyard all of his own"; another, Roscoe Bill, who sleeps with one ear out because of the rounders about, reports to the judge blandly that

> I didn't quite kill him, but I fixed him so dis mornin'
> He won't bodder wid me no mo'
> Dis mornin', dis evenin', so soon.

But the favorites, like such western desperadoes as Jesse James, Billy the Kid, and Sam Bass, stand up against the law. Railroad Bill (an actual outlaw of southern Alabama) "shot all the buttons off the sheriff's coat." On the manhunt, "the policemen dressed in blue, come down the street two by two." It took a posse to bring him in dead. Po' Lazarus also told the deputy to his face that he had never been arrested "by no one man, Lawd, Lawd, by no one man." Unlike his Biblical namesake in nature, Po' Lazarus broke into the commissary. The high sheriff sent the deputy to bring him back, dead or alive. They found him "way out between two mountains" and they "blowed him down."

> They shot Po' Lazarus, shot him with a great big number
> Number 45, Lawd, Lawd, number 45.

They laid Po' Lazarus on the commissary counter, and walked away. His mother, always worrying over the trouble she had with Lazarus, sees the body and cries.

> Dat's my only son, Lawd, Lawd, dat's my only son.

In contrast "Stackolee" ends on a hard note. At Stack's murder trial, his lawyer pleads for mercy because his aged mother is lying very low. The prosecutor states that

> Stackolee's aged mammy
> Has been dead these 'leven years.

Starting from a murder in Memphis in a dice game (some say over a Stetson Hat), Stackolee's saga has travelled from the Ohio River to the Brazos; in a Texas version, Stack goes to hell, challenges the devil to a duel—pitchfork versus forty-one revolver—and then takes over the lower world.

One of America's greatest ballads tells of John Henry. Based on the strength and courage of an actual hammer-swinging giant, though in spite of what folk-singers say, his hammer cannot be seen decorating the Big Bend Tunnel on the C. & O. Road, John Henry reflects the struggle of manual labor against the displacing machine. The ballad starts will ill omens. Even as a boy John Henry prophesies his death at the Big Bend Tunnel. But he stays to face it out. Pitting his brawn and stamina against the new-fangled steam drill, John Henry says to his captain:

> A man ain't nothing but a man.
> But before I'll let that steam driver beat me down
> I'll die with my hammer in my hand.

The heat of the contest makes him call for water (in one variant for tom-cat gin). When John Henry is momentarily overcome, his woman, Polly Ann, spelled him, hammering "like a natural man." At one crucial point, John Henry gave "a loud and lonesome cry," saying, "A hammer'll be the death of me." But the general tone is self confidence. John Henry throws the hammer from his hips on down, "Great gawd amighty how she rings!" He warns his shaker (the holder of the drill) that if ever he misses that piece of steel, "tomorrow'll be yo' burial day." His captain, hearing the mighty rumbling, thinks the mountain must be caving in. John Henry says to the captain: "It's my hammer swinging in the wind." Finally he defeats the drill, but the strain kills him. The people gather round, but all he asks is "a cool drink of water 'fo I die." Polly Ann swears to be true to the memory (although in another version she turns out to be as fickle as Mrs. Casey Jones). John Henry was buried near the railroad where

> Every locomotive come a-roarin' by
> Says, "There lies a steel-drivin' man, Lawd, Lawd;
> There lies a steel-drivin' man."

The topical nature of American balladry is seen in "Boll Weevil," a ballad that grew up almost as soon as the swarm of pests descended. "Come up from Mexico, they say."

The first time I seed the boll weevil
He was sitting on the square—

(The folk poet puns on the "square" of the cotton boll, and the familiar
southern town square.) A tough little rascal is celebrated who, when buried
in the hot sand, says "I can stand it like a man"; when put into ice, says:
"This is mighty cool and nice," and thrives and breeds right on, until
finally he can take over:

You better leave me alone
I done et up all your cotton,
And now I'll start on your corn.

The ballad has grim side glances; the boll weevil didn't leave "the farmer's
wife but one old cotton dress"; made his nest in the farmer's "best Sunday
hat"; and closed the church doors since the farmer couldn't pay the
preacher.

Oh, de Farmer say to de Merchant
I ain't made but only one bale
An' befo' I bring you dat one
I'll fight an' go to jail
I'll have a home
I'll have a home.

The stanzaic forms and general structure of "John Henry" and "The
Boll Weevil" are fairly developed. One of the best folk ballads, however,
is in the simpler, unrhymed African leader-chorus design. This is "The
Grey Goose," a ballad about a seemingly ordinary fowl who becomes a
symbol of ability to take it. It is a song done with the highest spirits; the
"Lord, Lord, Lord" of the responding chorus expressing amazement, flattery, and good-humored respect for the tough bird:

Well, last Monday mornin'
    Lord, Lord, Lord!
Well, last Monday mornin'
    Lord, Lord, Lord!

They went hunting for the grey goose. When shot "Boo-loom!" the grey
goose was six weeks a-falling. Then it was six weeks a-finding, and once in

the white house, was six weeks a-picking. Even after the great feather-picking he was six months parboiling. And then on the table, the forks couldn't stick him; the knife couldn't cut him. So they threw him in the hog-pen where he broke the sow's jawbone. Even in the sawmill, he broke the saw's teeth out. He was indestructible. Last seen the grey goose was flying across the ocean, with a long string of goslings, all going "Quank-quink-quank." Yessir, it was one hell of a gray goose. Lord, Lord, Lord!

WORK SONGS AND SOCIAL PROTEST

More work songs come from the Negro than from any other American folk group. Rowing the cypress dug-outs in Carolina low-country, slaves timed their singing to the long sweep of the oars. The leader, a sort of coxswain, chanted verse after verse; the rowers rumbled a refrain. On the docks Negroes sang sailors' chanteys as metronomes to their heaving and hauling. Some chanteys, like "Old Stormy," they took over from the white seamen; others they improvised. Along the Ohio and Mississippi water-fronts Negro roustabouts created "coonjine" songs, so-called after the shuf-fling dance over bucking gang-planks in and out of steamboat holds. Unless the rhythm was just right a roustabout and his bale or sack of cottonseed might be jolted into the brown waters. The singers cheered the speed of the highballing paddlewheelers: "left Baton Rouge at half pas' one, and got to Vicksburg at setting of de sun." But they griped over the tough captains "workin' hell out of me" and sang

> Ole Roustabout ain't got no home
> Makes his livin' on his shoulder bone.

For release from the timber and the heavy sacks there was always some city around the bend—Paducah, Cairo, Memphis, Natchez, and then

> Alberta let yo' hair hang low . . .
> I'll give you mo' gold
> Than yo' apron can hold . . .
> Alberta let yo' hair hang low.

These songs flourished in the hey-day of the packets; today they are nearly lost.

Another type of work song was chanted as a gang unloaded steel rails. Since these rails weighed over a ton apiece and were over ten yards long, any break in the rhythm of lifting them from the flat cars to the ground was a good way to get ruptured, maimed, or killed. So a chanter was employed to time the hoisting, lowering, and the getting away from it. He was a coach, directing the teamwork, and in self-protection the men had to learn his rhythmic tricks. In track-lining, a similar chanter functioned to keep the track straight in line. As he called, the men jammed their bars under the rails and braced in unison:

> Shove it over! Hey, hey, can't you line it!
> Ah shack-a-lack-a-lack-a-lack-a-lack-a-lack-alack (Grunt)
> Can't you move it? Hey, hey, can't you try.[5]

As they caught their breath and got a new purchase, he turned off a couplet. Then came the shouted refrain as the men strained together.

More widely spread and known are the Negro work songs whose rhythm is timed with the swing back and down and the blow of broad-axe, pick, hammer, or tamper. The short lines are punctuated by a grunt as the axe bites into the wood, or the hammer finds the spike-head.

> Dis ole hammer—hunh
> Ring like silver—hunh (3)
> Shine like gold, baby—hunh
> Shine like gold—hunh.

The leader rings countless changes in his words and melody over the unchanging rhythm. When he grows dull or forgets, another singer takes over. The song is consecutive, fluid; it is doubtful if any one version is ever exactly repeated. Ballads, blues, even church-songs are levied on for lines, a simple matter since the stanzas are unrhymed. Some lines tell of the satisfaction of doing a man's work well:

> I got a rainbow—hunh
> Tied 'round my shoulder—hunh—(3)
> Tain't gonna rain, baby—hunh
> Tain't gonna rain.

(The rainbow is the arc of the hammer as the sunlight glints on the moving metal.) Sometimes a singer boasts of being a "sun-down man," who can

5. Zora Neale Hurston, *Mules and Men* (Philadelphia, 1935), p. 322.

work the sun down without breaking down himself. Lines quite as popular, however, oppose any speed-up stretch-out system:

> Dis ole hammer—hunh
> Killt John Henry—hunh—(3)
> Twon't kill me, baby—hunh
> Twon't kill me.

Some lines get close to the blues: "Every mail day / Gits a letter / Son, come home, baby / Son, come home." Sometimes they tell of a hard captain (boss)

> Told my captain—hunh
> Hands are cold—hunh—(3)
> Damn yo' hands—hunh
> Let de wheelin' roll.

The new-fangled machine killed John Henry; its numerous offspring have killed the work songs of his buddies. No hammer song could compete now with the staccato roaring drill even if the will to sing were there. The steamboat is coming back to the Mississippi but the winches and cranes do not call forth the old gang choruses. A few songs connected with work survive such as the hollers of the lonely worker in the fields and woods, or the call boy's chant to the glory-hole.

> Sleeping good, sleeping good,
> Give me them covers, I wish you would.

At ease from their work in their bunkhouses, the men may sing, but their fancies ramble from the job oftener than they stay with it. Song as a rhythmic accompaniment to work is declining. John and Alan Lomax, whose bag of Negro work songs is the fullest, had to go to the penitentiaries, where labor-saving devices were not yet numerous, in order to find the art thriving. They found lively cotton-picking songs:

> A-pick a bale, a pick a bale
> Pick a bale of cotton
> A-pick a bale, a-pick a bale
> Pick a bale a day.[6]

6. The Library of Congress, Music Division. Archive of American Folk Song for this and the following quotations.

Slower songs came from gangs that were cutting cane or chopping weeds or hewing timber. Prison work is of course mean and tough: "You oughta come on de Brazo in nineteen-fo'; you could find a dead man on every turn-row." So the convicts cry out to the taskmaster sun:

> Go down, Ol' Hannah, doncha rise no mo'
> Ef you rise any mo' bring judgment day.

They grouse about the food: ever "the same damn thing," and at that the cook isn't clean. An old evangelical stand-by, "Let the Light of the Lighthouse Shine on Me," becomes a hymn of hope that the Midnight Special, a fast train, will some day bring a pardon from the governor. They sing of their long sentences:

> Ninety-nine years so jumpin' long
> To be here rollin' an' cain' go home.

If women aren't to be blamed for it all, they are still to be blamed for a great deal:

> Ain't but de one thing worries my min'
> My cheating woman and my great long time.

One song, like the best balladry, throws a searchlight into the darkness:

> "Little boy, what'd you do for to get so long?"
> Said, "I killed my rider in the high sheriff's arms."

From these men—long-termers, lifers, three-time losers—come songs brewed in bitterness. This is not the double-talk of the slave seculars, but the naked truth of desperate men telling what is on their brooding minds. Only to collectors who have won their trust—such as the Lomaxes, Lawrence Gellert and Josh White—and only when the white captain is far enough away, do the prisoners confide these songs. Then they sing not loudly but deeply their hatred of the brutality of the chain-gang:

> If I'd a had my weight in lime
> I'd a whupped dat captain, till he went stone blind.

If you don't believe my buddy's dead
Just look at that hole in my buddy's head.[7]

A prisoner is told: "Don't you go worryin' about forty [the years of your sentence], Cause in five years you'll be dead."

They glorify the man who makes a crazy dare for freedom; Jimbo, for instance, who escapes almost under the nose of his captain, described as "a big Goliath," who walks like Samson and "totes his talker." They boast: "Ef ah git de drop / Ah'm goin' on / Dat same good way / Dat Jimbo's gone / Lord, Lord, Lord."[8] They reenact with graphic realism the lashing of a fellow-prisoner; the man-hunting of Ol' Rattler, "fastest and smellingest bloodhound in the South"; and the power of Black Betty, the ugly bull-whip. They make stark drama out of the pain, and hopelessness, and shame.

All I wants is dese cold iron shackles off my leg.

It is not only in the prison songs that there is social protest. Where there is some protection or guaranteed secrecy other *verboten* songs come to light. Coal miners, fortified by a strong, truculent union, sing grimly of the exorbitant company stores:

What's de use of me working any more, my baby? (2)
What's de use of me working any more,
When I have to take it up at de company store,
My baby?[9]

Or they use the blues idiom with a new twist:

Operator will forsake you, he'll drive you from his do' . . .
No matter what you do, dis union gwine to stand by you
While de union growing strong in dis land.[10]

7. Josh White, *Chain Gang Songs* (Bridgeport, Conn., Columbia Recording Corporation), Set C-22.

8. Willis James, "Hyah Come de Cap'n," from Brown, Davis, and Lee, *The Negro Caravan* (New York, 1948), p. 469.

9. John and Alan Lomax, *Our Singing Country* (New York, 1941), pp. 278–288.

10. *Ibid.*

And the sharecroppers sharply phrase their plight:

> Go in the store and the merchant would say,
> 'Your mortgage is due and I'm looking for my pay.'
> Down in his pocket with a tremblin' hand
> 'Can't pay you all but I'll pay what I can,'
> Then to the telephone the merchant made a call,
> They'll put you on the chain-gang, an' you don't pay at all.[11]

Big Bill Broonzy is best known as a blues singer, but in the cotton belt of Arkansas he learned a great deal that sank deep. His sharp "Black, Brown, and White Blues" has the new militancy built up on the sills of the old folksong. In an employment office, Big Bill sings, "They called everybody's number / But they never did call mine." Then working side by side with a white man:

> He was getting a dollar an hour
> When I was making fifty cents.

Onto this new protest he ties an old vaudeville chorus, deepening the irony:

> If you's black, ah brother,
> Git back, git back, git back.[12]

Such songs, together with the blues composed by Waring Cuney and Josh White on poverty, hardship, poor housing and jim crow military service, come from conscious propagandists, not truly folk. They make use of the folk idiom in both text and music, however, and the folk listen and applaud. They know very well what Josh White is talking about in such lines as:

> Great gawdamighty, folks feelin' bad
> Lost everything they ever had.

PROSPECT

It is evident that Negro folk culture is breaking up. Where Negro met only with Negro in the black belt the old beliefs strengthened. But when

11. *Ibid.*
12. *People's Songs*, Vol. 1, No. 10 (November, 1940), 9.

mud traps give way to gravel roads, and black tops and even concrete highways with buses and jalopies and trucks lumbering over them, the world comes closer. The churches and schools, such as they are, struggle against some of the results of isolation, and the radio plays a part. Even in the backwoods, aerials are mounted on shanties that seem ready to collapse from the extra weight on the roof, or from a good burst of static against the walls. The phonograph is common, the television set is by no means unknown, and down at the four corners store, a jukebox gives out the latest jive. Rural folk closer to towns and cities may on Saturday jaunts even see an occasional movie, where a rootin'-tootin' Western gangster film introduces them to the advancements of civilization. Newspapers, especially the Negro press, give the people a sense of belonging to a larger world. Letters from their boys in the army, located in all corners of the world, and the tales of the returning veterans, true Marco Polos, also prod the inert into curiosity. Brer Rabbit and Old Jack no longer are enough. Increasingly in the churches the spirituals lose favor to singing out of the books or from broadsides, and city-born blues and jive take over the jook-joints.

The migration of the folk Negro to the cities, started by the hope for better living and schooling, and greater self-respect, quickened by the industrial demands of two world wars is sure to be increased by the new cotton picker and other man-displacing machines. In the city the folk become a submerged proletariat. Leisurely yarn-spinning, slow-paced aphoristic conversation become lost arts; jazzed-up gospel hymns provide a different sort of release from the old spirituals; the blues reflect the distortions of the new way of life. Folk arts are no longer by the folk for the folk; smart businessmen now put them up for sale. Gospel songs often become show-pieces for radio slummers, and the blues become the double-talk of the dives. And yet, in spite of the commercializing, the folk roots often show a stubborn vitality. Just as the transplanted folk may show the old credulity, though the sophisticated impulse sends them to an American Indian for nostrums, or for fortune-telling to an East Indian "madame" with a turban around her head rather than to a mammy with a bandanna around hers; so the folk for all their disorganization may keep something of the fine quality of their old tales and songs. Assuredly even in the new gospel songs and blues much is retained of the phrasing and the distinctive musical manner. Finally, it should be pointed out that even in the transplanting, a certain kind of isolation—class and racial—remains. What may come of it, if anything, is unpredictable, but so far the vigor of the creative impulse has not been snapped, even in the slums.

Whatever may be the future of the folk Negro, American literature as well as American music is the richer because of his expression. Just as Huckleberry Finn and Tom Sawyer were fascinated by the immense lore of their friend Jim, American authors have been drawn to Negro folk life and character. With varying authenticity and understanding, Joel Chandler Harris, Du Bose Heyward, Julia Peterkin, Roark Bradford, Marc Connelly, E. C. L. Adams, Zora Neale Hurston and Langston Hughes have all made rewarding use of this material. Folk Negroes have themselves bequeathed a wealth of moving song, both religious and secular, of pithy folk-say and entertaining and wise folk-tales. They have settled characters in the gallery of American heroes; resourceful Brer Rabbit and Old Jack, and indomitable John Henry. They have told their own story so well that all men should be able to hear it and understand.

Stray Notes on Jazz

~❧ IN 1916 the Victor Company offered a recording contract to the Original Creole Band, a group of New Orleans Negroes which for five years had been touring the country, playing the new "jazz" from Los Angeles to Coney Island. The leader, Freddie Keppard, rejected the offer: "We won't put our stuff on records for everybody to steal." His suspicion was costly. A white band from New Orleans, the Original Dixieland Jass [sic] Band, had just come to New York and was dazzling crowds at Reisenweber's Café. They jumped at the chance to record, and their records sold by the millions. The momentum of success carried them to England. Their early playings therefore can be heard today, while the punching trumpet of the more original Keppard is to be heard on only a few collectors' items, cut in Keppard's declining years. Contrary to accepted opinion, the Original Dixielanders were not the first white band to play jazz in New York, as they had been preceded by the Louisiana Five. But they were the first to record and to be well advertised, and they have given a name to a school of jazz. Their influence was strong: La Rocca on cornet inspired Bix Beiderbecke; Eddie Edwards on trombone inspired Georg Brunies; and Larry Shields showed the capacities of the jazz clarinet. Most important, however, was their balanced contrapunctal ensemble.

In Chicago another white band, the New Orleans Rhythm Kings, rivalled them in performance and fame. Two youngsters, Leon Rappolo on clarinet and Georg Brunies on trombone, were driving forces in this band. Rappolo died early, victim of drugs and hectic living; Brunies is still a favorite in the recording studios. Brunies has said that the best tunes for the early jazz were originated by New Orleans Negroes, and in many other respects these bands are indebted to Negro pioneers. But the music so derived became distinctive. "Dixieland moves, not like Negro jazz, smoothly, unpredictably, and with vast momentum, but jumpily like white ragtime playing. Nevertheless it moves and at its best can be a very exciting music. It never quite achieves the free, relaxed counterpoint of black music; it relies more on the solo; it has more harmony and less dissonance. Nor will the blues be found in it. . . ."[1]

Even if Keppard had recorded for Victor, it is unlikely that his Negro band could have garnered the fame and money that the Dixielanders did; the band would hardly have been engaged in the spots that assured popularity. Audiences at first did not know how to take the infectious rhythms and improvisation. It was looked on as a barnyard music, a misgiving reenforced by the Dixielanders' gay spoofing of "Livery Stable Blues" (no blues, of course, but the seed-corn from which Spike Jones has sprouted). Despite the sensation of the Original Dixielanders and the New Orleans Rhythm Kings, jazz was still too rough musically and too tough socially for people brought up on Sousa and Victor Herbert. There had to be compromise. So what has been aptly called the Whiteman era in jazz was ushered in with pomp and circumstance. Violins and saxophones sweetened and sentimentalized what seemed coarse and raucous. A solidly rocking rhythm was exchanged for a rapping tattoo; the beating of a tom-tom subsided to the rustling of a whisk broom over sand paper, semi-symphonic arrangements were attempted (and this line has led to Fred Waring and Lombardo). Tricky and arch, these arrangements were as far from symphonies as from jazz, but their rehearsed precision got them where New Orleans jamming might have pushed out the walls or summoned the police. Paul Whiteman laid down his fiddle for a baton and was crowned "king of jazz." Managers, worshipping mere "bigness," following Barnum's "A hundred—count 'em!" technique for packing them in, multiplied performers to multiply box-office receipts. A brass section of four trumpets and three trombones, drilled to rise and blast automatically, was thought to be three-and-a-half times as good as one trumpet-trombone team, seated around a piano feeling a song and trying their best to blow that feeling out truthfully, the way it was.

Otis Ferguson tells in *Jazzmen* how Bix Beiderbecke, the young man with the golden horn, wandered in amid the acre of brass in Whiteman's band, was called on for a startling solo, and then subsided forlornly, his good deed done. He was no more lost, however, than the true Negro idiom was. By popular logic what was Negro was conceived to be funny—Bessie Smith, the great blues singer, was first labelled as a "comedienne," for

1. Rudi Blesch, "Jazz Begins," *Jazzways*, I (1946), 120.

instance—and music in the Negro idiom was tricked out to stir laughter. Comic devices were urged by the entrepreneurs; cornets and trombones ejaculated laughter, and one clarinetist blew on three clarinets at one time. Master of the clowning of jazz, the "hokum," was Ted Lewis. He set a tophat on his head, blew bad clarinet, strutted about and beamed "Is everybody happy?" thereby contributing to an unhappy state of affairs. Lewis did hire good musicians like Muggsy Spanier, Fats Waller and Benny Goodman, and he imitated the Negro idiom as well as he knew how, but most of the playing in the Negro style was not an imitation but a caricature, as phoney as a vaudevillian's impersonation of a Negro.

The real jazz went underground, almost literally. But it throve. It was still sustained by a folk-life, unorganized now, but teeming with music. In Chicago, St. Louis, Detroit and Kansas City, the Negro migrants still had their stomps and blues and rocking spirituals. In Chicago King Oliver had one of the best small combinations with Crown Prince Louis Armstrong and Johnny Dodds counterpointing his driving cornet. Jimmy Noone, Sidney Bechet, Jelly Roll Morton, and Kid Ory were others who had spent *lehrjahre* in New Orleans, and were in Chicago on their *wanderjahre*. Free and open, Chicago was a good city for the exciting music to flourish in. Young white men (some still in Austin High School) hung around Negro dance-halls like the Dreamland and the Royal Gardens to learn the new musical language, the unorthodox but inventive techniques, and to assimilate the spirit of the playing. Benny Goodman, Muggsy Spanier, Jess Stacy, Joe Sullivan, Gene Krupa, Bud Freeman, Joe Marsala, and Frank Teschmaker were some who went to school to Negro jazzmen. One of the legends about Bix is that for hours on end he would listen to Bessie Smith's intoning of the blues. She was no comedienne to him.

Because Bessie Smith's music was the deeply felt music of the blues. Around themes of hard-luck, desperation, ironic contrasts between the hope and the actuality—"the blues ain't nothing but the poor man's heart disease"—grew up the Negro's secular songs of sorrow. Musically the blues were suited to carry the burden of grief. Comprising twelve or occasionally sixteen bars, involving certain simple harmonic changes, stressing the "blue note" in which the third and seventh are not pitched steadily but waver between flat and natural, they brought a poignance to American music. They lend themselves to improvisation and are basic to much hot jazz. W. C. Handy's best selling blues of Memphis and St. Louis introduced the blues to another America than their native haunts in turpentine camps and on the levees. Women of expressive voices as impelling as cornets, as subtle as clarinets, sang in the small Negro theatres and honky-tonks.

Among the best were Ma Rainey, Bessie and Clara Smith, and Ida Cox. In small towns people waited religiously for the latest blues records which sold like the hot platters they were. Louis Armstrong, Tommy Ladnier, Joe Smith, one of the most creative cornetists, Buster Bailey and Coleman Hawkins (who play so differently now) and James P. Johnson and Fletcher Henderson, great influences today, learned jazz from the roots by accompanying these singers. Men singers of the blues were Lonnie Johnson, Jim Jackson, Tampa Red, and Blind Lemon Jefferson, who was led about by a small boy named Josh White. Joe Turner was a wee baby then.

Boogie-woogie piano playing, another form close to the folk, also entered jazz history in the twenties. Starting from Southern origins as dim as those of the blues, boogie-woogie is another jazz invention created to fill a need. For the house parties of Chicago's Negro ghetto a piano player was hired to serve as a one-piece band all by himself. This made for musical discoveries, pursued with technical passion. Careless listening results in charging boogie-woogie with monotony. But one enthusiast writes: "Look, look, the artist seems to say. Look at all the things you can do with piano blues. You can make 'em ring out like chimes: you can make 'em cascade like falling icicles; you can make 'em sound like a train going over a bridge; you can make 'em whimper like a lost dog; you can make 'em stomp and holler and shout. . . . Look what you can do by fluttering this chord while the left hand maintains its beat!"[2]

Blesch characterizes boogie-woogie as "a primitive style of piano playing employing the twelve-bar blues form . . . almost percussive in effect, with the right hand chording very rhythmically over a basso ostinato of rising and descending chromatic chords or a similarly rising and descending 'walking bass' consisting of spread octaves."[3] "Pine-top" Smith, who popularized the name, and Jimmy Yancey, who inspired Meade Lux Lewis to compose a jazz classic, "The Yancey Special," were masters of the style in the twenties. Lewis and Al Ammons from Chicago, and Pete Johnson from Kansas City brought boogie-woogie to New York under the sponsorship of John Hammond, starting a lasting praise. Big bands such as Will Bradley, Tommy Dorsey and Lionel Hampton now have orchestrated boogie-woogie; Larry Adler blows it on his harmonica, and even Iturbi essays to play it, but the purest exponents of this style are the midwesterners mentioned, together with Cripple Clarence Loftow, Cow Cow Davenport

2. S. I. Hayakawa, "Reflections on the Development of Jazz," *Jazz Quarterly*, II: 4, p. 7.

3. Blesch, *This Is Jazz*, p. 25.

and Honey Hill of Chicago, Mary Lou Williams of Kansas City and Sammy Price of Texas.

In jazz history then, as the center for hot jazz in the twenties and early thirties, Chicago is second in importance only to New Orleans. Small bands were chiefly responsible for this. After making historic records with King Oliver, Louis Armstrong organized his Hot Five and Hot Seven with such stars as Kid Ory on trombone, Johnny Dodds on clarinet, and Lil Hardin, his second wife, and Earl Hines on piano. Jelly Roll Morton's Red Hot Peppers were cutting some of the hottest and least dated records of the era which make Morton's scoff at the various styles—"Man, they are *all* Jelly Roll's style"—seem less like egomania. Earl Hines, father of the trumpet-style piano, later recorded with Jimmy Noone, from whose expressive clarinet both Goodman and Artie Shaw have learned. Tops among white musicians before his early death was Bix Beiderbecke, a cornetist of fluent melodic ideas and brilliant jetting notes—"they were hit, like a mallet hits a chime," says his friend Hoagy Carmichael. But Bix did not have stellar musicians in his Wolverine Band as Louis Armstrong had, and the records of the Wolverines, for all of their historic importance, lack the prophetic quality of those made by Armstrong and Hines—"The West End Blues," for instance.

Bix and Louis, King Oliver, Earl Hines, Johnny Dodds, and Jimmie Noone stirred enthusiastic imitation. Soon Chicago's second line: Frank Teschmaker, Jimmy McParland, Goodman, Spanier, Stacy, Bud Freeman, Mezz Mezzrow and Art Hodes were contributing to Chicago Jazz—which if not a clearly defined style—is at least a period in jazz history. Most of the bands were pick-up bands for recording; the best-paying showplaces still kept up with the Isham Joneses. When Wingy Mannone, New Orleans trumpeter proud to be of Satchmo's School, fronted a big band with a baton (hoping to cash in on some of the ready dough) he was hooted by the lovers of the hot style: "Wingy, where did *you* learn to lead a band?" and he went back to playing the way he knew how. Perhaps the greatest unifying thread among the Chicagoans was a determination to play what they wanted, the way they wanted to play it. And that was generally in a style that fused the New Orleans jazz of Oliver and Armstrong with Dixieland. In spite of the Negro talent in the town, the term Chicago Jazz applies to white Chicagoan musicians, and not to all of them. Goodman, though a native of the city, is not a Chicago clarinetist, but Pee Wee Russell from Missouri is. Chicago style has no standardized meaning. To the New Orleans instrumentation, a saxophone (or two) was added (disturbing the New Orleans balance), and solos were favored over ensemble improvisation. Charles Smith holds that "the Chicagoans brought orchestral dynamics to the back room, welding them to stop-and-go tactics that had been features of white jazz since the Dixieland days.[4] There was an all-out ensemble climax, straight from New Orleans, a sort of "get-the-hell-off-of-my-note" ride-out. Eddie Condon's jam sessions and the Nicksielanders are the current development of the style. They are praised for "the warm, spontaneous, sometimes almost undisciplined ardor . . . with terrific tension generated by each man blowing off steam in his own way."[5]

Miff Mole, one of the standbys of the Nicksielanders, illustrates what New York brought to jazz history in the twenties, namely a high degree of musicianship. Skillful in the playing of a legato instead of a staccato trombone, he teamed up with Red Nichols to produce countless records in which technique and quiet assurance were the values instead of the fervor of the Hot Five and the out-of-this-world trance of the Chicagoans. With Jimmy and Tommy Dorsey, Glenn Miller and the precocious Benny Goodman, Nichols and Mole (sometimes Nichols and Teagarden, who had mastered blues and hot trombone deep in the heart of Texas) steadily enlarged the popularity of the new art. The records they made were more apt to be of the "Tea for Two" and "Avalon" type, rather than "Gin Mill Blues," and "Basin Street Blues," and "King Porter Stomp," but they generated enough heat to thaw out the young who huddled over phonographs and missed the ball-room palaces where bands performed in swallow-tails. Meanwhile in Harlem there were first-rate performers, like Johnny Dunn and Bubber Miley on trumpet, Tricky Sam and Jimmy Harrison on trombone, Bennie Carter and Coleman Hawkins on saxophone, studying nuances of expressiveness. And there was a good living playing at parlor socials for such pianists as Willie the Lion Smith, Lucky Roberts, James P. Johnson and Fats Waller, who in contrast to the self-taught boogie-woogie pianists in Chicago, were well-trained. Most important in New York jazz, however, were the bands of Fletcher Henderson and Duke Ellington. With a roster of some of the best musicians, Fletcher Henderson was leading the way in fusing jazz band arrangements with improvised hot solos. Louis Armstrong came over to join him. And at the Cotton Club, Duke Ellington, just arrived from Washington with the nucleus of the most famous jazz orchestra of all, was already introducing the distinctive ensemble pattern, arrived at by innumerable shadings of tone and subtleties of rhythm."[6]

4. Charles Smith, *et al.*, *The Jazz Record Book*, New York: Smith and Durrell Co., 1942, p. 162.
5. Anonymous, "Condon Mob," *Jazzways*, ed. by George S. Rosenthal, I:1, p. 102.
6. Smith, *et al.*, *The Jazz Record Book*, p. 62.

Whiteman's popularity had declined; Ted Lewis was old hat. But the big band was here to stay. Even in Chicago of the twenties there were big bands that struggled to play "hot" in the large dance halls—Erskine Tate's and Doc Cook's for instance. "The development of hot music from the New Orleans small group to the five brass, four reeds and four rhythms which Goodman used was a gradual evolutionary process rather than an abrupt revolutionary one."[7] White bands that illustrate the steps from both New Orleans-Chicago collective improvisation and semi-symphonic jazz, are the Ben Pollack band in which Goodman started, Glen Gray and the Casa Loma Band, and the Dorsey Brothers. When these brothers split up, Tommy the trombonist and Jimmy the saxophonist headed individual bands, each of which hit the jackpot. Other leaders helping in the triumph of swing were Artie Shaw, Charley Barnett who frankly imitates Ellington and Basie, Glenn Miller, Bob Crosby, the brother of Bing, but dedicated to Dixieland, and Woody Herman who metamorphosed Isham Jones's relicts into a blues-playing and today frenzied swing band. But Goodman "opened the door for the modern era of big bands with virtuoso leadership."[8] Negro bands, other than Henderson's and Ellington's that helped establish swing were led by Chick Webb at Harlem's Savoy, Cab Calloway, the hi-de-ho man, Lus Russell with whom Louis Armstrong played, Count Basie, and Andy Kirk.

To the question: "What is Swing?" Fats Waller once answered, "If you have to ask, you ain't got it." The critic Robert Goffin states that the word was "created to designate this artificial dynamism which replaced ensemble improvisation . . . a successful formula for commercial hot music."[9] Paul Eduard Miller believes that swing contains all the elements of jazz, and though he prefers the small sized groups he refuses to argue that "jazz written for large orchestras cannot also be great."[10] To Rudi Blesch, big bands, "an inevitable development in Jazz . . . spell the virtually complete dropping of the basic idea of *collective* improvisation." Gaining fullness and richness of tone and accuracy, big bands lose suppleness and rhythmic complexity. "No one has been able as yet to write the sort of free counterpoint which small bands improvise, nor arrange for even the most gifted sections to play it." Blesch finds swing bands relying more and more on powerful beats and repeated riffs (rhythmic phrases) that take the place of melodic developments. Often impressive, this can become "deadly monoto-

7. Frank Stacy, "Swing," *Jazzways*, p. 49.
8. Dale Curran, "Three Brass, Four Rhythm," *Jazzways*, p. 24.
9. Robert Goffin, *Jazz: From the Congo to the Metropolitan*, New York: Alfred A. Knopf, 1944, pp. 149ff.
10. Paul Eduard Miller, *Esquire's Jazz Book*, 1945, p. 24.

nous."[11] One defender of swing, even while praising the exciting musicianship of the new bands led by Woody Herman and Lionel Hampton, fears that swing may become static and exchange "the jazz birth-right . . . for a mess of box-office receipts."[12] In spite of the contemporary need that he believes is filled by swing, it is still at the mercy of commercialism.

Where the seven-brass, five reeds, and four rhythm band has perforce had to create a new tradition, small bands play closer to the parent style. In recommending certain jazz records B. H. Haggin writes: "What I am concerned with is the freely improvisatory 'hot' performances—which are what jazz is—that some of the players in one of these bands may indulge in when their night's work is over, either in private for their own pleasure or in the recording-studio for pleasure and the union-rate . . . under the conditions of relaxed freedom and intimacy which this improvisatory performance requires."[13] Benny Goodman's trios, quartette, and sextet, were distinctive alike for the chamber-music jazz they produced and for their interracial make-up. Teddy Wilson, Lionel Hampton, Charles Christian, Fletcher Henderson, and Cootie Williams are Negroes who have supported Goodman on jazz classics. Crosby's Bobcats, Dorsey's Clambake Seven, and Shaw's Gramercy Five are small recording outfits from large swing bands. Ellington's smaller units led by Johnny Nodges, alto saxophonist; Barney Bigard, clarinetist, Rex Stewart and Cootie Williams, trumpeters, are noted. From Basie's band, the Kansas City Six and Seven play an easier riding jazz than Basie's powerhouse riffing. Small Dixieland or Nicksieland groups make use of such men as Spanier, Teagarden, Bud Freeman, Max Kaminsky, Wild Bill Davison, Pee Wee Russell and Eddie Condon. Earlier, Fats Waller had an underestimated small combination; the rollicking buffoonery of the old master too often diverted attention from the fine musical backing. The recording groups of Red Norvo supporting Mildred Bailey and of Teddy Wilson supporting Billie Holiday created relaxed, skillful and emotionally persuasive music. Bunny Berigan and Gene Krupa recorded jazz classics with bands composed of Negro and white stars. A distinctively fluent small group was John Kirby's. Art Hodes, Red Allen, Edmond Hall and Benny Morton have for a long time led outstanding small bands; Joe Sullivan and Jack Teagarden have made fine records with small outfits. The small band tradition of the Hot Five and the Red Hot Peppers has never been lost, certainly not in the recording studios.

11. Blesch, *op. cit.*, p. 27.
12. Stacy, *loc. cit.* p. 105.
13. B. H. Haggin, *Music on Records*, New York: Alfred A. Knopf, 1945, p. 244.

And yet for a long time small bands "made musical history and laid a large financial egg,"[14] in the words of one historian. Small bands today, however, are laying golden eggs, especially on New York's Fifty-Second Street. During the war, nightspots sprang up like mushrooms in places so small that trios (especially piano, guitar, and bass) became standard. The King Cole Trio led in popularity, but soon trios starred men like Art Tatum, Eddie Heywood, Johnny Guarnieri, Herman Chittison on piano, Stuff Smith and Slam Stewart on strings, Ben Webster, Coleman Hawkins, Don Buas and Charlie Parker on saxophone and Dizzy Gillespie—especially Dizzy—on trumpet. The rationing of shellac and the Petrillo AFL ban on the recording by the major companies caused a sudden flurry of new recording firms which are concentrating on small all-star bands.

Does this mean that jazz has returned to the collective improvisation of New Orleans? It does not. The dominant aim on Fifty-Second Street seems to be exhibition of virtuosity, rather than ensemble improvising. Bunk Johnson likens the conventional tenor saxophone solo to a man "running up and down stairs with no place to go."[15] Dizzy Gillespie has become one of those single man influences on jazz, like Louis Armstrong and Father Hines in the twenties. Noted for brilliant facility (the leading swing bands of Woody Herman and Lionel Hampton are said to be on a "Dizzy kick"), Gillespie has been called "the most-discussed, most idolized and most imitated musician of the year."[16] The type of music played by Gillespie goes by the name of "be-bop" (not to be confused with the juke-box jingle—"Hey-ba-ba-re-bop"); it is marked by rapid-fire changes. One critic caustically wonders what might happen if a sudden veering of fashion left the band "stuck at 9:01 p.m. with an anachronistic 9:00 p.m. riff." Instead of playing fast as fury to keep abreast of the latest development, "be-bop" performers are urged to return to "playing a tune, just any old thing with a reasonable chord progression and everyone somewhere near it, in something resembling dance tempo, in a way that sounds pleasant, and without piercing an ear drum at twenty paces."[17]

Leonard Feather, who favors progressive jazz of the "be-bop" school applies the term "moldy figs" to all adherents of the New Orleans style. Nevertheless such jazz is being played and recorded increasingly. In these first years of Bunk Johnson's renascence, he and his band have been re-

14. Curran, *loc. cit.*, p. 18.
15. Blesch, *op. cit.*, p. 26.
16. Leonard Feather, "A Survey of Jazz Today," *Esquire's 1946 Jazz Book*, p. 71.
17. Carlton Brown, "Hey! Ba-Ba-Revolt," in *The Record Changer*, May, 1946, p. 26.

corded by five different companies; King Jazz, Inc., is recording the veterans Sidney Bechet and Mezz Mezzrow; Commodore, Blue Note and Disc Companies, while eclectically sponsoring jazz of all types, stress improvised jazz; out in California the Jazz Man Company is issuing the Dixieland of Lu Walters and the Crescent Company brings back Kid Ory to the turn tables. Numerous recently formed companies record small combinations, generally drawn from Fifty-Second Street. Interest in extending the boundaries of jazz goes on apace. The New Jazz Foundation in New York aims at ambitious concert jazz. Famous soloists have been giving jam sessions at San Francisco's Philharmonic; and Duke Ellington has presented his Black, Brown, and Beige Tone Parallel at Carnegie Hall. James P. Johnson, dean of jazz pianists, has been presented in frequent concerts, pleasing both long-hair critics and the jazz *aficionados*. Serious books and articles are now being written on jazz; magazines from the most popular to the most highbrow have articles on jazz and record reviews. One no longer has to read European aesthetes for interpretation of an American popular art.

Record collecting is now a fascinating and remunerative American hobby. A thriving magazine, *The Record Changer,* is dedicated to the collecting fraternity all over the world. Prices in the *Record Changer* sometimes run amazingly high. According to Gordon Gullickson, its editor, "Almost any King Oliver or Gennett or Okeh will, if in good condition, bring between $150 and $200." Joe Oliver, called the king of jazz by those who knew, though the early books on jazz do not mention him, died penniless in Savannah at the time of the triumph of swing. His sister had to use her rent money to get his body to New York. She wanted to buy a headstone for his grave, but her money ran out and the grave still lacks a stone. If she only had one of her brother's early records she might buy a fine marker for his resting place.

Reviews

Not Without Laughter

Not Without Laughter. By Langston Hughes. Alfred A. Knopf. $2.50.

◄ WE HAVE in this book, laconically, tenderly told, the story of a young boy's growing up. Let no one be deceived by the effortless ease of the telling by the unpretentious simplicity of *Not Without Laughter.* Its simplicity is the simplicity of great art; a wide observation, a long brooding over humanity, and a feeling for beauty in unexpected, out of the way places, must have gone into its makeup. It is generously what one would expect of the author of *The Weary Blues* and *Fine Clothes to the Jew.*

Not Without Laughter tells of a poor family living in a small town in Kansas. We are shown intimately the work and play, the many sided aspects of Aunt Hager and her brood. Aunt Hager has three daughters: Tempy, Annjee and Harriett. Tempy is doing well; having joined the Episcopalian Church she has put away "niggerish" things; Annjee is married to a likeable scapegrace, Jimboy, guitar plunker and rambling man; Harriett, young, full of life and daring, is her heart's worry. She has a grandchild, Sandy, son of Annjee and Jimboy. And about him the story centers.

Sandy with his wide eyes picking up knowledge of life about the house; Sandy listening to his father's blues and ballads in the purple evenings, watching his Aunt Harriett at her dancing; Sandy at school; Sandy dreaming over his geography book; Sandy at his job in the barbershop and hotel; Sandy at his grandmother's funeral; Sandy learning respectability at Aunt Tempy's,—and learning at the same time something of the ways of women from Pansetta; Sandy in Chicago; Sandy with his books and dreams of education—so run the many neatly etched scenes.

But the story is not Sandy's alone. We see Harriett, first as a firm fleshed beautiful black girl, quick at her lessons; we see her finally a blues singer on State Street. The road she has gone has been rocky enough. She has been maid at a country club where the tired business men made advances; she has been with a carnival troupe, she has been arrested for street walking. We follow Annjee in her trials, and Jimboy, and Tempy. And we get to know the wise, tolerant Aunt Hager, beloved by whites and blacks; even by Harriett who just about breaks her heart. Lesser characters are as clearly individualized and developed. We have Willie Mae, and Jimmy Lane, and Joe Willis, "white folks nigger," and Uncle Dan, and Mingo, and Buster, who could have passed for white. The white side of town, the relationships of employers with laundresses and cooks, all these are adequately done. The book, for all of its apparent slightness, is full-bodied.

One has to respect the author's almost casual filling in of background. The details are perfectly chosen; and they make the reader *see*. How representative are his pictures of the carnival, and the dance at which "Benbow's Famous Kansas City Band" plays, and the gossip over back fences! How recognizable is Sister Johnson's "All these womens dey mammy named Jane an' Mary an' Cora, soon's dey gets a little somethin', dey changes dey names to Janette or Mariana or Corina or somethin' mo' flowery than what dey had."

As the title would suggest the book is not without laughter. Jimboy's guitar-playing, Harriett's escapades, the barber shop tall tales, the philosophizing of the old sheep "who know de road," all furnish something of this. Sandy's ingenuousness occasionally is not without laughter. But the dominant note of the book is a quiet pity. It is not sentimental; it is candid, clear eyed instead—but it is still pity. Even the abandon, the fervor of the chapter called *Dance,* closely and accurately rendered (as one would expect of Langston Hughes) does not strike the note of unclouded joy. We see these things as they are: as the pitiful refuges of poor folk against the worries of hard days. It is more the laughter of the blues line—*laughin' just to keep from cryin'*.

The difference between comedy and tragedy of course lies often in the point of view from which the story is told. Mr. Hughes' sympathetic identification with these folk is so complete that even when sly comic bits creep in (such as Madame de Carter and the Dance of the Nations) the laughter is quiet—more of a smile than a Cohen-like guffaw. But even these sly bits are few and far between. More than Sandy's throwing his boot-black box at the drunken cracker, certainly a welcome case of poetic justice, one remembers the disappointments of this lad's life. Sandy went on Children's Day to the Park. "Sorry," the man said. "This party's for white kids." In a classroom where the students are seated alphabetically, Sandy and the other three colored children sit behind Albert Zwick. Sandy, in the white folks' kitchen, hears his hardworking mother reprimanded by her sharp tempered employer. And while his mother wraps several little bundles of food to carry to Jimboy, Sandy cried. These scenes are excellently done, with restraint, with irony, and with compassion.

Sandy knows the meaning of a broken family, of poverty, of seeing those he loves go down without being able to help. Most touching, and strikingly universal, is the incident of the Xmas sled. Sandy, wishful for a Golden Flyer sled with flexible rudders! is surprised on Christmas Day by the gift of his mother and grandmother. It is a sled. They had labored and schemed and sacrificed for it in a hard winter. On the cold Christmas morning they dragged it home. It was a home-made contraption—roughly carpentered, with strips of rusty tin along the wooden runners. "It's fine," Sandy lied, as he tried to lift it.

Of a piece with this are the troubles that Annjee knows—Annjee whose husband is here today and gone tomorrow; Annjee, who grows tired of the buffeting and loses ground slowly; and the troubles of Aunt Hager who lives long enough to see her hopes fade out, and not long enough to test her final hope, Sandy. . . . Tempy, prosperous, has coldshouldered her mother; Annjee is married to a man who frets Hager; Harriett has gone with Maudel to the sinister houses of the bottom. "One by one they leaves you," Hager said slowly. "One by one yo' chillen goes."

Unforgettable is the little drama of Harriett's rebellion. It is the universal conflict of youth and age. Mr. Hughes records it, without comment. It is the way life goes. Harriett, embittered by life, wanting her share of joy, is forbidden to leave the house. The grandmother is belligerent, authoritative, the girl rebellious. And then the grandmother breaks. . . . "Harriett, honey, I wants you to be good." But the pitiful words do not avail; Harriett, pitiless as only proud youth can be, flings out of doors—with a cry, "You old Christian Fool!" A group of giggling sheiks welcomes her.

Of all of his characters, Mr. Hughes obviously has least sympathy with Tempy. She is the *arriviste*, the worshipper of white folks' ways, the striver. "They don't 'sociate no mo' with none but de high toned colored folks." The type deserves contempt looked at in one way, certainly; looked at in another it might deserve pity. But the point of the reviewer is this: that Mr. Hughes does not make Tempy quite convincing. It is hard to believe that Tempy would be as blatantly crass as she is to her mother on Christmas Day, when she says of her church "Father Hill is so dignified, and the services are absolutely refined! *There's never anything niggerish about them—so you know, mother, they suit me.*"

But, excepting Tempy, who to the reviewer seems slightly caricatured, all of the characters are completely convincing. There is a universality about them. They have, of course, peculiar problems as Negroes. Harriett, for instance, hates all whites, with reason. But they have even more the problems that are universally human. Our author does not exploit either local color, or race. He has selected an interesting family and has told us candidly, unembitteredly, poetically of their joy lightened and sorrow laden life.

Langston Hughes presents all of this without apology. Tolerant, humane, and wise in the ways of mortals, he has revealed beauty where too many of us, dazzled by false lights, are unable to see it. He has shown us again, in this third book of his—what he has insisted all along, with quiet courage:

Beautiful, also, is the sun.
Beautiful, also, are the souls of my people. . . .

A Romantic Defense

〜 I'LL TAKE MY STAND, by Twelve Southerners, is a romantic defense of the agrarian tradition. These twelve articles, all of them ably written, would have served well enough for magazines, but cohering in a book they don't seem to be nearly so epochal as some would have us believe. In the last analysis, they are all fairly old stuff. At their worst they are Thomas Nelson Page; at their infrequent best they are Emerson (a 'damyank'), and diluted Matthew Arnold.

The thesis of this book is that in our mechanized age there is a great deal lacking. That is, what has been the common intellectual property from Ruskin and Carlyle down to Van Wyck Brooks, Randolph Bourne, Sinclair Lewis, and John Dewey (to mention only a few names), has now crossed the Potomac and reached Tennessee. Industrialism being a curse, it follows logically (?) that the only escape is a return to the blessing dispensed unto man in the shape of the Old South. Graciousness and culture and art and individual liberty are indigenous to agrarianism; the South was agrarian, and our only way out of perplexity therefore is a reassumption of the Southern way of life.

But just what *was* the Southern way of life is not so explicit as the Neoconfederate distrust of the machine. The contributors who are confident of what it was hand out many underripe assertions. Thus, 'the South has been non-acquisitive.' (With an oligarchy of planters ruining the past and future of their section!) 'It has been leisurely (praises be for euphemism), kindly, serene.' So we have heard Southerners insist heatedly and long. 'Only recently Northern interests have opened up the South to industry.' (The Birmingham of the last century is forgotten.) The frontier qualities of the Old South don't fit into the picture and artistically (or artfully) are left out. Old wives' tales, and gentlemanly colonels musing over mint juleps, are better sources than the other Page (Walter H.), Broadus Mitchell, T. S. Stribling, and Francis Pendleton Gaines.

God made the country (and in this case Dixie,—page Al Jolson) and man—the Damyank—made the town. And it's oh for the loss of the poor white's folk art! says the author who deals with the South's "forgotten man." He was happy once, whether hill billy or independent yeoman, or poor white trash; but now shades of the factory descend. Perhaps. But while it takes no perspicuity to see the present evils of industrialization, it does take a great imagination to see this peasant's paradise just as it does to see the whole mythical Arcadia—unless, of course, one happens to be an ancestor worshipper.

The chronicler suspected all along that there would be hidden somewhere the unreconstructed Southerner's attitude to the Negro—the proverbial African woodcarving in the lumber yard. One contributor Donald Davidson had written (italics mine)

> "Black man, . . . Though I am no longer
> A child, *and you perhaps unfortunately*
> *Are no longer a child*, we still understand
> Better maybe than others. . . .
> . . . But now I cannot
> Forget that I was master, and you can hardly
> Forget that you were slave.
> Let us not bruise our foreheads on the wall."

The suspicion based on the earlier writings of these twelve is justified. In "The Briar Patch" Mr. Warren, with all the metaphysics of his breed, and using all the connotations of the title,—tells the world about the Negro's place in that world. "Money has trickled down from the North to be invested in the negro's education. Southern states have doled out money from their all too inadequate educational funds. . . . For what is the negro to be educated? . . . Are most negroes to be taught to read and write, and then turned back on society with only that talent as a guaranty of their safety or prosperity? Are some others, far fewer in number, to be taught their little French and less Latin, and then sent packing about their business? The most urgent need was to make the ordinary negro into a competent workman or artisan and a decent citizen. . . . This remains, it seems, the most urgent need. . . . The Southern white man . . . wishes the negro well; he wishes to see crime, genial irresponsibility, ignorance and oppression replaced by an informed and productive negro community. . . . Let the negro sit beneath his own vine and fig tree. The relation of the two will not immediately escape friction and difference, but there is no reason to despair of their fate."

The white man's burden. Oh the pity of it, Iago. A separate community the ideal,—"Under his own vine and fig tree." (Which is a 'cultured' euphemism for ghetto.)—It seems to the chronicler that he's heard all of this, somewhere, before. . . .

"Caroling Softly Souls of Slavery"

~€ THE CHRONICLER, in rummaging about the attic, discovered a modestly bound, modestly printed small volume, published in 1897. This dusty relic was *Thirty Years a Slave*, the life story of one Louis C. Hughes. It served as the assembly call for many thoughts that have heretofore been even more scattered than they appear to be on this page.

Prof. William Dodd in *The Cotton Kingdom* says of the slaves: "Willingly or unwillingly, they increased its solidarity and lent enchantment to the life of the planter. They boasted of the limitless lands of their masters, of the incomparable horses of 'ol' massa,' of the riches of 'ol' massa's' table and the elegancies of 'ol' massa's great house.' *What their inmost thoughts were is not likely ever to be known.*" From *Thirty Years a Slave* these inmost thoughts are still not to be learned. The subtitle of this autobiography *From Bondage to Freedom, The Institution of Slavery As Seen on the Plantation and in the Home of the Planter* would indicate of course that the book deals with generalities rather than particularities. The author doesn't take us inside with him. We learn from what so many of the "Bondage and Freedom" narratives we have already learned: the size of the cabins, the differences between house and field servants, preparing cotton for markets, etc. E.g. "The overseer was a man hired to look after the farm and whip the slaves." "There was a section of the plantation known as 'the quarters' where were situated the cabins of the slaves."—These are the type of comments; fellow slaves go unnamed, uncharacterized, almost unmentioned. And all the time how much these things would have meant to us!—the things he actually saw and did, the 'real' things that fixed themselves forever in his mind—what he thought in those long hours hidden in the hold of the steamboat, what separation from his mother meant to him and what the whipping of his wife meant to him, what the joyous band on safely escaping from the plantation said to each other in the days of Jubilo.

It would be more than ungrateful to blame for sins of omission a gentleman who afforded one a quiet meditative vista into days nearly forgotten now, and put away by so many, forever. The chronicler realized well enough, on picking out the book, that this new friend was not likely to be a Douglass, in either life or letters. To expect the analyst, the register, the artist, of this hard pressed struggler for subsistence, decency, self respect and a fair measure of happiness would be foolish, of course; to expect more than what he gave from a man disclaiming in his preface any of the "adjuncts of literary adornment" would be futile.

But there's the rub. The chronicler realizes that this must be so—but the pity of it remains. If only! If only instead of an oft repeated generalized treatment the man had told us what he really *knew*. One fears that this narrative was recollected in too much tranquillity. The drama, the emotion, the personality, what one feels to be the essential truth is somehow missing.

Mr. Hughes' life certainly contained material enough. Cities and men he knew: Richmond slave mart, Mississippi plantations, Memphis big houses, Cincinnati, Milwaukee, Detroit in days after the war; life on plantation, in house service, on steamboats, in Federal and Confederate camps; the separation of families, frustrated breaks for freedom, courtship, marriage, running picket lines, self education, escaping slavery, working in hotels, in his own laundry business: much had he seen and known. He could have told us so much. Instead, and I quote his preface, "the narrator presents his story in compliance with the suggestion of friends, and hopes that it may add something of accurate information regarding the character and influence of an institution which for two hundred years, etc. etc." With all of his disclaimers one believes that he had too much of an eye on "literary adjuncts": he wanted to be important, and he should have been himself. In his portrait, which shows a kindly faced man with alert eyes and a humorous mouth—he wears the old styled coat—the "jim-swinger." Too many of his pages are "jim-swinger."

If only the impossible could have happened, that from this man's brothers and sisters there could have come simple, unvarnished accounts of what they *knew*. There it seems is a great loss to the full chronicling of American life, that this people—"leaving, soon gone" should have been either enforcedly silent or unable to reveal in terms that would stay alive what slavery really was to the slave. To an understanding of antebellum, civil war, and reconstruction days some of the finest talent in American literature has applied itself. Certainly the Negro artist could well follow, for an epic theme, where Evelyn Scott and Stephen Vincent Benet have led the way. There is room for a complement to the *Wave* done with the same integrity and artistry. In lieu of this treatment of course, there always remains the prime testimony of the spirituals—and of course for those who will have it—and one fears they are many—the picture vouched for by slaveowners of the perpetual and glorious holiday that antebellum life was.

But those artists, seeking as Jean Toomer once sought to "catch the plaintive soul, leaving, soon gone," will find that few and far between now are those who once could have told so much. And even with them—there is the slow, inevitable—and after all, not to be deplored—erasure of the years. Not to be deplored. . . . For the chronicler remembers his persistence in the face of an old gentleman's studied avoidance of pointed questions about cruelty. Finally, the old man said, "Was dey evah cruel? Certainly dey was cruel. But I don't want to talk about dat." And he closed his eyes. . . .

Imitation of Life:
Once a Pancake

～ IMITATION OF LIFE,* by Fannie Hurst, first appeared as *Sugar House* in the *Pictorial Review*. It was another American success story. Bea Pullman, a hard working, motherless girl, with a paralyzed father, forges her way, after her husband is killed in a railroad accident, from drab poverty, to Ducan Phyfe, Heppelwhite and Sheraton prosperity. She is grateful to life for her talent to "provide people with a few moments of creature enjoyment" in the shape of succulent waffles and maple syrup; she should be grateful to Delilah, upon whose broad shoulders she rode pickaback to affluence. Delilah, whose recipe and skill are the makings of the world famous enterprise, wants little but the chance, since she is full of "a rambunctious capacity for devotion," to be mammy to the whole world, and especially to Miss Bea. Her greatest trouble is her fair daughter Peola, who wants to be white in the worst way, and finally marries a young blond engineer, who, coincidentally, was never to know that he had called his mother-in-law "mammy" over a stack of wheats. Peola and husband disappear into Bolivia; Delilah obligingly dies after the business is established and Miss Bea, free at last for love, finds that it is too late, that her beloved has been swept away by her daughter, Jessie. It is, in the main, a tearful story.

Those who have seen the picture will recognize the differences in plot. The characterization and ideas, however, are little changed. Delilah, "vast monument of a woman," "her huge smile the glowing heart of a furnace," "her round black moon face shining above an Alps of bosom" is essentially the same, with her passion for rubbing "dem white little dead beat feet," the inebriation of her language, too designedly picturesque, her unintelligi-

*"Imitation of Life," by Fannie Hurst. Harper & Bros. $2.50.

ble character, now infantile, now mature, now cataloguing folk-beliefs of the Southern Negro, and now cracking contemporary witticisms. Her baby talk to the white child partakes too much of maple sugar; to her own, too much of mustard. Delilah's visions of going to glory recur in the book. To the reviewer they are not true folk-eloquence. "I'm paying lodge-dues an' I'm savin' mah own pennies for to be sent home and delivered to de glory of de Lawd wid plumes and trumpets blowin' louder dan rhubarb would make growin'." There is a great deal of talk on the text: "Never the Twain Shall Meet." Delilah is completely black, and therefore contented: "Lovers of de Lawd an' willin' servers is my race, filled with de blessings of humility" . . . "Glory be to Gawd, I's glad I's one of his black chillun, 'cause, sho' as heaven, his heart will bleed fust wid pity and wid mercy for his lowdown ones." Peola, near white, but with "not a half moon to her finger nails" is unhappy. *It's de white horses dat's wild, a'swimmin' in de blood of mah chile. . . . I wants to drown dem white horses plungin' in mah baby's blood.* Can one reader be forgiven, if during such passages, there runs into his mind something unmistakably like a wild horse laugh?

Remembering the book I was unprepared to believe the theatregoers and critics who urged the novelty, the breaking away from old patterns of the picture. Of course they had reasons. It is true that the picture is a departure from Stepin Fetchit. There is less of Octavus Roy Cohen in the film than in the book (perhaps the intrinsic dignity of Louise Beavers kept down the clowning). The bandana has been exchanged for a white chef's cap. There is a warm mutual affection between the two mothers; kindheartedness meets up with gratitude. Important roles, of some seriousness, were given to Louise Beavers and Fredi Washington, who are certainly deserving actresses. If their names on the screen were not quite in the largest type, they were still high up on the list, and will be remembered because of first rate performances. Moreover, Delilah is a preternaturally good woman, except for a little breadth of diction, and Peola's morality, in spite of her bitterness, is unimpeachable. Cabins and cottonfields are a long way from the suite (downstairs) of Delilah. Both Delilah and Peola can dress up, after a fashion. Poverty is back in the past, due to Miss Bea's midas-like touch (?) and her generosity (!) "Ain't you made life a white padded cell for Delilah?" The word "nigger" is not once used, even in places where logically it should occur. Minor problems are touched upon. All of these things are undoubtedly gladdening to our bourgeois hearts. But that doesn't make them new. However novel in Hollywood, they are old in literature. It requires no searching analysis to see in *Imitation of Life* the old stereotype of the contented Mammy, and the tragic mulatto; and the ancient ideas about the mixture of the races.

Delilah is straight out of Southern fiction. Less abject than in the novel, she is still more concerned with the white Jessie than with Peola. She has little faith in Peola's capacities: "We all starts out smart; we don't get dumb till later on." Resignation to injustice is her creed; God knows best, we can't be telling Him his business; mixed bloods who want to be white must learn to take it, must not beat their fists against life; she doesn't rightly know where the blame lies. When she refuses her twenty per cent (not because it was too little) she is the old slave refusing freedom: "My own house? You gonna send me away? Don't do that to me? How I gonna take care of you and Miss Jessie if I's away? I's yo' cook. You kin have it; I make you a present of it." She finally consents for some money to be put aside against a funeral. *"Once a pancake, always a pancake."* The "passing" episodes are as unbelievable. She is ignorant of the school attended by her daughter (in Atlantic City of segregated schools); she naively gives Peola away, insisting that she did not intend to. Later, finding her daughter passing as a cashier she announces, "I'se yo' mammy, Peola," although she could have spared the girl embarrassment by sending in Miss Bea. She is canny about the ways of men and women where Miss Bea is concerned; but when her daughter is yearning for music and parties, she says, "Come on, honey, I'll dance with you." The director would not even let Delilah die in peace. She must speak, in a tragic scene, well acted, comic lines about "colored folks' eyes budging out," and "not liking the smell of gasoline." Her idiom is good only in spots; I have heard dialect all my life, but I have yet to hear such a line as "She am an angel."

Peola, wistfully hearing the music upstairs, searching the mirror for proof of her whiteness, crying out her hatred of life, her vexation at her black mother, is the tragic octoroon, familiar to novels more than to life. She, too, is at times hard to believe in. For she never quite gets a grasp of the true problem. There was a chance for real bitterness when Miss Bea stops her as she is finally leaving her mother. But the tirade does not come, although Peola must have seen through the condescension and the gentle exploitation. It would be refreshing to have heard what a girl like Peola would really have said; I believe Miss Washington could have risen to heights in its delivery. There is a scene where Miss Bea goes upstairs while Delilah goes down. It is symbolic of many things. One is, that in *Imitation of Life* where Claudette Colbert has a role to bring out all that there is in her, both Miss Beavers and Miss Washington have, so to speak, to go downstairs; Miss Beavers to a much greater childishness, and Miss Washington to a much greater bewilderment than they would recognize in real life. But so Hollywood would have it; and so Hollywood gets something less artistic and less true.

To the reviewer the shots nearest to truth are the Harlem funeral scenes; the most memorable is the flash of the electric sign after the death of Delilah. The good old heart-broken soul dies, having made Miss Bea's road an easy one, for little more return than comfort and affection; Miss Bea goes on to wealth, love, and happiness, and Delilah gets her dubious immortality as an electrified trademark. The music of the quartette is stirring, although it is unfortunately synchronized with Delilah's dying, and is another instance of Hollywood's poor imitation of life. One of the worst shots is the renunciation finale in the romantic garden, with the lights on the river reminiscent of Venice.

It goes without saying that the picture has its moments of truth to American life. It is true, for instance, that in such a partnership, the white member, whose contributions were mild flirtations for business support, and energy, and "brains," would give the real power behind the enterprise a paltry twenty per cent. It is true that the white partner would most likely live upstairs, the black down; and that they would not ride side by side in the same automobile. It is true that after the death of the dearly beloved Mammy, the lost daughter, finding her friends again, would be gently comforted, and placed in the family car up front with the chauffeur. And it is true that for Jessie, business success would mean horse-shows, Switzerland, and finishing schools, where she could learn to stretch her eyes and simper, whereas for Peola it would mean a precarious future, remorse-ridden and threatening. All of this is true to the ways of America. But it hardly seems anything to cheer about.

"Luck Is a Fortune"

Their Eyes Were Watching God. By Zora Neale Hurston. J. B. Lippincott Company. $2.

✒ JANIE'S GRANDMOTHER, remembering how in slavery she was used "for a work-ox and a brood sow," and remembering her daughter's shame, seeks Janie's security above all else. But to Janie, her husband, for all his sixty acres, looks like "some old skull-head in de graveyard," and she goes off down the road with slick-talking Jody Sparks. In Eatonville, an all-colored town, Jody becomes the "big voice," but Janie is first neglected and then browbeaten. When Jody dies, Tea-Cake, with his contagious high spirits, whirls Janie into a marriage, idyllic until Tea-Cake's tragic end. Janie returns home, grief-stricken but fulfilled. Better than her grandmother's security, she had found out about living for herself.

Filling out Janie's story are sketches of Eatonville and farming down "on the muck" in the Everglades. On the porch of the mayor's store "big old lies" and comic-serious debates, with the tallest of metaphors, while away the evenings. The dedication of the town's first lamp and the community burial of an old mule are rich in humor but they are not cartoons. Many incidents are unusual, and there are narrative gaps in need of building up. Miss Hurston's forte is the recording and the creation of folk-speech. Her devotion to these people has rewarded her; "Their Eyes Were Watching God" is chock-full of earthy and touching poetry.

> Ah don't want yo' feathers always crumpled by folks throwin' up things in yo' face. And ah can't die easy thinkin' maybe de menfolks white or black is makin' a spit cup outa you: Have some sympathy fuh me. Put me down easy, Janie, Ah'm a cracked plate.

Though inclined to violence and not strictly conventional, her people are not naive primitives. About human needs and frailties they have the unabashed shrewdness of the Blues. It is therefore surprising when, in spite of her clear innocence, all the Negroes turn away from Janie at her murder trial.

But this is not *the* story of Miss Hurston's own people, as the foreword states, for *the* Negro novel is as unachievable as the Great American Novel. Living in an all-colored town, these people escape the worst pressures of class and caste. There is little harshness; there is enough money and work to go around. The author does not dwell upon the "people ugly from ignorance and broken from being poor" who swarm upon the "muck" for short-time jobs. But there is bitterness, sometimes oblique, in the enforced folk manner, and sometimes forthright. The slave, Nanny, for bearing too light a child with gray eyes, is ordered a terrible beating by her mistress, who in her jealousy is perfectly willing to "stand the loss" if the beating is fatal. And after the hurricane there is a great to-do lest white and black victims be buried together. To detect the race of the long-unburied corpses, the conscripted grave-diggers must examine the hair. The whites get pine coffins; the Negroes get quick-lime. "They's mighty particular how dese dead folks goes tuh judgment. Look lak they think God don't know nothin' 'bout de Jim Crow law."

An Annotated Bibliography of the Works of Sterling A. Brown

by Robert G. O'Meally

~ STERLING A. BROWN is a distinguished writer whose poems, short stories, reviews, and scholarly works have appeared for more than fifty years. His poetry reflects the innovative impulse of contemporary verse as well as the toughness, humor, and protest of black American folklore. And his reportorial narratives and sketches of the Southern scene are alive with black talk, and they convey vividly the terror and the irony of "living Jim Crow" during the forties. Brown has studied the role of blacks in American folklore, literature, and music since the New Negro Renaissance period. His work also has provided perspective to *New* New Negroes, including Black Aesthetic writers of the sixties and seventies.

This annotated bibliography, arranged according to subject and date of publication, is designed to assist readers in locating Brown's works, many of which are uncollected or out of print.

For assisting me in tracking down materials, I am indebted to Cornelia Stokes and Ahmos Zu-Bolton at Founder's Library, Howard University. Special thanks go to Sterling A. Brown, teacher, hero, friend.

I. POEMS

A. Poems included in *Southern Road*, but published previously:

"Challenge," "Odyssey of Big Boy," "Return," "Salutamus," "To a Certain Lady, in Her Garden." *Caroling Dusk*. Edited by Countee Cullen. New York: Harper and Brothers, 1927, pp. 130–139.

"Foreclosure." *Ebony and Topaz, A Collectanea*. Edited by Charles S. Johnson. New York: *Opportunity, Journal of Negro Life*,[1] 1927, p. 36.

"Old Man Buzzard." *The Carolina Magazine*, LVIII (May, 1927), 25–26.

---

1. Hereafter, *Opportunity, Journal of Negro Life* will be cited as *Opportunity*.

"When de Saints Go Ma'ching Home." *Opportunity*, V (July, 1927), 48.

"Thoughts of Death." *Opportunity*, VI (August 6, 1928), 242.

"Long Gone." *Anthology of Negro American Literature*. Edited by V. F. Calverton. New York: Modern Library, 1929, pp. 209–210.

"Riverbank Blues." *Opportunity*, VII (May, 1929), 148.

"Effie." *Opportunity*, VII (October, 1929), 304.

"Dark of the Moon," "Ma Rainey," "Southern Road." *Folk-Say, a Regional Miscellany*,[2] II. Edited by Benjamin A. Botkin. Norman, Oklahoma: University of Oklahoma Press, 1930, pp. 275–279.

"Memphis Blues," "Slim Greer," "Strong Men." *The Book of American Negro Poetry*. Edited by James Weldon Johnson. New York: Harcourt, Brace, 1931, pp. 248–266.

"Convict," "New St. Louis Blues," "Old King Cotton," "Pardners," "Revelations," "Slow Coon" (later published as "Slim Lands a Job"), "Tin Roof Blues." *Folk-Say*, III. Edited by Benjamin A. Botkin. Norman, Oklahoma: Oklahoma Folklore Society, 1931, pp. 113–123.

B. *Southern Road*. New York: Harcourt, Brace, 1932.

Brown's first book of poems.

C. Poems not in *Southern Road:*

"After the Storm." *The Crisis, a Record of the Darker Races*,[3] XXXIV (April, 1927), 48.

"A Bad, Bad Man," "Call Boy," "Long Track Blues," "Puttin' on Dog," "Rent Day Blues," "Slim in Hell." *Folk-Say*, IV. Edited by Benjamin A. Botkin. Norman, Oklahoma: Oklahoma Folklore Society, 1932, pp. 249–256.

"He Was a Man." *Opportunity*, X (June, 1932), 179.

"Let Us Suppose." *Opportunity*, XIII (September, 1935), 281.

"Southern Cop," "Transfer." *Partisan Review*, III (October, 1936), 220–221.

"Master and Man." *New Republic*, LXXXIX (November 18, 1936), 66.

"All Are Gay." *American Stuff*. New York: Viking Press, 1937, pp. 79–81.

"Break of Day." *New Republic*, LXXXV (May 11, 1938), 10.

"The Young Ones." *Poetry*, III (July, 1938), 189–190.

"Glory, Glory." *Esquire*, X (August, 1938), 78.

"Colloquy (Black Worker and White Worker)," "Conjured," "Old Lem." *This Generation*. Edited by George Anderson and Eda L. Walton. New York: Scott, Foresman, 1939, pp. 645–646.

"Sharecropper." *Get Organized*. Edited by Alan Calmer. New York: International Press, 1939, pp. 24–25.

2. Hereafter, *Folk-Say, a Regional Miscellany* will be cited as *Folk-Say*.

3. Hereafter, *The Crisis, a Record of the Darker Races* will be cited as *The Crisis*.

"Remembering Nat Turner." *The Crisis*, XLVI (February, 1939), 48.

"Bitter Fruit of the Tree." *The Nation*, CXLIX (August 26, 1939), 223.

"An Old Woman Remembers," "The Ballad of Joe Meek." *Freedomways*, III (Summer, 1963), 405–411. (These poems, according to a headnote, were "written over a score of years ago.")

"Crispus Attucks McCoy." *Ik Ben de Nieuwe Neger*. Edited by Rosie Pool. The Hague: B. Dakker, 1965, p. 49.

D. *The Last Ride of Wild Bill and Eleven Narrative Poems*. Detroit: Broadside Press, 1975.

Collection of ballads, including previously unpublished poems, "The Last Ride of Wild Bill" and "Slim Hears the Call"; "Sam Smiley" from *Southern Road* appears here as "Sam Yancy."

II. NARRATIVES AND SKETCHES

"Out of Their Mouths." *Survey Graphic*, XXI (November, 1942), 480–483.
Anecdotes, conversations, statements by black and white Americans on race relations.

"Words on a Bus." *South Today*, VII (Spring, 1943), 26–28.
Narrative about a black man who flirts with a black woman on a segregated bus.

"Farewell to Basin Street." *The Record Changer*, III (December, 1944), 7–9, 51.
Sketch in which a first-person narrator recalls a trip to New Orleans, which he found more of a monument to the past than a thriving jazz center.

"The Muted South." *Phylon, the Atlanta University Review of Race and Culture*,[4] VI (Winter, 1945), 22–34.
Five sketches of the South dealing with racism and the war as well as black American life styles and folk art forms.

"Georgia Sketches." *Phylon*, VI (Summer, 1945), 225–231.
Two sketches of Atlanta: one dealing with two blacks' attempt to visit Joel Chandler Harris's home, the other consisting of recollections of public jazz dances.

"Georgia Nymphs." *Phylon*, VI (Autumn, 1945), 362–367.
Sketch about two black men who happen upon bathing white women; the men leave town with caution and haste.

"And/Or." *Phylon*, VII (Fall, 1946), 269–272.
Narrative focusing upon a black collegiate's struggles to vote in segregated Alabama.

4. Hereafter, *Phylon, the Atlanta University Review of Race and Culture* will be cited as *Phylon*.

III. BOOKS OF CRITICISM

Outline for the Study of the Poetry of American Negroes. New York: Harcourt, Brace, 1931.

> Supplement to James Weldon Johnson's anthology, *The Book of American Negro Poetry;* includes topics for papers, study questions, definitions of poetic forms and elements, and an essay on contemporary American verse.

The Negro in American Fiction. Washington: Associates in Negro Folk Education, 1938.

> Critical essays on the portrayal of blacks in American fiction.

Negro Poetry and Drama. Washington: Associates in Negro Folk Education, 1938.

> Critical history of black American poetry and drama.

The Negro Caravan. Edited by Sterling A. Brown, Arthur P. Davis, and Ulysses Lee. New York: Dryden Press, 1941.

> Anthology of Afro-American writing from its folk foundations to 1940; includes critical and historical interchapters by the editors.

The Reader's Companion to World Literature. Edited by Lillian H. Hornstein and G. D. Percy. New York: New American Library, 1956.

> Dictionary of international writers and their major works; Brown contributed entries on Matthew Arnold, Charles Baudelaire, Emily Brontë, Robert Burns, Emily Dickinson. Ralph Waldo Emerson, Benjamin Franklin, Robert Frost, Heinrich Heine, A. E. Housman, Thomas Jefferson, Abraham Lincoln, Henry Wadsworth Longfellow, Herman Melville, *Moby Dick,* Edgar Allan Poe, Henry Thoreau, Mark Twain, and Walt Whitman.

IV. ESSAYS ON AMERICAN LITERATURE AND THE ROLE OF BLACKS IN AMERICAN LITERATURE

"Negro Literature—Is It True? Complete?" *The Durham Fact-Finding Conference,* Durham, North Carolina: Fact-Finding Conference, 1929, pp. 26–28.

> Statement in defense of realism in the portrayal of blacks in literature.

"Our Literary Audience." *Opportunity,* VIII (February, 1930), 42–46, 61.

> Criticism of readers who are put off by realistic portraiture of Negroes in literature.

"James Weldon Johnson." *The Book of American Negro Poetry.* Edited by James Weldon Johnson. New York: Harcourt, Brace, 1931, pp. 114–117.

> Biographical headnote preceding the selection of Johnson's poetry.

"A Literary Parallel." *Opportunity,* X (May, 1932), 152–153.

> Discussion of stereotypes in fiction and drama: English, Irish, American.

"In Memoriam: Charles W. Chesnutt." *Opportunity,* X (December, 1932), 387.

> Eulogy of Chesnutt and evaluation of his stories and novels.

"Negro Character As Seen by White Authors." *The Journal of Negro Education,* II (April, 1933), 179–203.

> Discussion of black stereotypes in American literature of the nineteenth and twentieth centuries; a few true portraits, "realizations," also noted.

"Problems of the Negro Writer." *Official Proceedings, National Negro Congress.* Washington: National Negro Congress Publications, 1937, pp. 18–19.

> Transcript of a speech advocating techniques and perspectives of realism in black writing.

"The Negro in American Literature." *James Weldon Johnson, a Biographical Sketch.* Nashville: Fisk University, 1938, pp. 20–28.

> Transcript of a speech surveying black literature; the contributions of Johnson are highlighted.

"The American Race Problem As Reflected in American Literature." *The Journal of Negro Education,* VIII (July, 1939), 275–290.

> Study of racial attitudes expressed in American writing of the nineteenth and twentieth centuries.

"The Negro Writer and His Publisher." *The Quarterly Review of Higher Education Among Negroes,* IX (July, 1941), 140–146.

> Discussion of the problems black writers face getting published, stressing their responsibility to practice their craft without excuse or compromise.

"Negro in the American Theatre." *Oxford Companion to the Theatre.* Edited by Phyllis Hartnoll. London: Oxford Press, 1950, pp. 672–679.

> Essay surveying the contributions of Afro-American actors and playwrights to American theatre from the colonial period to 1947.

"In the American Grain." *Vassar Alumnae Magazine,* XXXVI (February, 1951), 5–9.

> Essay tracing realism in American literature, from Emerson to Faulkner.

"Seventy-five Years of the Negro in Literature." *Jackson College Bulletin,* II (September, 1953), 26–30.

> Transcribed address at Jackson College, outlining American writers' uses and abuses of black folklore.

"The New Negro in Literature (1925–1955)." *The New Negro Thirty Years Afterwards.* Washington: Howard University Press, 1955.

> Transcript of a speech surveying American literature (1925–1955) by and about blacks.

"A Century of Negro Portraiture in American Literature." *The Massachusetts Review,* VII (Winter, 1966), 73–96.

> Essay on the treatment of racial themes and black characters in Post–Civil War literature.

"Arna Bontemps, Co-Worker, Comrade." *Black World,* XXII (September, 1973), 11, 91–97.

> Eulogy of Bontemps and appraisal of his writings.

V. ESSAYS AND COMMENTARIES ON BLACK FOLKLORE AND MUSIC

"Roland Hayes." *Opportunity,* III, 30 (June, 1925), 173–174.

> Brown's first published writing, an award-winning sketch of the renowned tenor.

"The Blues As Folk Poetry." *Folk-Say*, I. Edited by Benjamin A. Botkin. Norman, Oklahoma: University of Oklahoma Press, 1930, pp. 324–339.

Discussion of the forms and meanings of blues songs.

"The Folk Roots." *Vanguard* LP—VSD—47/48. Liner notes. Copyright 1973.

Excerpt from a speech on the blues given at the "Spirituals to Swing" concert at Carnegie Hall, December 24, 1939.

"Blues, Ballads and Social Songs." *Seventy-five Years of Freedom*. Washington: Library of Congress Press, December 18, 1940, pp. 17–25.

Discussion of the meaning and "mood" of Afro-American folk music.

"The Negro in American Culture." Unpublished memoranda, Carnegie/Myrdal study of blacks in America, 1940.

Survey of the contributions of blacks to American theatre, music, and sports.

"Stray Notes on Jazz." *Vassar Brew*, XXVII (June, 1946), 15–19.

Discussion of the influence of recording companies on jazz.

"Remarks at a Conference on the Character and State of Studies in Folklore." *Journal of American Folklore*, LIX (October, 1946), 506–507.

Transcript of Brown's speech on folklore, "living-people-lore," as important to artists, folklorists, and historians.

"Negro Folk Expression." *Phylon*, XI (Autumn, 1950), 318–327.

Analysis of the origins and meanings of Afro-American jokes and tales.

"Athletics and the Arts." *The Integration of the Negro into American Society*. Edited by E. Franklin Frazier. Washington: Howard University Press, 1951, 117–147.

Discussion of the struggles for integration by blacks in literature, art, music, dance, and sports.

"The Blues." *Phylon*, XIII (Autumn, 1952), 286–292.

Paper read at the "Post-Tanglewood Round Table on Jazz," Lenox, Massachusetts, August, 1952; deals with the underlying themes and the poetry of the blues.

"Negro Folk Expression: Spirituals, Seculars, Ballads and Work Songs." *Phylon*, XIV (Winter, 1953), 45–61.

Essay on the history, meanings, and poetic elements in the folk songs of Afro-Americans.

"Portrait of a Jazz Giant: 'Jelly Roll' Morton (1885?–1941)." *Black World*, XXIII (February, 1974), 28–49.

Essay on Morton's importance as composer, pianist, and singer.

VI. REVIEWS AND NOTES ON BOOKS, MOVIES, PLAYS

"Two African Heroines." *Opportunity*, VI (January, 1926), 24–26.

Review of David Garnett's novel, *The Sailor's Return*, and Louis Charbonneau's novel, *Mambu, et Son Amour*.

"The New Secession—a Review." *Opportunity*, V (May, 1927), 147–148.

Review of Julia Peterkin's novel, *Black April*.

"Our Book Shelf." *Opportunity*, VI (March, 1928), 91–92.

Review of *Dwellers in the Jungle*, a novel by Gordon Casserly.

"Fabulist and Felossofer." *Opportunity*, VI (July, 1928), 211–212.

Review of *Ol' Man Adam an' His Chillun*, a novel by Roark Bradford.

"Mamba's Daughters." *Opportunity*, VII (May, 1929), 161–162.

A review of DuBose Heyward's novel, *Mamba's Daughters*.

"Black Ulysses at War." *Opportunity*, VII (December, 1929), 383–384.

Review of *Wings on My Feet*, a novel by Howard Odum.

"Unhistoric History." *Journal of Negro History*, XV (April, 1930), 134–161.

Essay on historical fiction and biography focusing on *Quiet Cities* and *Swords and Roses*, novels by Joseph Hergesheimer; *Stonewall Jackson* and *Jefferson Davis*, biographies by Allen Tate; *John Brown*, a biography by Robert Penn Warren; *Abraham Lincoln*, a biography by Raymond Holden; and *The Tragic Era*, a novel by Claude Bowers.

"Not Without Laughter." *Opportunity*, VIII (September, 1930), 279–280.

Review of *Not Without Laughter*, a novel by Langston Hughes.

"Black Genesis." *Opportunity*, VIII (October, 1930), 311–312.

Review of *Black Genesis*, a collection of stories by Samuel G. Stoney and Gertrude M. Shelby.

"Chronicle and Comment." *Opportunity*, VIII (December, 1930), 375.

Notes on literary and scholarly works by Abram Harris, Carter Woodson, George Schuyler, and Randolph Edmonds.

"Folk Values in a New Medium." Co-author, Alain Locke. *Folk-Say*, II. Edited by Benjamin A. Botkin. Norman, Oklahoma: University of Oklahoma Press, 1930, pp. 340–345.

Review of two movies, "Hearts in Dixie" and "Hallelujah."

"The Literary Scene." *Opportunity*, IX (January, 1931), 20.

Notes on *Folk-Say* II, an annual collection of folklore materials, edited by Benjamin A. Botkin; *Short History of Julia*, a novel by Isa Glen; *Po' Buckra*, a novel by Marie Stanley; *Strike!* a novel by Mary Vorse; and essays and poems by Carl Carmer.

"The Literary Scene." *Opportunity*, IX (February, 1931), 53–54.

Notes on *The Black Worker*, a study of the relation of blacks to the American labor movement, by Abram Harris and Sterling Spero, and *Black No More*, a novel by George Schuyler.

"The Literary Scene, Chronicle and Commentary." *Opportunity*, IX (March, 1931), 87.

Notes on many books, including the scholarly works *Race Psychology* by Thomas R. Garth, and *The Negro Wage Earner* by Lorenzo Greene, a novel, *Jungle Ways* by William Seabrook; and a collection of stories, *Golden Tales from the South*, edited by May Becker.

"A Romantic Defense." *Opportunity*, IX (April, 1931), 118.

Review of *I'll Take My Stand*, a collection of essays by Twelve Southerners.

"An American Epoch." *Opportunity*, IX (June, 1931), 187.
> Review of Howard Odum's work. *An American Epoch, Southern Portraiture in the National Picture.*

"Our Bookshelf." *Opportunity*, IX (June, 1931), 199.
> Review of Arna Bontemps's novel, *God Sends Sunday.*

"As to 'Jungle Ways.'" *Opportunity*, IX (July, 1931), 219–221.
> Review of William Seabrook's novel, *Jungle Ways.*

"Caroling Softly Souls of Slavery." *Opportunity*, IX (August, 1931), 251–252.
> Commentary on Louis C. Hughes's autobiography, *Thirty Years a Slave.*

"Concerning Negro Drama." *Opportunity*, IX (September, 1931), 284–288.
> Comments on "The Green Pastures," "The Emperor Jones," and other plays of black life by white playwrights.

"Poor Whites." *Opportunity*, IX (October, 1931), 317, 320.
> Review of Erskine Caldwell's collection of stories, *American Earth;* John Fort's novel, *God in the Straw Pen;* and George Millburn's novel, *Oklahoma Town.*

"The Point of View." *Opportunity*, IX (November, 1931), 347–350.
> Discussion of "point of view" in literature with reference to Elizabethan drama, American minstrelsy, black folklore, and the fiction of William Faulkner, Roark Bradford, and DuBose Heyward.

"Pride and Pathos." *Opportunity*, IX (December, 1931), 381–384.
> Review of *The Carolina Low Country*, a collection of essays by Members of the Society for the Preservation of the Spirituals.

"Never No Steel Driving Man." *Opportunity*, IX (December, 1931), 382.
> Review of *John Henry*, a novel by Roark Bradford.

"Truth Will Out." *Opportunity*, X (January, 1932), 23–24.
> Review of Frederic Bancroft's *Slave Trading in the Old South*, a history.

" 'Never No More.'" *Opportunity*, X (February, 1932), 55–56.
> Review of James Millen's play, "Never No More."

"Weep Some More My Lady." *Opportunity*, X (March, 1932), 87.
> Comments on Louis Untermeyer's presentation of black folklore in his anthology, *American Poetry: From the Beginning to Whitman.*

"Joel Chandler Harris." *Opportunity*, X (April, 1932), 119–120.
> Review of *Joel Chandler Harris: Editor and Essayist*, a collection of Harris's essays, edited by Julia Collier Harris.

"More Odds." *Opportunity*, X (June, 1932), 188–189.
> Review of Edwin Embree's *Brown America*, a social history of blacks in America.

"Local Color or Interpretation." *Opportunity*, X (July, 1932), 223.
> Review of Julia Peterkin's novel, *Bright Skin.*

"A Poet and His Prose." *Opportunity*, X (August, 1932), 256.
> Commentary on Claude McKay's novels and stories.

"Signs of Promise." *Opportunity*, X (September, 1932), 287.
> Comments on *University of Michigan Plays*, an anthology edited by Kenneth T. Rowe.

"Amber Satyr." *Opportunity*, X (November, 1932), 352.
    Review of Roy Flannagan's novel, *Amber Satyr*.
"A New Trend." *Opportunity*, XI (February, 1933), 56.
    Comments on *Inchin' Along*, a novel by Welbourne Kelley, as well as *Free Born* and *Georgia Nigger*, novels by John L. Spivak.
"Alas the Poor Mulatto." *Opportunity*, XI (March, 1933), 91.
    Review of *Dark Lustre*, a novel by Geoffrey Barnes.
"Time for a New Deal." *Opportunity*, II (April, 1933), 122, 126.
    Review of *The Southern Oligarchy*, a study of the politics and economics of the American South by William Scaggs.
"Smartness Goes Traveling." *Opportunity*, XI (May, 1933), 154, 158.
    Review of Evelyn Waugh's narrative of travels in Africa, *They Were Still Dancing*, and his novel, *Black Mischief*.
"John Brown: God's Angry Man." *Opportunity*, XI (June, 1933), 186–187.
    Review of *God's Angry Man*, a biography of John Brown by Leonard Ehrlick.
"Banana Bottom." *Opportunity*, XI (July, 1933), 217, 222.
    Review of Claude McKay's novel, *Banana Bottom*.
"From the Southwest." *Opportunity*, XI (October, 1933), 313.
    Review of *Negrito*, a novel by J. Mason Brewer, and *Tone the Bell Easy*, a journal of folklore studies, edited by J. Frank Dobie.
"Kingdom Coming." *Opportunity*, XI (December, 1933), 382–383.
    Review of Roark Bradford's novel, *Kingdom Coming*.
"Arcadia, South Carolina." *Opportunity*, XII (February, 1934), 59–60.
    Review of *Roll, Jordan, Roll*, a narrative history and pictorial essay on black Americans, by Doris Ulmann and Julia Peterkin.
"Satire of Imperialism." *Opportunity*, XII (March, 1934), 89–90.
    Review of Winifred Holtby's novel, *Mandos, Mandos!*
"Six Plays for a Negro Theatre." *Opportunity*, XII (September, 1934), 280–281.
    Review of "Six Plays for a Negro Theatre," a collection of Randolph Edmond's plays.
"The Atlanta Summer Theatre." *Opportunity*, XII (October, 1934), 308–309.
    Commentary on Atlanta University's five dramatic productions, summer, 1934.
"Stars Fell on Alabama." *Opportunity*, XII (October, 1934), 312–313.
    Review of Carl Carmer's novel, *Stars Fell on Alabama*.
"Mississippi—Old Style." *Opportunity*, XII (December, 1934), 377–378.
    Review of *So Red the Rose*, a novel by Stark Young.
"Mississippi, Alabama: New Style." *Opportunity*, XIII (February, 1935), 55–56.
    Commentary on Southern novels by Thomas Wolfe, William March, and T. S. Stribling.
"The Negro in Fiction and Drama." *The Christian Register*, CXIV (February 14, 1935), 111–112.
    Review of fiction by Stark Young, William March, T. S. Stribling, Zora Neale Hurston, and Langston Hughes.
"Imitation of Life: Once a Pancake." *Opportunity*, XIII (March, 1935), 87–88.
    Review of *Imitation of Life*, a novel by Fannie Hurst.

"Mr. Sterling Brown." *Opportunity*, XIII (April, 1935), 121–122.
  Reply to Fannie Hurst's objections to the review of *Imitation of Life*.
"Correspondence." *Opportunity*, XIII (May, 1935), 153.
  Response to a letter to the editor about "Imitation of Life: Once a Pancake" and *Southern Road*.
"Come Day, Go Day." *Opportunity*, XIII (September, 1935), 279–280.
  Review of Roark Bradford's collection of short stories, *Let the Band Play Dixie*, and Richard Coleman's novel, *Don't You Weep, Don't You Moan*.
"Realism in the South." *Opportunity*, XIII (October, 1935), 311–312.
  Review of *Kneel to the Rising Sun*, a collection of short stories by Erskine Caldwell, and *Deep Dark River*, a novel by Robert Rylee.
"Southern Cross Sections." *Opportunity*, XIII (December, 1935), 380–385.
  Review of *Siesta*, a novel by Barry Fleming, and *South*, a novel by Frederick Wright.
"Shadow of the Plantation." *Journal of Negro History*, XXI (January, 1936), 70–73.
  Review of Charles S. Johnson's sociological study, *Shadow of the Plantation*.
"The First Negro Writers." *The New Republic*, LXXXVI (May 6, 1936), 376–377.
  Review of Benjamin Brawley's anthology, *Early Negro Writers*.
"Two Negro Poets." *Opportunity*, XIV (July, 1936), 216–220.
  Review of *Black Thunder*, a historical novel by Arna Bontemps, and *Black Man's Verse*, a collection of poems by Frank Marshall Davis.
"Book Reviews." *Opportunity*, XV (September, 1937), 280–281.
  Review of *The Negro Genius*, essays on black artists and intellectuals by Benjamin Brawley.
"Biography." *Opportunity*, XV (September, 1937), 216–217.
  Appraisal of Benjamin Brawley's *Paul Laurence Dunbar, Poet of His People*, a biography.
" 'Luck Is a Fortune.' " *The Nation*, CXLV (October 16, 1937), 409–410.
  Review of Zora Neale Hurston's novel, *Their Eyes Were Watching God*.
"Prize Winning Stories." *Opportunity*, XVI (April, 1938), 120–121.
  Review of *Uncle Tom's Children*, Richard Wright's collection of stories.
"From the Inside." *The Nation*, CLXVI (April 16, 1938), 448.
  Review of *Uncle Tom's Children*, Richard Wright's collection of stories.
"South on the Move." *Opportunity*, XVI (December, 1938), 366–369.
  Review of *A Southerner Discovers the South*, a travel book by Jonathan Daniels, and *Forty Acres and Steel Mules*, an economist's portrait of the South by Herman Clarence Nixon.
"Insight, Courage, and Craftsmanship." *Opportunity*, XVIII (June, 1940), 185–186.
  Review of Richard Wright's novel, *Native Son*.
"Foreword." *Place: America*, a play by Thomas Richardson. New York: NAACP Press, 1940, pp. 4–5.
  Introductory note, recommending this play.

"Three Ways of Looking at the South." *The Journal of Negro Education*, XIV (Winter, 1945), 68–72.

Review of William Percy's autobiography, *Lanterns on the Levee;* Anne Walker's study of Tuskegee Institute and town, *Tuskegee and the Black Belt;* and Ira De A. Reid's discussion of tenant farmers, *Sharecroppers All.*

VII. ON RECORD AND TAPE

"Readings by Sterling Brown and Langston Hughes." *Folkways* LP—FP90. Copyright 1952.

Recitation by Brown of "Break of Day," "Old King Cotton," "Old Lem," "Puttin' on Dog," "Sharecropper," "Slim in Hell."

"Anthology of Negro Poets, Edited by Arna Bontemps." *Folkways* LP—FL 9791. Copyright 1966.

Recitation by Brown of "Long Gone" and "Ma Rainey."

"Sixteen Poems of Sterling A. Brown." *Folkways* LP—FL 9794 Copyright 1978.

Recitation by Brown of poems published in *Southern Road* and in periodicals; also, "Cloteel," "Parish Doctor," and "Uncle Joe" are presented here for the first time.

"Sterling Brown Lectures." On file at the Institute for Arts and Humanities and the Afro-American Resource Center, Howard University, September 19 and October 10, 17, 31, 1973.

"Sterling Brown." Interview by Dyalsingh Sadhi. On file at the Institute for Arts and Humanities and the Afro-American Resource Center, Howard University, January 10, 1974.

Videotaped interview at Howard University concerning Brown's years at Lincoln University.

"Sterling Brown Poetry Recital." On file at the Institute for Arts and Humanities and the Afro-American Resource Center, Howard University, May 17, 1974.

Speech by Brown at the M. L. King Library, Washington, D.C., about the influences on his poetry; a reading of seventeen published poems.

"Sterling Brown." Interview by Steven Jones. On file at the Institute for Arts and Humanities and the Afro-American Resource Center, Howard University, May 4, 14, 1978.

Tape recorded interview at Brown's home concerning the poet's early years in Washington, D.C.

VIII. MISCELLANEOUS

"The Negro in Washington." *Washington: City and Capital.* Federal Writers' Project. Washington: Government Printing Office, 1937.

Collection of essays by Brown dealing with the political and cultural history of black Washingtonians.

The Negro in Virginia. Federal Writers' Project. New York: Hastings House, 1940.

Collection of essays on the history and folklore of blacks in Virginia. Although as Federal Writers' Project Editor for Negro Affairs (1936–1940) Brown helped edit virtually every Project essay dealing with black life, he worked most extensively on *The Negro in Virginia*, even writing entire sections himself.

"Poetry Corner." Mary Strong. *Scholastic*, XXXVI (April 29, 1940), 25, 27.
 Strong's discussion of Brown's life and poetry includes lengthy statements by the poet himself.

"Saving the Cargo (Sidelights on the Underground Railroad)." *The Negro History Bulletin* (April, 1941), 151–154.
 Historical essay on the trials of Underground Railroad conductors and riders.

"The Contributions of the American Negro." *One America*. Edited by Frances Brown and Joseph Roucek. New York: Prentice-Hall, 1945, pp. 588–615.
 Essay surveying the Negro's contributions to American political and cultural history.

"Count Us In." *Primer for White Folks*. Edited by Bucklin Moon. Garden City: Doubleday, 1945, pp. 364–395.
 Essay on segregation and prejudice, with focus on the black serviceman.

"Ralph Bunche—Statesman." *The Reporter*, I (December 6, 1949), 3–6.
 Biographical sketch.

"Negro, American." By Sterling A. Brown, John Hope Franklin, and Rayford Logan. *Encyclopaedia Britannica*, XVI. Chicago: William Benton, 1968, pp. 188–201.
 Essay on the role of blacks in American life, from slavery through the mid-1960s.

"The Teacher . . . Sterling Brown, the Mentor of Thousands . . . Talks About Art, Black and White." Sterling A. Brown and Hollie West. *The Washington Post*, CXIII, 346 (November 16, 1969), pp. F1–F3.
 Interview dealing with black folklore, music, and the relation of blacks and whites.

"Appendixes." *The American Slave: From Sunup to Sundown*. Edited by George Rawick. Westport, Connecticut: Greenwood, 1972, pp. 172–178.
 Outlining certain WPA procedures for interviewing ex-slaves, these official memoranda (1937) were influenced by the Project's Editor for Negro Affairs, Sterling Brown.

"Sterling Brown, a Living Legend." Genevieve Ekaete. *New Directions*, I (Winter, 1974), 4–11.
 Tribute by Ekaete, containing statements by Brown on culture and politics.

"A Son's Return: 'Oh Didn't He Ramble.' " *Berkshire Review*, X (Summer, 1974), 9–30.
 Transcript of a talk in which Brown recalls his student years at Williams College.

"Blacks in Brookland." *The Washington Star* (April 18, 1979), A-17.
 Letter to the Editor defending Brown's neighborhood in Washington as something more than a "ghetto."

Index

Davis, Frank Marshall, 66, 194, 199–200
Dawson, Mary Cardwell, 114
Demby, William, 198
Democracy, 25–26, 87–89, 94, 97, 195
Dempsey, Richard, 119
Depression, Great, 7, 191, 192
Dew, Thomas R., 151–52, 154
Dialect, 145–46, 156, 165; Gullah, 174, 175, 202, 227; local color, 174–75
Dixon, Thomas, 59, 62, 141, 168
Dodd, William, 284
Dodds, Johnny, 269
Dodson, Owen, 131, 198, 200
Dollard, John, 242
Dorrington, Art, 107
Dorsey, Thomas, 249
Dorsey, Tommy, 270
Douglass, Frederick, 35, 51–52, 133, 214, 247
Dover, Cedric, 130
Dowson, Ernest, 19
Dred (Stowe), 51, 170–71
Drew, Charles, 71
Du Bois, W. E. B., x, xii, xv, 3, 10, 16, 61–62, 126, 133, 188; on spirituals, 248
Dunbar, Paul Laurence, 35, 60, 126, 128, 131, 190
Duncan, Todd, 113
Dutton, George, 3, 14–15, 16

Eakins, Thomas, 117
Edmonds, Randolph, 122
Edmondson, Emily, 28, 30
Edmondson, Mary, 28
Education, 29–30, 33–34, 42–43, 79–80
Ellington, Duke, xii, 43, 109, 111, 121, 270
Elliott, Robert Brown, 34
Ellison, Ralph, xii, 124, 198–99
Emancipation Proclamation, 31, 56, 97
Emperor Jones, The (O'Neill), 123, 140–41, 185–86
Employment, 29, 31, 39, 70–71
Engel, Carl, 213
Ethridge, Mark, 81–82
Europe, James Reese, xi, 115
Extinction, 159, 160

Fair Employment Practices Committee (FEPC), 70, 77, 80, 89, 92, 96
Farm Security Administration, 69, 96

Fauset, Arthur Huff, 226–27, 229, 236
Fauset, Jessie, xv, 188
Feather, Leonard, 273
Federal Writer's Project (FWP), ix, xviii, 194–95, 200
FEPC, 70, 77, 80, 89, 92, 96
Ferguson, Otis, 266
Fine Clothes to the Jew (Hughes), 189
Firbank, Ronald, 186
Fire in the Flint (White), 63, 188
Fisher, Rudolph, 63, 188
Fisk Jubilee Singers, 113, 207–8
Fisk University, 3, 128
Flournoy, J. J., 52
Folk literature: of Africa, 234–36; animal tales, 236–40; aphorisms, 218–19, 234–42; ballads, 219–21, 252–57; deceptive bargain tales, 241; and folk Negro, 188–90, 233–34n1, 262–64; folk tales, 226–29, 234–42; Irish, 239; irony in, 241; jokes, 242; outlook for, 262–64; about racial origins, 240–41; Reynard cycle, 235, 236; sermons, 229–30; sharecropping tales, 241–42; trickster Jack, 239; "why" stories, 240. *See also* Literature; Seculars; Spirituals
Folk Negro, 188–90, 233–34n1, 262–64
Folk-Say, 174
Fool's Errand, A (Tourgee), 60
Forrest, Edwin, 162
Forten, Charlotte, 207
Frank, Waldo, 186, 190
Frazier, E. Franklin, 2, 107, 192
Free Joe (Harris), 160
Free Negroes, 56; business ownership, 29; and education, 29–30; in literature, 50–51, 66–67; and prosperity, 30–31, 32; and religion, 30; and seculars, 251–52; and slave codes, 28–29; Southerners' concept of, 55; spirituals of, 207
Freedmen. *See* Free Negroes
Frost, Robert, 19–21
Fugitive Slave Bill, 51, 54, 74

Gabbin, Joanne V., xix, xx
Gaines, F. P., 152, 182
Gardiner, William, 26
Garfield, Harry, 6
Garrison, Lucy McKim, 207, 211
Gates, Henry Lewis, Jr., xiii
Gellert, Lawrence, 222, 260
Georgia: Unfinished State (Steed), 68

Race riots, 29, 38, 62, 75, 79, 84
Races of Mankind, The, 79
Rainbow Round My Shoulder (Odum), 181
Rainey, Ma, xii, 189, 223, 268
Ramsey, Frederick, 201–2
Randolph, John, 26–27
Rankin, John, 70, 80, 89
Ransom, John Crowe, xx
Rape, 59, 79, 83, 85, 168, 178
Raper, Arthur, 86
Really the Blues (Mezzrow), 110
Reconstruction, 56–60
Red Cross, 70–71
Red Rock (Page), 58, 167
Redding, J. Saunders, 2, 128–29, 196, 201
Regionalism, 188–90, 194–95, 228
Reid, Ira, 86, 91
Religion, 30, 41–42
Republican Party, 35
Rice, T. D., 163
Rickey, Branch, 101
Rider of Dreams, The (Torrence), 180
Riggs, Marlon, xix
River George (Lee), 66, 193
Roberts, Needham, 38
Robeson, Paul, x, 16, 189
Robinson, Edwin Arlington, 15
Robinson, Jackie, 100, 101–2
"Roland Hayes," xii
"Romantic Defense, A," xx
Roosevelt, Eleanor, 77–78
Rosskam, Edwin, 196
Rourke, Constance, 162
Rowan, Carl, 201
Russell, Irwin, 156, 164, 174
Rylee, Robert, 193

Sale, John B., 174–75, 189, 228
Sancton, Thomas, 76, 91
Sartre, Jean-Paul, 129, 132
Savoy, Willard, 196
Saxon, Lyle, 171, 174
Schuyler, George, 141, 147, 192
Scott, Emmett J., 37
Scott, Evelyn, 181
Scott, Ralph Winfield, 6, 8, 9
Scottsboro boys, 81, 194
Seabrook, William, 177, 186
Seculars, 216–18, 249–52; coon-songs, 253; devil tunes, 217, 250; dirty dozens, 252; of freedmen, 251–52; sources for, 252–54

Segregation, xviii, 6–7, 39–40, 44–46; absurdity of, 86–87; biracial parallelism, 93–94; and blood banks, 70–71; on buses, 74, 76–77, 90; and fear of harm, 82–83; in military, 74, 76–77; in music, 110–11; Negro support for, 92–93; and religion, 30; Southern liberal support for, 81–82
"Self Determination (The Philosophy of the American Negro)" (Hill), 61
Selling of Joseph, The (Sewall), 50
Sewall, Samuel, 50
Shaw, Nate, xii
Shelby, Gertrude, 175, 228, 236
Short Symphony (Swanson), 115
Sign for Cain, A (Lumpkin), 64, 193
Simms, William Gilmore, 153
Sinclair, Upton, 62
Slave Songs of the United States (Allen, Ware, Garrison), 207, 211
Slavery: biological justification for, 52–54; British view of, 52; Compromise of 1850, 27; and democracy, 25–26; economic justification for, 151–52; as normal condition, 57–58; political justification for, 54, 59; slave codes, 28–29; theological justification for, 54, 151–52, 166–67; in Washington, 28
Smith, Bessie, 109–10, 189, 201, 223, 232–33, 266
Smith, Gerald L. K., 83–84
Smith, Lillian, 69
Smith, Mamie, 23, 189
Smith, W. L. G., 55, 56, 174
Smith, William Gardner, 127, 197, 199
Soby, James Thrall, 118
"Son's Return, A," xxi
Souls of Black Folk, The (Du Bois), 126, 133
Southern Negro Conference, 90–91, 93
Southern Plantation, The (Gaines), 152
Southern Road, xiii
Spencer, Anne, xii
Spencer, Onah L., 229
Spirituals, 230–31, 243–49; apocalyptic imagery in, 244–45; Biblical imagery in, 245–47; composition of, 208–9; double meanings in, 214, 247–48; emotional content of, 214–66; and freedom, 207, 247; gospel songs, 249, 263; and jazz, 216; lyrics, 212–13, 243–44; modern imagery in, 248–49; music of,

209–11; origin of, 209–10, 243; as oth-
erworldly, 244–45; performances of,
215–16; popularity of, 232–33; record-
ings of, 211; and slavery, 213–15, 248
Sport of the Gods, The (Dunbar), 60
Spy, The (Cooper), 50, 162–63
St. Louis Woman, 121
"Stackolee," 254–55
Statistics, 68–69
Stearns, Marshall, 108–9
Steed, Hal, 68
Stephens, Nan Bagby, 182
Stepto, Robert Burns, xv, 1, 6
Stereotypes, 78, 126, 144, 149–50, 179–
80, 287–88
Stoney, Samuel, 175, 228, 236
Stowe, Harriet Beecher, 30, 50–51,
170–71
Straight, Michael, 94–95
Strange Fruit (Smith), 197
Strauss, Theodore, 64
"Stray Notes on Jazz," xix
Stribling, T. S., 181
Student Army Training Corps, 4–5
Sumner, Charles, 28, 34, 57
Sumner, William Graham, 82
Supreme Court, 89
Swallow Barn (Kennedy), 54, 152–53,
163, 176
Swanson, Howard, 115
Syphax, Maria, 32
Syphax, William, 34

Talley, Thomas W., 218, 236
Talmadge, Eugene, 73, 78–79, 80, 83, 92
Tanner, Henry O., 117
Tate, Allen, xx, 81, 161
Taubman, Howard, 113
Teaching, 11–16
Their Eyes Were Watching God (Hurston),
xx, 132, 193, 291–92
There Is Confusion, xvi
Thirty Years a Slave (Hughes), xxi, 284–86
This Side of Jordan (Bradford), 173
Thompson, Era Bell, 201
Thompson, Stith, 235–36
Thompson, William, 55
Thomson, Virgil, 114
Thorpe, Will, 12
Thurman, Wallace, 63, 187, 192
Tidwell, John Edgar, xiv
Tinker, E. Larocque, 174

"To America" (Johnson), 62
Tolson, M. Beaunorus, 200
Toomer, Jean, xvi, 127, 147, 186–87, 190
Torrence, Ridgeley, 180
Torrey, Jesse, 26, 27
Toulouse-Lautrec, Henri, xiii
Tourgee, Albion, 60
Trade unions, 96
Tree Named John, The (Sale), 174–75
Tropic Death (Walrond), 187
Tubman, Harriet, 27, 50, 248
Turner, Nat, 30
Turner, Patricia, xix
Turpin, E. Waters, 193
Twain, Mark, 59, 60
"Twelve Million Black Voices" (Wright),
196
"Two Men and a Bargain: A Parable of the
Solid South" (Smith), 69

Uncle Remus, 58, 157–58, 226–27, 232,
236–38. *See also* Harris, Joel Chandler
Uncle Robin in His Cabin (Page), 55
Uncle Tom's Cabin (Stowe), 48, 50–51,
119, 154, 156, 170–71; dramatic ver-
sions of, 164
Uncle Tom's Children (Wright), 66,
193–94
Underground Railroad, 27, 74
Untermeyer, Louis, xiii, 213

Van Doren, Carl, 185
Van Evrie, C. J. H., 53, 57–58, 112–13,
167
Van Vechten, Carl, 126, 176–77, 186, 187,
190, 192
Vandercook, John, 174, 186
Voting, 89, 90

Walker, James, 37
Walker, Margaret, 200
Wallaschek, Richard, 209
Waller, Fats, 110, 270, 272
Walrond, Eric, 127, 187
Ward, Artemus, 63
Ward, Theodore, 121
Ware, Charles P., 207, 211
Warren, Robert Penn, xx
Washington, Booker T., 37, 61
Washington, City and Capitol, xviii
Washington, D.C., 25; arts, 36–37; athlet-
ics, 41; crime rate in, 32–33; disfran-

chisement act, 34; and domestic slave traffic, 26–29; health concerns in, 33, 40; housing in, 30–32, 39–40; neighborhoods, 32; recreation in, 40–41; social life, 36, 44–45; suffrage in, 46

Ways of White Folks (Hughes), 66, 193

Weary Blues (Hughes), 189

Weaver, Mortimer, 9, 15

Weir, Reginald, 106

Wells, Ida B., xii

West, Dorothy, 196

White, George, 207–8

White, Joshua, 199, 201, 221, 233, 253, 260, 262, 268

White, Newman, 210, 213, 214

White, Walter, 63, 102, 188

White Supremacy and Negro Subordination (Van Evrie), 167

White supremacy movement, 77–79, 89, 167–68

Whiteman, Paul, 109, 266

Whitman, Walt, 56–57, 139

Whitney, Eli, 151

Wickham, Harvey, 179, 190

Wild Duck, The (Ibsen), 121

Wilkinson, Garnet C., 42

Wilkinson, Horace, 77–78

Willbanks, Alexander, 42

Williams, Chancellor, 197

Williams, Ephraim, 11

Williams College, ix, xvi, 2–21; fraternities, 8; religious services, 8–9; segregation in, 6–7; sports, 10–11

Willkie, Wendell, 95, 97

Wolfe, Bernard, 129–30

Woolson, Constance Fenimore, 57

Work, Henry C., 251

World War II, xviii

Wormley, William H. A., 34

Wright, Richard, 66, 122, 135, 193–96, 201

Yankee Slave Dealer, The, 155, 160

Yemassee (Simms), 153

Yerby, Frank, 127, 132, 133, 199